AF608068

EMOTIONS, COMMUNITY, AND CITIZENSHIP

Cross-Disciplinary Perspectives

Emotions, Community, and Citizenship

Cross-Disciplinary Perspectives

EDITED BY REBECCA KINGSTON,
KIRAN BANERJEE, JAMES MCKEE,
YI-CHUN CHIEN, AND
CONSTANTINE CHRISTOS VASSILIOU

UNIVERSITY OF TORONTO PRESS
Toronto Buffalo London

Toronto Buffalo London
www.utppublishing.com

ISBN 978-1-4426-4552-3

Library and Archives Canada Cataloguing in Publication

Emotions, community, and citizenship : cross-disciplinary perspectives/ edited by Rebecca Kingston, Kiran Banerjee, James McKee, Yi-Chun Chien, and Constantine Christos Vassiliou.

Includes bibliographical references.
ISBN 978-1-4426-4552-3 (cloth)

1. Emotions. 2. Emotions – Social aspects. I. Kingston, Rebecca, author, editor II. Banerjee, Kiran, 1983–, author, editor III. McKee, James, 1970–, editor IV. Vassiliou, Constantine Christos, editor V. Chien, Yi-Chun, 1983–, editor

BF531.E486 2017 152.4 C2016-906137-X

University of Toronto Press acknowledges the financial assistance to its publishing program of the Canada Council for the Arts and the Ontario Arts Council, an agency of the Government of Ontario.

Canada Council for the Arts   Conseil des Arts du Canada

Funded by the Government of Canada   Financé par le gouvernement du Canada   Canada

Contents

Acknowledgments vii

Preface: Social Implications of Emotions ix
KEITH OATLEY

Introduction 3
REBECCA KINGSTON, KIRAN BANERJEE, YI-CHUN CHIEN, AND JAMES MCKEE

Part I: Interpretive Perspectives

1 Virtue and Emotional Education in Ancient Greece 35
RYAN K. BALOT

2 Renaissance Discourses of Emotions 52
JAN PURNIS

3 Wittgenstein and the Social Science of Emotion 75
JOHN G. GUNNELL

Part II: Naturalistic Approaches

4 Current Emotion Research in Philosophy 107
PAUL E. GRIFFITHS

5 Are Our Emotional Feelings Relational? 126
GEORG NORTHOFF

6 The Interpersonal Is the Political: The Role of Social Belongingness in Emotional Experience and Political Orientation 154
KRISTINA TCHALOVA AND GEOFF MACDONALD

7 Revising Emotions of Three Post-9/11 Moments 176
JOSEPH F. FLETCHER AND JENNIFER HOVE

Part III: Emotions and Citizenship

8 Constructing Indignation: Anger Dynamics in Protest Movements 201
JAMES M. JASPER

9 Compassion and the Public Sphere: Hannah Arendt on a Contested Political Passion 215
SOPHIE BOURGAULT

10 Envy, Shame, and Self-Respect: Situating the Emotions in the Work of John Rawls 241
KIRAN BANERJEE AND JEFFREY BERCUSON

Part IV: Seeking Common Ground

Epilogue: Integrating Multiple Perspectives into the Study of Emotions 265
REBECCA KINGSTON

Contributors 285

Acknowledgments

We would like to thank all those who have helped in the production of this edited volume. First of all, we thank the contributors for their many hours of hard work. Thanks is also due to the Jackman Humanities Institute at the University of Toronto, which hosted the symposium on which this collection was based, as well as the Social Sciences and Humanities Research Council of Canada Insight Grants program. We are particularly grateful for the work of Ethel Tungohan as well as the support staff at the Department of Political Science of the University of Toronto. In addition, we would like to thank Daniel Quinlan, Stephanie Stone, and those who have worked on the production of the volume at the University of Toronto Press.

Chapter 4, "Current Emotion Research in Philosophy" by Griffiths, was first published in the journal *Emotion Review* 5 (2), April 2013: 215–22, and Chapter 8, "Constructing Indignation: Anger Dynamics in Protest Movements" by Jasper, appeared in *Emotion Review* 6 (3), July 2014: 208–13. Both are reprinted with permission.

Preface: Social Implications of Emotions

KEITH OATLEY

Emotions have been discussed by the founders of Western philosophy: Plato, Aristotle, and René Descartes; by the most influential of biologists, Charles Darwin; as well as by the father of American psychology, William James. Despite this, it is only in about the last 60 years that the topic of emotion has come fully onto the agendas of psychology, psychiatry, and neuroscience; of history, sociology, and politics; and of literary theory (Oatley 2004). In psychology, there has been a concentration on issues of how individual emotions are elicited, what processes are involved, and what effects they have; in the current book, the widening of focus to the contexts in which emotions occur is therefore welcome. In this volume are contributions on emotions from political science as well as from psychology, sociology, neuroscience, philosophy, classics, and literature.

Emotions deserve a place at the centre of how we think about ourselves because, following the analysis of Aristotle, they are about the judgments we make. And so, says Aristotle, in *Rhetoric*,

> The emotions are all those feelings that so change [people] as to affect their judgements, and that are also attended by pain or pleasure. Such are anger, pity, fear, and the like, with their opposites. (1378a, lines 21–3)

Aristotle gives an example of the cognitive makeup of a particular emotion.

> Anger may be defined as a desire accompanied by pain, for a conspicuous revenge for a conspicuous slight at the hands of [people] who have no call to slight oneself or one's friends ... it must always be felt towards some

> particular individual ... because the other has done or intended to do something to him or one of his friends. (1378a, line 31 to 1378b, line 2)

In the case of anger, the emotion occurs because someone's action is evaluated as diminishing a person's status. From anger we learn, shockingly perhaps, that for us humans, status is rather important.

An emotion occurs generally when an event is evaluated as affecting a significant concern. It then typically imparts an urge to do something about what has happened, and it tends to direct our thoughts.

So, as Robert Solomon (e.g., 2007) has argued, from the idea of evaluation it becomes clear that emotions are principal sources of value in our lives: in our loves, in our strivings and satisfactions, in our commitments and contentments, in our antagonisms and conflicts. Most important (as Georg Northoff argues in this volume), emotions are relational: they relate the environment to the self.

Bodily effects in emotional life have been discussed for centuries – for instance, in the theory of the humours, which were thought to give rise to such states as being sanguine, feeling melancholy, and so on, as discussed in this volume by Jan Purnis. Bodily changes were important to James (1884), who thought that emotions were perceptions of these changes. Although emotions may often have biological and bodily bases, a feature stressed in this volume by Paul Griffiths in his overview of recent work in philosophy, they are not like a sneeze. A sneeze is local and almost entirely bodily. In contrast, emotions can be far reaching, and they (as some argue) are not just bodily. Because emotions relate events to concerns, they are necessarily dependent on context: internal context of what our concerns may be and external context of the implications of events. Hence, the reason for the present book.

The Social-Relational Context of Emotions

Philosophers, psychologists, and neuroscientists have started to recognize that alongside questions of how emotions work in the individual, the question of their roles in interpersonal and social life is perhaps even more critical. This recognition has wide implications, and it involves interdisciplinary research that includes psychology and neuroscience in partnership with sociology, history, and the humanities.

A long-standing issue in the Western history of ideas is how we humans might be able to regulate problematic aspects of our emotions. An early example was the *Meditations* of Marcus Aurelius (ca. 170). But as we start to think about this issue of regulation, not just in terms of the issues of anger about which Marcus Aurelius was exercised in himself, but in relation to civil violence and international warfare, it turns out that here, too, the issues are best conceptualized not as individual but social, and hence often political.

Emotions configure the cognitive system to match recurring kinds of goal-relevant event: progress in plans, losses, frustrations, dangers, and so on. If, as recent evidence indicates, most emotions are social, the critical question arises of what our social goals are. Jennifer Jenkins and Keith Oatley (see Keltner, Oatley, and Jenkins 2013) have proposed that three such social goals are predominant: assertion, attachment, and affiliation. There is also an antisocial goal: to exclude others.

Attachment is a basic social goal for mammals, and a parallel system exists for birds. Attachment is a biologically based structuring of a relationship between a mother (or other caregiver) and an infant, which enables the immature infant to be nurtured and kept safe. It was discovered and named by the psychoanalyst John Bowlby. His work, starting with his (1951) book, *Child Care and the Growth of Love,* can be thought of as ushering in the modern conception of emotion. The biologically based system of mother-infant love keeps the infant close to the caregiver, imbues the relationship with trust and contentment for both partners, and makes for intense anxiety in each partner when a separation occurs. In the current volume, Kristina Tchalova and Geoff MacDonald use attachment theory as a basis for their exploration of emotions of social exclusion.

Evolutionarily older than attachment, but strong in mammals, is assertion. In sociology and politics, it is called power. It is the social goal of achieving and maintaining status in hierarchies in different domains. In each domain, there tends to be a leader and subordinates at different social distances from the leader. If attachment is about safety, with its emotions of trust and anxiety, assertion is about conflict with its emotions of anger and shame, as highlighted by James Jasper in this volume. One might say that the aim of political science is to understand such issues. It is not insignificant that the best account we have of a contest between two male chimpanzees for alpha status in the hierarchy of a social group – a contest that involved allies and antagonists – is called *Chimpanzee Politics,* by Frans De Waal (1982). In the current volume, several authors explore themes that derive from hierarchy and the privileges associated with hierarchical status. For instance, Ryan Balot discusses democracy, and Kiran Banerjee and Jeffrey Bercuson discuss justice, both issues in which modifications to basic hierarchical arrangements have been seen as essential to well-functioning human societies.

Evolutionarily much newer than attachment and assertion is the social goal of affiliation. Our close relatives the apes have this goal, but its most substantial development is in humans. Indeed, it could be thought that this social goal characterizes our species. We do not just affiliate with each other, we are also able to know what others are thinking and feeling (which apes cannot), and we can make arrangements to do things together that we are unable to do alone (which again apes cannot); for instance, we can work cooperatively to formulate joint plans and pursue them. These abilities form the emotional bases for the human development of cultures, of the technologies of food provision, housing, transport, and communication. The kind of cooperation among disciplines envisaged by Rebecca Kingston, Kiran Banerjee, Yi-Chun Chien, and James McKee (in this volume) would not be possible without this affiliative goal.

A baleful attribute of humankind is our antisocial goal to displace and eliminate others, particularly others in groups perceived to be different from our own. This goal may have been important in earlier stages of hominid evolution. It is likely, for instance, to have worked to separate social groups from each other and thereby to have applied pressure to explore and disperse. One can imagine, too, that benefit to the human species derived from our forebears being able to drive other hominid groups into extinction, most recently the Neanderthals (Mellars 2004). Now, however, this goal with its accompanying proclivities to warfare and genocide can only be seen as the most serious threat to the continuing existence of the human species. In this volume, in relation to the dynamics of this eliminative goal, Joseph Fletcher and Jennifer Hove have investigated emotional reactions to the ramifications of the 9/11 attacks on the United States, while Sophie Bourgault has investigated the idea of compassion in politics in relation to the work of Hannah Arendt.

Emotions occur as we move in the world in relation to social and antisocial goals, our own and others'. As we do so, emotions configure our relationships. I have put it like this (Oatley 2009). An actor on the stage has a script of words and uses these to guide the enactment of emotionally based relationships with other characters in a play or film. In ordinary life, a kind of inverse occurs. We have scripts of emotionally based relationships for which we find the words. If someone smiles at us, we tend to feel empathetically happy and disposed to cooperate. If we sense anger in the other, we feel angry, disposed to conflict. If we see someone sad, we tend to feel sad, too, disposed to help. If we see someone fearful, we often feel anxious about a shared danger. If we see people in a group to which we do not belong, we may despise and shun them.

Psychologists and neuroscientists have not always been able to engage sufficiently deeply with issues that are raised by the social implications of emotions. The fact that such issues are now becoming of interest to disciplines in the wider social sciences is important. Although some, such as John Gunnell (in this volume), are sceptical of social scientific approaches to emotion, the general trend towards making emotions central to our understanding in such disciplines as political science is of considerable significance. Only, I think, when people in different disciplines cooperate will we be able to understand the contexts in which emotions occur in human life. And only when we take such contexts into account will we be properly able to understand the many-faceted phenomena of human emotions.

REFERENCES

Aristotle. 1984. *Complete Works of Aristotle: The Revised Oxford Translation*. Edited by Jonathan Barnes. 2 vols. Bollingen Series. Princeton, NJ: Princeton University Press. Original works mostly composed between 335 and 322 BC.

Aurelius, Marcus. 1964. *Meditations*. Translated by Maxwell Staniforth. London: Penguin. Originally published ca. 170.

Bowlby, John. 1951. *Child Care and the Growth of Love*. Harmondsworth, UK: Penguin.

De Waal, Frans. 1982. *Chimpanzee Politics*. New York: Harper & Row.

James, William. 1884. "What Is an Emotion?" *Mind* 9 (34): 188–205. http://dx.doi.org/10.1093/mind/os-IX.34.188.

Keltner, Dacher, Keith Oatley, and Jennifer M. Jenkins. 2013. *Understanding Emotions*. 3rd ed. Hoboken, NJ: Wiley.

Mellars, Paul. 2004. "Neanderthals and the Modern Human Colonization of Europe." *Nature* 432 (7016): 461–5. http://dx.doi.org/10.1038/nature03103.

Oatley, Keith. 2004. *Emotions: A Brief History*. Oxford: Blackwell. http://dx.doi.org/10.1002/9780470776322.

Oatley, Keith. 2009. "Communications to Self and Others: Emotional Experience and Its Skills." *Emotion Review* 1 (3): 206–13. http://dx.doi.org/10.1177/1754073909103588.

Solomon, Robert. 2007. *True to Our Feelings: What Our Emotions Are Really Telling Us*. New York: Oxford University Press.

EMOTIONS, COMMUNITY, AND CITIZENSHIP

Cross-Disciplinary Perspectives

Introduction

REBECCA KINGSTON, KIRAN BANERJEE,
YI-CHUN CHIEN, AND JAMES McKEE

Most people can understand what it is to feel or to emote, and they can understand others when they give an account of their feelings, but researchers across academic disciplines conceptualize and make sense of the emotions in very different ways. Given some basic agreement on the phenomena as experienced, yet the diverse and often quite divergent ways we tend to make sense of it on reflection, there is hardly a better area for thinking about the possibility of cross-disciplinary dialogue. The purpose of this volume is to continue this dialogue in critical fashion among fields of scholarship often represented in the study of emotions. The idea of context is also a theme pursued capaciously here as we explore emotions in the context of competing areas of research, but also with particular emphasis on the different ways that disciplines study emotions in the social and political contexts in which they are experienced.

Of course, there is no template for cross-disciplinary study, given that the field of investigation is always situated in some conceptually defined area of knowledge. The editors of this volume are all political scientists, and we have chosen the pieces included here as a means of shedding light on the wider dialogues possible between political science and other fields of study with respect to the emotions. This selection of chapters is meant to serve four purposes in particular: in the first instance, the collection demonstrates one possible cross section of the wide diversity of approaches possible in the field of emotion studies relevant to politics, and it identifies some of the key points of difference and possible dispute among these approaches; second, the collection demonstrates how political issues of context and human interrelatedness have a thematic place in studies on emotion outside the discipline of political science; third, the collection demonstrates how other work in emotion studies broadly conceived has had an impact on both the empirical and the normative issues taken up in the discipline of political science; and fourth, the collection provides reflection on the possibility of a field of emotion studies that looks to address questions surrounding the study of emotions from broader cross-disciplinary perspectives. This collection took root in a cross-disciplinary symposium on the emotions held at the University of Toronto in the fall of 2011, drawing from a number of outstanding scholars in the field in different departments across the university. We have supplemented the collection of core chapters from this symposium with work from other scholars to meet the full objectives of this work.

There is no question that, over the past ten to fifteen years, there have been significant advances enhancing our understanding of and appreciation for the emotions. In the humanities and social sciences, emotion is construed as a phenomenon that expresses a deep connection between the body and cognition, evokes fundamental aspects of the human person, sheds light on our ties to others, and tests the strength of the link between our normative theories of politics and society and our practice. In medical science, increased accessibility to functional magnetic resonance imaging (fMRI) and positron emission tomography (PET) scans, among an array of new technologies in brain science, offers researchers more insight into neurological patterns associated with emotional experience. In experimental psychology, increased attention is being paid to the possibility of a science of human well-being and its links to emotion. In philosophy, a number of scholars have acknowledged that emotions are not always disruptive and have deep connections to motivation, to a sense of meaning, and to the very process of reasoning itself. In the social sciences, there is increased appreciation of the complexity and centrality of our emotional experience, at both the individual and the social levels as well as in politics.

Given these concurrent developments, there is clearly a need to think in greater detail about how the findings in one domain might inform and facilitate analysis in others – and, in more basic terms, how the themes of differing approaches might interconnect. Yet a great deal of this work has yet to be done. While as editors we are sceptical of the presumption that an overarching perspective is possible, we do harbour the hope that pursuit of emotion studies from a more informed cross-disciplinary perspective will help deepen our understanding. Contributors to this volume fully accept their disciplinary enclave, yet despite their different approaches and objectives, they present a number of interlocking themes.

We hope by this introduction to do two things. The first is to provide a generalized account of the state of scholarship across a number of different fields. This will serve to situate our particular contributions in their disciplinary focus as well as to provide one articulation (largely humanist inspired) that might facilitate cross-disciplinary questions. As it cannot be claimed that the contributions to this volume are fully representative of their respective disciplines, given that the diversity within the disciplines does not allow for any one fully representative contribution, the broader survey offered in this introduction serves to contextualize the contributions and provide a perspective that might serve as a springboard for cross-disciplinary questions.

The second purpose of this introduction is to raise two questions that emerge from this juxtaposition of chapters from diverse disciplines and that inform the structure of the book and the ordering of the chapters. The first question structuring the collection is, What sort of account might help us to understand the various invocations of emotion across disciplines? Is it just a matter of contingent vocabulary, or is there a core phenomenon evoked by the term *emotion*, and, if so, what sort of linkage or relation helps us to best account for it? Given that emotion can often be conceptualized as pointing beyond itself in accounts of its essence or in its impact – with links to the body, to the environment, to personality or disposition, to the social setting, and to broader political structures and choices – is there something that we can say is deemed to be essential to emotion? The second question structuring the collection is, What emotions and what emotional dispositions are normatively best associated with the context of liberal democratic citizenship? While liberal democratic citizenship has traditionally been interpreted as allowing citizens the liberty to pursue competing conceptions of the good, there has been increasing acknowledgment that granting citizens this liberty requires the development of particular dispositions and emotional qualities. Through a consideration of varied practices and thinkers, the contributions of this volume provide competing accounts of how best to think about the contours and possibilities of emotions for sustaining democratic practice.

Of course, there is a great deal of overlap in these matters, so in this sense, all the chapters in the volume are relevant to a broader deliberation. For example, it may be that an understanding of emotion that is relational yet also amenable to cognitive modification has a more effective place in normative political theory. For those projects of mapping human behaviours that appear to hold regardless of our conscious awareness, it may be that a more embodied and less cognitive understanding of emotion may hold. The breadth of research in the social sciences appears to suggest that the academic task is not to unquestionably champion one conception of emotion over all others, but rather to map their various manifestations and to argue for when the evocation of one may be more appropriate than another.

As a preliminary step, it might be helpful to take stock, as it were. What, if anything, can we consider to be a given in the realm of emotion? Can conclusions about emotions from the world of science really provide insights for the humanities and social sciences, as has recently been attempted in a number of ways? What are the most important questions about the emotions that are being explored across the various disciplines? How might we identify some of the tensions between the perspectives of the humanities and social sciences on the issue of emotional experience? And how might the insights of social science and philosophy contribute, if at all, to the questions pursued in more scientific settings?

This introduction offers an overview of some of the most important trends and developments in the study of emotions. While a crude synthesis, this introductory essay can stand as a justification for more cross-disciplinary consideration of emotions, given the new insights across the various fields, as well as a resource for exploring new avenues of enquiry. We begin with an overview of some of the most important contributions in the field of experimental science, followed by a consideration of scholarly trends in the social sciences, and rounded up by an overview of more recent trends in the humanities, classics, and philosophy.

Reflections on the Science of Emotion

A plurality of perspectives characterizes engagement with the study of the emotions in the sciences. Indeed, how we come to know the basic nature of emotion is itself a matter of controversy.

> Let's take the example of someone waving when she sees a friend across a room. We can describe this action purely in terms of mechanics – the tensing of muscles gives rise to a lifting of the arm etc. In contrast, a description of the same event at a social level might be put in terms of how the

> person is welcoming her friend. Both of these levels of analysis are accurate and provide qualitatively different descriptions of the same phenomenon. (Fox 2008, 150)

Elaine Fox uses this example to argue that the neurologist working on the chemical and mechanical components of emotion must not ignore, or be ignored by, the cognitive psychologist working at the level of the processing of information. This is certainly true if one's objective is to give as full an account of the phenomenon of emotion as possible. To develop this full account, there is a need to gather information from as many perspectives as possible to sort out what exactly is going on. It would appear to be the standard academic reflex.

Yet when it comes to emotion, the questions of what science is doing, and whether and how what it is doing is relevant to other questions of meaning, both individually and socially, are controversial ones. And these questions are not limited to the humanities and social sciences, where there are debates about the applicability of the findings of science, but are found within the bounds of science itself.

The science of emotion is both vast and multifaceted. Not only is the scientific, or experimental, study of emotion spread over a vast number of disciplines, ranging from biology, psychology, neuroscience, genetics, and psychiatry, but also, the focus of what is central to emotion shifts both within and among these disciplines. The wide diversity of approaches and methods even in the field of experimental work on the emotions may lead one to be initially sceptical of those in the social sciences and humanities who claim in somewhat uncategorical terms that experimental science in the realm of emotion can do little to shed light on the true nature of human emotional experience (Tallis 2011).

Of course, any general overview of the science of emotion study as offered here will not do full justice to the field and will certainly not capture most of the subtleties and range of arguments. However, some understanding of the breadth and depth of the field is important, especially for those who study emotion from outside the realm of experimental science, in part to deepen their analysis and in part to adequately judge those arguments in the humanities and social sciences that engage with the question of what experimental science can offer to our knowledge of emotions.

Experimental focus in the study of emotion can range across localizing the relevant spot in the brain for specific emotional processing, analysing the structure and behaviour of a single molecule or chemical particle in the brain, exploring the genetic basis for emotional disposition, and studying complex physiological and chemical processes in the brain or in the brain's interaction with the mind and body. Other experimental scientists may focus on the behaviour associated with emotional response, whether in facial expression or other outward manifestations of an emotional state. Yet another level of experimental work is focused on the cognitive and/or subjective aspects of emotional experience, looking at the functioning of the mind and the way in which emotional experience unfolds. For the purpose of analysis and at the risk of oversimplification, we can sort the science (coming from a vast array of academic disciplines, including neuroscience, chemistry, behavioural biology, anthropology, and psychology) into five broad approaches – i.e., brain science, science of behaviour and emotional response, science of physiology and emotion, science of mind, and a broader component process model. It is sometimes the case that this division also corresponds with other criteria – namely, the degree of specificity given to human emotion.

The first category encompassing those scientific researchers who explore various brain circuits appears to be grounded in a broadly evolutionary understanding of emotion – suggesting that the faculty of emotion stems from very basic needs of individual and collective survival. This approach involves, at a preliminary level, locating where certain types of emotional processing occur in the brain (either by mapping changes in blood flow using fMRI and PET or mapping metabolic activity in general with PET or electrical activity in the brain with magnetoencephalography) and then exploring and explaining how it occurs. While the limbic system (including the structures of the cingulate cortex, hippocampus, thalamus, hypothalamus, and amygdala) has often been targeted in this work, it is now acknowledged that other circuits and systems are also involved in the processing of emotion.

A focus on the subcortical region is offered in the work of Jaak Panksepp, whose approach is cited and further nuanced by Georg Northoff in chapter 5 of this volume (Panksepp 1998). Panksepp suggests that the same basic emotional system functions across all animal species and that the study of these systems in rodents can shed important light on the working of human emotion. Even here, the areas of study are multiple and could be very crudely broken down into the types of processes deemed to be most important, with attention paid to elements of the anatomy, the physiology, as well as the neurochemical processes found in the brain. The processes are obviously complex, and, despite an acceptance of the genesis of emotion in basic needs, many researchers also acknowledge systems of adaptation and brain plasticity (where brains can perform the same functions through different circuits). Some researchers suggest that, physiologically, the human experience of emotion is unique, with the cortical regions playing an important role and with greater possibility of flexibility and compensatory processes in the functioning of human brains than in the brains of animals. So while it may be conceded that both humans and animals have similar forms of background and/or primary emotions, the greater complexity of the human mind allows for different types of secondary emotions (or emotions about our emotions – for example, shame, pride, and guilt), which have no counterpart in the animal world.

Often central to these approaches is the idea that emotions emerge from processes centred in the brain, with discrete and distinct patterns of neural networks identified with particular emotions, and that these emotions can be identified by these processes regardless of our consciousness or sense of our own body and feeling. Thus, for these researchers, we must distinguish between emotions and feelings. While *emotions* "are specific and consistent collections of physiological responses triggered by certain brain systems when the organism represents certain objects or situations," *feelings* refer only to those instances when we perceive emotion (Damasio 2000, 15). Although there is no one definition of emotion agreed on in the differing fields of scientific research (some would even deny that any form of mental representation is required for an emotion to be possible), much of the experimental scientific community accept that having an emotion does not require consciousness of that experience as an emotion. This can be revealed in experiments that demonstrate how individuals can be brought to perceive ostensibly neutral images in a negative light by cultivating negative associations with an object (through the split-second flashing of images) under the radar of conscious awareness. These individuals are then tested to demonstrate how emotion can be shaped below or beyond the level of advanced cognition. In more general terms, it is acknowledged that sometimes the physiological and behavioural changes associated with emotion can occur while we are not aware of them subjectively, or at least not immediately.

A second feature of emotion treated experimentally is the physiological dimension. While clearly the neural focus on the brain involves discussion of some physiological dimension to emotional experience, more broadly construed approaches explore changes in the body as a whole, including chemical release into the bloodstream, and the targeting of certain organs, such as water in the eyes or increasing heart rate. This focus is often subject to an important distinction between the sympathetic autonomic nervous system, associated with features of physical arousal, and the parasympathetic autonomic nervous system, associated with effects linked to rest. Arousal in turn has been seen to have an impact on patterns of attention. While greater emotional stimulation can often be shown to heighten attentiveness to the stimuli giving rise to emotion, it may also narrow the range of focus of attention. Still, it is also acknowledged that not all emotional states will be linked to a particular physiological pattern.

A third category of experimental research looks at similarities of behaviour related to emotion, whether between humans and other living species or specifically related to human life. Some experimental work in animal behaviour, such as that of Frans de Waal, seeks to demonstrate that basic primate tendencies to empathy and cooperation are embedded in our biology.[1] Another famous approach to exploring emotion through behavioural response is the work of Paul Ekman, who studies the expression of emotion on faces (Ekman 2007). Inspired initially by the work of Charles Darwin on the expression of emotion, Ekman works with the understanding that there are templates for emotion that are shared by the whole human species and that are processed quasi-automatically in the brain, at least with respect to what he identifies as the six basic emotions: sadness, happiness, surprise, anger, disgust, and fear (Darwin 1999). In this experimental approach, the universality of some basic emotional reactions is considered proof that a core set of emotional systems is given to us by nature. Still, while the experience of these emotions is universally shared and ultimately linked to common features of brain structure, emotional response can mean a number of things, from physiological readiness to action tendencies. Some responses are considered by nature automatic, others made automatic by habitual behaviour or cultural transmission, yet others a matter of more conscious management – something indeed acknowledged by Darwin himself.

The fourth focus of emotion research is on subjective experience, or the feeling and more general awareness that we can report. While subjective report clearly plays a crucial role in helping to validate certain emotional states, scientific researchers tend to believe that there is more to emotion than what can be gained through introspection. Subjective accounts, therefore, tend not to be the central focus of scientific investigation on the emotions. One exception is those experimental researchers who hold to a dimensional approach to emotion – that is, those who suggest that one cannot identify different emotions according to distinct neural networks. Fox (2008, 114) argues that the neural and physiological features of emotion provide only vague indicators of valence (i.e., positive or negative associations given to emotions in a way not generally felt with other forms of perceptions) and intensity and that the specific quality of emotion must be traced to alternative factors, such as language or judgment or psychological processes or appraisal (even when we are not conscious of them, as argued by Richard Lazarus [1994] as well as Stanley Schachter and Jerome Singer [1962]). It is a general tendency to minimize the importance of the subjective dimension in the exploration and understanding of emotion that makes scientific and experimental approaches controversial in the eyes of some emotion researchers from disciplines in the humanities and social sciences.

A fifth experimental approach, sometimes called the component process model, developed initially by Klaus Scherer, is used by those who take a broad view of emotions and seek to analyse them more holistically according to the changes that can be mapped in five important subsystems – i.e., cognitive component (appraisal), neurophysiological component (bodily symptoms), motivational component (action tendencies), motor expression component (facial and vocal expression), and subjective feeling component (emotional experience) (Fox 2008, 26). These components, while operating often independently of one another, become coordinated for a short time in an emotion. Exploring emotions with this broad template in mind makes investigation much more general and also more complicated, but it does allow for a certain flexibility in analysis – for example, in acknowledging that different emotions may demonstrate very different interactions among these subsystems and in considering that no one subsystem is more fundamental than any other in all instances of emotional experience. This broader overview allows for greater reflection on the interaction of brain systems, including recognition of the important role that affect in general may play in good cognitive functioning, but also how affect may shape the contours of perception and attention as well as later stages of processing information, such as judgment and memory.

The wide array of scientific approaches and methods evoked in the study of emotions makes it very difficult to both summarize and judge. The diversity noted here also poses a particular challenge to those scholars in the humanities and social sciences who may wish to draw on scientific findings to enhance their own work. The disputed nature of many of these scientific claims, even those advanced on the grounds of scientific research, makes their status as evidence in other fields of enquiry quite unstable, for they may not have the status of verifiable truth claimed for them by those who evoke them, a point also noted by John Gunnell in this volume. Without a good understanding of the broader scientific context, findings in the science of emotion may not be taken into other disciplines with an appropriate degree of critical regard. So one of the questions posed by the studies in this book is, How might we or should we consider the relation between these experimental approaches to the study of emotion and those driven by narrative and history?

There are clearly limits to what the findings of brain science can tell us. For example, the snapshot portrait that comes from fMRI scans cannot provide an overview over time of what the brain is doing, and there is still no clear evidence that such brain changes, even if mapped accurately, can really explain both the emotion and the behaviour often associated with it. As argued by Raymond Tallis, the fact that emotion can be correlated with varying forms of brain activity cannot demonstrate that brain activity is a sufficient condition or cause of emotion. Nonetheless, the insights of this experimental field, especially in neuroscience, have driven new excitement, especially in the developing field of "affect studies," in which scholars can reconsider and re-conceptualize the nature of embodiment and bring a new understanding to an account of how non-conscious forces can help to shape our relations with others (Massumi 2002; Gregg and Seigworth 2010). This has also been argued as providing focus for a new direction in historical research.[2]

In general terms, the diversity of scientific exploration in these various fields of research should open us to the possibility of a wide variety of phenomena connected with the broad term we tend to call *emotion*. It may be that emotion is not one neural and biological mechanism at all, but a broad range of possible mechanisms (a position previously argued by Paul Griffiths). This should also lead us to acknowledge that we should not seek to rule out the findings of neuroscience on the basis that scientific explanation may not always suitably account for the meaning or conscious feel of emotion.

Reflections on the Study of Emotion in the Humanities

Given their centrality to human experience, affect and the emotions have been a permanent focus of investigation among the fields of the humanities. Grappling with the status and place of emotions in human experience has constituted an important concern of philosophers, poets, and historians since antiquity. Yet at the same time, as in the social sciences, a number of fields have undergone a recent "emotions turn," in which the subject of affect has been taken up in novel ways or opened new avenues of research.

In the humanities, few disciplines have had as sustained and varied an engagement with the subject of the emotions than philosophy. Whether that field of study is interrogating the status of emotions as part of the human psyche and embodied experience or evaluating their role in ethics, aesthetics, judgment, and political life, the subject of affect has remained a perennial concern of philosophy since its inception, although in a number of different ways. In recent times, philosophy as a discipline has been most serious in adjudicating the claims of science with regard to the nature of emotion.

Susan James in *Passion and Action* (1997) and Martha Nussbaum with *The Therapy of Desire* (1994) helped to establish a new focus in the history of philosophic thought. Part of the challenge of this intellectual and philosophical history is to make sense of terms through which various thinkers reflected on emotions, for the terms of the discourse have shifted significantly throughout history, a point also highlighted by Thomas Dixon (2003).

Philosophical work on emotion from an analytical perspective has tended to present itself as a dichotomy between those who espouse the work and language of natural science and those who hold that the essence of emotion is more phenomenal and requires the work of philosophical reflexivity to explore its nature. On the naturalistic side, there are various accounts that, to some degree, mirror the scientific explanations available. One of the key distinctions is between those who identify emotions by their phenomenal, or "felt," quality and those who think of emotions within the framework of what one might call an "affect system" or the patterns of stimulation in the brain. Espousal of the James-Lange view, in which emotion is identified subjectively with feeling, characterizes in broad terms the work of Jesse J. Prinz (2006, 2013) as well as Peter Goldie (2000) (although Prinz does incorporate into his analysis of "somatic markers" some idea of affective appraisal).

Still, there are some philosophers whose analyses point to the possibility that this division between emotion as feeling and emotion as an affect system may be somewhat of a false dichotomy. Ekman, for example, follows Darwin (1999) with a focus on emotional expression as a product of processes considered both automatic and habitual. It is also suggested that even for those theorists who equate emotion with feeling, there is the recognition that one can have instances of not being fully aware of or not acknowledging what one is feeling, or misrepresenting it, as a child might (Deonna, Rodogno, and Teroni 2012). From this perspective, emotion may offer more the possibility or potential of a particular type of feeling, rather than having to be directly equated with the feeling itself. From another perspective, Northoff in this volume suggests that an affect system approach can, in fact, work in the service of a "feeling" approach and indeed provide the grounds for demonstrating the relation of the emotions to a broader environmental context, or what is sometimes called the intentionality of emotion.

The cognitivists are foremost among those who are more sceptical of naturalistic and scientific approaches to the study of emotions. This view, in which emotion is likened to some form of judgment that can be made available for articulation, a vision first articulated by the Stoics, has been held into present times by such thinkers as Robert Solomon (1976) and Jeremy Neu (2002) as well as Nussbaum (2001). While, in simple terms, cognitivists hold that some form of judgment is a component of emotional experience, there is a large range of possibilities allowing for different ways of understanding the nature of the implied judgment (e.g., should we understand it as a proposition requiring advanced mental capacity? Or a less definite aesthetic form of appraisal? Requiring language capacity or not? How is it combined with other propositional content such as beliefs and desires?), although all do face the challenge of accounting for the somatic, or bodily, features of emotional experience. Another class of challenges to the more naturalistic views ties the most crucial features of meaning in an emotion to cultural and linguistic factors. The idea of the social construction of emotions traced to judgments embedded in cultural outlooks has been defended by James Averill (1985) and Rom Harré (1986), among others. The Wittgensteinian approach offered by Gunnell in chapter 3 of this collection can be linked with this perspective.

Some recent philosophical literature on the emotions seeks to bridge the divide between the feeling and interpretive approaches in various ways. The notion of "affective appraisal," or what is sometimes called a "perceptual" approach, linking somatic feeling in emotion with some idea of motivational or attitudinal shift, offers some middle ground between the theories of pure feeling and judgment, although defenders of the notion of appraisal in emotion reject any cognitivist basis for this (Robinson 2007; Prinz 2006). The challenge here is to provide a theory of emotion that can account for some of the idiosyncrasies of emotional experience, such as bodily manifestation that may have the potential for being experienced as feeling, along with attitudinal shifts that are amenable to questions for justification (e.g., why am I feeling sad when I should be happy?), along with some, albeit complicated, scale of valence. Julien Deonna, Raffaele Rodogno, and Fabrice Teroni offer their attitudinal theory, suggesting that emotion can be understood as a bodily attitude towards a given object and as an experience that helps to form judgments and evaluations, which are subsequently used to justify the emotion (Deonna, Rodogno, and Teroni 2012).

Griffiths, both in chapter 4 of this volume and elsewhere (1997, 2013), goes further in seeking to overcome the naturalistic and interpretivist divide in arguing that the name *emotion* does not constitute only one phenomenal process and that it is quite likely that affect programs looked at objectively have a certain salience for explaining some basic emotions, while more feeling, cognitivist, and social constructive accounts may work in understanding others. Other theorists suggest that Griffiths's division does not conform to actual experience, in which there is a complex interaction between cognitive judgments and affect systems at all levels of emotional experience, so that the basic fears of inarticulate children do not always have to be qualitatively different from fears triggered by more developed cognitive faculties in adults (Deonna, Rodogno, and Teroni 2012). In broad terms, contemporary analytical reflection on the emotions leaves many issues open for discussion, but it can be suggested that philosophers are developing accounts that seek to do better justice to the complexities associated with emotional experience, and, through this, they appear to be breaking down to some extent the stark divisions that can be prevalent in other disciplines when it comes to the study of emotions.

In the field of classics, the emotions loom large in studies of conceptions of the self, virtue ethics, and moral psychology. Scholars have suggested that Greek and Roman writers offer an understanding of the place of emotion in the human condition, yielding insight that ought to deepen our appreciation of the complex nature of social and political life. In *Shame and Necessity* (1993), Bernard Williams draws on the cultural resources of ancient Greece to develop an alternative perspective on ethics, one in which shame plays a crucial role; his project has proved to be an important point of departure for more recent work in the field. Christina Tarnopolsky (2010) articulates a multivalent and complex account of shame as inspired by Plato's *Gorgias*, suggesting that some manifestations of shame allied with self-respect can be ethically constructive and harnessed to a project of liberal democratic citizenship.

Beginning with *The Therapy of Desire* (1994), Nussbaum argues for a practical and compassionate vision of philosophy as therapy, drawing on the works of Hellenistic writers to draw attention to the embodied and worldly aspects of human life, while also developing a broadly cognitive account of the emotions. In subsequent work spanning classics, philosophy, and literature, Nussbaum argues that we need to place attentiveness to the emotional dimensions of human experience at the centre of our ethical thinking, including in *Political Emotions: Why Love Matters for Justice* (2013).

In a related although distinct vein, a number of classicists have developed extensive reconstructions of the emotions in ancient public and private life by drawing on a myriad of classical sources, including courtroom and political orations, literature, and drama. William Fortenbaugh's *Aristotle on Emotion* (1975) argues for recovering a cognitive perspective of the emotions from Aristotle's thought, for which emotions entail judgment, a theme that is further pursued in his more recent *Aristotle's Practical Side* (2006). A deep engagement with Aristotle's view of the interplay between cognition and feeling in emotion, as well as an exploration of its place in political persuasion, is found in Jamie Dow's *Passions and Persuasion in Aristotle's "Rhetoric"* (2015).

David Konstan (2006) has unpacked a broad range of emotional expression in the context of ancient Greece, while also putting his work in conversation with contemporary theorists of the emotions, such as Georg Simmel. In earlier work, Konstan (2001) offers an extensive study of pity; his subsequent work articulates a cognitivist view of the emotions, while also insisting on the socially embedded nature of affective dispositions. William Harris (2002) has also developed a careful contextual approach to the place of anger and its control in the classical world.

There have also been a number of recent studies tracing broader historical approaches to the emotions. In a study moving from antiquity to early Christianity, Richard Sorabji (2000) offers careful analysis of the shifting status of the emotions from the thought of Plato to the transformation of Stoic ideas by Christian writers, while also putting such analysis in conversation with contemporary discussions in cognitive science and philosophy. Simo Knuuttila (2004) traces the development of philosophical accounts of the emotions from antiquity up to the fourteenth-century context of the High Middle Ages. It is also worth noting that a number of scholars have turned to the place of emotions as part of broader projects concerned with reconstructing the cultural and social practices of antiquity. Here Ryan Balot's (2002) study of the relation of greed and injustice in classical Athenian society and democratic life, as well as Fiona McHardy's (2008) work on revenge and violence in ancient Athens, may be taken as representative of scholarship in classics, taking the historical manifestation of emotions as a serious focus of study.

The origins of the study of the emotions in the discipline of history can be traced to the pioneering work of the Annales historians, who advocated a new object of history, including curiosity for the daily activities of life and changing popular attitudes. The work of Norbert Elias (1994) also had an important role. A central assumption of most emotion history, apart from perhaps the controversial work of Daniel Smail (2008), is the idea that emotions are, to an important degree, shaped (if not generated) by culture and thereby that they can change significantly over the course of time. Susan Matt (2011) suggests that a triangulation of the work of Peter Stearns (1994, 1999, 2006) and Peter and Carol Stearns (1986), with a focus on what Stearns has called "emotionology," or the dominant patterns of feeling within a cultural context; of Barbara Rosenwein (2007), with her focus on "emotional communities," or the varying models of feeling and acting that exist in one historical community; and of William Reddy (2001), exploring the idea of "emotives," or the way in which language itself can shape feeling, has served to map the broad contours of the current trends in emotion research in history.

In this context, it is worth noting that there is a certain tendency in both history and the wider humanities to characterize the place of emotion in contemporary culture as a pathology. This can take the form of acknowledging that psychological styles, or "structures of feeling" (to cite Raymond Williams), particularly in the wake of greater commercialism and media culture, have made it more difficult for people to manage their psychological lives in meaningful or effective ways (Berlant 2011; Illouz 2007; Stearns 1994; Woodward 2009) or that the emotional disparities in contemporary societies reflect and help entrench deeper social, racial, and economic inequalities (Frevert 2011; Gross 2007; Hochschild 1983).

An attentiveness to emotion has remained characteristic of literary studies. Indeed, a number of other disciplines in the humanities and beyond – most notably, philosophy – have drawn directly on the resources offered by the study of literature and fiction in attempting to interrogate the emotions. This is in part because of the powerful ability of literary narratives to bring about affective responses and trigger processes of moral learning. There has been widespread recognition from outside the field that literature provides one of our greatest resources for helping to think through subjective emotional experience. Indeed, the apparent detachability of belief and affective response captured in works of fiction – that we can be powerfully moved by stories that we at the same time know to be untrue – has remained a perennial point of interest in the philosophy of literature, while the implications of this have made interdisciplinary engagements with literature a particularly fertile mode for thinking about the emotions. Consequently, there have been a number of philosophers and social scientists who have appealed to literature to shed light on emotional experience.

Perhaps one of the more notable developments in the field of the humanities in relation to the study of emotion is the rise of what is called "affect theory." While *affect* is a term that carries diverse meanings in its uses in the field, affect theory generally distinguishes itself by emphasizing an often unarticulated but tonal background that shapes our interrelations. Affect theorists often insist that affect should be understood in its raw presence, coming before language, consciousness, and even to some degree perception. This emphasis is sometimes thought of as a greater attunement to the embodied nature of our relation to other people and things.

The rise of affect studies in the humanities has been greatly influenced by developments outside the field. Silvan Tomkins, who trained in both philosophy and psychology and published *Affect Imagery Consciousness* (1962), focused on affect as an independent factor in helping to shape human interactions, in part as an alternative to the hegemony of Freudian narratives in the field. He sought to identify a basic affect system – a set of eight primary motives (fear, distress, anger, shame, contempt, interest, enjoyment, and surprise) found in both human beings and animals – paying special attention to the face, where the affective response was thought to be often visible (Tomkins 1981). The presumption was that each affect was associated with a specific set of responses, which were innately programmed in the muscles (although subject to some conscious and cultural manipulation), and that feeling preceded thinking or any form of cognitive judgment or even intentionality, much like what was presumably witnessed in a baby. Deborah Gould (2010) has identified affect as the non-cognitive, non-conscious, non-linguistic, and non-rational qualities of emotion – that is, unnamed but nevertheless registered through the experiences of bodily energy and intensity that arise in response to the impinging of stimuli on the body. For most affect theorists, it appears that these instances of affect or intensity of bodily response often come with a certain indeterminacy of meaning, which only latterly become more determinate in meaning when they are taken up and processed as a form of emotive experience channelled through a number of cultural and social norms.

In 1995, Eve Sedgwick published a reader devoted to Tomkins, a move that appeared to formally initiate the "affective turn." The approach has been important for theorists in feminist studies and queer theory, especially insofar as it appeared to bring back a form of subjectivity often missing from traditional post-structuralist accounts, while still retaining a certain critical function. In cultural theory, Sara Ahmed's *The Cultural Politics of Emotion* (2004) has been particularly effective in harnessing the approach of affect theory to critical theory. Another strand of affect theory is associated with the work of the philosopher Brian Massumi (2002), who has translated and been inspired by the work of Gilles Deleuze (1980) as a source of contributions to modern social theory. A distinction between Ahmed's and Massumi's general approach to affect theory appears to be that Ahmed allows for a degree of cognitive and interpretative agency in the affective moment ("How we arrive, how we enter this room or that room, will affect what impressions we receive. To receive is to act. To receive an impression is to make an impression" [Ahmed 2010, 40; Ahmed 2012, 48]). In contrast, Massumi tends to emphasize the fully preconscious nature of affect. While affect theory has garnered a great deal of support and influence across the humanities and social sciences, opposition to some of the assumed presumptions of this approach has been voiced by critics like Ruth Leys (2011) as well as Gunnell in this volume. Among an array of concerns, critics have tended to question whether any sort of recognizably human meaning can be ascribed in any valid way to what is generally taken to be a precognitive and prelinguistic state of mind.

Reflections on the Study of Emotion in the Social Sciences

There has not been one social scientific approach to the study of emotion. While attention to emotion has arrived relatively recently to the disciplines of political science and sociology (for in this crude classification, we include a discussion of historical approaches in the camp of the humanities), it has provided important challenges to traditional approaches to these disciplines. In the study of politics, paying concerted attention to the place of emotion has led to a deeper questioning of the long-standing normative ideals of a fully rational, deliberative community as a model of good politics, but it has also led to new types of reflection on the ways to manage peace building and development. Still, as demonstrated by Joseph Fletcher and Jennifer Hove (chapter 7) in this volume, one cannot assume that the same emotions function in the same way in different political contexts. As they demonstrate, while grief for the death of service personnel and empathy for their families may work in some cases to increase support for military campaigns, it may also work in a different context to undermine popular support for military missions, even if justified publicly for peaceful ends. In sociology, analysis of the workings of emotion in society has led to a deeper critical analysis of the manifestations of social power and inequalities, as explored by James Jasper (chapter 8) in this volume. There has also been, following Williams, further consideration of how to characterize the emotional climate in our era of advanced capitalism (Williams 1978).

In political science, emotion is often studied as one facet of political culture or political behaviour helping scholars to understand policy preferences, voting patterns, the psychology of leadership, and even the "emotional temperaments" of international politics. Others have begun to reconsider fundamental assumptions about rationality and decision making as they pertain to established fields of study in international relations and foreign policy, for example.

Three key areas are highlighted here: the study of individual citizen attitudes in the light of liberal democratic norms, the place of emotion in regulating conflict in the courts or in peace building, and the question of happiness as an objective of public policy. The "affective intelligence" theory of George E. Marcus, W. Russell Neuman, and Michael MacKuen (2000) stands as one current and widely cited example of an influential approach to the study of emotion in political science. In this and his subsequent work on emotion, Marcus (2002, 2013) brings the insights of certain strands of neuroscience to bear on questions of political behaviour. He acknowledges that there is a great deal of citizen behaviour that is ruled by processes that occur below our conscious radar. For Marcus, this applies not only in the realm of very basic human action but also in the political realm for such things as voting habits and traditional partisan behaviour. It forms part of what he terms the "disposition system," which characterizes the ways in which citizens rely on traditional emotional and cognitive patterns in their public lives. In times when traditional patterns are being challenged or changed, an alternative system called the "surveillance system" is activated so as to provoke reflection and deliberation. The upshot is that politics is both affective and deliberative and that anxiety can be productive in politics as it helps to encourage a more reflective public.

> We misunderstand politics if it is reduced to a domesticated form of combat (using votes rather than weapons of war to achieve victory of "us" over "them"). And we also misunderstand politics if we require that it be limited to thoughtful deliberation over what the circumstances require, freed from the grip of convictions and established loyalties. Democratic politics is both of these. (Marcus 2013)

The work of Marcus and other scholars on the place of emotion in politics has led some to a rethinking of the norms of democratic life and a consideration of the ways that emotion can work positively in politics.

Another focus of the work in political science on emotion concerns the place of emotion in the courtroom, in peace building, and in a good practice of citizenship (Baron-Cohen 2011; Nussbaum 2013). There has been discussion of the nature and desirability of shaming practices in legal punishment (Nussbaum 2004; Deonna, Rodogno, and Teroni 2012) and of the need for empathy as a basic condition of proper legal judgment and civic friendship. The literature on peace building has explored the place of empathy as well as other emotions and the institutions that might promote and sustain them in facilitating transitions to post-conflict stability (Kaindaneh and Rigby 2012).

A third, newer branch of reflection in politics and development is the current project of various social scientists to develop measurements of happiness as an objective of public policy (Helliwell, Layard, and Sachs 2012). While happiness economics has been in development for a longer while, bodies such as the Organisation for Economic Co-operation and Development have recently issued detailed reports offering guidance for governments seeking happiness measurements of policy effectiveness. In these measurements, subjective assessments of mood and self-reports of emotion are supplemented by standard measures of development, such as educational levels and income. Governments such as the United Kingdom's have now followed the lead of Bhutan in announcing that happiness will become an expressed goal and measure of policy effectiveness. This development is becoming the object of broad political and philosophical commentary.

A focus on emotions was introduced into sociology with the work of Arlie Hochschild (1983), who understood emotions as deriving from a set of social relations. Hochschild's idea of "emotional labour" acknowledged how capitalist economies have spawned a set of jobs, such as flight attendants, store greeters, and caregivers, jobs that require workers to display their emotions as their primary responsibility. The sociological perspective linking emotion to social structures has often favoured an interpretivist approach to emotion.

Hochschild's pioneering work spawned a vast literature exploring the nature and place of emotion in broad social circles from a deeply critical perspective. Laura Suski (2012), for example, explores how the seemingly benign emotion of humanitarianism masks a certain form of neocolonialism and dubious politics as it transforms a question of justice into a question of feeling and assumes that the suffering of the other can be fully understood and made our own simply through a process of our imagination.

There is some discussion in the sociological literature regarding how to characterize the patterns of emotion in late capitalism. Is it the case that the "iron cage" has subsumed us in greater ways and that our emotional lives are becoming more shallow and less meaningful in the face of hyper-commercialism – when sending a greeting card can replace our need to express an active emotion? Or is our era one of heightened emotional intensity, given the increased public display of emotion in the media? Alan Hunt (2012) suggests that the greeting card phenomenon is evidence of a shallower form of emotional life in broader social circles, accompanied by greater emotional intensity and expectations of expressive display of emotion with intimates, a dichotomy that we experience as a tension in contemporary life. It is a landscape characterized somewhat differently by Kathleen Woodward (2009), who sees the media and commercial culture as subjecting us to increasingly ramped-up intensities of feeling, although sometimes at the expense of our psychological and individualized emotions. These ways of thinking through the features of our era raise the question of the public-private divide in emotional patterns, a question that is also addressed through political theory by Sophie Bourgault (chapter 9) in this collection.

Overview of the Contributions to the Volume

In the context of this brief overview of major contributions to the field of emotion studies, the array of chapters presented in this volume offers a distinct contribution. While not committed to any one view or account of emotional phenomena, all the authors of these chapters acknowledge that emotion can be understood as an analytically distinct category, or at the very least as a term standing in for phenomena sharing some form of family resemblance. However, it is almost impossible to disentangle an experience of emotion from the language used to make sense of it, the nature of the community or environment in which it is felt, or the broader cultural and political structures that help to set the terms of understanding and the competing narratives of personal meaning from which emotional experience gets it force.

Part I of this volume is dedicated to interpretive approaches to the study of emotion, either by exploring the conceptualizing of emotion in different historical periods or through a reasoned philosophical defence of the interpretive approach in the field of social science. In the first chapter, Balot explores ancient discussions around courage – considered to be both a secondary, and moral, emotion regulating an individual's response to fear and one of the four cardinal virtues. He situates Plato's discussion of the education for courage as presented in *The Republic* in the context of competing approaches to the training of warriors represented by the Spartan and Athenian models. Despite evidence that Plato was greatly inspired by the Spartan example in his discussion of education in the early books of the dialogue, Balot suggests that, ultimately, Plato drew from a theory of emotion and model of education implicit in the practices of Athenian democracy. While Spartan warriors were taught to feel courage by observing strict habits and authoritative codes, Athenians were offered role models at a young age from which courageous attributes could be modelled, followed by the possibility of discursive reflection on the nature of courage and its place in a democratic community. Similarly, Plato teaches his young guardians to feel courage through a carefully considered set of influences, and he only subsequently develops their cognitive understanding of the virtue and its connection to a broader account of the truth and goodness. In this manner, despite Plato's attempt to undo the uncertainties connected with democratic practice, the basic structure of emotional education as instilling right feeling, followed by discursive and cognitive reflection on emotion and character, shows more affinity with the democratic Athenian model than the Spartan. This discussion suggests that courage can function distinctly in competing cultural contexts. In addition, it raises questions of the specific nature of courage compatible with the practice of democratic citizenship as well as the means to instil it.

In the second chapter, Jan Purnis provides a study of a historically situated conception of emotion in its ties to a culturally specific understanding of the body. This chapter highlights both particularities of the Renaissance perspective on emotion as well as continuities with certain modern scientific stances. The question this raises is whether it vindicates the position taken by Antonio Damasio and others that emotions are to be considered biologically determined, transhistorical processes to be best explored and explained through the methods of contemporary science or whether the patterns of both continuity and discontinuity provide evidence of the largely cultural (and thereby somewhat contingent) roots of contemporary scientific ideas and practices.

The third chapter in Part I provides a sceptical articulation of the modern attempt to explain emotion through scientific methods and, in particular, the work of neuroscience, which has been a touchstone for much recent commentary on the emotions in the social sciences. Gunnell, adopting a basic Wittgensteinian framework in what he calls a discursive view of emotion, suggests that evoking the term *emotion* hides a multiplicity of approaches and paradigms, with no clear link to any one underlying phenomenon. This offers a challenge to the pretensions of modern social scientists, who, he suggests, should stay true to the interpretive nature of the field and not seek to ground their enquiries in other scientific disciplines. In addition, it suggests that there are great, if not insurmountable, challenges in the work of interdisciplinary dialogue in the realm of emotion, for the task must involve historical consideration of the discipline and close critical assessment of its basic vocabulary and presuppositions, along with careful consideration of the findings. As a principled defender of an interpretive approach to the study of emotion, Gunnell argues that the attempt to explain emotion in scientific terms is a futile one given the phenomenon of language as being most central to our experience.

Part II of this collection is devoted to a presentation of various naturalistic accounts of emotion from the fields of neuroscience, philosophy, psychology, and political science, but they are naturalistic accounts with a bit of a twist; that is, they offer universal accounts of human psychology in which the emotion or affect system functions with deep ties to other facets of the human person and the environment. Griffiths in chapter 4 continues to uphold an approach with which he is often associated: that emotion is a conceptual category encompassing analogous but, at bottom, quite varied processes. Still, he continues to defend broad, naturalistic claims for a large part of what we call emotion. In his contribution here, while providing his perspective on major recent developments in the field of emotions in the philosophy of mind, he weighs competing accounts of intentionality and of attempts to square these developments with moral philosophy. For the latter, he sees promise in "enactive" theories, which, alongside perceptual theories of emotion, demonstrate how moral emotions are directly elicited in the act of perception rather than processed secondarily or separately.

In chapter 5, Northoff provides a neurophilosophical account of emotion that extends and deepens the traditional James-Lange account (attributing emotion to the experience of feeling change in the body) with the argument that there is a phenomenal experience of emotion preceding bodily feeling and representation. He suggests that the environment can be considered to be constitutive of what he calls a relational conception of emotion (one that subsumes the embodied conception of the James-Lange approach). One might suggest that this view harbours similar logic to the accounts of affect theory as Northoff nods to Panksepp's notion of "affective consciousness," which can precede awareness of feeling in the body. He suggests that the scientific evidence more clearly supports this notion of a direct link between environment and emotion – that is, the idea that neural processing associated with emotion goes on before bodily feeling and representation. This picture, he argues, provides a better understanding of the often-indeterminate nature of raw bodily feeling and helps to account for the element of intentionality missing from the traditional James-Lange approach.

Kristina Tchalova and Geoff MacDonald in chapter 6 offer some reflection on the relation in neurophysiological systems between bodily pain and social pain to suggest that, in the context of social exclusion, these systems work together. Still, the authors' main concern is to explore the relation between social environments broadly construed and generalized patterns of feeling. From the perspective of attachment theory, psychological dispositions are formed through a relation to a particular nurturing environment, and, in particular, to the specific behaviours of caregivers, and subsequently give rise to how a social environment is perceived phenomenally and emotionally. Tchalova and MacDonald demonstrate how two distinct emotional types, those who demonstrate attachment anxiety and those who demonstrate attachment avoidance, may respond differently to the same social environment, thereby suggesting that while environments can impact directly on emotion, they can do so in divergent ways given divergent personality traits. The authors further seek to explore the relation between these distinct attachment personalities and political orientation, suggesting that anxiously attached individuals have a tendency towards a greater sense of victimization, greater coldness to transgressors and those in need, and a propensity to favour leaders who give an image of strength. Those considered to demonstrate attachment avoidance are deemed to be particularly prone to depression and feelings of helplessness under conditions of stress, but often prioritize self-reliance and non-interference in their political orientations. The more general point is that a disposition to certain emotional patterns appears to be related to particular types of political choices.

In chapter 7, Fletcher and Hove explore how emotion works through an empirical study of citizen attitudes in contemporary liberal democracy. In particular, they explore how emotion has had an impact on policy preference in the realm of Canadian foreign policy. The general finding of the empirical study is that the emotions of sadness and pride can have a modifying effect on opinion. In one of their case studies, images of flag-draped coffins of repatriated soldiers from the Afghan mission in 2009 served in many instances to enhance support for the war. We see from this the direct impact of emotion on policy preference. Still, the same type of images in the different political climate of the United States generated similar emotions but precipitated greater opposition to the war; as a result, the authors acknowledge that it is important to reflect on the nature of the "emotional community," which helps to filter, somewhat like the personality types explored by Tchalova and MacDonald, both the perception and the impact of shared emotional events.

Part III of the volume explores the question of the emotions that do or should sustain the practice of citizenship in the context of democracy. James Jasper in chapter 8 explores the varying ways in which emotion plays a central role in the sociology of protest. He discusses how recent literature has explored the pairing of emotions in experiences, such as shifts from collective shame to pride or mobilization through transitions from fear to anger. He recommends paying attention to the variety of forms that the anger of protest can take with the implicit suggestion that anger can play a particularly important role as a public emotion.

The question of the public-private divide in emotional display is also raised in Bourgault's assessment (chapter 9) of Hannah Arendt's rejection of compassion as a public virtue of contemporary democracy. According to Arendt, compassion appears to work in prelinguistic and invisible ways, thereby robbing politics of its important quality of revealing personality through speech and action. Bourgault suggests, contrary to established interpretations, that Arendt is neither anti-compassion nor anti-affective. Rather, because of the hidden nature of compassion, Arendt sees it best relegated to the private realm of contemporary political life, to the realm of sentimentality. The emotions suited for revelation in the public realm, such as courage, a love of honour, and a desire for equality, are nurtured in private, but they show themselves fully only when individuals step onto a public stage and display their unique qualities. Thus, while not indicting compassion fully, Arendt's views on emotion do lead to certain distinct policy implications, implications that sit rather uneasily with the ideological commitments of some of her defenders in political theory. The deeper question, then, raised by this discussion of Arendt is the degree to which the distinct nature of politics requires devoted democratic citizens to follow her move in disqualifying compassion as a legitimate motivation in public life. This relates to a broader theme common to these engagements: what sort of sentiments and emotions are most salutary to political life? As Balot acknowledges, part of the practice of democratic citizenship will involve not only the discussion of the nature of democratic emotions but also which emotions to include and which to leave out.

In chapter 10, Kiran Banerjee and Jeffrey Bercuson take up a similar discussion of the appropriate emotions for a good practice of democratic citizenship through their study of the work of John Rawls. Similar to the scholarship on Arendt, Rawls has often been subjected to the criticism of neglecting or rejecting the emotions in his normative account of justice. Banerjee and Bercuson seek to defend Rawls against these criticisms, first by showing the affective motivations required by citizens in Rawls's understanding of the social contract (as has been argued before), and second, by demonstrating that Rawls requires a certain moral psychology of citizenship as an ongoing and regulative feature of a liberal-democratic community. In particular, Banerjee and Bercuson focus on the need that Rawls has to mitigate envy (as it is associated with feelings of inequality) and cultivate self-love, self-esteem, and empathy. The upshot of this discussion is that a defence of some form of virtue ethics resonates even in this most liberal of thinkers. The chapter implies that the self-understanding of liberalism as devoid of any particular commitment to cultivation of character and emotion is misguided. Still, the full array of the emotional psychology required for a good practice of contemporary liberal-democratic citizenship is clearly a matter of ongoing deliberation.

In general, this volume raises several distinct questions and seeks to extend the literature on emotions in a couple of new directions. In the first instance, it addresses head-on the question of the benefits and potential dangers of engaging in a more concerted interdisciplinary approach with regard to the emotions. We do not assume that all interdisciplinary dialogue will be fruitful, but we do suggest that it offers the possibility of new perspectives, which can enhance enquiry in our own disciplinary enclaves.

A second awareness highlighted by this collection is that there is a great deal of complexity in trying to make sense of the sources of emotion. One can look to the body, the brain, the environment, personality type, culture, and language as only a few possible sources among many referred to in this collection. Of course, not all these sources need to be mutually exclusive.

In the context of contemporary liberal democracy, we have begun a more concerted discussion of the nature of the emotions best suited for citizenship and of the means to best promote them. It would appear that some form of deliberative practice around the commemorations and occasions for the display of civic sadness and pride, as well as around the choice of appropriate heroes, constitutes an important facet of the emotional infrastructure of a well-functioning liberal-democratic community. Further research incorporating contemporary discussions of the nature of shame, empathy, moral courage, and a sense of irony would fill out a broader sense of the emotional template aimed at in democratic education.

In the epilogue to this collection, we address in greater depth some of the issues raised by this cross-disciplinary array of chapters. In particular, we identify several points of continuity and contrast and suggest avenues for further exploration both for the field of emotion studies and for thinking about the place of emotion studies in the discipline of political science.

NOTES

1 See his most recent work, *The Age of Empathy: Nature's Lessons for a Kinder Society* (2009). An excellent discussion of some of the implications of his work can be found in *Primates and Philosophers: How Morality Evolved* (Ober and Macedo 2007).

2 Daniel Smail (2008). As he notes in this work, "Culture, in some fundamental sense, has been revealed as a biological phenomenon. Wired in

neurophysiology, taking shape in the form of neural networks and receptors, culture can operate in a relatively mechanistic, quasi-biological fashion" (154).

REFERENCES

Ahmed, Sara. 2004. *The Cultural Politics of Emotion*. London: Routledge.

Ahmed, Sara. 2010. *The Promise of Happiness*. Durham, NC: Duke University Press.

Ahmed, Sara. 2012. "Sociable Happiness." In *Emotions Matter: A Relational Approach to Emotions*, edited by Dale Spencer, Kevin Walby, and Alan Hunt, 40–62. Toronto: University of Toronto Press.

Averill, James R. 1985. "The Social Construction of Emotion: With Special Reference to Love." In *The Social Construction of the Person*, edited by Kenneth J. Gergen and Keith E. Davis, 89–109. New York: Springer-Verlag.

Balot, Ryan. 2002. *Greed and Injustice in Classical Athens*. Princeton: Princeton University Press.

Baron-Cohen, Simon. 2011. *Zero Degrees of Empathy*. London: Allen Lane.

Berlant, Lauren. 2011. *Cruel Optimism*. Durham, NC: Duke University Press.

Damasio, Antonio. 2000. "A Second Chance for Emotion." In *Cognitive Neuroscience of Emotion*, edited by Richard D. Lane and Lynn Nadel, 12–23. New York: Oxford University Press.

Darwin, Charles. 1999. *The Expression of Emotions in Man and Animals*. London: Harper Collins.

Deleuze, Gilles, and Felix Guattari. 1980. *A Thousand Plateaus: Capitalism and Schizophrenia*. Minneapolis: University of Minnesota Press.

Deonna, Julien A., Raffaele Rodogno, and Fabrice Teroni. 2012. *In Defense of Shame: The Faces of an Emotion*. Oxford: Oxford University Press.

De Waal, Frans. 2009. *The Age of Empathy: Nature's Lessons for a Kinder Society*. New York: Harmony.

Dixon, Thomas. 2003. *From Passions to Emotions: The Creation of a Secular Psychological Category*. Cambridge: Cambridge University Press.

Dow, Jamie. 2015. *Passions and Persuasion in Aristotle's "Rhetoric."* Oxford: Oxford University Press.

Ekman, Paul. 2007. *Emotions Revealed: Recognizing Faces and Feelings to Improve Communication*. New York: Times Books.

Elias, Norbert. 1994. *The Civilizing Process*. Oxford: Blackwell. First published 1939 by Verlag Haus zum Falken, Basel.

Fortenbaugh, William. 1975. *Aristotle on Emotion*. Bristol: Bristol Classical Press.

Fortenbaugh, William. 2006. *Aristotle's Practical Side*. Leiden, The Netherlands: Brill.

Fox, Elaine. 2008. *Emotion Science*. London: Palgrave Macmillan.
Frevert, Ute. 2011. *Emotions in History: Lost and Found*. Budapest: Central European University Press.
Goldie, Peter. 2000. *The Emotions: A Philosophical Explanation*. Oxford: Clarendon Press.
Gould, Deborah. 2010. "On Affect and Protest." In *Political Emotions*, edited by Janet Staiger, Janet Cvetkovich, and Ann Reynolds, 18–44. London: Routledge.
Gregg, Melissa, and Gregory Seigworth, eds. 2010. *The Affect Theory Reader*. Durham, NC: Duke University Press.
Griffiths, Paul E. 1997. *What Emotions Really Are: The Problem of Psychological Categories*. Chicago: University of Chicago Press.
Griffiths, Paul E. 2013. "Current Emotion Research in Philosophy." *Emotion Review* 5 (2): 215–22.
Gross, Daniel. 2007. *The Secret History of Emotion*. Chicago: University of Chicago Press.
Harré, Rom, ed. 1986. *The Social Construction of Emotions*. Oxford: Blackwell.
Harris, William. 2002. *Restraining Rage: The Ideology of Anger Control in Classical Antiquity*. Cambridge: Harvard University Press.
Helliwell, John, Richard Layard, and Jeffrey Sachs, eds. 2012. *World Happiness Report*. New York: Earth Institute, Columbia University.
Hochschild, Arlie. 1983. *The Managed Heart*. Berkeley: University of California Press.
Hunt, Alan. 2012. "The Civilizing Process and Emotional Life." In *Emotions Matter: A Relational Approach to Emotions*, edited by Dale Spencer, Kevin Walby, and Alan Hunt, 137–60. Toronto: University of Toronto Press.
Illouz, Eva. 2007. *Cold Intimacies: The Making of Emotional Capitalism*. London: Polity Press.
James, Susan. 1997. *Passion and Action: The Emotions in Seventeenth-Century Philosophy*. Oxford: Oxford University Press.
Kaindaneh, Steven, and Andrew Rigby. 2012. "Peace-Building in Sierra Leone." In *Politics and the Emotions*, edited by Simon Thompson and Pauk Hoggett, 157–80. London: Continuum.
Knuuttila, Simo. 2004. *Emotions in Ancient and Medieval Philosophy*. Oxford: Oxford University Press.
Konstan, David. 2001. *Pity Transformed*. London: Duckworth.
Konstan, David. 2006. *The Emotions of the Ancient Greeks: Studies in Aristotle and Classical Literature*. Toronto: University of Toronto Press.
Lazarus, Richard. 1994. *Passion and Reason: Making Sense of Our Emotions*. New York: Oxford University Press.

Leys, Ruth. 2011. "The Turn to Affect: A Critique." *Critical Inquiry* 37 (3): 434–72.

Marcus, George E. 2002. *The Sentimental Citizen: Emotion in Democratic Politics.* University Park: Penn State University Press.

Marcus, George E. 2013. "Reason, Passion, and Democratic Politics: Old Conceptions – New Understandings – New Possibilities." In *Passions and Emotions,* edited by James E. Fleming, 127–88. NOMOS LIII. New York: New York University Press.

Marcus, George E., W. Russell Neuman, and Michael MacKuen. 2000. *Affective Intelligence and Political Judgment*. Chicago: University of Chicago Press.

Massumi, Brian. 2002. *Parables for the Virtual: Movement, Affect, Sensation.* Durham, NC: Duke University Press.

Matt, Susan. 2011. "Current Emotion Research in History: Or, Doing History from the Inside Out." *Emotion Review* 3 (1): 117–24.

McHardy, Fiona. 2008. *Revenge in Athenian Culture.* Bristol: Bristol Classical Press.

Neu, Jeremy. 2002. *A Tear Is an Intellectual Thing.* Oxford: Oxford University Press.

Nussbaum, Martha. 1994. *The Therapy of Desire: Theory and Practice in Hellenistic Ethics.* Princeton, NJ: Princeton University Press.

Nussbaum, Martha. 2001. *Upheavals of Thought: The Intelligence of Emotions.* Cambridge: Cambridge University Press.

Nussbaum, Martha. 2004. *Hiding from Humanity: Disgust, Shame and the Law.* Princeton, NJ: Princeton University Press.

Nussbaum, Martha. 2013. *Political Emotions: Why Love Matters for Justice.* Cambridge, MA: Harvard University Press.

Ober, Josiah, and Stephen Macedo, eds. 2007. *Primates and Philosophers: How Morality Evolved.* Princeton, NJ: Princeton University Press.

Panksepp, Jaak. 1998. *The Foundations of Human and Animal Emotions.* New York: Oxford University Press.

Prinz, Jesse J. 2006. *Gut Reactions: A Perceptual Theory of Emotion.* Oxford: Oxford University Press.

Prinz, Jesse J. 2013. "Constructive Sentimentalism: Legal and Political Implications." In *Passions and Emotions,* edited by James Fleming, 3–18. NOMOS LIII. New York: New York University Press.

Reddy, William. 2001. *The Navigation of Feeling: A Framework for the History of Emotions.* Cambridge: Cambridge University Press.

Robinson, Jenefer. 2007. *Deeper than Reason.* Oxford: Oxford University Press.

Rosenwein, Barbara. 2007. *Emotional Communities in the Early Middle Ages.* Ithaca, NY: Cornell University Press.

Schachter, Stanley, and Jerome Singer. 1962. "Cognitive, Social, and Physiological Determinants of Emotional State." *Psychological Review* 69 (5): 379–99.

Smail, Daniel. 2008. *On Deep History and the Brain*. Berkeley: University of California Press.

Solomon, Robert. 1976. *The Passions*. New York: Doubleday.

Sorabji, Richard. 2000. *Emotion and Peace of Mind: From Stoic Agitation to Christian Temptation*. Oxford: Oxford University Press.

Stearns, Peter. 1994. *American Cool: Constructing a Twentieth Century Emotional Style*. New York: NYU Press.

Stearns, Peter. 1999. *The Battleground of Desire: The Struggle for Self-Control in America*. New York: NYU Press.

Stearns, Peter. 2006. *American Fear*. London: Taylor and Francis.

Stearns, Peter, and Carol Stearns. 1986. *Anger: The Struggle for Emotional Control in America's History*. Chicago: University of Chicago Press.

Suski, Laura. 2012. "Humanitarianism as a Politics of Emotion." In *Emotions Matter: A Relational Approach to Emotions*, edited by Dale Spencer, Kevin Walby, and Alan Hunt, 124–36. Toronto: University of Toronto Press.

Tallis, Raymond. 2011. *Aping Mankind: Neuromania, Darwinitis and the Misrepresentation of Humanity*. Durham, UK: Acumen.

Tarnopolsky, Christina. 2010. *Prudes, Perverts and Tyrants: Plato's Gorgias and the Politics of Shame*. Princeton, NJ: Princeton University Press.

Tomkins, Silvan. 1962. *Affect, Imagery, Consciousness*. New York: Springer.

Tomkins, Silvan. 1981. "The Quest for Primary Motives: Biography and Autobiography of an Idea." *Journal of Personality and Social Psychology* 41 (2): 306–29.

Williams, Bernard. 1993. *Shame and Necessity*. Berkeley: University of California Press.

Williams, Raymond. 1978. *Marxism and Literature*. New York: Oxford University Press.

Woodward, Kathleen. 2009. *Statistical Panic: Cultural Politics and Poetics of the Emotions*. Durham, NC: Duke University Press.

PART I

Interpretive Perspectives

1 Virtue and Emotional Education in Ancient Greece

RYAN K. BALOT

Ancient Greek thought has played a particularly crucial role in the rediscovery of the virtues and the emotions in political theory. There has always been a striking contrast between the centrality of these concepts in classical political philosophy and the comparative absence of them in modern liberal-democratic thought. Alasdair MacIntyre's *After Virtue* illustrated the usefulness of bringing these traditions together. Following MacIntyre, many have highlighted, in particular, the potential of Aristotelian thought to supplement or challenge contemporary political, ethical, and psychological theory (MacIntyre 1984; Nussbaum 1988, 1990, 2002; Salkever 1974, 1990, 2002; Galston 1991; Beiner 1992; Frank 2005; Collins 2006). Aristotle closely linked ethical life to political realities in ways that challenge the predominantly liberal-democratic presuppositions of our era. Moreover, Aristotle's *Ethics*, *Politics*, and *Rhetoric* arguably constituted a single "course of lectures," as Stephen Salkever has written, which attractively unified individual freedoms with a theory of social justice and political participation (Salkever 2009). Aristotelian theory offers these advantages, in fact, without inviting the criticisms usually levelled against the language of rights[1] and without compromising the modern commitment to social diversity (Nussbaum 1988, 1990, 2002).[2]

In the present essay, however, I want to take a different approach and concentrate on the psychological formation of citizens envisioned in classical Athenian democratic discourse and in the political philosophy of Plato. The political ideology of democratic Athens (508–322 BC) presents us with a robustly egalitarian and democratic account of the virtues and emotions.[3] In studying this ideology, we gain direct access to the workings of democracy as such, access unimpeded by the need to disentangle democracy from liberalism or to grapple with the extraordinary diversity of the modern democratic experience at institutional, cultural, and religious levels. By examining the political ideology of democratic Athens, moreover, we will uncover certain striking continuities between this ideology and Platonic political philosophy.[4] Perhaps democracy is "prior" to philosophy not only in the pragmatic interpretation of Richard Rorty (1993), but also in the sense that the practical (i.e., political and ethical) philosophy of Plato, not to mention Aristotle, originates, in its essential framework, in the democratic ideology to which it has frequently been opposed.

To make this investigation sufficiently concrete, I focus on the virtue of courage and its associated emotions, particularly shame. Courage – or *andreia*, which literally means "manliness" in ancient Greek – was the virtue that embodied a cluster of specifically "manly" ideals. This virtue had, of course, always been central to the self-understanding of Hellenic men, from the Homeric epics through the conquests of Alexander the Great and beyond. But the Athenians contended that they had constructed a new and specifically democratic paradigm of courage by linking courage to freedom, equality, and collective rationality. They distinguished democratic courage from the courage of non-democratic societies by emphasizing the citizens' grasp of why, when, and how they should act courageously.[5]

To understand this novel ideal, consider the account of democratic courage offered in the Periclean Funeral Oration in Thucydides' *History*.[6] Contrasting Athens with Sparta, Pericles says, "Those would rightly be judged most courageous who understand both the fearful and the pleasant and on account of this do not turn away from risks" (Thuc. 2.40).[7] Despite the Spartans' widespread reputation for courage, Pericles argued, it was the Athenians who possessed courage that was genuine in that it was rooted in self-understanding and political wisdom rather than unreflective subscription to the city's traditions or the fear of shame and other harsh punishments. Pericles' account of courage was intended to be specifically democratic in that it derived courage from the institutional practices that were characteristic of democracies as opposed to other forms of political regime.

By highlighting the cognitive elements of courage, Pericles implicitly rejected more traditional accounts that emphasized the fear of legal punishment and the fear of shame or disgrace. He strove to discredit the Spartans' unthinking adherence to traditional pugnacity and machismo. Pericles wanted, in fact, to distinguish the Athenians from the entire Hellenic tradition in these respects, including the societies depicted in the Homeric epics. Hence, he declared that Athens's accomplishments were self-evidently glorious and did not require the praise of celebratory poets such as Homer (Thuc. 2.41). Pericles presented a seemingly clear set of ideological oppositions, which located the Athenians on the side of rationality, intelligence, and deliberation and the Spartans and other, non-democratic Greeks on the side of shame, anger, and other passions construed as traditional and non-cognitive. In erecting these oppositions, Pericles also emphasized that the rational direction of one's life was not effeminate or incompatible with audacity or bold action (2.39–40); instead, any boldness worth having could arise only from a rationally governed and harmonious soul.

Despite Pericles' emphasis on rationality, however, the Athenians embraced the idea that their courage had both cognitive and emotional components; Pericles, in particular, recognized that reason and passion should not be as sharply distinguished as the European philosophical tradition, until recently, has suggested.[8] According to Pericles, in fact, the fallen Athenian soldiers "ran away from the word of shame" (*to men aischron tou logou ephugon*) (Thuc. 2.42.4), "longed to punish their enemies" (ibid., adapted), and "kept their sense of shame in battle" (*en tois ergois aischunomenoi*) (2.43, adapted). In making these arguments, Pericles emphasized that his audience should keep before their minds' eyes the courage and the accomplishments both of the fallen soldiers and of the city's previous generations. The current generation was expected to live up to their example. To further his presentation of the Athenian self-image in a specifically emotional register, Pericles also suggested that the Athenians had always had the habit of cultivating reverent attitudes towards the laws and towards appropriate objects of shame, respect, and honour, as follows: "As for public affairs, we respect the law greatly and fear to violate it, since we are obedient to those in office at any time, and also to the laws – especially to those laws that were made to help people who have suffered an injustice, and to the unwritten laws that bring shame on their transgressors by the agreement of all" (2.37). In addition to their cognitive understanding, therefore, the Athenians had also internalized emotions that were well known among, and widely admired by, their non-Athenian contemporaries, including both the Spartans and, later, Plato and Aristotle.[9]

Did the Athenians have a particular way of coordinating their rational decisions with their finely calibrated emotional responses? How can an ideal of courage based on shame be compatible with Pericles' emphasis on the Athenian democracy's discursive, deliberative, and rationalistic conception of courage? Could Pericles successfully unify not only thought and action, but also reason and emotion, in a specifically democratic way?

We can begin to answer these questions if we recognize, with Bernard Williams, Gabriele Taylor, and others, that shame is an emotion that derives from our sense of ourselves as selves.[10] As an emotion tied closely to our aspirations and hopes for the kinds of people we want to be, shame is founded on the sense that our self or self-image can be threatened by the judgments of social "others." As Williams has observed,

> Shame looks to what I am. ... By giving through the emotions a sense of who one is and of what one hopes to be, it mediates between act, character, and consequence, and also between ethical demands and the rest of life. Whatever it is working on, it requires an internalized other, who is not designated merely as a representative of an independently identified social group, and whose reactions the agent can respect. At the same time, this figure does not merely shrink into a hanger for those same values but embodies intimations of a genuine social reality – in particular, of how it will be for one's life with others if one acts in one way rather than another. (Williams 1993, 93, 102)

This account helps us to distinguish between the Spartans' less thoughtful experience of shame and the Athenians' more sophisticated social realization of this emotion in the production of courage (cf. James Jasper's discussion of paired negative and positive emotions in directing moral action in chapter 8 of this volume). The Athenians collectively deliberated about, thought through, and understood their self-images, even their "internalized others," as Williams puts it, in a richer, more self-conscious, and more complete way than their non-democratic counterparts. The Athenian democracy was distinctive in that, through its institutions, practices, public monuments, and literature, it invited all democratic citizens to take responsibility for the constituents of their self-image, such as their shared role models, their publicly avowed ideals, and their collectively formed aspirations as a polis.[11] This invitation to public reflection on shame and honour took place in the democracy's courtrooms, in its public assemblies, in its comic and tragic theatre, in its religious processions, and in its state-funded monuments and artwork. In other, related writings, I have shown that this process can be illustrated in the interpretation of Attic oratory and of tragedies funded by the Athenian demos – such as Euripides' *Suppliants* and Aeschylus's *Agamemnon*.[12] The Athenians effectively united reason and emotion, as well as thought and action, in constructing a novel and distinctively democratic ideal of courage.

By emphasizing both the Athenians' deliberative rationality and their subscription to honourable shame and reverence for the law, Pericles responded directly, if implicitly, to democracy's critics.[13] Yet how did these critics manage to find fault with such an apparently reasonable understanding of courage? In Plato's *Republic*, to take one important example, Socrates skewered the democracy for creating citizens without "order" or "necessity," citizens who indulged themselves in whatever random desires occurred to them (561cd).[14] They were so free that they attended to all desires equally. Their freedom, in fact, led to an inversion of the standard virtues. Democratic citizens, Plato said, "call reverence foolishness and moderation cowardice" and cast these virtues outside the soul's citadel (560cd). With a view to exiling the virtues more generally, they "give fine names" to bad habits, "calling insolence good breeding, anarchy freedom, extravagance magnificence, and shamelessness courage" (560e). Emphasizing both the emotions and the vices, Socrates maintained that the democratic regime was too free – that is to say, anarchic – and failed altogether to cultivate virtue in the citizenry.

Despite these criticisms, however, Socrates' presentation of the guardians' education owed a great deal to the Athenian ideology exemplified by Pericles' speech. Plato's own way of synthesizing reason and emotion owed a significant debt to the democratic Athenian models of understanding courage and the other virtues in their relation to both the emotions and familiar cognitive processes. The Athenians thought through the specific emotional qualities and normatively desirable characteristics of the Athenian citizenry, based on their articulate discussions of what courage demanded in their lives as a whole. Like the Athenians, Plato's Socrates envisioned both cognitive and emotional training for the best citizens, he explicitly raised the question of which qualities the educational system should highlight in its role models, and he considered the wider ethical context of courage to be a central political question. In these ways, the structure of Plato's ethical and psychological imagination was decisively informed by the Athenians' democratic ideology. It is crucial to take this point into account, because scholars have tended to present the Homeric character Achilles, and the epic tradition more generally, as Plato's chief reference point in his attempt to transform courage and its associated emotions.[15] While

Achilles undoubtedly looms large in the *Republic*, so too do the educational strategies, concepts, and ideals that Plato absorbed from the Athenians' own informal public education of the citizens.

To be more specific, Plato's Socrates maintains that courage, properly understood, must be explained with reference to a variety of elements corresponding to the complexity of our souls and to the world in which we find ourselves. Both intellectual and emotional excellences are necessary for the possession of courage and other virtues because our souls themselves are diverse; they are made up of different "parts," of different capacities and drives. All these parts must operate harmoniously if the fullest expressions of human excellence are to be realized. On the one hand, courage requires deep intellectual understanding of the intrinsic merits of being courageous and acting courageously – that is, of the goodness of courage itself. On the other hand, courage requires significant emotional training in respect of both desire (what Plato calls *to epithumētikon*) and spiritedness (what Plato calls *thumos* or *to thumoeides*). To lead flourishing lives, Socrates argues, we must understand and desire what is good for both ourselves and others. In addition, the *thumos* – the home of our sense of shame, our self-assertion, our self-respect, and our anger – must be educated to conform to the demands of moderation and justice so that we will not be indignant or angry in unjust or selfish ways, but rather at the right time, to the right extent, and for the right reasons.[16] To be sure, Socrates' anatomy of the soul is tripartite, by contrast with Pericles', but we will discover that his account of the motivations, parts, desires, and beliefs of the soul is unexpectedly similar to that of Pericles.[17]

To clarify these connections, and to pinpoint the relevance of the democratic legacy, it is helpful to begin by enquiring into the nature and status of courage, as Socrates sees it. What is courage, and how can it be produced reliably? In Book IV, Socrates says initially that courage is "that preservation of the belief that has been inculcated by the law through education about what things and sorts of things are to be feared. I mean preserving it and not abandoning it because of pains, pleasures, desires, or fears" (429cd). Socrates' definition of courage emphasizes its cognitive foundations ("belief") and its relationship to emotional experiences of pain, pleasure, desire, and fear. Along with correct beliefs, the citizens will be trained to respond in emotionally desirable ways to temptations, fears, and distractions. Socrates is quick to qualify his statement, however, by observing that this type of courage is his "account of *civic* courage" (430c). This "civic courage" is what the city cultivates in its warriors and future philosophers through the elaborate musical and physical education described in Books II–III of the work (429e–430a). By means of this education, the citizen-soldiers learn to hold fast to the beliefs inculcated in them, like dye, by the law, despite the assaults of pleasure, pain, fear, and desire (430ab).

It is illuminating to ask why this type of courage is qualified as "civic." The most plausible response is that Socrates imagines, by contrast, another, unqualified, type of courage, which is possessed not by the "guardians" or "warriors," but rather only by the philosopher-rulers.[18] This unqualified courage is superior to "civic courage" because it is based on knowledge rather than mere beliefs inculcated by the laws – even if those beliefs are true. Socrates thus agreed with the democratic Athenians that courage could vary in its quality and expression depending on the level of understanding that meaningfully informed it. To understand fully why this point matters, we would need to grapple with Socrates' distinctions between knowledge and belief at the end of Book V and his detailed account, imagistic though it may be, of knowledge and opinion in Books VI–VII. Let it suffice to say that a minority of the guardians educated in the manner described in Books II–III will be talented enough to receive further intellectual training, which is expected to culminate in a rational and dialectically powerful grasp of the "Forms." Their knowledge of the Form of the Good will enable them to understand the goodness of courage and its necessary interconnections with the other virtues; and it will enable them to see precisely how to instantiate courage in particular circumstances in the evolving world of "becoming."[19] By contrast, Callipolis' warriors will be guided by the philosophers' teachings without understanding these difficult subjects for themselves.

Working within a framework that he shared with the democratic Athenians, Socrates innovated in such a way as to emphasize the superior intellectual – and hence ethical – achievements of the city's philosophers. The emotional training of Callipolis' upper two classes requires the "cognitive inputs" of the philosopher-rulers, who grasp just how to produce the proper balance, or harmony, among the rational and non-rational elements of the soul, even if they do not themselves write poetry, stage dramas, or compose myths (378e–379a). By contrast with classical Athens, Callipolis will rely on educated experts, rather than ordinary citizens, to produce this cognitive framework. Hence, Socrates envisions the citizens as unequal in their capacity to embody authentic courage. Moreover, the knowledge or wisdom that guides courage results from philosophical dialectic rather than open public discourse among all citizens. Even so, the multidimensional and integrated psychology of Callipolis' citizens is envisioned in ways that are reminiscent of the psychology outlined in Pericles' Funeral Oration and in Athenian political ideology more generally.

Intriguingly, though, many readers have noted that Socrates' description of the Callipolis, in Books II–III, is loosely based on the institutional structure, not of democratic Athens, but rather of classical Sparta.[20] At least in these two books, it looks as though Socrates has taken over the rigorous Spartan system of education (which was called the *agōgē*) and adapted it to his own unusual purposes. As we understand from a variety of ancient sources, the Spartan *agōgē* impressed on young citizens the sense of shame, fearlessness in battle, toughness, austerity, and dedication to the city that made the Spartans so famous for "virtue," at least among most ordinary Greeks, throughout antiquity. However, Socrates transformed the Spartan *agōgē* by emphasizing that genuine courage required a lucid understanding of human excellence – even of the "Good" itself – along with normatively desirable emotions. Sparta was lacking in both these respects: as Thucydides represents them, for example, the Spartans were both hostile to public discussion and reflection on their traditions and overwhelmed by their fear of public shame or legal sanctions (e.g., 1.86–88). To motivate his own emergent citizens, by contrast, Socrates relied not on ignorance and fear but rather on a well-developed and positive vision of what is worthwhile in human life. As a result of the proposed training, the emergent citizens of Callipolis would be able to act virtuously – either on the basis of knowledge, ultimately, or true belief, in the case of those who remained only warriors. Ideally, at least, they would avoid the experience of serious internal conflict and the necessity constantly to overcome wayward desires and emotions that fail to harmonize with the agent's own conception of his flourishing (401e–402a).

To establish the need for Callipolis' elaborate educational system, Socrates and his interlocutors begin with pragmatic details related to the city's position in an aggressive and anarchic international world. They agree that the city will need to be defended, and so it must have warriors; and these warriors must be not only "spirited" with regard to the city's enemies but also necessarily "gentle" towards their fellow citizens (375a–e). The participants agree further that to produce this kind of character, they will rely on traditional modes of "physical" and "musical" (i.e., musical, literary, and, above all, poetic) education to unify the apparently antithetical attributes of spiritedness and gentleness (376e). Their students will have to be not only capable of balancing these attributes but also able and willing to learn – i.e., "philosophical" in at least a general sense (375e–376b) – because they must recognize, to begin with, the identities of friends and enemies (376b). Both the non-philosophical warriors and the warlike philosopher-rulers will have to unify in their souls the emotions (trained by music and poetry as well as physical exercise) relevant to both courage and moderation (399c; cf. 399e). In this way, they will emotionally, as well as behaviourally, balance the daring of courage with the more peaceful elements of moderation; or, rather, they will come to see that one must possess and use both virtues at once if he or she is to possess or use either one individually. As we have seen, such a unification of apparently opposing qualities was also central to Pericles' vision of the virtuous Athenians.[21]

In his exploration of early childhood education, Socrates is especially concerned to cultivate appropriate feelings of shame, self-restraint, and reasonable fear so as to make his citizenry courageous. Before grasping the goodness of the virtues conceptually, both the future philosophers and the warriors must "imitate" appropriate role models (cf. 409d), thereby coming to internalize and to acquire for themselves the correct emotional responses to danger, pleasure, pain, and so on.[22] Just as the democratic Athenians idealized their ancestors and mythical heroes such as Theseus, Socrates focused on the characters, good or bad, that might appear on the theatrical stage. That is why, for example, Socrates advises the educators not to frighten the children with terrifying stories of the gods, which would make them cowardly (381de). More important, and more tangibly, the city has to eliminate otherwise attractive characters who might lament their friends' and relatives' deaths excessively (387de): neither Achilles nor Priam should be shown disgracing himself by bathing in ashes or rolling in dung, as in Homer, because of their losses, respectively, of Patroclus and Hector. The heroes praised by poetry in Callipolis, such as Diomedes, must be characterized by self-restraint, discipline, and reverence toward the rulers and the laws (389e–390c). Achilles must not be presented as greedy (390e); Odysseus's admirable steadfastness must be valorized in the eyes of the citizens-in-training (390cd). The point is to idealize individuals, even fictional characters, whose attitudes the citizens in training can internalize so that they feel a suitable sense of shame and self-restraint (388d). (Socrates' provisions may call to mind significant questions regarding the types of propositions or concrete images necessary to elicit emotion; Paul Griffiths discusses this aspect of DeLancey's work in the contemporary philosophy of mind in chapter 4.)

As Pericles had indicated in his Funeral Oration, Socrates maintains that our desires and our spirit (*thumos*) are penetrated by thoughts about both what is good for us and what is just. The philosopher-rulers rationally discuss and reach conclusions about what is good for their fellow citizens, and they then attempt to embody their ideas in the musical and literary education offered to the guardians in training. It is in this way that they attempt to rebuke, to mould, and to persuade the desiring and spirited parts of the soul, even though those parts are not fully rational. For example, Socrates points out that the *thumos* becomes furious when a person perceives that someone has acted unjustly or tried to inflict harm, as follows: "But what happens if, instead, he believes that someone has been unjust to him? Isn't the spirit within him boiling and angry, fighting for what he believes to be just?" (440c). In its anger, the spirit is first responsive to the perception of injustice, and it is later open to the persuasion of reason, as the *thumos* calms down when it is commanded to do so by reason, "like a dog by a shepherd" (440cd). The *thumos* can answer to reason in these ways because it contains elements of cognition and judgment that enable it to be persuaded and conditioned appropriately.[23] This point is exemplified variously throughout the text. In the notorious case of Leontius, who struggled with himself to avoid looking at corpses lying on the road, spirit allied itself with reason and made Leontius angry with his desires (439e–440b). Later, however, *thumos* is shown working against what is objectively good for the individual, precisely because it is informed by misguided beliefs. Socrates' description of the timocratic youth in Book VIII shows that this young man, dominated by *thumos*, has a particular (albeit misguided) conception of the good, which consists in the love of honour and the love of victory (548d–549a). He is educated by what he hears in the city: from his mother, that his father is not manly enough (549d); from others, that he should take revenge and be more of a "man" than his father (549e–550a). His *thumos* – the home of shame, anger, the desire for honour, and other emotions of "self-assessment" – is shot through with ideas about what is good, even if it lacks the capacity to reflect deeply on or to change those ideas by itself.[24]

Socrates' emphasis on emotional education makes the following point very clear: even in the unlikely event that this young man should somehow come to appreciate the intrinsic merits of moderation, justice, courage, and wisdom, his badly fashioned desires and aspirations will always draw him away from what is best. Because he suffers from a kind of psychological dissonance, he will never take unqualified joy or pleasure in behaving correctly. In the language of Athenian democratic ideology, he might act justly, moderately, and courageously, but he will not do so in a "wholehearted" and "zealous" way.

By contrast, a minority of Callipolis' young people, both male and female, will be chosen to receive a more robustly philosophical training, which will enable them to avoid the problems encountered by the timocratic youth. Through that training, they are expected to form a more adequate conception of why their goodness lies in being attracted to, and repulsed by, just the models that their education has disposed them to have strong feelings about (402a). In Socrates' idealized vision, they will readily take pleasure in doing the things that they now understand to be intrinsically good for them: the acts of moderation, justice, courage, and so on that their teachers have praised all along. For example, Glaucon and Adeimantus, Socrates' chief interlocutors in the dialogue, are presented as having been educated reasonably well from childhood onward and as being genuinely (if not exclusively) attracted by what is just and virtuous; but they are working still to achieve a deeper philosophical understanding of why their attractions and repulsions are the best ones for human beings to have. In the economy of the dialogue, however, it is clear that only very few – and probably not, after all, those who resemble Glaucon and Adeimantus – will be capable of the philosophical depth required to arrive at a completely lucid grasp of human excellence. As Book I of the dialogue reveals, in fact, one of the chief problems with having only a correct emotional or prerational education, however great a good that may be, is that the convictions of people of this description can be upset by sophistic questioning, such as that of Thrasymachus (cf. 538a–539a). Only the philosophers of Callipolis will embody the carefully reasoned, well-grounded, self-conscious and deliberate, as well as emotionally correct, virtues prized by Socrates and his interlocutors: wisdom, courage, moderation, and justice.

On the basis of this all too brief discussion of Plato's *Republic*, it is possible to conclude that Plato's Socrates, in this dialogue at least, adapted the Athenian conception of courage for his own purposes. In his presentation, it emerges with great clarity that the emotions associated with courage are penetrated by cognition, that they are susceptible to persuasion, and that they are closely tied to our vision of the good.

Even so, as Socrates argues, emotions are not themselves articulate and well-reasoned statements of our beliefs. Rather, they have to be educated for the production of courageous individuals, even if courageous individuals will require, above all, a deeply cognitive and articulate understanding of the purposes, ends, and manner of genuine courage. Even the warriors will need the philosophers' cognitive inputs simply to approximate to genuine, well-founded courage.

By contrast with most of the citizens envisioned in Socrates' Callipolis, the Athenians took upon themselves the project of developing correct cognitive inputs by continually reflecting on the ways in which their own characters were shaped by life in their city. They recognized that we should always remain vigilant regarding the ends that make sense of our emotions as well as the domains in which, and styles through which, our emotions are expressed. Yet rather than relying on philosopher-rulers to design an educational system, the Athenians held that their public conversations about virtue and vice, and the emotions related to them, were themselves educational for the citizenry as it participated in democratic self-government and attended the democratically funded theatre. Theirs was a more political, and a more egalitarian and democratic, conception of the rationality and emotions that play a role in producing courage. Be that as it may, we are now in a strong position to conclude that Plato himself, whether wittingly or not, adapted the Athenians' attention to both reason and emotion as the central elements of an education to courage – and to virtue altogether.

NOTES

1 For discussion of this point, see Galston (1991) and Beiner (1992).
2 On the question of diversity in ancient Greek thought altogether, see Saxonhouse (1992).
3 See Balot (2009, 2014) for further discussion of this point.
4 For the basic idea, see Balot (2001, esp. 521–2). I have explored other aspects of this relationship in Balot (2013, 2014). For earlier treatments on which I have built, see Monoson (2000), Tarnopolsky (2010), and Euben (1997). Landauer (2016) criticizes Balot (2013) for assimilating Socratic ideas too closely to those of democratic Athens.
5 These arguments are made more fully in Balot (2014). To clarify the legacy of these democratic ideas, I will have to rehearse briefly certain arguments that I have laid out in greater detail in several recent publications.

6 This "anatomy" is the central theme of Balot (2001); cf. also Balot (2014, chap. 2). For arguments that this speech, albeit a Thucydidean construction, captures the essentials of the Athenian ideology, see Balot (2014).
7 Woodruff (1993, adapted). All citations refer to this edition.
8 By contrast, Jeffrey Rusten has argued that Pericles presents Athens's fallen soldiers as "reaching a complex, dignified and intensely rational decision to offer their lives: they must choose between the long life and material prosperity desired by the individual ... and the claims of the state which must occasionally supersede personal desires" (Rusten 1989, 161). In emphasizing the Athenians' "intensely rational decision," however, Rusten does not adequately attend to the Athenians' own emotional responses, as Pericles represented them. For further considerations along these lines, see Balot (2001, 2014).
9 I explore these themes, in particular, further in Balot (2014, chap. 10, 11).
10 See Williams (1993), Taylor (1985), and Tarnopolsky (2010).
11 On the Athenians' use of role models in public oratory, see Balot (2014); on Theseus in Greek tragedy, see Walker (1995); on role models in Platonic politics and ethics, especially Achilles, see Bloom (1968, 354–60), Annas (1981, 96–7), and Hobbs (2000, 59–68), with my discussion below.
12 See Balot (2010, 2014, esp. chap. 11–13).
13 Cf. Ober (2001), which discusses both Pericles' and Demosthenes' responses to democracy's critics along these lines.
14 Grube (rev. Reeve 1992). All citations refer to this edition.
15 See Bloom (1968), followed by Hobbs (2000, e.g., 7–8, 175–219), and, with interesting variations, Rabieh (2006, 95–160). These very different interpreters argue that Plato's predecessor in investigating *andreia* and *thumos* was Homer. Hence, they neglect the importance of these ideas in the democratic Athenian discourse of Plato's own time. Two partial exceptions are Monoson (2000) and Schofield (2006, e.g., 39–41).
16 In his *Republic,* Plato developed a conception of the *thumos* as the home of shame, self-respect, and anger; cf. Cooper (1999a) for the argument that it is a distinct source of motivation, based on competitiveness and self-respect. Socrates' presentation of the *thumos* is continuous with Athenian democratic conceptions of shame, pride, emulation, and anger (Balot 2014); cf. Casey (1990, 57–8), who uses the concept of the "spirited" to grapple with facets of "courage" related to anger and shame.
17 On Socrates' tripartite soul as a "self in dialogue" – in which reason, spirit, and appetite continually interact with and prove responsive to one another – see Gill (1996, 240–320; for our purposes, cf. esp. 268–70, 294–5).

18 Cf. Cooper (1999b, 140); Annas (1981, 114). At 414b, Socrates first distinguishes between the "complete" guardians and the "auxiliaries"; for the sake of convenience, I will refer to these two groups, respectively, as the "philosophers" and the "warriors," even though it will emerge that the city's philosopher-rulers will also be warriors. See Craig (1994) for a full treatment of the philosophers as warriors. On the description of both philosophers and warriors as "moderate and courageous warrior-athletes," see 416de.

19 Such is the model for the teleological description of the virtues that Socrates advances in the dialogue; it is reasonable, however, to remain agnostic or even dubious about whether Socrates actually possessed a coherent theory of the Forms. For further consideration of these issues, see Cooper (1999b), along with Smith (2006, 100–3), which offers an interpretation of Strauss's approach to the *Republic*, and, above all, Strauss (1964).

20 A recent reconsideration of the links between Platonic political thought and Sparta – an idea that goes back at least as far as Plutarch – is provided by Futter (2012); cf. also Schofield (2006, 32–43).

21 On Pericles' unification of opposites, see further Balot (2001). For a helpful perspective on this kind of opposition (and balance) within the wider Hellenic framework, and also in Plato's corpus, see North (1966). With regard to the *Republic*, see also Strauss (1964, 97), Bloom (1968, 350), Craig (1994, 7–9), and Hobbs (2000, 229–33). As Hobbs points out, this balance results in an "internalization of proportional beauty" (Hobbs 2000, 230), which derives from the appropriate shape of the warriors' early education. Hobbs (2000, 227) is correct, I believe, to link this notion of proportional beauty, ultimately, to the Form of the Good.

22 Cf. note 11 above, along with Gill (1996, 307–20) and Hobbs (2000, chap. 7 and 8), both of which provide helpful analyses of Socrates' appropriation of traditional role models.

23 For further discussion of the idea that the soul's parts, including *thumos*, possess their own judgments as well as their own specific emotional features, see Annas (1981, 126–31), Cooper (1999a, 130–6), Hobbs (2000, 19–23, 57–9), and Gill (1996, 251–2); for an explanation of why these judgments are not equivalent to the judgments of the "reasoning part" itself, see Cooper (1999a, 132–5).

24 The term "emotions of self-assessment" comes from Taylor (1985).

REFERENCES

Annas, Julia. 1981. *An Introduction to Plato's Republic*. Oxford: Oxford University Press.

Balot, Ryan K. 2001. "Pericles' Anatomy of Democratic Courage." *American Journal of Philology* 122 (4): 505–25. http://dx.doi.org/10.1353/ajp.2001.0048.

Balot, Ryan K. 2009. "The Virtue Politics of Democratic Athens." In *The Cambridge Companion to Ancient Greek Political Thought*, edited by Stephen Salkever, 271–300. Cambridge: Cambridge University Press. http://dx.doi.org/10.1017/CCOL9780521867535.011.

Balot, Ryan K. 2010. "Democratizing Courage in Classical Athens." In *War, Culture, and Democracy in Classical Athens*, edited by David Pritchard, 88–108. Cambridge: Cambridge University Press.

Balot, Ryan K. 2013. "Democracy and Political Philosophy: Influences, Tensions, Rapprochement." In *The Greek Polis and the Invention of Democracy*, edited by Johann P. Arnason, Kurt A. Raaflaub, and Peter Wagner, 181–204. Chichester, UK: Wiley-Blackwell.

Balot, Ryan K. 2014. *Courage in the Democratic Polis: Ideology and Critique in Classical Athens*. New York: Oxford University Press.

Beiner, Ronald S. 1992. "Moral Vocabularies." In *What's the Matter with Liberalism?*, edited by Ronald Beiner, 39–79. Berkeley: University of California Press.

Bloom, Allan. 1968. *The Republic of Plato*. New York: Basic Books.

Casey, John. 1990. *Pagan Virtue: An Essay in Ethics*. Oxford: Clarendon Press.

Collins, Susan. 2006. *Aristotle and the Rediscovery of Citizenship*. Cambridge: Cambridge University Press. http://dx.doi.org/10.1017/CBO9780511498633.

Cooper, John M. 1999a. "Plato's Theory of Human Motivation." In *Reason and Emotion*, edited by John M. Cooper, 118–37. Princeton, NJ: Princeton University Press.

Cooper, John M. 1999b. "The Psychology of Justice in Plato." In *Reason and Emotion*, edited by John M. Cooper, 138–50. Princeton, NJ: Princeton University Press.

Craig, Leon H. 1994. *The War Lover: A Study of Plato's Republic*. Toronto: University of Toronto Press.

Euben, J.P. 1997. *Corrupting Youth: Political Education, Democratic Culture, and Political Theory*. Princeton, NJ: Princeton University Press.

Frank, Jill. 2005. *A Democracy of Distinction: Aristotle and the Work of Politics*. Chicago: University of Chicago Press.

Futter, D. 2012. "Plutarch, Plato, and Sparta." *Akroterion* 57 (2012): 35–51.

Galston, William A. 1991. *Liberal Purposes: Goods, Virtues, and Diversity in the Liberal State*. Cambridge: Cambridge University Press. http://dx.doi.org/10.1017/CBO9781139172462.

Gill, Christopher. 1996. *Personality in Greek Epic, Tragedy, and Philosophy: The Self in Dialogue*. Oxford: Clarendon Press.

Grube, G.M.A. 1992. *Plato: Republic*. Revised by C.D.C. Reeve. Indianapolis, IN: Hackett.

Hobbs, Angela. 2000. *Plato and the Hero: Courage, Manliness, and the Impersonal Good*. Cambridge: Cambridge University Press. http://dx.doi.org/10.1017/CBO9780511551437.

Landauer, Matthew. 2016. "Democratic Theory and the Athenian Public Sphere." In *Approaches and Methods in Greek Political Thought*, edited by Ryan K. Balot, 31–51. Special issue, *Polis: The Journal for Ancient Greek Political Thought* 33, no. 1.

MacIntyre, Alasdair. 1984. *After Virtue*. 2nd ed. Notre Dame, IN: University of Notre Dame Press.

Monoson, S. Sara. 2000. *Plato's Democratic Entanglements: Athenian Politics and the Practice of Philosophy*. Princeton, NJ: Princeton University Press.

North, Helen. 1966. *Sophrosyne: Self-Knowledge and Self-Restraint in Greek Literature*. Ithaca, NY: Cornell University Press.

Nussbaum, Martha. 1988. "Nature, Function, and Capability: Aristotle on Political Distribution." In *Oxford Studies in Ancient Philosophy*, supplementary volume, 145–84. Oxford: Oxford University Press.

Nussbaum, Martha. 1990. "Non-Relative Virtues: An Aristotelian Approach." In *The Quality of Life*, edited by Martha Nussbaum and Amartya Sen, 242–69. Oxford: Clarendon Press.

Nussbaum, Martha. 2002. "Aristotelian Social Democracy." In *Aristotle and Modern Politics: The Persistence of Political Philosophy*, edited by Aristide Tessitore, 47–104. Notre Dame, IN: University of Notre Dame Press.

Ober, Josiah. 2001. "The Debate over Civic Education in Classical Athens." In *Education in Greek and Roman Antiquity*, edited by Y.L. Too, 175–207. Leiden, The Netherlands: Brill. http://dx.doi.org/10.1163/9789047400134_007.

Rabieh, Linda. 2006. *Plato and the Virtue of Courage*. Baltimore, MD: Johns Hopkins University Press.

Rorty, Richard. 1993. "The Priority of Democracy to Philosophy." In *Prospects for a Common Morality*, edited by Gene Outka and John Reeder, 254–78. Princeton, NJ: Princeton University Press.

Rusten, Jeffrey. 1989. *Thucydides: The Peloponnesian War – Book II*. Cambridge: Cambridge University Press.

Salkever, Stephen. 1974. "Virtue, Obligation and Politics." *American Political Science Review* 68 (1): 78–92.

Salkever, Stephen. 1990. *Finding the Mean: Theory and Practice in Aristotelian Political Philosophy*. Princeton, NJ: Princeton University Press.

Salkever, Stephen. 2002. "The Deliberative Model of Democracy and Aristotle's Ethics of Natural Questions." In *Aristotle and Modern Politics: The Persistence of Political Philosophy*, edited by Aristide Tessitore, 342–74. Notre Dame, IN: University of Notre Dame Press.

Salkever, Stephen. 2009. "Reading Aristotle's *Nicomachean Ethics* and *Politics* as a Single Course of Lectures: Rhetoric, Politics, and Philosophy." In *The Cambridge Companion to Ancient Greek Political Thought*, edited by Stephen Salkever, 209–42. Cambridge: Cambridge University Press. http://dx.doi.org/10.1017/CCOL9780521867535.009.

Saxonhouse, Arlene W. 1992. *Fear of Diversity: The Birth of Political Science in Ancient Greek Thought*. Chicago: University of Chicago Press.

Schofield, Malcolm. 2006. *Plato: Political Philosophy*. Oxford: Oxford University Press.

Smith, Steven B. 2006. *Reading Leo Strauss: Politics, Philosophy, Judaism*. Chicago: University of Chicago Press. http://dx.doi.org/10.7208/chicago/9780226763903.001.0001.

Strauss, Leo. 1964. *The City and Man*. Chicago: University of Chicago Press.

Tarnopolsky, Christina H. 2010. *Prudes, Perverts, and Tyrants: Plato's Gorgias and the Politics of Shame*. Princeton: Princeton University Press.

Taylor, Gabriele. 1985. *Pride, Shame, and Guilt: Emotions of Self-Assessment*. Oxford: Clarendon Press.

Walker, Henry J. 1995. *Theseus and Athens*. New York: Oxford University Press.

Williams, Bernard. 1993. *Shame and Necessity*. Berkeley: University of California Press.

Woodruff, Paul. 1993. *Thucydides on Justice, Power, and Human Nature*. Indianapolis, IN: Hackett.

2 Renaissance Discourses of Emotions

JAN PURNIS

The Renaissance provides an interesting historical period on which to focus for a study of emotion in an interdisciplinary context because it was, in many ways, an interdisciplinary period, a period when disciplinary boundaries were more fluid.[1] Of current debates about the nature and taxonomy of emotion, the editors of *Reading the Early Modern Passions* (Paster, Rowe, and Floyd-Wilson 2004) observe that, as a topic, emotion "does not exist in terms recognizable from one discipline to another in part because the very formation of distinct disciplines (and bounded bodies) erased the interstices that had formerly comprised emotion." Indeed, some contributions to that collection "provocatively suggest," in the words of the editors, that "the history of emotion is also a history of fixing aesthetic or disciplinary boundaries." Renaissance emotions, they argue, "resist the dualist categories that underwrite the formation of separate fields of study: literal and metaphorical, physiological and spiritual, inner and outer, passive and active, affect and affection" (18).

Focusing on the Renaissance period additionally highlights the important role that historical and cultural contexts play in theories of emotion and in emotional experience itself. Scholars of the Renaissance who apply the methodology known as historical phenomenology – an approach that aims to be less universalizing than the phenomenology of Edmund Husserl, Martin Heidegger, and Maurice Merleau-Ponty, on which it is based – suggest that "the very language of physiology – from Galenic humoralism to Ficinian cosmology to Cartesian categories to modern cognitive science – helps determine phenomenology"; or, put simply, "the way we describe the workings of our bodies and minds, and how we characterize our habitation in the world, may shape and color our emotional experiences" (Paster, Rowe, and Floyd-Wilson 2004, 16).

In what follows, I focus on Thomas Wright's 1604 *The Passions of the Minde in Generall*[2] as a means of offering insight into Renaissance understandings of the passions in the period before the mind-body dualism associated with René Descartes had become more pervasive,[3] before older medical and scientific models of the world had been replaced, and before disciplinary boundaries had become more strictly demarcated. I pay particular attention to the perceived relationship between biology and culture presented in articulations of what the emotions were and how they worked. The relationship between biology and culture in emotional experience – and whether emotion is primarily biological or socially constructed – is, as noted in the introduction to this collection, a question debated by modern theorists of emotion; examining Renaissance perspectives is particularly relevant in this regard as it is often easier to observe the ways that cultural values influence not only the experience of emotion but also theorizations of that experience – no matter how seemingly objective – when examining explanatory models that no longer hold sway and that employ descriptive language that is often more obviously value laden.

The terminology used to describe emotions has changed since the Renaissance, highlighting the challenge posed by language in historical but also cross-cultural and interdisciplinary work and drawing attention to the relationship between language and theory more generally. For example, neuroscientist Antonio Damasio (1999) observes that "emotion, as the word indicates, is about movement, about externalized behavior, about certain orchestrations of reactions to a given cause, within a given environment" (70). According to the *Oxford English Dictionary*, however, in the Renaissance the term *emotion* could be used to describe "political agitation, civil unrest; a public commotion or uprising," "a migration of people from one place to another," or "an agitation of mind; an excited mental state," only later taking on the meaning of a "strong mental or instinctive feeling, as pleasure, grief, hope, fear, etc., deriving esp. from one's circumstances, mood, or relationship with others."[4] Instead of *emotions*, English Renaissance writers usually used *passions*, *affections*, or *perturbations*, often interchangeably, although the terms were not exactly synonymous with each other (or with the modern use of *emotions*, which itself has different connotations, including being differentiated from *feelings* by Damasio). *Motion* and *commotion* were other terms used, and, like *emotion*, they are derived from the

Latin for "to move"; indeed, the passions were frequently described as being "moved," although the sense is usually of internal movement (cf. the place of emotions in the mobilization and demobilization of contemporary social movements in James Jasper's discussion in chapter 8 of this volume).

It is important that *commotion* and *motion* as well as *perturbation* were, like *emotion*, also used in the Renaissance in the political sense of civil unrest or uprising, highlighting how discourses of emotion overlap with other discourses, including political discourse. This overlap is especially evident in the long-standing tradition of the metaphor of the body politic, which, while now a dead metaphor, was very much alive in the Renaissance.[5] The body-state analogy worked to naturalize sociopolitical structures by comparing the state to the body in political writings or comparing the body to the state in medical and other texts. Thus, for example, in *Troilus and Cressida* William Shakespeare describes inner turmoil as civil strife. "Kingdom'd Achilles in commotion rages / And batters 'gainst himself" (1974, 2.3, 164–5), and Wright laments that uncontrolled passions "either rebell against Reason their Lord and King" or "oppose themselves one against another," which he likens to rebellion and sedition, respectively (1971, 69). Not only does such language express an opinion about the effect of emotions, but the metaphors also underline the way in which we experience our bodies and emotions in a sociopolitical context. The more literal manifestations of this intersection of the emotions with the political realm are explored by several contributors to this collection as well as by Renaissance writers like Wright, who discussed the role of the passions – and the rhetoric used to sway them – in the public sphere.[6]

Related to the body-state analogy was the equally commonplace Renaissance image of the human body as a microcosm of the world. In this model, the passions were frequently depicted as strong winds or rough seas: a "passionate man," Wright remarks, is "tossed like the Sea with contrary windes" (1971, 71). Gail Kern Paster describes the Renaissance correspondence of inner and outer as part of a "premodern ecology of the passions" (2004, 9). Noting modern psychological and anthropological research which argues that affective responses are "in part inborn and in part shaped on a minute-to-minute basis by the myriad social and natural stimuli that constitute culture" (8), her focus on the "transactional" relationship between the body and its natural environment in the microcosm-macrocosm context complements Georg Northoff's examination in chapter 5 of the person-environment interaction, in what he describes as the relational concept of emotional feeling.[7]

Like the body-state analogy, the body-world analogy foregrounds the way in which the experience of emotion occurs in and is shaped by the environment, whether natural or social. Furthermore, Renaissance descriptions literalize this relationship: more than simply an analogous relationship between body and world, "In an important sense, the passions actually *were* liquid forces of nature because, in this cosmology, the stuff of the outside world and the stuff of the body were composed of the same elemental materials. This is a literal early modern understanding of the relation of body to world, as old as Greek thought and derived ultimately from it" (Paster 2004, 4; emphasis original).

European Renaissance understandings of the emotions more specifically were influenced by both classical and Christian traditions. Richard Strier (2004) notes that although "it is often taken as a basic truth about the whole 'Western Tradition' that the control of 'passion' by 'reason' is its fundamental ethical-psychological ideal," this claim, in its focus on a very severe version of a Socratic or Stoic position, "obscures another strand in 'the tradition': the praise of passion," which can be found in the Aristotelian and the Judeo-Christian traditions (23). For example, Ryan Balot demonstrates in his discussion of Plato and Socrates in chapter 1 in this volume that the ancient Greeks assigned a positive role to the emotions,[8] particularly courage, in shaping citizens, while in the Christian tradition, many authors observed that Christ had experienced passions, although they affected him differently. Francis Bacon (1627) asserts in his essay "Of Anger," "To seek to extinguish anger utterly, is but a bravery of the Stoics." Quoting from the Bible, he adds, "We have better oracles: Be angry, but sin not. Let not the sun go down upon your anger" (111).

Both strands of the tradition – Stoicism and anti-Stoicism – were revived in the Renaissance, but the forms they took were shaped by specific social and political factors. Michael Schoenfeldt observes of England that the fact that, for the English, "the Renaissance was also experienced as a religious reformation only heightens the agitation between the comparative ethical value of classical Stoic apathy and Christian affect, between the rigorous self-control that temperance demands and the absolute dependence on God that Protestantism counsels" (1999, 18). In a related observation, political circumstances in England meant that Neostoicism took a different form there, becoming "a vehicle of political discontent, rather than the absolutist code it had become on the Continent" (19). The distinction was "heightened by the fact that in the seventeenth century, the English royal court came to define itself in terms of the kinds of sensual indulgence that Neostoicism castigated" (19).

Writers in the period who engaged with the topic of the emotions did so in these and other cultural contexts. Wright published *The Passions of the Minde in Generall* in 1604 as an enlarged and revised version of the 1601 first edition. For John Staines, Wright's volume is an "archetypal text" in the history of Renaissance rhetoric and politics because of its "development of a theory and practice of rhetoric that makes room for the proper use of both reason and passion" (2004, 93–4). Wright's text is often viewed as a predecessor of Robert Burton's influential compendium, *The Anatomy of Melancholy*. First published in 1621 and presented as a medical text devoted to melancholia, Burton's *Anatomy* is encyclopedic in the number and diversity of sources incorporated and the range of subjects discussed.[9] Both works are considered early efforts in the science of psychology, although there are important differences between the two authors due to Wright's focus on rhetoric and their religious backgrounds (Sloan 1971, xii): Wright was Catholic and had trained as a Jesuit at a time of strong anti-Catholic sentiment and persecution of Jesuits, while Burton was Anglican. In addition to being an early English work of proto-psychology, Wright's text is also significant for his pre-Baconian call for the use of method in the art of communication and for his own attempt to "scientize" and methodize his discussion of the passions (Sloan 1971, xiv).[10] Because *The Passions of the Minde* offers an extended analysis of the passions as Wright understands them, it provides useful insight into Renaissance attitudes towards the emotions – including how they operated, the function they served, their relationship to the body – and the influences that shaped them.

Although Wright's and Burton's texts have been described as early works in psychology, it is important to remember that psychology and physiology had not yet become separated. The mind and body were understood as being powerfully intertwined, and the soul (often used interchangeably for the mind) was thought to operate throughout the body, directing its functions. In a system derived from Thomas Aquinas's engagement with Aristotelian philosophy, the soul was believed to consist of three faculties, arranged on a hierarchical scale: the vegetative soul, which existed in plants, animals, and humans; the sensitive soul, which existed in animals and humans; and the intellective, or rational, soul, which existed in humans. The vegetative soul was responsible for nutrition, growth, and generation, the sensitive soul for sensation, motion, and emotion. The intellective soul (comprising understanding and will) was responsible for reasoning and memory, for example; it absorbed the other two souls and was immortal (Sloan 1971, xxvi; Burton 2001, 1.1.2.5, 155).[11]

The sensitive faculty of the soul was of primary concern in discussions of the passions. Wright explains how this faculty has two "appetites" or "inclinations," which form the basis of emotional response. The two appetites are the *concupiscible,* which he translates as "coveting," "desiring," or "wishing," and the *irascible,* which he translates as "anger," "invading," or "impugning" (1971, 19). As Burton puts it, "All affections and perturbations arise out of these two fountains, which, although the Stoics make light of, we hold natural, and not to be resisted" (2001, 1.1.2.8, 161). The coveting appetite is the inclination to seek out what is necessary and to avoid what is harmful, while the irascible appetite comes into play when there is an obstacle to overcome in obtaining what is needed or resisting what is harmful. Wright explains the relationship between the concupiscible and irascible powers as follows:

> God and Nature gave men and beasts these natural instincts or inclinations, to provide for themselves all those things that are profitable, and to avoid all those things which are damnifiable: and this inclination may be called, *concupiscibilis,* coveting; yet because that GOD did foresee, that oftentimes there should occurre impediments to hinder them from the execution of such inclinations, therefore he gave them another inclination, to helpe themselves to overcome or avoid those impediments, and to invade or impugne whatsoever resisteth: for the better execution whereof he hath armed all beasts, either with force, craft or flight, to eschew al [sic] obstacles that may detain them from those things which they conceive as convenient. Wherefore, to the Bull he hath imparted hornes, to the Boare his tuskes, to the Lion, clawes, to the Hare her heeles, to the Fox craft, to men their hands and witte. (1971, 21–2)

As Paster notes, this kind of argument, with its emphasis on the biological functionality of the passions, sounds very much like the interest of modern cognitive science in the evolution of the emotions (2004, 18n34).[12] Wright's description of the coveting and invading powers as "natural instincts" strengthens this sense of the passions as being biologically useful since God imprints onto every creature an inclination "to conserve it selfe, procure what it needeth, to resist and impugne whatsoeuer hindereth it" of what appertains "unto his good and conservation" (1971, 11–12). The naturalness of the emotions is also strengthened through the comparison with other natural forces. The idea of appetites, "believed to be principles inhering in any natural attraction or repulsion between things," was, as Thomas O. Sloan remarks, "crucial to the science of a pre-Newtonian world intrigued by such matters as the action of magnets, the rising of fire, or the image of man as a microcosm" (1971, xxvii). To explain the natural appetite, Wright uses the example of fire rising to avoid the coldness of earth and water, although elements and plants do not experience passions; nor do "inanimate creatures" experience pleasure and pain as beasts and humans do (1971, 12–13). This similarity stresses the naturalness of the passions, as does the comparison of the coveting and invading inclinations to animal defence mechanisms that are biological/physical as opposed to culturally constructed. Evolutionary theory is some ways in the future, but Wright's connection between animal defence mechanisms and emotional response, although here clearly given by God, strengthens the impression of emotions as biologically crucial to the survival of not only the individual but also the species. After all, he observes, "who would attend to eating or drinking, to the act of generation, if Nature had not joyned thereunto some delectation?" (13).

Although Wright believed that all passions could be reduced to just six – love, desire, pleasure, hatred, fear, and sadness – he is in general agreement with Aquinas's distinction of eleven basic emotions. Aquinas identified six concupiscible passions: "three pairs of opposites, love and hatred, desire and aversion, and joy and sadness," and five irascible ones, which included "two pairs of opposites – hope and despair, and fear and boldness – as well as a fifth passion that has no direct opposite – anger" (Schoenfeldt 2004, 50). Wright uses an example from the animal kingdom to outline these eleven basic passions. For the concupiscible passions, he uses the wolf-sheep relationship.

> First, the Wolfe loveth the flesh of the Sheep; then he desireth to have it; thirdly, he rejoyceth in his prey when he hath gotten it: Contrariwise, the Sheepe hateth the Wolfe, as an evill thing in himselfe, and thereupon detesteth him, as hurtfull to herselfe; and finally, if the Wolfe seaze upon her, she paineth and grieveth to become his prey: thus we haue love, desire, delight, hatred, abhomination, griefe, or heavinesse, the sixe passions of our coveting appetite. (1971, 23)

To demonstrate the irascible passions, Wright adds to the scenario a shepherd and his dogs, and he describes the circumstances under which the wolf will experience the five passions of the invading appetite: hope, boldness, anger, fear, and desperation (23–4).

This focus on animal passions draws attention to the assumption of shared emotional experience and continues to foreground the naturalness of those emotions and their importance to the survival of individual and species. Again, this perspective is reminiscent of some modern research into animal emotions. As the editors of this volume note in the introduction, Jaak Panksepp has suggested that animals and humans share the same basic emotional system and that study of how this system functions in rodents can offer insight into human emotions. More than poetic personification, Wright's portrayal of a wolf experiencing the full range of basic emotions, from love to joy to hope and courage, reflects fundamental beliefs about both animal and human emotion and about the "self-love" they have in common through the shared appetites of the sensitive soul.

Explaining the role of reason in human emotion, Wright employs analogies from the political and household realms to emphasize that God intended the reasonable soul, "like an Empresse," to "govern the body, direct the senses," and "guide the passions as subjects and vassals," but self-love allies itself with the senses and revolts, giving rise to the evils of the world (1971, 13). Wright explains that "passions and sense are like two naughty servants, who oft-times beare more love one to another, then [sic] they are obedient to their Master" (8). One reason for this alliance is that passions and sense are more alike, being both "drowned in corporall organs and instruments" (8); another is that they have a longer acquaintance because reason does not come into "possession of her kingdome" until after infancy and childhood (9). Oftentimes, the senses and passions persuade reason to join them, and reason, to please sense, then invents "tenne thousand sorts of new delights, which the passions never could have imagined" (10). Of arguments like this in Renaissance writing, Paster notes, "In high contrast to the rational-choice theory that underpins so many contemporary explanations of behavior, the early modern moralists strongly doubted the force of reason as an encompassing or even an adequate rationale for behavior" (2004, 19).

Wright, though, arguing against the Stoics, acknowledges, "Passions well used, may consist with wisedome, against the Stoicks, and if they be moderated, to be very serviceable to vertue" (1971, 18). Emphasizing the point with the examples of Christ's experience of passions (15) and the fact that the scriptures "exhort us to these passions" (of anger and fear) (16), Wright reiterates, "Passions, are not only, not wholy to be extinguished (as the Stoicks seemed to affirme) but sometimes to be moved, & stirred up for the service of vertue, as learnedly *Plutarch* teacheth" (17). Thus, in addition to biological-survival instincts designed for self-preservation and the survival of the species, the passions can also serve useful social functions: fear acts as a deterrent to sin, shame prevents "many loose affections," the appetite for honour leads military men to undertake dangerous exploits for the good of their countries, sadness brings about repentance, and compassion can lead to pity (17). Much of Wright's treatise is dedicated to instructing people how to discover the passions of others through their behaviour and external actions, including their speech, their gestures, their feasting, and their writing; and to instructing readers how to move the passions of others: the passions are moved through the bodily humours, by the senses, and by the commandment of reason (149).

Wright's views on how the passions are moved and their effects on the body are grounded in the predominant medical theory of his age. The Renaissance inherited a medical tradition based on the writings of Galen, a Greek physician who practised medicine in the second century but was influenced by an older tradition stretching back at least to Hippocrates. Although the brain has for some time been considered the most important organ in the body when it comes to emotional experience – from, for example, phrenology in the nineteenth century, which located specific emotions in specific regions of the brain, to current experiments by cognitive scientists, who employ functional magnetic resonance imaging, positron emission tomography, and magnetoencephalography in studies of brain function and activity – the Renaissance understandings of the body and the body-mind relationship were not cerebrocentric in the way the cognitive sciences tend to be. (John Gunnell notes in chapter 3 in this volume that the tendency simply to substitute "brain" for "mind" in cognitive science can be interpreted as a variation of the old mind-body dualism.)

In Renaissance adaptations of Galen, the body was generally divided into three regions, each controlled by one of the three principal organs: the liver in the belly, the heart in the chest, and the brain in the head. The principal organs were given relative value on a hierarchical scale, according to which the brain, located highest in the body, was considered superior to the heart, which was in turn considered superior to the liver. Helkiah Crooke asserts in a 1615 medical text that the opinion held by Aristotle and his followers, that there was only one principal organ of the body, the heart, has been "long since hissed out of the Schooles of the Physitians, and banished from amongst them" (1615, 40); however, as Scott Manning Stevens (1997) observes in an examination of the cultural significance of the heart in the Renaissance, while "for most of us today, the affective and the intellectual are both located in the brain," in the Renaissance "affect and intellect (which includes the imagination) were, according to the majority of authorities, located in the heart and head respectively" (267). In answer to the question of whether there is "any Part of the bodie, wherein peculiarly the passions of the mind are effected," Wright (1971, 33) responds that "the very seate of all Passions, is the heart, both of men and beasts." Common experience of emotion leads Wright to this conclusion: "for who loveth extreamely, and feeleth not that passion to dissolve his heart? who rejoiceth, and proveth not his heart dilated? who is moyled with heavinesse, or plunged with paine, and perceiveth not his heart to be coarcted? whom inflameth ire, and hath not heart-burning?" (33).

Although the heart was thus central to emotional experience, the liver and digestive organs played important roles as well.[13] In Galenic theory, digestion was believed to give rise to four humours: blood, phlegm, choler (or yellow bile), and melancholy (or black bile). Each of these humours served a specific physiological function: blood nourished the parts, phlegm moistened them, choler aided the natural heat and senses and assisted in the expelling of excrements, and melancholy nourished the bones and preserved choler and blood (Burton 2001, 1.1.2.2, 148). These fluids were classified along a temperature and moisture axis and corresponded to one of the four elements: black bile, cold and dry, corresponded to earth; phlegm, cold and moist, to water; yellow bile, hot and dry, to fire; and blood, hot and moist, to air. As part of what has been called the "psychological materialism" or "psychophysiology" of this model of the body-mind relationship, the humours were believed to contribute powerfully to emotional experience and personality. The proportion of the humours in an individual affected one's temperament, or complexion, making a person choleric, melancholic, phlegmatic, or sanguine. For example, those in whom choler predominated were hot-tempered and easily angered as well as quick-witted; melancholy made one unsociable, brooding, and prone to unprovoked anger; phlegmatic characteristics included calmness and imperturbability, sluggishness, or apathy; while sanguine people tended to be courageous, hopeful, and amorous.

Spirits were also an important part of the Galenic mind-body model. Spirits were thin substances made from the purest blood: natural spirits were made in the liver (the organ believed to produce blood from ingested food), while vital spirits were refined, or further digested, in the heart from the natural spirits, and animal spirits were even further refined in the brain from the vital spirits. The spirits acted as "a common tie or medium between the body and the soul," with natural spirits moving through the veins to perform natural actions, including nourishment; vital spirits, without which life ceased, moving through the arteries; and animal spirits moving through the nerves, enabling sense and motion (Burton 2001, 1.1.2.2, 148). Levinus Lemnius (1581) describes the humours and spirits as "incensours and stirrers forwarde of the minde" and remarks that they "obtayne and receive their nature" from foods, especially those that "ingender good bloud & juice" (5r), and from digestion of those foods. He explains that the spirits, either through their quantity or their quality, "engender & bring forth sundry affects in us, and manyfestly alter the state as well of body as of mynde" (15v–16r). Paster (1997) has argued that Renaissance explanations of the role played by the spirits reveal "how easily physiological knowledge intersects with early modern behavioral thought to produce somatically based theories of desire and affect" (118).

While humours and spirits affected and effected emotional experience, in the Galenic tradition the passions themselves were categorized as one of the six "non-naturals" that "together determined the immediate state of well-being in a given body" (Paster 2004, 4). The non-naturals, "so much spoken of amongst physicians," as Burton explains, are also categorized as being necessary "because we cannot avoid them, but they will alter us, as they are used or abused" (2001,1.2.2.1, 216). The other non-naturals are diet, retention/evacuation, air, exercise, and sleeping/waking. This categorization of the passions offers additional insight into important differences between earlier understandings of emotions and current ones. "For us, air and diet do not consort readily in conceptual categories also inhabited by the emotions. Air, diet, and the passions – though all may be considered determinative of health – do not work on the body in analogous ways because we tend not to imagine the emotions ... as part of the *fabric* of the body" (Paster 2004, 5; emphasis original). Burton stresses for his Renaissance readers that diet and retention/evacuation are "more material" than the other non-naturals because they either make new matter or keep or expel it (2001, 1.2.2.1, 217).

Wright offers a detailed explanation of the physiology of emotional experience based on the Galenic model of the body. He writes,

> First then, to our imagination commeth by sense or memorie, some object to be knowne, convenient or disconvenient to Nature, the which being knowne (for *Ignoti nulla cupido*) in the imagination which resideth in the former part of the braine, (as we prove) when we imagine any thing, presently the purer spirits, flocke from the brayne, by certaine secret channels to the heart, where they pitch at the dore, signifying what an object was presented, convenient or disconvenient for it. The heart immediately bendeth, either to prosecute it, or to eschew it: and the better to effect that affection, draweth other humours to helpe him, and so in pleasure concurre great store of pure spirits; in paine and sadnesse, much melancholy blood; in ire, blood and choller; and not onely (as I said) the heart draweth, but also the same soule that informeth the heart residing in other parts, sendeth the humours unto the heart, to performe their service in such a worthie place: ... in the hunger of the heart, the splene, the liuer, the blood, spirits, choller, and melancholly, attend and serue it most diligently. (1971, 45–6)

Emotional response thus begins as a reaction to an object, the impression of which has been received by the imagination in the brain from either the senses or memory. The imagination then sends a representation of the object to the heart by way of the spirits. Acting according to the concupiscible or irascible inclination (depending on whether or not an impediment exists), the heart undertakes either to seek after the object, if it is convenient, or to avoid it, if inconvenient. Different spirits and humours are used in achieving the heart's goal and are drawn by the heart as well as sent by the soul. While the heart plays an important role in affective response to stimuli, much of the body is involved, including the liver and spleen, revealing just how much emotional reaction is conceived as a whole-body experience. In Renaissance tradition, as in ancient Greek culture, organs like these were associated not only with substances crucial to emotional response but also with specific passions: the spleen, for example, was considered the seat of both morose feelings and mirth,[14] while the liver was associated with desire as well as courage: cowards were believed to have white livers.[15]

This description of emotional response outlined by Wright, which Burton later summarizes in *The Anatomy of Melancholy*, presents what appears to be a universal biological reaction to stimuli. However, while these writers agree that the passions are part of the human and animal condition and that they are natural in the sense that they perform basic survival functions, nonetheless there were numerous factors that influenced how different individuals experienced, for example, hope or fear. The factors are both biological and environmental. Wright adds to his description of emotional response quoted above the important point that "the diversities of complexions wonderfully increase or diminish Passions; for, if the imagination be very apprehensive, it sendeth greater store of spirits to the heart, & maketh greater empression: likewise if the heart be very hote, colde, moist, tender, cholericke; sooner, and more vehemently it is stirred to Passions thereunto proportionated; finally, if one abound more with one humour than another, he sendeth more fewell to nourish the Passion, and so it continueth the longer, and the stronger" (1971, 46).

Concentrating on anger, Wright explains that different people experience anger differently, depending on their humoral complexion. Phlegmatic men are "not so soone angrie, nor yet soone pleased," while those with a sanguine complexion are commonly called "goodfellowes" because, although they are "soone angrie," they are also "soone friended." Melancholy men, on the other hand, are "hardly offended, and afterward, with extreame difficulty reconciled," while those of a choleric nature are "all fiery, and in a moment, at every trifle they are inflamed, and, till their hearts be consumed (almost) with choller, they never cease, except they be revenged" (1971, 37). (In contrast, modern cognitive science appears to downplay humoral predispositions focusing on the relative universality and sameness of complex emotions across individuals. See Paul Griffiths's discussion in chapter 4 of this volume.)

In the Galenic model, however, individuals had a degree of control over the physiological components of their emotional response system. Beyond controlling the passions through facial expression, or applying reason, or diversion of the emotions, individuals could in theory alter certain qualities in their bodies, like the humours and spirits – and thus affective response – through other of the non-naturals. Humoral imbalance or excess was addressed through purgations, including bloodletting, induced vomiting, or use of laxatives. In addition, because foods, like the humours they gave rise to, were classified as hot or cold and wet or dry, different foods were considered suitable for different temperaments, and diet played an important role in medical treatments, whether for physical or mental ailments.

As Schoenfeldt observes, "In early modern England, the consuming subject was pressured by Galenic physiology, classical ethics, and Protestant theology to conceive all acts of ingestion and excretion as very literal acts of self-fashioning" (1999, 11). Beef, for example, was thought to be "dangerous to melancholics, leading to dry skin diseases and depression among other noxious conditions," but spices, on the other hand, because classified as hot, were good for melancholics since such foods "heat up the blood and dissolve the heavy 'crudities' that might otherwise clog it" (Appelbaum 2006, 61, 62). Some foods, like garlic, were more controversial than others, while many were quite complex: eggs, for instance, could be both hot (the yolk) and cold (the white) (62–3).[16] Furthermore, if the digestive organs did not function properly, "impure" spirits could result, which negatively affected the body and mind, potentially provoking chiding and brawling (Lemnius, 1581, 9v), and digestive function was negatively affected by the body's temperature since digestion was understood as primarily heat driven rather than primarily a chemical process, as in later theory. Quantity and quality of food and drink ingested also had an impact, and moderation was constantly advised by both medical doctors and preachers.

In *Eating Right in the Renaissance,* Ken Albala makes a claim about the relationship between food and culture in all eras. "All cultures create a nutritional ideal that reflects their particular values and in turn conditions their expectations of how their bodies will behave. And bodies do behave differently in different times and places" (2002, 9). Bringing emotion into the equation, he describes how the Renaissance "fear of melons" campaign by medical authorities was successful because "people went on eating them, just as we go on eating everything we are told is bad for us, but the guilt experienced after indulgence was a sure sign that the physician's message had been internalized" (12). In his own study of food in the period, Robert Appelbaum (2006) describes what he calls the Renaissance doctrine of sensory affect, and he claims that it "requires us to imagine not only a theory but a regime of sensation that we can no longer experience. It suggests to us that individuals could actually feel their bodies in the experience of eating differently from how we feel them now, and that they felt their bodily experience in this way because of an idea, a language, or a semiotic structure" (52). Given their belief in the powerful link between diet and the material underpinnings of emotion, they may well have experienced their guilt or other emotions relating to food differently too.

Although different people were affected by passions differently, general principles were believed to exist in relation to such factors as age, size, class, gender, and ethnicity. Since "the manners of the soul follow the temperature of the body" (Wright 1971, 38), it follows that, generally speaking, "Old men are subject to sadnesse, caused by coldnesse of blood" (39) because, as people aged, the body's natural heat waned. Inversely, young men, in whom heat "aboundeth," are generally "arrogant, proud, prodigall, incontinent, given to all sorts of pleasure" (38), and the hottest among them will be most subject to these passions. Experience plays a role, too, however, as Wright adds that the pride of young men, for example, "proceedeth from lacke of experience" of how "fraile" the "strength, beauty, and witts" are of which they boast (38). Old men, "by reason of long experience, wherein they have often beene deceived," are prone to "suspect ill" (39). Small men are inclined towards impatience and anger: "a little man having his heate so united and compacted together, and not dispersed into so vast a carkasse as the great man, therefore he, by temperature, possesseth more spirits, and by them becommeth more nimble, lively, chollerike, hasty, and impatient" (44).

In a physiological theory in which heat played a crucial role in the body's proper functioning and being hotter than the temperate ideal was considered better than being colder, women were believed to be categorically colder than men and more likely to be phlegmatic.[17] Owen Felltham (2001) interprets this female lack of heat positively, claiming that women are "by constitution colder than the boiling man" and therefore "more temperate" and "naturally the more modest," in contrast to the male tendency towards "immoderation and fury" as well as "savage and libidinous violence" (289).[18] Similarly, Wright declares that women, "by nature, are enclined more to mercie and pitie than men, because the tendernesse of their complexion moveth them more to compassion." In addition, they are not "so prone to incontinency as men, for lacke of heate, and for a native shamefastnesse." However, "foure passions greatly possesse them": pride, self-love, envy ("the daughter of pride"), and inconstancy (1971, 40).[19] Pregnant women were believed to be prone to especially powerful and dangerous emotions. Wright observes, "It is wonderfull what passionate appetites raigne in women when they be with childe," adding that he agrees with the opinion that "most of these appetites proceeded from women extreamly addicted to follow their owne desires, and of such a froward disposition, as in very deede, if they were crossed of their willes, their passions were so strong, as they undoubtedly would miscarry of their children; for vehement passions alter vehemently the temper and constitution of the body, which cannot but greatly prejudice the tender infant lying in the womb" (74–5).

In addition to describing the conditions of age, size, and gender, Wright acknowledges other circumstances, including social status, that influence general patterns of behaviour and emotion. Although he does not go into detail, in the introduction to *The Passions of the Minde* he claims he might "declare, what Passions they are subject unto, whom Nature monstrously hath signed [by which he means those born deformed], what affections rule Rustickes, possesse Citizens, tyrannize over Gentlemen; which are most frequented in adversity, and which in prosperity." Wright also suggests that nationality plays a role in emotional experience, noting that he "might discourse over Flemings, Frenchmen, Spaniards, Italians, Polans, Germans, Scotishmen, Irishmen, Welshmen, and Englishmen, explicating their nationall inclinations good or bad" (1971, 44). In the preface to the 1604 edition, Wright (1971) explains that Italians, Spaniards, and other inhabitants "beyond the Alpes" consider Flemings, Englishmen, Scots, and other nations on the English side of the mountains to be "simple, uncircumspect, unwarie," easily deceived, and even "uncivill and barbarous," despite the fact that there are numerous examples of learned English scholars (lvii–lviii). The reasons why those of northern climates are considered simple and unwary when compared with the "craftie" Spaniards and Italians are natural inclination and constitution of the body, as well as education (lx). Natural inclination and bodily constitution are influenced by climate: those who live in colder climates, he argues, have a "naturall inclination to Vertue and honestie," "the first step unto prudence" that is misinterpreted by those of hotter climates as "a passion of ignorance" (lviii–lix). Hotter climates, on the other hand, "inclineth and bendeth them of hotter Countries more unto craftinesse and warinesse than them of colder Climates," a point he claims is strengthened by the fact that even within Italy or Spain, those who dwell in the hotter parts of the country will be craftier than the rest, just as some animals "by their naturall instinct, are more wilie than others, as Foxes, Monckies, and Apes" (lxi).

In her 2003 study *English Ethnicity and Race in Early Modern Drama*, Mary Floyd-Wilson explored the ways in which the ancient medical theory of humoralism profoundly and often inconsistently informed conceptions of ethnicity and race. Floyd-Wilson describes the nexus of climate, humoral theory, and national identity as "geohumoralism," and she argues that the English had to rework and work within this inherited belief structure about northerners – who were marginalized in classical theory –to legitimate the Atlantic slave trade. In an essay specifically addressing English emotion in this context, Floyd-Wilson (2004) remarks, "Ethnicity in the early modern period is defined more by emotional differences than by appearance: distinctions rest on how easily one is stirred or calmed – on one's degree of emotional vulnerability or resistance – or one's capacity to move others" (133). One's environment affected one's personality, either analogously (in Hippocrates, northern peoples like the Scythians were considered colder and moister, or phlegmatic, like their weather, and "typically denigrated for their effeminacy and cowardice") or inversely (many early moderns challenged Hippocrates' theory with the view of Aristotle and Pliny that colder climates sealed in the body's humours and heat, making northerners hotter and moister as well as full of "thick, gross matter") (136). Either way, northerners were contrasted with their southern neighbours, who were believed to have "drier and more civilized wits" in comparison with northerners' humour-clouded minds, which negatively affected their ability to control themselves emotionally (137–8).

The influence of the natural environment on personal and national characteristics is complemented by – and almost a literalization of – the influence of the social and cultural environment on emotional qualities. (These cultural approaches could be compared with the contemporary constructionist theories of emotion discussed by Griffiths in chapter 4 of this volume.) When it comes to the shaping influence of education, Wright (1971) notes that "prudence and policie are wonne by experience, experience by practise, practise by conversation, conversation by communication with people," and, therefore, those who dwell in cities of greater commerce will be craftier than rural people (lix). Italians and Spaniards prefer to dwell in cities and so become "very politique and craftie"; most Englishmen, however, dwell in the country or in small cities (lx). English youth are also raised with "too much feare and terrour" because their parents or schoolmasters are too severe, whereas Spanish and Italian parents allow their children greater liberty, with the result that they are "bold and audacious" at sixteen or seventeen, while the English at that age are "drooping with feare and timiditie" (lxi). Wright is careful, though, to add that these are generalizations since he knows some English who far surpass any Italian or Spaniard in "subtiltie and warinesse" (lxii). Generally, though, "those Nations surpasse ours in a certaine politique craftinesse, the which Nature first bred in them, Education perfited, Vertue amendeth, and Art discovereth" (lxiii). A key purpose of Wright's treatise is to try to help his English readers learn how to discover other men's passions and how to behave themselves when overcome with strong emotion, which is the "fittest mean to attayne unto religious, civil, & gentlemenlike conversation, which is vertuous" (lxii).

In conclusion, Renaissance understandings of the emotions were influenced by the classical and Christian tradition and by an ancient medical theory that differed significantly from our own. Examining some of the attitudes towards the emotions that existed in the Renaissance reveals that, despite many differences, there are some similarities with modern interests, one being the diversity of opinions on the topic. It is worth noting that although we no longer subscribe to Galenic medicine, with its humours and spirits and individualized body temperatures, the English language retains vestiges of that model in its emotion language: "hot tempered," "high spirited," and "melancholy," for instance. Attending to this language raises questions about the relationship between language and the body that are more generally relevant to thinking about the emotions and the relationship between the experience of emotion and descriptions of that experience and about the relationship among language, culture, and science. For some linguists, metaphors are fundamental to human thought and grounded in bodily processes, while for others, cultural models form the basis of metaphors and not the other way around (Niemeier 2008, 350). Of language used to describe emotions specifically, Gail Kern Paster, Katherine Rowe, and Mary Floyd-Wilson (2004) outline how linguist Zoltán Kövecses offers the similarity of expressions like "hothead" in different languages to describe emotional experience as evidence of the influence of both culture and shared physiology, while Dirk Geeraerts and Stefan Grondelaers counter this, offering a "crucial diachronic dimension to the cultural study of emotion" by highlighting the continuing influence of ancient humoral physiology on many languages and suggesting that this humoral theory may itself have been influenced by "a prior metaphorical understanding of a physiological experience, along the lines of 'anger as fire'" (2004, 17).

Importantly, the Renaissance period, one in which the English lexicon expanded significantly, also contributed new vocabulary still used to describe specific emotions. In a recent article presenting part of a larger project called "Inventing Emotion," Benedict Robinson (2014) explains, "A whole series of words we still use to name and to know our emotions first entered the language between 1580 and 1700: disgust, self-esteem, resentment, anxiety, panic, embarrassment" (555). Robinson argues that each of these words represents "a new distinction within some prior field" (distinguishing anxiety from fear, or disgust from loathing, for example), "but also pushes the theory of the passions in new directions, demanding new accounts of experience, new ways of thinking about the relations between soul and body, and new concepts of what passion is" (555). Renaissance texts like Wright's *The Passions of the Minde* thus highlight the significance of terminology to theory and the interplay between physiological and cultural models in explanations of emotional experience. They also illustrate the ways in which discourses of emotion overlap with other discourses, including those of gender, ethnicity, class, and politics.

NOTES

1 I am grateful to the anonymous reader for UTP for comments on an earlier version of the essay as well as to the editors of the collection and the copy editor for their feedback.

2 When quoting from Renaissance sources, I have generally retained original spelling and capitalization, except when quoting from modernized editions. I have silently altered the long *s*, expanded abbreviations, and substituted *u* for *v* and *j* for *i*, where applicable, for clarity.

3 In *Rethinking the Mind-Body Relationship in Early Modern Literature, Philosophy and Medicine* (2016), Charis Charalampous nuances conceptions about pre- and post-Cartesian thought, noting, "Too many readers have been content to assume simplistically that mind and body were conjoined until Descartes, and then suddenly they were separated" (1).

4 *Oxford English Dictionary* online, s.v. "emotion," definitions 1a, 2, 3a, accessed 2013.

5 For more on the body politic metaphor, see, for example, David Hale, *The Body Politic: A Political Metaphor in Renaissance English Literature* (1971); Leonard Barkan, *Nature's Work of Art: The Human Body as Image of the World* (1975); Annabel Patterson, *Fables of Power: Aesopian Writing and Political History* (1991), particularly the chapter called "Body Fables"; Jonathan Gil Harris, *Foreign Bodies and the Body Politic: Discourses of Social Pathology in Early Modern England* (1998).

6 See, e.g., John Staines's engagement with and revision of Jürgen Habermas in "Compassion in the Public Sphere of Milton and King Charles" (2004) and Victoria Kahn's challenge to Albert Hirschman's theory about the emergence of a positive view of self-interest and acquisitive passions in "The Passions and Interests in Early Modern Europe: The Case of Guarini's *Il pastor fido*" (2004).
7 Cf. Northoff, ch. 5.
8 Cf. Balot, ch. 1.
9 Burton continued to revise and add to his *Anatomy* through successive editions. The modern edition employed here is based on the posthumously published 1651 sixth edition (the last to include Burton's suggested alterations), collated with the fifth edition.
10 Thomas O. Sloan (1971) adds, however, that this methodization was not achieved in any significant way until Descartes's *The Passions of the Soul* (1649), which was more in line with the new science and thus was less religious and rhetorical in emphasis (xiv).
11 When citing Burton, I include part, section, member, and subsection, followed by the page number.
12 For more on Paster's interpretation of Wright's comments on animal emotions, see *Humoring the Body* (2004, ch. 3).
13 For more on the role of the digestive organs in emotional experience, and analysis of how gender, ethnicity, and class hierarchies are mapped onto discourses of the stomach, see Jan Purnis, "The Stomach and Early Modern Emotion" (2010).
14 *Oxford English Dictionary* online, s.v. "spleen," definitions 1b, c, accessed 2013.
15 In Shakespeare's *The Merchant of Venice,* Bassanio, deliberating on which casket to choose in the hopes of winning Portia's hand, comments on the common discrepancy between outer appearance and inner nature, employing this belief about the liver in doing so. He remarks, "How many cowards, whose hearts are all as false/As stairs of sand, wear yet upon their chins/The beards of Hercules and frowning Mars,/Who inward search'd, have livers white as milk" (1974, 3.2, 83–6).
16 Robert Appelbaum (2006) notes that "though the humors were manufactured out of the concoction [digestion] of foodstuffs in the belly, the humors were not in the foodstuffs themselves. This principle accounts for the fact both that the same foods had different effects on different people and that one could not explain the temperamental effects of foodstuffs in the body simply by their obvious sensory qualities" (50–1).
17 This defect of heat theory was used to explain differences in male and female genitalia: according to this theory, women lacked the heat to push

the genitals outwards. For more on this, see Thomas Lacquer, *Making Sex: Body and Gender from the Greeks to Freud* (1990, esp. 25–35).

18 Women who were hotter and more choleric, like Shakespeare's Katherina in *The Taming of the Shrew*, were often labelled "scolds" or "shrews," evidence, Felltham (2001) affirms, of a double-standard he describes as "injustice" (289).

19 Juan Huarte (1594) contributes to this gendering of emotions with his comments on how men are commonly of "better wit" than women because women have tenderer flesh, which is the result of the humours of phlegm and blood, both moist, and which Galen says "make men simple & dullards," whereas the humours of choler and melancholy make the flesh harder and "hence grow the prudence and sapience which are found in man" (80).

REFERENCES

Albala, Ken. 2002. *Eating Right in the Renaissance*. Berkeley: University of California Press.

Appelbaum, Robert. 2006. *Aguecheek's Beef, Belch's Hiccup, and Other Gastronomic Interjections: Literature, Culture, and Food among the Early Moderns*. Chicago: University of Chicago Press. http://dx.doi.org/10.7208/chicago/9780226021287.001.0001.

Bacon, Francis. 1627. "Of Anger." From "Essays of Francis Bacon," no. 57. The Literature Page. Edited by Michael Moncur. Accessed July 2012. http://www.literaturepage.com/read/francis-bacon-essays-111.html.

Barkan, Leonard. 1975. *Nature's Work of Art: The Human Body as Image of the World*. New Haven, CT: Yale University Press.

Burton, Robert. 2001. *The Anatomy of Melancholy*. Edited by Holbrook Jackson. Introduction by William H. Gass. New York: New York Review Books.

Charalampous, Charis. 2016. *Rethinking the Mind-Body Relationship in Early Modern Literature, Philosophy and Medicine*. New York: Routledge.

Crooke, Helkiah. 1615. *Microcosmographia: A Description of the Body of Man*. London.

Damasio, Antonio. 1999. *The Feeling of What Happens: Body and Emotion in the Making of Consciousness*. New York: Harvest.

Felltham, Owen. 2001. "Of Woman (from *Resolves*)." In *The Broadview Anthology of Seventeenth-Century Verse & Prose*, vol. 2, edited by Alan Rudrum, Joseph Black, and Holly Faith Nelson, 289–90. Peterborough, ON: Broadview Press. First published 1623.

Floyd-Wilson, Mary. 2003. *English Ethnicity and Race in Early Modern Drama*. Cambridge, MA: Cambridge University Press.

Floyd-Wilson, M. 2004. "English Mettle." In *Reading the Early Modern Passions: Essays in the Cultural History of Emotion*, edited by Gail Kern Paster, Katherine Rowe, and Mary Floyd-Wilson, 130–146. Philadelphia: University of Pennsylvania Press.

Hale, David. 1971. *The Body Politic: A Political Metaphor in Renaissance English Literature*. The Hague, NL: Mouton.

Harris, Jonathan Gil. 1998. *Foreign Bodies and the Body Politic: Discourses of Social Pathology in Early Modern England*. Cambridge, MA: Cambridge University Press.

Huarte, Juan. 1594. *The Examination of Men's Wits*. Translated by R. Carew. London.

Kahn, Victoria. 2004. "The Passions and Interests in Early Modern Europe: The Case of Guarini's *Il pastor fido*." In *Reading the Early Modern Passions: Essays in the Cultural History of Emotion*, edited by Gail Kern Paster, Katherine Rowe, and Mary Floyd-Wilson, 217–39. Philadelphia: University of Pennsylvania Press.

Lacquer, Thomas. 1990. *Making Sex: Body and Gender from the Greeks to Freud*. Cambridge, MA: Harvard University Press.

Lemnius, Levinus. 1581. *The Touchstone of Complexions*. Translated by Thomas Newton. London.

Niemeier, Susanne. 2008. "To Be in Control: Kind-Hearted and Cool-Headed – The Head-Heart Dichotomy in English." In *Culture, Body, and Language: Conceptualizations of Internal Body Organs across Cultures and Languages*, edited by Farzad Sharifian, René Dirven, Ning Yu, and Susanne Niemeier, 349–72. Berlin: Mouton de Gruyter.

Paster, Gail Kern. 1997. "Nervous Tension." In *The Body in Parts: Fantasies of Corporeality in Early Modern Europe*, edited by David Hillman and Carla Mazzio, 107–25. New York: Routledge.

Paster, Gail Kern. 2004. *Humoring the Body: Emotions and the Shakespearean Stage*. Chicago: University of Chicago Press. http://dx.doi.org/10.7208/chicago/9780226648484.001.0001.

Paster, Gail Kern, Katherine Rowe, and Mary Floyd-Wilson. 2004. Introduction to *Reading the Early Modern Passions: Essays in the Cultural History of Emotion*, edited by Gail Kern Paster, Katherine Rowe, and Mary Floyd-Wilson, 1–20. Philadelphia: University of Pennsylvania Press.

Patterson, Annabel. 1991. *Fables of Power: Aesopian Writing and Political History*. Durham, NC: Duke University Press. http://dx.doi.org/10.1215/9780822382577.

Purnis, Jan. 2010. "The Stomach and Early Modern Emotion." *University of Toronto Quarterly* 79 (2): 800–18.

Robinson, Benedict. 2014. "Disgust c. 1600." *ELH: English Literary History* 81 (2): 553–83.

Schoenfeldt, Michael. 1999. *Bodies and Selves in Early Modern England: Physiology and Inwardness in Spenser, Shakespeare, Herbert, and Milton.* Cambridge: Cambridge University Press.

Schoenfeldt, Michael. 2004. "'Commotion Strange': Passion in *Paradise Lost*." In *Reading the Early Modern Passions: Essays in the Cultural History of Emotion*, edited by Gail Kern Paster, Katherine Rowe, and Mary Floyd-Wilson, 43–67. Philadelphia: University of Pennsylvania Press.

Shakespeare, William. 1974. *The Merchant of Venice*. In *The Riverside Shakespeare*, edited by G. Blakemore Evans, 250–85. Boston, MA: Houghton Mifflin.

Shakespeare, William. 1974. *The Taming of the Shrew*. In *The Riverside Shakespeare*, edited by G. Blakemore Evans, 106–142. Boston, MA: Houghton Mifflin.

Shakespeare, William. 1974. *Troilus and Cressida*. In *The Riverside Shakespeare*, edited by G. Blakemore Evans, 443–98. Boston, MA: Houghton Mifflin.

Sloan, Thomas O. 1971. Introduction to *The Passions of the Minde in Generall*, by Thomas Wright, xi–xlix. Chicago: University of Illinois Press.

Staines, John. 2004. "Compassion in the Public Sphere of Milton and King Charles." In *Reading the Early Modern Passions: Essays in the Cultural History of Emotion*, edited by Gail Kern Paster, Katherine Rowe, and Mary Floyd-Wilson, 89–110. Philadelphia: University of Pennsylvania Press.

Stevens, Scott Manning. 1997. "Sacred Heart and Secular Brain." In *The Body in Parts: Fantasies of Corporeality in Early Modern Europe*, edited by David Hillman and Carla Mazzio, 263–82. New York: Routledge.

Strier, Richard. 2004. "Against the Rule of Reason: Praise of Passion from Petrarch to Luther to Shakespeare to Herbert." In *Reading the Early Modern Passions: Essays in the Cultural History of Emotion*, edited by Gail Kern Paster, Katherine Rowe, and Mary Floyd-Wilson, 23–42. Philadelphia: University of Pennsylvania Press.

Wright, Thomas. 1971. *The Passions of the Minde in Generall.* Reprint based on the 1604 edition. Introduction by Thomas O. Sloan. Chicago: University of Illinois Press.

3 Wittgenstein and the Social Science of Emotion

JOHN G. GUNNELL

Introduction

In recent years, there has been an increased interest among the social sciences in the phenomena of emotion and how emotions are involved in the explanation of human action and interaction. This has, in part, been the consequence of a renewed awareness, and concern, about the role of emotions in political life as well as a reaction against what is sometimes perceived as the dominance of rational choice analysis and the prominence of normative arguments, such as the work of John Rawls, about the possibilities for public reason and deliberative democracy.[1] This wave of a social scientific approach to emotion has been significantly inspired by recent research in neuroscience and sociobiology, which has reinforced, and reawakened, in both philosophy and social science, the long-standing proclivity to seek a naturalistic explanation of social phenomena. The manner in which emotion has been analysed in much of this literature has tended to parallel and reflect claims about "emotional intelligence" (Goleman 1995) and popular arguments such as those of Malcolm Gladwell (2005) about the importance of "thinking without thinking." These claims have, however, often been quite uncritically received, and among the social sciences, this approach to the study of emotion has remained more an image and aspiration than an actual research program. I will explore some of the deficiencies of this approach, but what is more important, I will examine and defend an account of emotion that has, in part, been inspired by the philosophy of Ludwig Wittgenstein and explore aspects of its potential contribution to social enquiry.

My point is not to challenge the basic theoretical and experimental research in cognitive neuroscience, but rather to question some of the social scientific derivations and philosophical extrapolations. There are many reasons to encourage interdisciplinary research, but there is sometimes a failure to recognize that despite the use of the same word, such as *emotion*, quite different concepts may be involved. Simply because cognitive scientists use *emotion* as a naturalistic concept does not mean that they are addressing the same phenomenon that social scientists are confronting. The basic problem with much of the contemporary discussion is that it begins with asking what emotions are, in the sense of what they *really* are, as if what we are typically witnessing when we see something such as a social expression of fear is only an appearance, similar to what a physicist might say about common sense perceptions of temporality. Although emotions, like many forms of human behaviour, have biological foundations, correlates, and consequences, it is a mistake, in the context of social enquiry, to conceive emotions as neurological and physiological events, which can be isolated as the causes, or the underlying reality, of overt forms of what human beings say and do. This mistake would not be dissimilar to claiming that because the human brain is wired to facilitate language, we can understand linguistic meaning by studying the brain.

It is important to recognize that even philosophers such as Daniel Dennett, as well as scientists such as Richard Dawkins, who have strongly defended the biological foundations of human consciousness, stress the emergent autonomy of social phenomena and social enquiry. Dennett, for example, recommends what he refers to as "heterophenomenology" (2005, 36), which would be a somewhat anthropological third-person study of first-person reports and expressions of such things as emotion. Unlike some neuroscientists, who attempt to overlay their research with philosophical implications, and some philosophers and social theorists, who attempt to ground their arguments on experimental findings, Dennett and Dawkins recognize that the "hardware" of the brain does not determine what we might characterize as the cultural constructions in the social "software" and that the latter can have a recursive effect on the former.

Contemporary uses of "emoticons" in social media are only one manifestation of how emotions are manifest in language and action and explicable in the context of the conventions constituting what Wittgenstein referred to as the social "weave of life." Although much of the current literature in neuroscience, and its echoes in the social sciences, continues to construe emotions as hidden internal phenomena of which public behaviour is an indicator, Wittgenstein frontally challenged such an account and provided a basis for defending the autonomy of social enquiry. He was not, however, advancing an alternative theory of what emotions *really* are, but only clarifying conceptually what constitutes a certain dimension of social meaning and interaction. He approached emotions, like human speech and action, as conventional phenomena and stressed that various terms characteristically designating emotions gain meaning neither from first-person introspection nor from references to neurological states and processes. If emotions are theorized in the manner that Wittgenstein suggested, it implies an interpretive mode of enquiry that is very different from that associated with natural science.

Concepts of Emotion

Part of the confusion attending recent discussions of emotion is a consequence of the fact that many terms, such as emotion, used by psychologists and neuroscientists, have a prior, pre-scientific meaning. These realms of meaning tend to become conflated, and this encourages the implication that science has isolated what is represented in the public language. Wittgenstein illustrated this point by noting how a scientific concept such as that referred to by "solidity" did not provide an answer to the various social uses of such a word and the contexts in which it was meaningful. Lack of clarity about how emotions are involved in various forms of social life is also the consequence of a failure to recognize that *emotion* is a word that, over time, as well as in contemporary literature, has referred to some quite different kinds of things. The English word connotes a range of phenomena including thoughts, feelings, and bodily events and processes, but there is considerable historical and cultural variation among uses of what might be understood as the same or a comparable term. In Western society, accounts of emotion have been particularly influenced by a long tradition of "psychophysiological symbolism" (Averill 1996), which locates emotion in what is often conceived as an inferior or visceral part of the body.

While some philosophers and neuroscientists, from William James to the present, discuss at length what they claim is the relationship between emotions and physical feelings, there really is no exact distinction in, for example, the German language.[2] Further semantic slippage arises from the manner in which *emotion* often functions as a generic or classificatory term that, while sometimes used somewhat restrictively to refer to psychological states, is employed in many instances more expansively to include things such as primal instinctive responses to certain stimuli. There is also a tendency to confuse an analytic term, which specifies a taxonomic kind, with a theoretical term, which posits a natural or substantive kind. When we encounter contemporary books that seek to locate emotions physiologically, such as *The Emotional Brain* (LeDoux 1996) and *What Emotions Really Are* (Griffiths 1997), we should take this less as the announcement of an empirical discovery than as a claim about the kinds of things to which we should properly apply the word *emotion*. So in studying emotion, the important question is whether we are interested in social phenomena or physical phenomena.

Although the physiological account of emotion has become increasingly popular, Wittgenstein's work has contributed significantly to a less prominent, but competing, account, which is sometimes referred to as the "discursive theory" of emotion (e.g., Harré 1986; Harré and Gillett 1994; Harré and Parrott 1996). It claims that emotions are less unconscious adjuncts to public expressions than social constructions that themselves represent, and are involved in, forms of judgment and appraisal. What is sometimes referred to as the "cognitivist thesis" (not to be confused with the field of cognitive science) claims that "emotions are a kind of judgment – or rather, a complex of interlocking judgments, desires, and intentions" (Solomon 2004, 76; also 2002, 2007). For example, the historian William Reddy has coined the term "emotives" to refer to emotions as a form of utterance that can be studied culturally and historically (2001). He rejects the idea of reducing emotions to physiological phenomena and claims that even sexual desire is, in some respects, a cultural rather than "hard-wired" experience and that some research in cognitive science actually "confirms the claims historians, anthropologists, and others have made about the powerful impact of cultural factors[3] on perceptions and practice;" he accords with Wittgenstein's account of emotion as part of a social and linguistic "form of life" (2008, 2009).

It is always appealing, and often important, to seek an interdisciplinary approach, such as that of Jon Elster (1999, 2000), who recommends approaching the study of emotion in a manner that combines neurobiology, culture, and the study of strategic choice. Such eclecticism, however, too often assumes that emotions are an object on which one can have various perspectives, when the underlying issue actually involves incommensurable theoretical claims about the concept of emotion and the class of things to which emotion belongs. Such positions are not necessarily in conflict, but when a conflict arises, there is, as Thomas Kuhn argued, no neutral empirical resolution, and, in the end, as both Kuhn and Wittgenstein claimed, the matter can be settled only by persuasion (Wittgenstein 1969, 262, 612). There are, however, some significant immanent weaknesses in certain theoretical accounts of emotion that have been based on neuroscientific research and that have gained prominence in the social and human sciences.

When Gladwell and others claimed that there is an important unconscious dimension of appraisal and judgment that supplements, and is often superior to, conscious thought and deliberation, he drew heavily on the work of individuals such as the experimental physiologist Antonio Damasio. Although Gladwell's claims might be passed off by some as "pop science," many social scientists have followed the same path. Gladwell presented many examples of what he referred to as the "adaptive unconscious," or the apparent capacity that some people possess to reach sound conclusions on the basis of what is often colloquially referred to as "gut feeling," but this reflected a view that had been advanced by some philosophers (e.g., Prinz 2003) who analysed cases in which a person could not articulate a "rational" basis for reaching "snap decisions."

While some view emotions as supplementing conscious judgment, others have taken an even more reductive approach. The cognitive scientist Mark Turner has argued that, because of research in neuroscience, social enquiry "is in a position something like biology before the theory of evolution" and that to explain the meaning of social phenomena, it is necessary to access the "neurocognitive level at which these meanings emerge" (2001, 11–12). The philosopher Paul Churchland (e.g., 1995) has embraced connectionism in neuroscience and claimed that this kind of study of the brain can not only explain human behaviour but also yield a science of public policy and put the study and practice of morality on a scientific basis. Drawing on the work of Churchland, the sociologist Stephen Turner (2002) has claimed that the findings of neuroscience can serve to underwrite an individualist social ontology as well as a critical social science and provide a basis for core concepts, which can be replaced by references to nodes in a neural network.

The current enthusiasm for applying cognitive science to the subject of emotion is, however, only one element of a considerable renaissance, during the past few years, in the study of emotion and its place in both philosophy and social enquiry (e.g., Blackburn 1998; Goodwin, Jasper, and Polletta 2001; Clarke, Hoggett, and Thompson 2006). Although much of this literature has little connection to the study of emotion in cognitive science and is sometimes pointedly at odds with that approach, it claims that political judgment, and practical reason as a whole, are not, as "traditionally" assumed, matters relating to what is loosely referred to as rational deliberation, but are significantly informed by affect, sentiment, and emotion. It would, however, be difficult to sustain the claim that this is really a recent discovery. Neither in the history of political philosophy nor in more contemporary disciplinary studies of politics, as well as in journalism and popular media, has the emotional dimension of politics been neglected. A recent book on "bringing the emotions back in" (Kingston and Ferry 2008) was, in large part, devoted to recapitulating how much attention in the classic canon of political thought had, in fact, been devoted to emotions, and a great deal of attention has been given to the study of how emotions are socially constituted and interpreted (see also Koziak 2000; Sokolon 2006). Many social scientists have, nevertheless, fastened on a limited dimension of the literature on emotion and particularly on the arguments of Damasio (1994, 1999) and similar claims about the physiological nature of emotion and the manner in which it features as an unconscious aspect of judgment. Although this has extended to fields as diverse as economics and ethics, it has been especially prominent in the study of politics. Politics seems to be a world in which emotion is particularly salient, and consequently, political scientists and political theorists have been prone to seeking support from the experimental results and philosophical embellishments of cognitive science.

There are, however, several specific problems involved in attempts to apply the findings of neuroscience to social and political enquiry and particularly to the study of emotion (for a more detailed critical discussion, see Gunnell 2007, 2011, 2012). First, cognitive neuroscience is not a specific field of study, but a conceptually and empirically diverse, and sometimes contentious, amalgam of research areas. It is not organized around a dominant unifying theory, and claims about how it might be adapted to social and political enquiry have been varied as well as sometimes confused, if not, in some cases, simply mistaken, in their account of the literature on which they rely. Second, some of the literature in neuroscience, such as the work of Damasio, has often been entangled with, but insensitive to, various highly contested issues in both psychology and the philosophy of mind. Third, the social scientific borrowings have typically been highly selective and ad hoc, sometimes contradictory, and often chosen to support prior ideological and research agendas. Fourth, significant contemporary challenges, emanating from both philosophy and psychology, as well as from neuroscientists themselves, to some of the treatments of mental concepts have seldom been taken into account. And finally, it is often unclear exactly how knowledge of brain states and processes could be practically used in research on collective social behaviour. Once we have assembled reports about what people claim is, for example, their anger about what is happening in politics and after describing what might be classed as angry behaviour, it is difficult to determine exactly how we could go about accessing the physiological and neural foundations.

Why Damasio's work has featured so prominently among the claims of social scientists is probably because it is written in a relatively popular and accessible style and focuses on dramatic stories such as that of the unfortunate Phineas Gage, whose injuries to the ventromedial frontal cortex of his brain resulted in lapses in rational judgment accompanied by erratic emotional responses. Although individuals such as Damasio claim to expose Descartes's "error" regarding the divide between mind and body, they actually tend to posit a new form of dualism, one that substitutes the brain for the mind. The brain is viewed as distinct from the rest of the body and as something to which psychological attributes can be ascribed. Damasio actually still retains the category of the mind, even though it is no longer conceived in Cartesian terms as an immaterial substance. He characterizes the "mind" as an ontologically distinct emergent phenomenon, or inner "eye." While Cartesian dualism posited a non-extended mental activity, cognitive science posits extended mental activity. The mental realm remains hidden behind the externally observed body and inferred from public behaviour, but known, at least partially, to the actor by introspection. Finally, dualism reappears in the form of things such as emotions attributed to a subconscious realm interacting with the conscious dimension of human agency. A recent popular book titled *The Future of the Mind* (2014), by the physicist Michio Kaku, is actually a book about the brain. He focused on how the amygdala is the "seat of the emotions" from which come "rapid decisions made independently … without permission from the top" (20), while, as opposed to the "conscious emotions" that are located in the cingulate cortex (34), "irrational" emotions spring from the limbic system (231). It might not be an exaggeration to say that the brain has become the last refuge of an image of the mind as a separate realm, one that has endured from Plato to contemporary philosophers such as John Searle (1992).

Damasio defines emotion as a change in a brain state that is a response to an image in the thought process, but, he claims, it is reducible to a pattern of physiological responses. Consequently, emotions are taken to be experimentally observable even if the subject is not aware of the emotion. Some emotions are equated with general background affects that are common to animals (e.g., fear), and some are parsed as social and cultural, even though often shared by humans and animals. While Damasio describes emotions as expressions, he designates feelings as experiences. Feelings are posited as private and mostly conscious, and they consist of mental, perceptual images of a bodily state based on a neural map. They may arise from an emotion (like a feeling of sadness), but they can be wrong and not reflect an actual bodily state. Although Damasio's account of emotion is in many ways similar to that of William James, the latter claimed that a bodily change results from the perception of an "exciting" fact and that the feeling of that change is the emotion. This difference between Damasio and the early nineteenth-century James-Lange theory simply indicates how much conceptual ambiguity there is in the discussion of emotion and its relationship to concepts such as feelings. Simply stipulating the meaning of a term such as *feeling* does not explain the meaning of what is involved when, for example, voters say that they have a positive feeling about a candidate.

Another typical argument about "the emotional brain," on which some social scientists have also relied, has been advanced by Joseph LeDoux (1996), whose work, along with that of Damasio, has been defended as confirming a version of James's basic physicalist account of emotion. LeDoux argued that Damasio's study of the "rationality of emotions," as well as complementary studies, have demonstrated that "the left hemisphere" of the brain is engaged in "unconscious information processing" and "making emotional judgments without knowing what was judged" and that this unconscious activity performs functions such as detecting danger and reinforcing positive choices. Although he designated emotions as "things that happen to us" and that usually evoke bodily responses, he claimed that it is also possible to "turn our mind's eye inward on our emotions" and survey our "cognitive unconscious" and the manner in which "emotions intrude into our conscious mind" (15, 19, 22, 30, 36). As in the case of Damasio, however, much of this was less a report of experimental data than a thinly articulated philosophy of mind and often a reversion to what are now such highly criticized psychological concepts as introspection. But all these arguments flow from the assumption that the meaning of words designating emotions must refer to some object that can be scientifically located. It was a critique of such a limited account of meaning that was the central theme of Wittgenstein's *Philosophical Investigations* (2001).

On the last page of the *Investigations*, Wittgenstein famously stated that "the confusion and barrenness of psychology is not to be explained by calling it a 'young science'; its state is not comparable with that of physics, for instance, in its beginnings … for in psychology there are experimental methods and *conceptual confusion*. … The existence of the experimental method makes us think that we have the means of solving the problems that trouble us; though problem and method pass one another by" (2001, p. 197).[4] The cognitive scientist Max R. Bennett and the Wittgensteinian scholar Peter M.S. Hacker (2003) collaborated in a challenge to the conceptual coherence of much of the literature deriving from neuroscience and particularly the work of individuals such as Damasio. The problems they noted have reappeared, and often been compounded, in the work of a number of social theorists who have drawn on this work.

Although Bennett and Hacker did not quarrel with most of the basic experimental findings, which they often found interesting and provocative, they focused on the conceptual confusions in the philosophical elaborations and justifications as well as on the manner in which these confusions sometimes became embedded in certain research programs. These basic criticisms have been amplified in detail by others (e.g., Coulter and Sharrock 2007; Hacker 2009; Racine and Müller 2009; Gustafsson, Kronquist, and McEachrane 2009), but one of the principal points was that, despite the emphasis on identifying the mind with the brain, much of this work perpetuates the Cartesian legacy, which Wittgenstein had done so much to undermine. Bennett and Hacker claimed that a principal aspect of conceptual confusion arises from what they refer to as the "mereological fallacy" of ascribing psychological attributes to the brain/mind. Although human capacities and abilities have physiological correlates, psychological attributes, including perception, experience, intention, judgment, belief, and emotion, attach to persons or agents as a whole, not to either a mind or a brain – or a heart or a gut. Metaphors such as "gut feeling" and "mind's eye" lead us astray and suggest that something such as the "embodied mind" can be the subject of mental predicates. Bennett and Hacker argued that although there is logical asymmetry between first- and third-person claims, this is not because of individual subjectivity and the ability of persons to look "inside" themselves and observe their thoughts and sensations. Following Wittgenstein, they claimed that what is mental is inner only in the sense that one can conceal it, as in the case of the sensation of pain, the articulation of a thought, and the experience of an emotion, but this is not because these are events that take place in a Cartesian theatre of the mind. The fact that one can conceal one's emotions presupposes that they were at first not concealed.

Emotions as Social Phenomena

There are many debates and sub-debates in various disciplines and fields associated with cognitive science, but one fundamental split is between those who hold to some form of the subconscious biological conception of emotion as a brain state or somatic reaction and those who argue that emotions are a class of affections that involve intentionality (in the philosophical senses of both directiveness, or "aboutness," and agency) and normativity, manifest in judgments and appraisals. The latter theorists argue that although we extend emotion talk metaphorically to things other than persons and to functionally equivalent behaviour in animals, human emotions, for the most part, involve the mastery of language and are conventionally constituted phenomena that are integral to, and manifestations of, things such as moral judgment (e.g., Taylor 1985; Nussbaum 2001, 2004). Ronald de Sousa has argued that "reason and emotion are not natural antagonists," but are also not just complementary and mutually exclusive elements of judgment. Emotions are "learned rather like a language," and although he suggests that "physiology does have something to contribute to our understanding of emotions," he maintains that "this can itself be sorted out only in terms of higher level functions" (1987, xv–xvi; see also Goldie 2000).

This argument has been supported by philosophers of psychology such as Rom Harré, who argue that, during the past two decades, a "second cognitive revolution" has been taking shape and presents a challenge to the idea of the mind as a machine, which has dominated so much of the cognitive science that has become popular among social scientists. At the core of this revolution is what he refers to as the theory of the "discursive mind," or the "rediscovery of the human mind," which he claims has benefited significantly from Wittgenstein's analysis of mental concepts (Harré and Gillett 1994; Harré and Parrott 1996; Harré and Tissaw 2005) as well as from the work of diverse individuals ranging from Aristotle to the social theories of mind in the work of George Mead and Lev Vygotsky, which together suggest a social or symbolic account of mind. Discursive theorists claim that psychological phenomena are neither brain states and processes nor things rooted in a hidden language of thought, or "mentalese," operating behind public language. This position does not deny the neural foundations of discursive behaviour, but it stresses the manner in which such behaviour also shapes and restructures the pathways in the brain. The principal point, however, is to defend the theoretical autonomy of conventional phenomena. The *mind* refers to the abilities and capacities that define the discursive dimension of social activity. With respect to the particular issue of emotions, this position rejects the idea that emotion, as displayed in social life, is a manifestation of bodily states of individuals and physiological reactions to external stimuli. This position has sometimes been identified as "the social construction" of emotion (Harré 1986), but the basic argument is that while Aristotle, who viewed what we call emotions, despite their physiological dimension, as integrally involved with judgments, may stand out as an exception, more typical has been the Platonic tendency to situate emotions in the body and oppose them to the workings of the soul and reason lodged in the head.

Advocates of a discursive approach to emotions conceive them as socially variable and operating within a set of beliefs and a particular moral order, and although acknowledging that certain things that are often designated as emotions, such as reacting to a loud noise, are physiological and the product of ethological rather than ethnological phenomena, they claim that there is little experimental evidence of specific physical events that reliably differentiate emotions. The variability of cultural expressions of emotion has been well documented in anthropological research and was even noted by Darwin. In some cultures, what might be classed as emotions have little physical symbolism attached to them, and even many Western images of emotion are not identified in terms of physical criteria. While philosophers such as Kant wished to keep emotions from intruding on rational moral judgment, and while emotivist philosophers of ethics argued, on the contrary, that such judgments were simply the verbal expression of emotions, both viewed them naturalistically and as distinct from and prior to rational or discursive decision.

There is much more that can be said about this broad division in the theoretical literature about emotion, but much of what might be broadly termed "the discursive view" was inspired by Wittgenstein. Hacker, for example, followed Wittgenstein in systematically attempting to map the conceptual terrain represented in the language of emotion and its relationship to other mental terms, and Joachim Schulte carefully examined elements of Wittgenstein's discussion (2009). Both focused on the manner in which the study of emotion presupposes the background of specific social and cultural forms of human life. Since so much of the critique of the neuroscientific account of emotion as well as the formulation of the discursive account have been based on Wittgenstein's work, it is important to examine his position more closely and consider more directly the manner in which his treatment of emotion could be, and possibly should be, a guide for social science.

Wittgenstein on Emotion

Wittgenstein did not advance what might typically be classified as a philosophical theory of the mind, discursive or otherwise, but he had a great deal to say about the "grammar" of mental concepts, including those we typically associate with emotion, sensation, and feeling. Wittgenstein's remarks about psychology, especially in the last sections of the *Investigations* (2001), were an extension of what are arguably the two most prominent themes running through his later work: his critiques of the assumption that words gain their meaning primarily by naming objects, which are in turn pictured in the mind, and the assumption that there is a private language for first-person references to mental states and events. One of the important dimensions of his later work was the claim that although thought and language were categorically different, they had the same content – that is, that there is no ontological distinction. His critiques bear on the use of mental terms in the literature of psychology and social science and particularly in cognitive science and its social scientific and philosophical applications. What he challenged were the assumptions, first, that in using terms such as *emotion, idea, intention*, and the like, we must seek a distinct thing to which these terms refer; second, that speech and action have antecedent and parallel mental states and processes as accompaniments; and third, that what mental terms refer to and represent are first-person-accessible internal events.

We typically use the word *emotion* to refer to various actions, words, and bodily expressions of individuals, but we also speak, for example, of something, such as a rise in respiration rate, which may be a correlate of overt performances, as an emotional response. We might then assume that we are talking about the same thing or that the one is a cause of the other. The word *emotion*, however, is not restricted to a specific object or even to a particular kind of object, but rather belongs to a quite diverse family of language-games. It is necessary to explore the grammar of emotion and its kinship to other grammars, such as those relating to thoughts and mental images – and not to confuse these language regions. It is only what Wittgenstein referred to as our "craving for generality" (1958, p. 17) and a wish to emulate what we believe are the methods of natural science that lead us to seek a fundamental sameness underlying the application of a term such as *emotion*. When we ask, for example, what constitutes a feeling and how it relates to an emotion, we are often not talking about neural maps, but about grammatical maps of the historically and culturally diverse language of human experience and expression. Much of the difficulty, however, is that the issue is still framed within the mind/body and inner/outer paradigm, which Wittgenstein so frontally challenged.

Wittgenstein noted that "in science it is usual to make phenomena that allow of exact measurement into defining criteria for an expression; and then one is inclined to think that the proper meaning has been *found*" (1967, 438). In the case of emotion, this often results in quite arbitrarily assuming that what, in some cases, may be a physical correlate of an expression of emotion is actually the meaning of *emotion*. Furthermore, not only emotion itself but also types of emotion, such as fear, anger, etc., are very generic concepts, and it is important to resist reifying the terms and applying the paradigm of a physical state and assuming that we can explain emotions by specifying some physical event, either internal or external, as a cause. These mistakes engender the kind of picture that Wittgenstein referred to as holding us captive (2001, 118). When confronted with a "substantive" part of speech such as *mind* or *emotion*, the temptation is "to look for a thing that corresponds to it" and "to look about you for some object which you might call the 'meaning'" (1958, p. 1).

Maybe Wittgenstein's most general and important argument was his insistence on the theoretical or ontological autonomy of language, which can be extended to social or what may be called "conventional objects" in general (Gunnell 1998). His point was simply that language gains its meaning neither as a medium for representing prior thoughts, as individuals as diverse as St. Augustine, William James, and many proponents of cognitive science have pictured it, nor as a token for physical and mental objects, but rather through the rules, customs, and conventions that inform its uses in various human practices and "forms of life." This is not to say that the world, or what is accepted in natural science as a discovery about the world, does not or should not influence the use of a term such as *emotion*, but if it is decided that the term should be applied to a bodily state rather than to public actions and assertions, which are the phenomena of social investigation, we would have to find other words for the latter. For Wittgenstein, the respective autonomy of language and the world did not imply the lack of a relationship between language and the "very general facts of nature" or a denial of the assumption that if those facts were different, many of our concepts might be different too (2001, 142, p. 195). His point was that the facts with which philosophy – and we can add social science – are concerned are conceptual facts manifest in social practices. Among such facts are emotions. "What is an emotion?" is first of all a conceptual query and not an empirical question, and the latter actually presupposes the former.

The path to understanding the phenomena we associate with emotion begins with Wittgenstein's general consideration of mentalistic language. Already in the early sections of the *Investigations*, he attempted to demolish the assumption that language is primarily a medium for naming and expressing prior thoughts. He concluded that the meaning of words is, in most cases, primarily a function of their "use" in a multiplicity of sentences or propositions, which in turn belong to various, and changing, "language-games" and "forms of life." He then confronted the related assumption that terms such as *understanding* gain their meaning by reference to a "mental process" that takes place "in the brain and the nervous system" (2001, 43, 153–8). This belief in the existence of such a "queer process" is, he argued, the consequence of failing to account for how the grammar of mental concepts is employed in the context of "the common behavior of mankind," which is grounded in forms of agreement manifest in rules, customs, and conventions (196, 199, 206, 242). We do not find the meaning of a term such as *pain* by looking inside ourselves to ascertain what it refers to or by examining nerve endings. Pain talk emerges as a refinement of more primitive expressions of sensations, and while pains are private and internal in the sense that they are experienced and reported by a particular person and vouchsafed by first-person authority, and can be concealed, feigned, imagined, etc., the language of pain is separate from what any particular person is experiencing. There is no private "language which describes my inner experience and which only I myself can understand" (256). Wittgenstein's claims about the impossibility of a private language are often misconstrued or viewed as more mysterious than they actually are. The core point was simply that the idea of private language is oxymoronic – that is, language is a public phenomenon.

It was at this point in the *Investigations* that he offered his well-known hypothetical account of several people simultaneously claiming that they had a beetle in a box and describing the insect – just as people might say that they were experiencing pain (and, we could add, emotion) or behaving as people do when they are confronted with beetles (if there is any such typical behaviour). The upshot was that there could be perfectly reasonable beetle talk whether or not people had the same sort of beetle, or even actually had a beetle, in their box. There could be beetle-talk only because of the existence of a public language for talking about beetles. Since there was only the public language for speaking about beetles and pain, it was the case that "if we view the grammar of an expression of a sensation on the model of 'object and designation' the object drops out of consideration as irrelevant." This did not mean that a beetle was simply a linguistic construction or that pain was just pain talk and "pain behaviour," but only that although the grammar and expression of pain has a function, it is not to report on, or convey thoughts about, an internally observed object or event. Wittgenstein did not, as some have argued, endorse behaviourism, but rather argued that "inner" and "outer" were not spatial, but logical distinctions and represented different aspects of human beings. He did not wish to deny the existence of "mental processes," whatever that terminology might actually refer to, but he insisted that reference to "an 'inner process' stands in need of outward criteria." The image of an "inner process" equated with capacities such as remembering or understanding had no particular "experiential content" (2001, 281, 293, 308, 571, 580, p. 196). And we could say the same about emotion.

Wittgenstein posed the question of how the "philosophical problem about mental processes and states and about behaviorism arise," and he noted that "we talk of processes and states and leave their nature undecided as we attempt to learn more about them." This, however, "commits us to a particular way of looking at the matter" and to an idea of what this would entail, and at this point, "the decisive move in the conjuring trick has been made." Emotions, and mental terms in general, are not something apart from their expression. For example, as opposed to the thesis in Gladwell's *Blink* (2005), if asked to explain the phrase "sudden understanding," the "answer is not to point to a process that we give this name to." And "when I think in language, there aren't 'meanings' going through my mind in addition to the verbal expressions: the language is itself the vehicle of thought" (Wittgenstein 2001, 329). If asked what constituted a thought or an intention before its expression, one could only repeat the expression. "An intention is embedded in its situation, in human customs and institutions," and "thinking is not an incorporeal process which lends life and sense to speaking" or accompanies speech (304–8, 329, 330–9, p. 185). Whether a "machine can think" and whether animals have consciousness are not empirical issues, but conceptual ones revolving around the concept of a human being. As Wittgenstein said, "*essence* is expressed in grammar," but he stressed that apart from playing make-believe and using analogies, "we only say of a human being and what is like one that it thinks," by which he meant that language, in the broad sense of symbolic capacities, constituted what we typically mean by "thinking" and "consciousness." Wittgenstein found nothing problematic in talking about brain processes as part of experimental science, but such discussions become problematic when "misleading parallels" intrude. The assumption emerges that "psychology treats of processes in the psychical sphere, as does physics in the physical," when, in fact, "seeing, hearing, thinking, feeling, willing, are not the subject of psychology *in the same sense* as that in which the movements of bodies, the phenomena of electricity etc. are the subject of physics" (359–60, 371, 412, 571).

Wittgenstein was quite unequivocal about what can be the bearer of an emotion. He asked whether one could "imagine an animal angry, frightened, unhappy, happy, startled," and although he found no real bar to these attributions if they were framed in terms of the paradigm of behaviour, it was more difficult to conceive of a dog as "believing," "hoping," or expressing "grief" because these "are modes of this complicated form of life" that we associate with linguistic and symbolic capacities. His basic point was that professing or otherwise expressing hope was identical with what we might wish to call the mental state of hoping and that a dog could not really hope without possessing the concept of hope. Yet he suggested that "the human body is the best picture of the human mind" and that if we wished to know whether someone could understand something or play chess, we would not be looking for an "inner process," but rather for the manifestation of a certain ability and grasp of rules. "If God [or a cognitive scientist] had looked into our minds he would not have been able to see there whom we were speaking of" (2001, pp. 148, 152, 155, 185). With respect to emotion, the central point was "to remove the temptation to think that there '*must* be'" some mental process, such as that of hoping, that was independent of the process of expressing a hope (1958, p. 41).

In the years preceding his death, Wittgenstein increasingly turned to issues in psychology, and it was in this context that he most fully developed his analysis of emotion. Some of the main elements of this work found their way into what was eventually published as Part II of the *Investigations*. In the *Investigations*, he tended to use the term "feeling" (*Gefühl*) generically to include what we would typically refer to as emotions. He used the more singular term *Gemütsbewegung*, which may be the best equivalent for the English word "emotion," only twice (2001, 321, p. 163), even though he discussed what he would later refer to as the specific emotions of anger, grief, joy, fear, hope, happiness, etc. This change in strategy is significant in several respects. It reflected his increasing concern with differentiating more clearly among mental terms such as *sensations*, *feelings*, and *emotions* as well as with demonstrating that there was no essence to emotion apart from the grammar attaching to these particulars. The connection was typical of what he referred to as a "family resemblance" (67). And his treatment gave added prominence to the social context of emotion.

Much of this latter work was devoted to further demonstrating that the difference between the "inner," or mental, realm and the "outer," or physical was more a matter of grammar rather than a fundamental dualism regarding what was visible and invisible. He pointed out that "the difficulty is to know one's way about among the concepts of 'psychological phenomena'" and to realize that "thinking in terms of physiological processes is extremely dangerous in connexion with the clarification of conceptual problems in psychology." He suggested that maybe "the best prophylactic against this is the thought that I don't know at all whether the humans I am acquainted with actually have a nervous system" (1980a, 1054, 1063). The problem was that there had developed a picture of something going on inside a person that was accessible only to that person and that "psychology was now the theory of this inner thing." What was involved, however, were "two language-games" that bore a complicated relationship to each other rather than the problem of finding the physiological referents of psychological phenomena.

To question the existence of such referents was not to fall back on the assumption of "a mind *alongside* the body, a ghostly mental nature" (1980a, 289, 692), and he once again noted that "the human being is the best picture of the human mind" (281). In the case of emotion, the problems revolved around such things as mistakenly assuming, because people might say they "feel depressed," that depression is a "bodily feeling" known by introspection (135). Although if we saw an ape tearing things up, we might wonder what was going on "inside" him, it would not be much different than wondering about how much grief was in our heart (347, 439). Grief, joy, and hope are, no more than belief, not things we inwardly observe, but rather matters of what we say and how we behave (446, 450, 460). We might choose not to speak and act in a particular manner that expresses emotion, but this presupposes that we *could* speak and act in that manner. What we might consider to be instances of thinking to oneself or calculating in one's head are only logically different from writing it down (577, 583).

Wittgenstein posed the question of why we treat fear or hope as an emotion, but do not do so in the case of belief, and his basic answer was that the former is somewhat like pain in its first-person use – that is, a concept for the expression of experiences (*Erlebnisbegriffe*) – while beliefs, as well as intentions, have no particular characteristic form of expression. Emotions might reasonably be broadly spoken of as experiences, but not as something that "happens" to one or what one "undergoes," like an "impression" (1980a, 596, 836). Wittgenstein noted that "I would like to speak of a genealogical tree of psychological concepts" (722), and he undertook a quite extended "classification of psychological concepts" (1980b, 148; see also 1967, 472–525), in which he distinguished emotions – that is, *Gemütsbewegungen* – from dispositions, moods, and sensations (*Empfindungen*) such as pain – although when he said that "pain is not a *something*, but not a *nothing* either!" (2001, 304), he might as well have said the same about emotion. There is, however, a difference between pain and certain other psychological concepts, such as those relating to emotion. There is experience of both pain and emotion, but while it is possible to experience pain without having a concept of pain, many terms related to emotion are conceptually dependent.

It is important to be clear about the fact that what Wittgenstein was really doing was not categorizing and describing objects, but clarifying the grammar or application of words, even though he recognized considerable overlap in usage. What, he claimed, is common to emotions (such as joy, fear, and depression) was "duration" and often a tendency to follow a "course" involving appearing, abating, and so on. Unlike sensations, emotions "do not give us any information about the external world," and despite metaphorical phrases such as "sick at heart" and of similar "content" such as the "darkness of depression," they are neither "localized" nor "diffuse." Like sensations, however, emotions often have characteristic behavioural and facial expression, and they may be accompanied by certain sensations, but, he stressed, "sensations are not emotions. (In the sense in which the numeral 2 is not the number 2.)" Among emotions, it is important to distinguish those that are typically "directed," such as fear, from those, such as anxiety, that tend to be "undirected." In addition to emotions and sensations, he recognized "dispositions." For Wittgenstein, these various language-games were not insulated from one another, but he characterized love and hate as "emotional dispositions" and "attitudes," which could be distinguished by features such as capable of being "put to the test" and which could also, in some cases, include "chronic" as opposed to "acute" fear, but, he again pointed out, "fear is not a sensation" (1980, 148).

Wittgenstein then went on to elaborate on these remarks. He claimed, for example, that it was cogent to speak about how emotions such as sadness, hope, and fear might "*colour* thoughts," or even constitute thoughts, such as those that we might categorize as "misgivings," while this was not true of sensations, and that it would not make much sense to speak of something such as "toothachey thoughts" (1980, 153). He claimed that most emotions represent what could be called "mental states" (*Seelenzuständen*), which subjects can report much as they report pain, but unlike James, who viewed emotion as composed of sensations, Wittgenstein noted that although a sensation such as pain resembles an emotion in that it is expressed in facial expressions, gestures, noises, and the like, "it did not follow from this that our bodily feeling" is the emotion (1980, 177, 321, 499). In most cases, it is "essential to what we call emotion" that we do not simply observe physical changes such as "facial contortions" from which we "*make the inference* of grief, joy, etc., but immediately perceive a face as expressing an emotion." Just as in the case of all of what he termed "aspect-seeing," like his famous use of the "duck/rabbit" figure, "we *see* emotions" (1980b, 570) – we do not typically first see facial expressions and then infer emotions any more than, in a realistic drawing, we see marks and infer, for example, a rabbit. If people were brought up not to register emotion by either expression or report, we would have to say, "I have no idea of what is going on inside them" (568), but that would only really be a statement of an "external fact" and not a failure to penetrate some hidden space (570).

In his final writings on the philosophy of psychology, Wittgenstein focused yet further on the general dilemma of the "inner and the outer," including the concept of emotion. The thrust of his argument was, once again, in the direction of demonstrating that emotions are not subliminal phenomena, of which we see traces in what people say and do, but rather are an essential part of their conventional repertoire and that, like other aspects of human behaviour, which we sometimes locate as belonging to an "inner" dimension, they gain "meaning only in the stream of life." He noted that, in many instances, what is involved in saying that the "'inner is hidden' would be as if one said: 'All that you *see* in a multiplication is the outer movement of the figures; the multiplication is hidden from us,'" or, as in the case of people speaking to themselves, the "words only have meaning as elements of a language-game." In most cases, "there is an *unmistakable* expression of joy and its opposite," and when an emotion is hidden, "it is not hidden because it is inner," but because it is not expressed. What "inner" and "hidden" really mean is that, as of feelings in general, there is asymmetry between the first-person experience and third-person knowledge of a person's feelings and the "logic" of the respective claims (1992, pp. 28, 30, 32, 33, 35, 36, 62, 63). Emotions are part of "the whole swirl [*Gewimmel*] of human actions," along with concepts, judgments, and the like. We are sometimes uncertain about these things, but "we don't need the concept 'mental' (etc.) to justify some of our conclusions that are undetermined, etc. Rather this indeterminacy, etc., explains the use of the word 'mental'" as well as how uncertainty about the "outer" corresponds to uncertainty about the "inner." It was simply the comparison of the language-games dealing respectively with mental and behavioural concepts and the uncertainty involved in attempting to know other "minds" that led to the false picture of an inner and outer dualism. He once again insisted that "I presuppose the *inner* in so far as I presuppose a *human being*," and that is the person who smiles, not a body or an inner face. In the end, he concluded that what we often refer to as "the 'inner' is a delusion. That is, the whole complex of ideas alluded to by the word is like a painted curtain drawn in front of the scene of the actual word use" of terms such as *emotion* (66, 69, 78, 79, 84).

If emotions are conceived in the manner suggested by Wittgenstein, it is necessary to confront the issue of how we cognitively access these phenomena. If they are not like the objects of natural science, but rather conventional or discursive phenomena, they are objects of interpretation. The recognition of the importance of emotion and the rise of cognitive science has once more pulled social theory back in the direction of amalgamating the social and natural sciences, but Wittgenstein's work provides the basis of a more unified and autonomous vision of social enquiry – that is, one that views social enquiry as interpretive and addressed to phenomena that are irreducible. When we confront the case of what might be termed meta-practical enquiry (Gunnell 1998) – that is, practices devoted to the study of other human practices, in fields such as philosophy and the social sciences – we are confronting the problem of conceptualizing concepts and conveying their meaning. This forces us to deal with the concept of interpretation and how closely his analysis of emotion is tied up with the idea of an interpretive social science.

Understanding and Interpreting Emotions

Wittgenstein did not, of course, speak directly about social science, but his work after the *Tractatus* moved increasingly in the direction of conceiving philosophy itself as a form of social enquiry (Gunnell 2014). More than a half-century ago, Peter Winch (1958) presented an "idea" of a social science inspired by Wittgenstein's work. Although Winch's argument is usually, and correctly, understood as a paradigm case of the rejection of a positivist image of social science and its view of the unity of scientific method, what was more fundamental, but less noted, were his claims about the logical symmetry between social science and philosophy. Wittgenstein often likened his philosophical method to anthropology, and his concern with achieving an account of the "language-games" constituting various "forms of life" suggests grounds for addressing the ongoing controversy in the social sciences about whether to employ interpretive or scientific methods. It is important, however, to recognize that the social sciences are by their very nature interpretive enterprises – whatever the methods to which they subscribe.

Although the words *interpretation* and *understanding* are often used to refer to the same concept, there is an important distinction that is sometimes elided, and it is of particular importance in thinking about emotions. A great deal of social interaction involves *understanding* emotion, conveyed both in action and in language, and although in particular cases, this sometimes requires individuals to step back and *interpret* one another, most of the time, as in the case of linguistic communication, we simply understand one another. Some philosophers, ranging from W.V.O. Quine to, from a quite different philosophical perspective, Jacques Derrida, tend to explicitly equate understanding with interpreting and suggest that the latter "goes all the way down." There are, however, reasons, such as those Wittgenstein adduced, for challenging such an equation, and in doing so, to point to the fundamental difference between engaging in a human practice and giving an account of that practice.

Already in *The Big Typescript* (2005), where much of his final work was adumbrated, Wittgenstein had noted that "an interpretation is a supplementation of the interpreted sign with another sign" and, for example, "in receiving an order we do not normally interpret it," but hear or grasp it (2005, 16). In the *Investigations*, he spent a great deal of time sorting out more fully the difference between the grammars of "understanding" (*Verstehen*) and "interpretation" (*Deutung*) (Gunnell 2011, ch. 6). "Understanding," he claimed, involves the capacity to act in a language and the "mastery of a technique" (Wittgenstein 2001, 150), while an "interpretation still hangs in the air along with what it interprets, and cannot give it any support" because interpretations are not, in the first instance, the source of meaning (198). It would be natural to ask whether understanding is a prerequisite for interpreting, and for individuals such as Winch and Kuhn, the task of the historian or social scientist is one of, first, understanding another discursive realm and then, second, interpreting or representing it and conveying it, even though there may be limits to accessing the realm of understanding that constitutes a particular object of interpretation.

Wittgenstein often distinguished between his aims and those of natural science, and the underlying distinction revolved around the fact that although we might think of natural science as *representing* nature, it is really *presenting* nature. After the theories of natural science have presented a picture of the world, there is no way to check whether the picture is correct, and the only way to challenge it is to propound or embrace incommensurable alternative theories or an alternate vision of the world, such as that of religion. According to Wittgenstein, it is philosophy that is, strictly speaking, in the business of interpreting and representing. What an interpretation aims to produce is a "perspicuous representation" (a synopsis) (2001, 122) that achieves clarity about a prior and autonomous conceptual realm. This is the very aim of philosophy – and, it follows, of meta-practices as a whole, including social science. Wittgenstein had said at one point that "savages have games ... for which there are no written rules. Now let's imagine the activity of an explorer traveling throughout the countries of these peoples and setting up lists of rules for their games. This is completely analogous to what the philosopher does" (2005, 313). He pointedly denied that "philosophy is ethnology," but he claimed that it is essential to "look at things from an ethnological point of view," which "means that we are taking up a position outside, an interpretive position, so as to be able to see things *more objectively*" (37).

One of Wittgenstein's most controversial and disparately interpreted remarks was that "philosophy may in no way interfere with the actual use of language; it can in the end only describe it. For it cannot give it [such as the practice of mathematics] any foundation either. It leaves everything as it is." A philosophical claim does not, as such, change its object of enquiry, but "simply puts everything before us" (2001, 124–6). His point was that the practical relationship between an interpretation and its object is contingent. Unlike conceptual or theoretical moves *within* a practice, such as natural science, philosophical investigations, which are "grammatical" and "conceptual investigations" of other linguistic domains, do not necessarily have such effect. Whether they might or should was an open question about which Wittgenstein was somewhat ambivalent (2001, 90; 1967, 458).

The essential business of meta-practical investigation is representational in that its object of enquiry is not internally generated, but stands apart, just as much as the landscape is different from what is represented by the landscape painter. Wittgenstein used the term "explanation" (*Erklärung*) in a variety of familiar ways – often with respect to explaining the meaning or uses of a word (e.g., 2001, 71, 87, 533), but he stressed that such philosophical or grammatical explanation was a matter of "describing" the use of signs rather than explaining in the sense of positing something deeper or establishing through "experiment" a "causal connection" (126, 169, 496). Although he consistently rejected the idea that he was doing anything like natural science, he suggested that he was conducting something like a "natural history of human beings" in the sense of describing the variety of conventional performances. He insisted, however, that there was often a need to "invent fictitious natural history for our purposes" – that is, for the purposes of interpretation.

What Wittgenstein was driving at when he claimed that he was not "doing natural science," and maintaining that his "considerations could not be scientific ones" or concerned with "empirical problems" and with "*explanation*" in the sense of advancing a "theory," was that natural history, as opposed to natural science, is more observational and taxonomic than experimental. To the extent that it is explanatory, it is in the sense that it involves "description" and is interpretive, holistic, non-reductive, and ecological. It does not treat its immediate subject matter as epiphenomenal and seek an ideal that transcends particularity. He often spoke of what he did as "explaining" meaning, and since he seldom used the word *theory*, not much should be made of his putative rejection of theorizing. When he did talk about theory, it was, as already noted, usually with respect to theories in natural science or with respect to general philosophical theories such as realism and idealism, which were at the very core of his rebellion in the field of philosophy (2001, 25, 81, 89, 109, 392, 415, p. 195).

If we want to understand such a method, the best place to start is in terms of Wittgenstein's account of a perspicuous representation *(übersichtliche Darstellung*), which was his "method" of interpretation (2001, 50). He suggested that what was required in giving an account of a *Lebensform* and *Weltbild* was something like "sketches of a landscape," something that "produces just that understanding which consists in 'seeing connections.'" The kind of representation that he sought would be accomplished by "inventing *intermediate cases*" that determined "the way we look at things." The subject matter consisted of "language-games" embedded in various social practices and forms of life, but he recommended, and saw the necessity of creating, second-order language-games that would be "set up as *objects of comparison*" and that were "meant to throw light on the facts ... by way not only of similarities, but also dissimilarities." Here one might generalize in the sense of seeking "family resemblances," but not succumb to the search for generalization that characterized so much of philosophy and modern thought in general. Such a model would, again, be "a measuring rod" and "not as a preconceived idea to which reality *must* correspond" (67, 122, 130, 131). Such typifications were central to the activity of interpretation. Interpretation involved seeing something, but in addition, seeing it in a certain way, and thus the necessity to first "*see*" something and then "*interpret* it" (p. 193).

What we should take away from his discussion of interpretation with respect to the subject of emotion is, first, that there is considerable historical and cultural variability in the repertoire and expression of emotion and, second, that in the social and human sciences, the study of emotion is primarily a matter of understanding and interpreting a dimension of the conventional objects that constitute social phenomena.

Conclusion

Part of what is involved in the problems attaching to the contemporary practice of the social sciences is that these disciplines, as they took institutional and academic form in the nineteenth century, were largely the legacy of moral philosophy and social reform movements. The scientific quest that attended these fields, from their origins, was rooted less in some abstract concern with explanation than in establishing an authoritative cognitive identity that would underwrite their claims to a capacity for critical evaluation and judgment in matters relating to social policy. Although this legacy has receded from view, the ideological context of social science and its normative concerns are still reflected in the turn to neuroscience, as well as in some of the literature of neuroscience itself, and it is important to understand the manner in which these issues have shaped discussions of issues such as the nature of emotion. The social sciences have continually searched outside themselves for both a vision of science and an account of their subject matter. As long as social science denies the theoretical autonomy of its subject matter and fails to come concretely to grips with its cognitive and practical relationship to that subject matter and with the issues attaching to what is necessarily involved in interpretation as a mode of enquiry, it will find itself continually in the position of chasing after whatever appears to offer an authoritative foundation of enquiry.

NOTES

1 Cf. Kiran Banerjee and Jeffrey Bercuson, chap. 10.
2 Cf. Georg Northoff, chap. 5.
3 Cf. Ryan Balot, chap. 1.
4 References to Wittgenstein refer to numbered remarks unless otherwise indicated.

REFERENCES

Averill, James. 1996. "An Analysis of Psychophysiological Symbolism and Its Influence on Theories of Emotion." In *The Emotions: Social, Cultural, and*

Biological Dimensions, edited by Rom Harré and W. Gerrod Parrott, 204–28. Thousand Oaks, CA: Sage Publications.

Bennett, Max R., and Peter M.S. Hacker. 2003. *Philosophical Foundations of Neuroscience*. Oxford: Blackwell.

Blackburn, Simon. 1998. *Ruling Passions: A Theory of Practical Reasoning*. Oxford: Oxford University Press.

Churchland, Paul. 1995. *The Engine of Reason, the Seat of the Soul: A Philosophical Journey into the Brain*. Cambridge, MA: MIT Press.

Clarke, Simon, Paul Hoggett, and Simon Thompson, eds. 2006. *Emotion, Politics, and Society*. New York: Palgrave Macmillan. http://dx.doi.org/10.1057/9780230627895.

Coulter, Jeff, and Wes Sharrock. 2007. *Brain, Mind, and Human Behavior: Critical Assessments of the Philosophy of Psychology*. Lewiston, NY: Edwin Mellen Press.

Damasio, Antonio. 1994. *Descartes' Error: Emotion, Reason, and the Human Brain*. New York: Putnam and Sons.

Damasio, Antonio. 1999. *The Feeling of What Happens: Body and Emotion in the Making of Consciousness*. New York: Harcourt Brace.

Dennett, Daniel. 2005. *Sweet Dreams*. Cambridge, MA: MIT Press.

De Sousa, Ronald. 1987. *The Rationality of Emotion*. Cambridge, MA: MIT Press.

Elster, Jon. 1999. *Alchemies of the Mind: Rationality and the Emotions*. Cambridge: Cambridge University Press.

Elster, Jon. 2000. *Strong Feelings: Emotions, Addiction, and Human Behavior*. Cambridge, MA: MIT Press.

Gladwell, Malcolm. 2005. *Blink*. Boston, MA: Little-Brown.

Goldie, Peter. 2000. *The Emotions: A Philosophical Exploration*. Oxford: Oxford University Press.

Goleman, Daniel. 1995. *Emotional Intelligence*. New York: Bantam.

Goodwin, Jeff, James M. Jasper, and Francesca Polletta. 2001. *Passionate Politics: Emotion and Social Movements*. Chicago: University of Chicago Press. http://dx.doi.org/10.7208/chicago/9780226304007.001.0001.

Griffiths, Paul E. 1997. *What Emotions Really Are*. Chicago: University of Chicago Press. http://dx.doi.org/10.7208/chicago/9780226308760.001.0001.

Gunnell, John G. 1998. *The Orders of Discourse: Philosophy, Social Science, and Politics*. Lanham, MD: Rowman and Littlefield.

Gunnell, John. G. 2007. "Are We Losing Our Minds? Cognitive Science and the Study of Politics." *Political Theory* 35 (6): 704–31.

Gunnell, John G. 2011. *Political Theory and Social Science: Cutting against the Grain*. New York: Palgrave Macmillan. http://dx.doi.org/10.1057/9780230117587.

Gunnell, John G. 2012. "Unpacking Emotional Baggage in Political Theory." In *Essays in Neuroscience and Political Theory*, edited by Frank Vander Valk, 91–116. New York: Routledge.

Gunnell, John G. 2014. *Social Inquiry after Wittgenstein and Kuhn: Leaving Everything as It Is*. New York: Columbia University Press. http://dx.doi.org/10.7312/columbia/9780231169400.001.0001.

Gustafsson, Ylva, Camilla Kronquist, and Michael McEachrane, eds. 2009. *Emotions and Understanding: Wittgensteinian Perspectives*. New York: Palgrave Macmillan.

Hacker, Peter M.S. 2009. "The Conceptual Framework for the Investigation of Emotion." In *Emotions and Understanding: Wittgensteinian Perspectives,* edited by Ylva Gustafsson, Camilla Kronquist, and Michael McEachrane, 43–59. New York: Palgrave Macmillan

Harré, Rom, ed. 1986. *The Social Construction of Emotion*. New York: Oxford University Press.

Harré, Rom, and G. Gillett. 1994. *The Discursive Mind*. Thousand Oaks, CA: Sage Publications.

Harré, Rom, and W. Gerrod Parrott, eds. 1996. *The Emotions: Social, Cultural, and Biological Dimensions*. Thousand Oaks, CA: Sage Publications.

Harré, Rom, and M. Tissaw. 2005. *Wittgenstein and Psychology*. Aldershot, UK: Ashgate.

Kaku, Michio. 2014. *The Future of the Mind: The Scientific Quest to Understand, Enhance, and Empower the Mind*. New York: Doubleday.

Kingston, Rebecca, and Leonard Ferry. 2008. *Bringing the Passions Back In: The Emotions in Political Philosophy.* Vancouver: UBC Press.

Koziak, Barbara. 2000. *Retrieving Political Emotion: Thumos, Aristotle, and Gender*. College Park: Pennsylvania State University Press.

LeDoux, Joseph. 1996. *The Emotional Brain: the Mysterious Underpinnings of Emotional Life*. New York: Simon and Schuster.

Nussbaum, Martha. 2001. *Upheavals of Thought*. Cambridge: Cambridge University Press. http://dx.doi.org/10.1017/CBO9780511840715.

Nussbaum, Martha. 2004. "Emotions as Judgments of Value and Importance." In *Thinking about Feeling: Contemporary Philosophers on Emotion*, edited by Robert C. Solomon, 183–99. Oxford: Oxford University Press

Prinz, Jesse. 2003. *Gut Reactions: A Perceptual Theory of Emotion*. Oxford: Oxford University Press.

Racine, Timothy P., and Ulrich Müller, eds. 2009. "Mind, Meaning, and Language: Wittgenstein's Relevance for Psychology." *New Ideas in Psychology* 27 (2): 107–304.

Reddy, William M. 2001. *The Navigation of Feeling: A Framework for the History of Emotions*. Cambridge: Cambridge University Press. http://dx.doi.org/10.1017/CBO9780511512001.

Reddy, William M. 2008. "Emotional Styles and Modern Forms of Life." In *Sexualized Brains: Scientific Modeling of Emotional Intelligence from a Cultural Perspective*, edited by Nicole Karafyllis and Gotlind Ulshöfer, 81–100. Cambridge, MA: MIT Press.

Reddy, William M. 2009. "Saying Something New: Practice Theory and Cognitive Neuroscience." *Arcadia* 44 (1): 8–23. http://dx.doi.org/10.1515/ARCA.2009.002.

Schulte, Joachim. 2009. "Wittgenstein on Emotion." In *Emotions and Understanding: Wittgensteinian Perspectives*, edited by Ylva Gustafsson, Camilla Kronqvist, and Michael McEachrane, 27–42. New York: Palgrave Macmillan.

Searle, John. 1992. *The Rediscovery of the Mind*. Cambridge, MA: MIT Press.

Sokolon, Marlene K. 2006. *Political Emotions: Aristotle and Symphony of Reason and Emotion*. DeKalb: Northern Illinois Press.

Solomon, Robert C., ed. 2002. *What Is an Emotion?* Oxford: Oxford University Press.

Solomon, Robert C. 2004. "Emotions, Thoughts, and Feelings: Emotions as Engagements with the World." In *Thinking about Feeling: Contemporary Philosophers on Emotion*, edited by Robert C. Solomon, 1–18. Oxford: Oxford University Press.

Solomon, Robert C. 2007. *True to Our Feelings: What Our Emotions Are Really Telling Us*. Oxford: Oxford University Press.

Taylor, Charles. 1985. *Human Agency and Language*. Cambridge: Cambridge University Press. http://dx.doi.org/10.1017/CBO9781139173483.

Turner, Mark. 2001. *Cognitive Dimensions of Social Science: The Way We Think About Politics, Economics, Law, and Society*. New York: Oxford University Press.

Turner, Stephen. 2002. *Brains/Practices/Relativism: Social Theory after Cognitive Science*. Chicago: University of Chicago Press.

Winch, Peter. 1958. *The Idea of a Social Science and Its Relation to Philosophy*. London: Routledge and Kegan-Paul.

Wittgenstein, Ludwig. 1958. *The Blue and Brown Books*. New York: Harper.

Wittgenstein, Ludwig. 1967. *Zettel*. Berkeley: University of California Press.

Wittgenstein, Ludwig. 1969. *On Certainty*. New York: Harper and Row.

Wittgenstein, Ludwig. 1980a. *Remarks on the Philosophy of Psychology*. Vol. 1. Oxford: Blackwell.

Wittgenstein, Ludwig. 1980b. *Remarks on the Philosophy of Psychology*. Vol. 2. Oxford: Blackwell.

Wittgenstein, Ludwig. 1992. *The Inner and the Outer*. Vol. 2, *Last Writings on the Philosophy of Psychology*. Oxford: Blackwell.

Wittgenstein, Ludwig. 2001. *Philosophical Investigations*. Oxford: Blackwell.

Wittgenstein, Ludwig. 2005. *The Big Typescript*. Oxford: Blackwell. http://dx.doi.org/10.1002/9780470752906.

PART II

Naturalistic Approaches

4 Current Emotion Research in Philosophy

PAUL E. GRIFFITHS

Much philosophical work on the emotions is pursued by adherents of philosophical naturalism, the view that philosophy deals in knowledge of the natural world no different in principle from that revealed by the sciences. These philosophers look to the sciences of the mind to illuminate philosophical questions about emotion. In many areas of philosophy, naturalism is uncontroversial. The philosophy of physics proceeds by the analysis of historical and contemporary physics. The same can be said of the philosophy of biology or the philosophy of economics. But it cannot be said of the philosophy of mind. Many philosophers still believe that important truths about the mind can be discovered using distinctively philosophical methods and working independently of the sciences of the mind. Some also believe that these truths are different in kind from those revealed by the sciences.

Two recent books on disgust exemplify these two approaches to the philosophy of emotion. Colin McGinn's *The Meaning of Disgust* (2011) sets out to identify the essence of disgust – that which all disgusting things have in common – by reflecting on the author's ideas about what is disgusting. McGinn concludes that disgust is produced by objects that mix death and life. This "death-in-life" theory is to be preferred to rival theories because it alone allows disgust to be defined with necessary and sufficient conditions. McGinn also offers an evolutionary explanation of disgust. It is a uniquely human emotion and developed because the insatiability of human desire required a special emotion to control our limitless appetites. McGinn imagines an evolutionary past in which, for example, humans lacking disgust engaged in necrophilia as an expression of their limitless sexual desire. Reviews of McGinn's book have found it puzzling that he does not consider the most widely discussed theory of disgust in contemporary psychology, according to which disgust evolved as a response to potential sources of infection, and that he largely ignores the scientific literature on disgust and its evolution.

The second book, Daniel Kelly's *Yuck! The Nature and Moral Significance of Disgust* (2011), could not be more different in this respect, being based on a thorough survey of that literature. Kelly argues that disgust combines a taste-aversion mechanism with a mechanism for avoiding infection and parasitism. Kelly sees disgust as a uniquely human emotion, but his account of its uniqueness and its evolutionary origin is very different from McGinn's. Disgust is a typical example of the co-option and developmental entanglement that occurs as an evolving lineage confronts new adaptive challenges and must solve them by modifying existing features. Both elements of the disgust response have homologues or analogues in other species – it is their entanglement that creates a uniquely human emotion. Moral disgust represents a further piece of evolutionary tinkering, in which the emotion of disgust was co-opted to help enforce conformity with in-group norms.

Philosophers who work in these two modes can be very critical of one another. Kelly concludes his review of McGinn, whose theory he describes as "coherent, if incredible," with the observation,

> Despite rather quaint use of the word "data" to describe the examples of what he deems to be disgusting ... nowhere does he consult current empirical literature for evidence about disgust, cross-cultural or otherwise. The resulting book is as disappointing as it is irresponsible. (Kelly 2012, n.p.)

McGinn has not, to my knowledge, reviewed Kelly's book, but naturalistic work on the emotions is regarded by its critics as unduly reductive, as a manifestation of scientific imperialism, and as unable or unwilling to address the real questions about emotion.

Among the questions that naturalistic approaches are supposedly unable to address, the role of the emotions in moral psychology is perhaps the most prominent. This critique is at the heart of Robert C. Roberts's *Emotions: An Essay in Aid of Moral Psychology* (2003). Roberts rejects the conventional view of conceptual analysis as the study of our own concepts (Jackson 1998). Instead, "conceptual analysis of the emotions [is] the investigation of them from the point of view of a human participant" (Roberts 2003, 37). Its focus on rich human experience is similar to "literary and psychoanalytic examinations of emotion and a rather strong contrast with biological and neuroscientific examinations" (5). Roberts opens his book with an example of literary insight into moral character – namely, Anthony Trollope's 1876 description of his character Ferdinand Lopez, a London share trader. Roberts contrasts the answer to the question, what is an emotion? implicit in this passage with answers from the sciences and suggests that the former is more suited to moral psychology (19). To be frank, I found little moral insight in this bit of Trollope and a good deal of stereotyped Victorian anti-Semitism. I have no desire to decry the value of humanistic approaches to the emotions, but the special value of those approaches for moral psychology needs to be defended, not merely asserted. This is particularly true in light of the recent flowering of naturalistic moral psychology, which looks to the sciences of the mind in exactly the same way as the naturalistic philosophy of emotion (Prinz 2007; Sinnott-Armstrong 2008).

About twenty years ago, there was an upsurge of naturalistic work in the philosophy of emotion. My own *What Emotions Really Are: The Problem of Psychological Categories* (Griffiths 1997) pursued an ethological and evolutionary approach to the emotions. Its central thesis was that the psychological processes encompassed by the vernacular category of *emotion* are too diverse to make emotion per se a useful category for scientific investigation. Like memory, emotion is a collection of different psychological processes. Unsurprisingly, my book devoted a good deal of attention to the work of Paul Ekman and his collaborators. Ekman's "basic emotions" were treated as an example of the value of carving out a subset of the vernacular category of emotion and analysing them on their own terms. The basic emotions were also used as a case study of psychobiological classification. The book argued that the basic emotions are homologues – categories defined by shared evolutionary origins. The basic emotion of fear, for example, exists in many mammalian species, and it is the same thing in each, just as the femur or the hypothalamus is the same thing – it has a shared evolutionary origin in the common ancestor of those species. This approach to categorization is very different from classification by shared function, which would place in the category of fear any psychological mechanism designed to detect and respond to danger. Biologists call such categories *analogies*. Homology and analogy are both useful, and indeed complementary, principles of classification, but it is essential to distinguish them and to use each appropriately.

Craig DeLancey's *Passionate Engines: What Emotions Reveal about Mind and Artificial Intelligence* (2001) also focused on the basic emotions and on Ekman's claim that each of these corresponds to an "affect program," a coordinated array of physiological and behavioural reactions. DeLancey used affect program theory to offer a new approach to the intentionality of emotion. This has been a central topic in the philosophy of emotion since the 1960s, when Anthony Kenny was the most prominent of several philosophers to argue that emotions are subject to normative standards of "fit" to the world – they can be appropriate or inappropriate, reasonable or unreasonable. This suggests that emotions have intentional objects – it is inappropriate and unreasonable to fear things that are not dangerous because fear represents the world as dangerous (Kenny 1963). This, in turn, was widely held to refute theories that identified an emotion with a sensation or a physiological state per se (ibid.). Robert Solomon's influential *The Passions* (Solomon 1976), which argued that emotions are constituted by judgments about the significance for the subject of the situation confronting them, was the mature expression of a consensus that had developed in philosophy in the intervening years.

However, the view that emotions are judgments creates a dilemma. Commonly accepted statements of the content of emotional judgments involve sophisticated social and normative concepts. For example, anger is the judgment that the agent has suffered "a demeaning offense against me and mine" (Lazarus 1991, 222; endorsed by Nussbaum 2001; Prinz 2004b). The intentionality of emotions is thus placed in tension with the plausible claim that adult human anger has something deeply in common with anger in frustrated infants or the anger of a dominant monkey towards a subordinate. Either these agents possess the concepts of *demeaning* and *self*, or they are not angry in the true sense of the word. This problem is made worse by evidence that emotions in adult humans can be produced by low-level processes that seem equally implausible locales for such concepts.

DeLancey responds to this dilemma by arguing for the "heterogenous intentionality" of basic emotions (DeLancey 2001, 89–98). Basic emotions can be intentionally directed at a state of affairs, so that their content is a proposition. For example, I may be afraid *that this dingo will bite me*. But the very same emotion may be intentionally directed at what DeLancey calls a "concretum," meaning an object as such, rather than as an element in a proposition. For example, I may be afraid of this dingo. This is where affect program theory comes in. Because emotions are intrinsically action directing, an emotion whose content is a concretum can nevertheless explain action. I flee the dingo because I am afraid of it. To flee, I do not need a proposition about the dingo, such as that it is dangerous or that it will bite me, combined with a desire to avoid danger or to not be bitten. I just need to be afraid and for the target of my fear to be the dingo. What we have in common with other animals, DeLancey argues, is the ability to have emotions that are intentionally directed at a concretum. What distinguishes us is the ability to have emotions intentionally directed at propositions. This ability introduces a far greater flexibility into our emotional responses. An instance of this flexibility, which I think DeLancey could emphasize more strongly, is that the ability to have proposition-directed emotions allows emotions to occur as the result of a chain of reasoning, with the relevant proposition as its conclusion.

A third, influential naturalistic treatment of emotions was Jesse Prinz's *Gut Reactions: A Perceptual Theory of Emotion* (2004b). Prinz's theory builds on the "somatic marker hypothesis" (Damasio 1994), which is itself a development of the late-nineteenth-century James-Lange theory that emotions are perceptions of the body's automatic reactions to stimuli. In this vein, Prinz argues that emotions are perceptions of aroused states of the body, or gut reactions. Prinz gives a distinctive account of the intentionality of these gut reactions. Although emotions are not propositional representations, their content is correctly represented by the propositional descriptions with which we are familiar. The content of anger is that a demeaning offence to me or mine has been committed. To assign such complex intentional contents to gut reactions, Prinz embraces a form of teleosemantics. This is the view that the content of a representation is the state of affairs that is the function of that representation to detect. The actual "vehicle" of representation can be very simple as long as that vehicle was designed to fulfil the right function. In an earlier book, Prinz argued that all mental representations are perceptual images and that these images can be used to represent the whole range of topics about which we are capable of having thoughts (Prinz 2002). Applied to the emotions, this implies that they are perceptual images of the subject's body, which are used to represent the significance for the subject of the situation confronting them. Although anger itself is a perception of the body, its function is to detect demeaning offences. What Prinz calls the *nominal content* of anger is an aroused body, but its *real content* is the proposition that a demeaning offence has been committed against me or mine.

At the heart of Prinz's theory is a small range of basic emotions, but he builds on these to explain the whole range of human emotions. More complex emotions are simply basic emotions triggered by acquired sets of associations. Prinz calls these sets of associations "calibration files." He argues that these files are not part of the emotion itself, properly understood, but merely its causes. The emotion in itself is only the representation of the bodily state, and hence all emotions are fundamentally gut reactions.

The methodological disagreement that I have described does not align neatly with positions on other issues. In the remainder of this article, I will canvass three questions that have featured in the philosophical literature of the last decade. Naturalists and their critics will be found on both sides.

According to Prinz, "All emotions are constituted by embodied appraisals alone. ... Emotions are a natural kind in a strong sense. They share a common essence. It is rare for nature (and folk psychology) to offer such a neat category" (Prinz 2004b, 102). However, having a neat definition, or even an essence, is not enough to make a category a natural kind. On the view of natural kinds that both Prinz and I accept, "natural kinds" are categories that admit reliable extrapolation from samples of the category to the whole category or, in other words, categories that are productive objects for scientific investigation. Aristotle thought that objects outside the orbit of the moon formed such a category. He was wrong, despite the neat definition of superlunary objects. I have continued to argue that the overall category of emotion is not a natural kind (Griffiths 2004a, 2004b). It is instructive to compare emotion to memory. In light of distinctions like that between working memory and long-term memory, or episodic and procedural memory, a neat definition of memory would not show that these processes are essentially the same. All it would do is neatly capture the similarities of function that explain why these processes are referred to by the same vernacular term. A definition of memory might be based on shared process or mechanism, but then it would probably not include all and only the things covered by the vernacular term.

The two main arguments for the view that emotion is a natural kind are what I will call the "entanglement argument" and the "argument from affective neuroscience." The substantive argument that backs up Prinz's assertion quoted above is an example of the argument from affective neuroscience. According to Prinz, affective neuroscience shows that at the core of every emotion is a perception of a bodily registration of the significance of a stimulus. The difference among more or less cognitively sophisticated emotional responses is only in the way they are caused, not in the emotion itself. Louis Charland's version of the argument from affective neuroscience does not depend on a specific theory of emotion. Charland argues that neuroscience has identified a set of core processes that map reasonably well onto the vernacular category of emotion. These mechanisms capture what is common to a wide range of organisms and that leads us to recognize them as having an emotional life (Charland 2001, 2002). It can be seen that Prinz, Charland, and I are asking the same fundamental question: what big-picture lessons about the nature of emotion can be derived from the current state of the sciences of the mind?

An important variant of the argument from affective neuroscience has been proposed by philosopher and cognitive scientist Jason A. Clark, who has argued that basic emotions and more cognitively sophisticated forms of the same emotion may be homologous to one another (Clark 2010a, 2010b). The idea that emotions are homologous across species (taxic homology) is a familiar one. The facial expression of anger and the brain regions that produce anger have homologues in other primates, so why should anger itself not have psychological homologues? Clark's innovation is to propose that simple and complex emotions in the same species may be homologous. The same evolved developmental patterns are used twice, just as the developmental patterns that produce skeletal elements are used twice in our arms and legs (serial homology). Clark proposes that both a form of shame similar to that in other primates and a more cognitively sophisticated form unique to humans are found in humans. We have two different kinds of shame in the same way that bats have two different kinds of phalanges: those in their feet, which are similar to those in other mammals, and those in their hands, which are dramatically specialized for their unique lifestyle. Despite their dramatic differences, these bones are fundamentally the same anatomical part – phalanges. Clark proposes that radically different forms of shame (and pride) may nonetheless be fundamentally the same emotion.

The entanglement argument is somewhat different from the argument from affective neuroscience, although the work of the neuroscientist Antonio Damasio is often cited to back it up. It proposes that the different processes involved in emotion are so bound up in natural episodes of human emotion that they cannot or should not be separated. The argument is presented at length by Roberts in "the most comprehensive defence to date of the coherence of the category 'emotion'" (Döring 2007, 372). His target is my (Griffiths 1997) presentation of the view that experimental disassociations between cognition and emotion reveal the existence of separable, low-level processes that are capable of triggering an affect program response (Öhman 1999; Zajonc 1980, 2000). These phenomena are often discussed in psychology under the heading of "multilevel appraisal" (Scherer 1999; Teasdale 1999). I used such work to argue that there are two or three fundamentally different processes going on in *emotion* that, while they can occur together, can also occur independently of one another and that the way forward for the study of emotion is to distinguish these processes, rather than studying emotion as a whole.

In reply, Roberts describes intuitively plausible cases in which higher cognitive processes cause affect program responses. Such cases are so devastating that I was "shy to acknowledge" them, and my book "seems to try to prevent the reader from looking at the obvious evidence" (Roberts 2003, 26–7). Roberts is unimpressed by my own discussion of cognition-emotion relations. I discussed Ekman's well-known work on display rules, the use of cognitive management strategies to modulate emotional response, and various ways in which affect programs can be triggered by higher cognitive processes. My discussion, however, was "evasive and reducing" (25) because the word *triggering* glosses over cases where "the object of an affect program emotion is wholly and fundamentally presented by higher cognition and could be presented in no other way" (26).

But this idea is ambiguous. On one interpretation, it could mean that there are some emotion episodes in which an affect program response is triggered by a high-level appraisal process that makes use of concepts that could not plausibly be attributed to lower-level processes (or to simpler organisms). On this first interpretation, the idea is uncontroversial and is entirely consistent with the claim that, on other occasions, the same affect program is produced by low-level appraisal. Alternatively, Roberts might mean that these sophisticated concepts are present in the affect program itself, so that it could not occur without them, and no simpler organism without such concepts could have the same emotional response. This second, stronger interpretation is supported by the fact that Roberts also takes his cases to refute the idea that affect programs are informationally encapsulated (Roberts 2003, 28). But so far as I can see, Roberts has not argued for this stronger interpretation or against the experimental evidence that the same affect program response can be triggered by different levels of appraisal.

Supporters of the entanglement thesis often cite the work of Damasio as evidence that no distinction can be drawn between higher- and lower-level emotional processes. The eminent philosopher Simon Blackburn writes,

> Empirically, the suggestion that we split the operation of the affect program from "higher cognitive emotion" seems to ignore the most fascinating result of Damasio's work, which is the extent to which "higher-order" decision making has to harness the limbic system in order to work at all. (Blackburn 1998, 129)

But empirically the operation of higher- and lower-level processes in emotion *can* be split, in phobias and in the experiments reported in the literature on multi-level appraisal (Öhman 1999, 2002; Teasdale 1999) and "affective primacy" (Zajonc 1980, 2000). The interaction of affect and cognition is a flourishing field of research (e.g., Forgas 2001), but this does not mean that the two are so entangled that they should be treated as one.

There is a fundamental difference between the use of Damasio's work as part of the argument from affective neuroscience and its use in the entanglement argument. The former seeks to identify a core of basic processes that play a role in all emotions. If that idea is correct, it is in real tension with the claims of my 1997 book. The entanglement argument, however, seeks to show that lower- and higher-level emotional processing cannot be separated. Roberts thinks this is adequately demonstrated by Damasio's work and that my failure to see this is "another example of [Griffiths's] evasiveness."

> Damasio's basic thesis that organs like the amygdala can be triggered by higher cognitive processes is almost certainly correct and devastating for the basis thesis of Griffiths's book. One would expect Griffiths to aim all his firepower at that thesis, but instead he presents arguments against the weaker parts of Damasio's picture, arguments that create a bit of smoke to keep the reader from seeing that Griffiths did not clearly answer the crucial argument against his view that the affect programs and the higher-cognitive emotions are two completely discrete classes of things. (Roberts 2003, 27–8)

Roberts apparently believes that the issue is whether emotional episodes come in two discrete and non-overlapping kinds – those that involve higher cognition and those that do not. His version of the entanglement argument is like denouncing the distinction between working memory and long-term memory because items in working memory sometimes pass into long-term memory.

As we have just seen, philosophers who do not adopt a naturalistic approach to the philosophy of emotion are nevertheless enthusiastic about the work of Damasio. Martha Nussbaum is another eminent figure who praises his "nonreductionistic" approach to neuroscience (Nussbaum 2001, 115). Opinion among naturalistic philosophers is more divided. Prinz has shown how the somatic marker theory can be expanded into a general account of the emotions (Prinz 2004b) and of the role of emotion in moral psychology (Prinz 2007). Others philosophers have emphasized the gap between the actual findings of Damasio and his collaborators and the broad picture of the role of emotion in mental life painted in his popular books and adopted wholesale by some philosophers. Giovanna Colombetti distinguishes two versions of the somatic marker hypothesis. In the first, somatic markers are the fundamental source of valence in decision making. In the second, somatic markers have a specific role in thinking about distant outcomes. Colombetti argues that neither hypothesis is supported by the data from Damasio's key experimental paradigm, the Iowa gambling task (Colombetti 2008).

Philip Gerrans, on the other hand, defends the second hypothesis and argues that Damasio's subjects had a specific deficit in the ability for "mental time-travel" (Gerrans 2007, 459). There is nothing unusual about the existence of this kind of gap. Scientists need to go beyond what is immediately implied by their data if they are to develop theoretical frameworks that guide future experimentation. One aim of naturalistic philosophy is to stand back from any particular research program and ask to what extent some broad conclusion is supported by the current state of knowledge. The work of Stefan Linquist and Jordan Bartol suggests that the broad conclusion drawn by Blackburn (see quotation above) is not well supported.

> First, contrary to conventional wisdom there is no single somatic marker hypothesis. Even within the writings of its chief proponent, Antonio Damasio, somatic markers are assigned a variety of different functions. … A second myth concerns the stages of practical decision making at which

> somatic markers are most likely engaged. The received view is that the available evidence suggests a role for somatic markers in the "core stages" of decision making, where a subject generates, evaluates and selects among alternative courses of action. We argue that Damasio's own evidence suggests otherwise. Somatic markers appear to be involved (if at all) in the "peripheral" stages of decision making: one possibility is that they are engaged early on, in notifying the subject that a decision-point has been reached; another possibility is that somatic markers are engaged at the terminal stage, in motivating the subject to execute a decision. (Linquist and Bartol 2013)

The pattern(s) of interaction between affect and cognition remain an important topic for philosophy. Some leading figures continue to argue that emotions are judgments (e.g., Nussbaum 2001). Andrea Scarantino has forcefully restated the view that this is inconsistent with empirical evidence that emotional responses can be triggered by low-level appraisal (Scarantino 2010). Scarantino argues that judgmentalists have responded to this evidence, and also to the existence of animal emotions, by stretching the concept of judgment until it becomes trivial. "All instances of emotions eventually manage to find room in the unboundedly malleable and arguably unprincipled notion of judgment" (Scarantino 2010, 746).

According to one philosopher, the experimental evidence Scarantino (2010) adduces is irrelevant to the issue of whether all emotions involve higher cognition because the experiments involve placing a subject in abnormal conditions or using subjects with damaged brains. Charles Starkey argues that responses produced under these conditions do not count as emotion. Emotion should be restricted to states that occur when the system is intact and operating under the conditions for which it was designed (Starkey 2007). Psychologists will be relieved to know that Starkey does not intend a wholesale rejection of the experimental method: his point is purely about the definition of emotion. However, I think it is fair to say that most researchers working in this area do not think of their work as merely the creation of abnormal phenomena in the laboratory, but as throwing light on the relative independence of different levels of emotional appraisal in normal life.

A good deal of philosophical discussion has been provoked by the rise of core affect theory in psychology. Psychological constructionists like James A. Russell and Lisa Feldman Barrett deny that subordinate-emotion categories like fear and anger are natural kinds. (This is consistent with thinking that the superordinate category of emotion is a natural kind.) Constructionists identify pleasure and arousal as affective primitives that combine into core affect, a blend of hedonic and arousal values that is "the most basic building block of emotional life" (Barrett 2006, 48). All affective states are built out of core affect, perhaps with other ingredients. Mood is "prolonged core affect without an object" (Russell 2003, 149). Discrete emotions emerge from a conceptual act of categorization of core affect (Barrett 2006). A core affective state of high pleasantness and high arousal may be categorized as happiness, a state of low pleasantness and high activation as fear, a state of low pleasantness and low arousal as sadness, and so forth. "Categorizing the ebb and flow of core affect into a discrete experience of emotion corresponds to the colloquial idea of 'having an emotion'" (Barrett 2006, 49). The key idea here is that discrete categories are imposed on underlying psychological processes that are continuous in nature. This general idea is not new, but by constructing a detailed model and presenting evidence in its support, core affect theory has become an important player in the contemporary psychology of emotion.

There have been some productive interactions between psychologists and philosophers about core affect theory. Scarantino has argued that much of the evidence for the artificiality of discrete-emotion categories targets the vernacular categories used in everyday life. The real target of core affect theory, however, is the scientific taxonomy of discrete emotions represented by Ekman's list of basic emotions (e.g., Ekman 1999). Core affect theorists have evidence of the artificiality of that taxonomy too, but Scarantino's point is that proper assessment of the relative merits of basic emotion theory and core affect theory requires that the disputants separate the question of whether our existing, vernacular categories of emotion are natural from the question of whether there are natural categories to be found (Scarantino 2009; see also Scarantino and Griffiths 2011). Colombetti has argued, using her dynamical systems account of emotion, discussed in what follows, that discrete emotions are "softly assembled" as reasonably consistent patterns that emerge as the brain interacts with its context (Colombetti 2009a). Colombetti argues that her proposal can do justice to both the evidence for discrete emotion types and the evidence of the variability and context-dependence of emotion mustered by core affect theorists.

In the exchange that followed, two things became clear (Barrett, Gendron, and Huang 2009; Colombetti 2009b). First, the disagreement between basic emotion theorists and core affect theorists is as much about the data itself as about which framework best explains that data. Barrett and collaborators do not regard it as an advantage that Colombetti's framework can explain the evidence for discrete emotions: they do not think there is much to explain! Second, Barrett and collaborators emphasize that the categorization of core affect is not a superficial overlay on the underlying process. Categorization is at the heart of what brains do, and even highly culturally specific emotion categories may be implicit in the way the brains of enculturated individuals process emotional stimuli.

Is Emotion a Form of Perception?

Perceptual theories of emotion have become increasingly popular in philosophy (for a review, see Salmela 2011). Perceptual theories seem to combine the best features of the traditional feeling theory of emotion and the judgmentalist theories that have dominated since the 1960s. Perceptual states have intrinsic phenomenology – the fact that it feels like something to experience emotion does not need to be added as an afterthought. But perceptual states are also intentional – they represent the world as being a certain way. As such, they can be accurate or inaccurate, appropriate or inappropriate – the feature that attracts philosophers to judgmentalist theories of emotion. The idea that emotions are perceptions of evaluative properties has additional attractions for some moral psychologists. It suggests that emotions may be a source of evaluative knowledge. Michael Tye is one author who argues that evaluative qualities are directly given to us in our perceptual experience – we *see* that something is dangerous or disgusting (Tye 2008).

The idea that emotions are perceptions of evaluative properties can be used to understand how emotions motivate actions. I described above DeLancey's proposal that basic emotions can explain action directly, rather than by combining with a desire to attain some goal. A basic emotion both represents the world as being a particular way and embodies an action tendency. Sabine Döring has developed a theory that is structurally similar, although in a very different philosophical tradition (Döring 2003, 2007). Her concern is whether emotion can rationally explain action without the assistance of belief or desire. Can someone who has the emotion but does not perform the action be considered to have acted irrationally merely because of the intentional content of that emotion? Döring suggests that emotions can play this role because, as well as motivating a particular kind of action, an emotion represents the world as having a property in the light of which that action is rational.

In a later article, Döring builds on these ideas to address a key debate in moral psychology. Externalist accounts of moral motivation hold that an agent who judges that an action is morally right will not be motivated to act unless they desire to do the right thing. Internalist accounts hold that someone who judges that an action is morally right thereby has a motive to act: moral judgments are intrinsically motivating. Döring uses a perceptual theory of emotion to uphold internalism.

> Emotions are affective perceptions. They have motivational force so that they can contribute to the explanation of action. At the same time they can rationalise actions because they have an intentional content which resembles the content of sensory perception in being representational. ... Doing the right thing is much more a matter of seeing things right than of drawing the right inferences. Seeing things right, in its turn, is not only to justify an action: it necessarily implies to be motivated to act accordingly. (Döring 2007, 363)

Emotions are being asked to do an extraordinary amount of work in this form of moral psychology. They are both a key element in moral epistemology – perceptions of evaluative properties, and a key element in moral motivation – linking evaluative properties to action. To my mind, this makes it even more important to show that there actually are mental processes that play these roles and that we are not merely projecting the desiderata of our ethical theories onto the emotions.

Colombetti has defended a very different approach to emotional perception (Colombetti 2007). *Enactive* theories of perception argue that organisms perceive by acting in the world and that perceptual skills are, in part, motor skills (Hurley 1998; Noë 2004). Applying this theory to emotional appraisal leads Colombetti to suggest that bodily arousal and action are means by which the organism appraises emotional significance. For example, becoming aroused and orienting to the stimulus are part of the process by which a subject determines that they are confronting danger. At the heart of Colombetti's work is a dynamical systems approach to cognitive science: the mind is the emergent pattern of activity of the brain and the body. The best way to conceptualize emotional episodes is as self-organizing, dynamical patterns of the whole organism (Colombetti 2009a).

There are some similarities between the enactive approach and Prinz's theory of gut reactions, and both theorists talk of *embodied* emotions (Prinz 2004a; Colombetti 2014). But their understanding of embodiment is very different. For example, Prinz follows Damasio in allowing that the brain can substitute for the absence of an actual bodily state through a neural "as-if loop." In Colombetti's view, it would be extremely surprising if the brain, uncoupled from the body, could recreate the dynamics of the whole system. Prinz's proposal that appraisal is carried out by "calibration files" of learned associations is also at odds with the enactive perspective, according to which appraisal is not a separate process that occurs before other aspects of becoming emotional.

As well as being embodied, emotion for Colombetti is *embedded* because the brain-body system is in continual commerce with the environment as an emotional episode unfolds. The course of the emotion depends on this exchange. I am not sure how far Colombetti would endorse the *situated* emotion perspective, according to which emotional competence – the ability to have the right emotion at the right time – depends on scaffolding by the physical and social environment (Griffiths and Scarantino 2009; Parkinson, Fischer, and Manstead 2005).

Colombetti's work introduces to the philosophy of emotion the ideas and issues that have dominated the philosophy of cognitive science for the past decade – the so-called three Es of embodiment, embeddedness, and enaction. This is likely to set a new direction for the field (see also Greenwood 2012, 2015). Philosophers have found much work unpacking what these ideas really mean and where they can plausibly be applied to cognition, and their application to emotion will raise the same questions.

Conclusion

Despite the at-times heated methodological disagreement between naturalistic philosophers of emotion and other philosophers of emotion, the central concerns of their work remain quite similar. For example, the integration of the purely philosophical literature on emotion-as-perception with naturalistic approaches to emotional perception is the obvious way to meet the concern expressed above that there may be no actual psychological processes that play the role moral psychologists look to the emotions to play. Conversely, such integration will help ensure that naturalistic work continues to address important philosophical questions.

REFERENCES

Barrett, Lisa Feldman. 2006. "Are Emotions Natural Kinds?" *Perspectives on Psychological Science* 1 (1): 28–58. http://dx.doi.org/10.1111/j.1745-6916.2006.00003.x.

Barrett, Lisa Feldman, Maria Gendron, and Yang-Ming Huang. 2009. "Do Discrete Emotions Exist?" *Philosophical Psychology* 22 (4): 427–37. http://dx.doi.org/10.1080/09515080903153634.

Blackburn, Simon. 1998. *Ruling Passions: A Theory of Practical Reasoning*. Oxford: Oxford University Press.

Charland, Louis C. 2001. "In Defence of 'Emotion.'" *Canadian Journal of Philosophy* 31 (1): 133–54.

Charland, Louis C. 2002. "The Natural Kind Status of Emotion." *British Journal for the Philosophy of Science* 53 (4): 511–37. http://dx.doi.org/10.1093/bjps/53.4.511.

Clark, Jason A. 2010a. "Hubristic and Authentic Pride as Serial Homologues: The Same but Different." *Emotion Review* 2 (4): 397–8. http://dx.doi.org/10.1177/1754073910374663.

Clark, Jason A. 2010b. "Relations of Homology between Higher Cognitive Emotions and Basic Emotions." *Biology & Philosophy* 25 (1): 75–94. http://dx.doi.org/10.1007/s10539-009-9170-1.

Colombetti, Giovanna. 2007. "Enactive Appraisal." *Phenomenology and the Cognitive Sciences* 6 (4): 527–46. http://dx.doi.org/10.1007/s11097-007-9077-8.

Colombetti, Giovanna. 2008. "The Somatic Marker Hypotheses, and What the Iowa Gambling Task Does and Does Not Show." *British Journal for the Philosophy of Science* 59 (1): 51–71. http://dx.doi.org/10.1093/bjps/axm045.

Colombetti, Giovanna. 2009a. "From Affect Programs to Dynamical Discrete Emotions." *Philosophical Psychology* 22 (4): 407–25. http://dx.doi.org/10.1080/09515080903153600.

Colombetti, Giovanna. 2009b. "Reply to Barrett, Gendron & Huang." *Philosophical Psychology* 22 (4): 439–42. http://dx.doi.org/10.1080/09515080903153642.

Colombetti, Giovanna. 2014. *The Feeling Body: Affective Science Meets the Enactive Mind*. Cambridge, MA: MIT Press. http://dx.doi.org/10.7551/mitpress/9780262019958.001.0001.

Damasio, Antonio R. 1994. *Descartes' Error: Emotion, Reason and the Human Brain*. New York: Grosset / Putnam.

DeLancey, Craig. 2001. *Passionate Engines: What Emotions Reveal about Mind and Artificial Intelligence*. New York: Oxford University Press.

Döring, Sabine A. 2003. "Explaining Action by Emotion." *Philosophical Quarterly* 53 (211): 214–30. http://dx.doi.org/10.1111/1467-9213.00307.

Döring, Sabine A. 2007. "Seeing What to Do: Affective Perception and Rational Motivation." *Dialectica: International Journal of Philosophy of Knowledge* 61 (3): 363–94. http://dx.doi.org/10.1111/j.1746-8361.2007.01105.x.

Ekman, Paul. 1999. "Basic Emotions." In *Handbook of Cognition and Emotion*, edited by Tim Dalgleish and Mick Power, 45–60. Chichester, UK: John Wiley and Sons.

Forgas, Joseph P., ed. 2001. *Handbook of Affect and Social Cognition*. Mahwah, NJ: Lawrence Erlbaum.

Gerrans, Philip. 2007. "Mental Time Travel, Somatic Markers and 'Myopia for the Future.'" *Synthese: An International Journal for Epistemology, Methodology and Philosophy of Science* 159 (3): 459–74.

Greenwood, Jennifer. 2012. "Wide Externalism and the Roles of Biology and Culture in Human Emotional Development." *Emotion Review* 4 (4): 423–31. http://dx.doi.org/10.1177/1754073912445813.

Greenwood, Jennifer. 2015. *Becoming Human: The Ontogenesis, Metaphysics, and Expression of Human Emotionality*. Cambridge, MA: MIT Press.

Griffiths, Paul E. 1997. *What Emotions Really Are: The Problem of Psychological Categories*. Chicago: University of Chicago Press. http://dx.doi.org/10.7208/chicago/9780226308760.001.0001.

Griffiths, Paul E. 2004a. "Emotions as Natural Kinds and Normative Kinds." *Philosophy of Science* 71 (5): 901–11. http://dx.doi.org/10.1086/425944.

Griffiths, Paul E. 2004b. "Is Emotion a Natural Kind?" In *Thinking about Emotion: Contemporary Philosophers on Emotion*, edited by Robert C. Solomon, 233–49. Oxford: Oxford University Press.

Griffiths, Paul E., and Andrea Scarantino. 2009. "Emotions in the Wild: The Situated Perspective on Emotion." In *Cambridge Handbook of Situated Cognition*, edited by Philip Robbins and Murat Aydede, 437–53. Cambridge: Cambridge University Press.

Hurley, Susan. 1998. *Consciousness in Action*. Cambridge, MA: Harvard University Press.

Jackson, Frank C. 1998. *From Metaphysics to Ethics: A Defence of Conceptual Analysis*. Oxford: Oxford University Press.

Kelly, Daniel. 2011. *Yuck! The Nature and Moral Significance of Disgust*. Cambridge, MA: MIT Press.

Kelly, Daniel. 2012. Review of *The Meaning of Disgust*, by Colin McGinn. *Notre Dame Philosophical Reviews* (June 23). http://ndpr.nd.edu/news/31351-the-meaning-of-disgust/.

Kenny, Anthony. 1963. *Action, Emotion and Will*. London: Routledge & Kegan Paul.

Lazarus, Richard S. 1991. *Emotion and Adaptation*. New York: Oxford University Press.

Linquist, Stefan, and Jordan Bartol. 2013. "Two Myths about Somatic Markers." *British Journal for the Philosophy of Science* 64 (3): 455–84. http://dx.doi.org/10.1093/bjps/axs020.

McGinn, Colin. 2011. *The Meaning of Disgust*. New York: Oxford University Press. http://dx.doi.org/10.1093/acprof:oso/9780199829538.001.0001.

Noë, Alva. 2004. *Action in Perception*. Cambridge, MA: MIT Press.

Nussbaum, Martha. 2001. *Upheavals of Thought: The Intelligence of Emotions*. Cambridge: Cambridge University Press. http://dx.doi.org/10.1017/CBO9780511840715.

Öhman, Arne. 1999. "Distinguishing Unconscious from Conscious Emotional Processes: Methodological Considerations and Theoretical Implications." In *Handbook of Emotion and Cognition*, edited by Tim Dalgleish and Mick Power, 321–52. Chichester, UK: John Wiley and Sons.

Öhman, Arne. 2002. "Automaticity and the Amygdala: Nonconscious Responses to Emotional Faces – Current Directions in Psychological Science." *Emotion Review* 5 (2): 62–6.

Parkinson, Brian, Agneta H. Fischer, and Antony S.R. Manstead. 2005. *Emotions in Social Relations: Cultural, Group and Interpersonal Processes*. New York: Psychology Press.

Prinz, Jesse. 2002. *Furnishing the Mind: Concepts and Their Perceptual Basis*. Cambridge, MA: MIT Press.

Prinz, Jesse. 2004a. "Embodied Emotions." In *Thinking about Feeling: Contemporary Philosophers on the Emotions*, edited by Robert C. Solomon, 44–59. Oxford: Oxford University Press.

Prinz, Jesse. 2004b. *Gut Reactions: A Perceptual Theory of Emotion*. Oxford: Oxford University Press.

Prinz, Jesse. 2007. *The Emotional Construction of Morals*. Oxford: Oxford University Press.

Roberts, Robert C. 2003. *Emotions: An Essay in Aid of Moral Psychology*. Cambridge: Cambridge University Press. http://dx.doi.org/10.1017/CBO9780511610202.

Russell, James A. 2003. "Core Affect and the Psychological Construction of Emotion." *Psychological Review* 110 (1): 145–72. http://dx.doi.org/10.1037/0033-295X.110.1.145.

Salmela, Mikko. 2011. "Can Emotion be Modelled on Perception?" *Dialectica: International Journal of Philosophy of Knowledge* 65 (1): 1–29. http://dx.doi.org/10.1111/j.1746-8361.2011.01259.x.

Scarantino, Andrea. 2009. "Core Affect and Natural Affective Kinds." *Philosophy of Science* 76 (5): 940–57. http://dx.doi.org/10.1086/605816.

Scarantino, Andrea. 2010. "Insights and Blindspots of the Cognitivist Theory of Emotions." *British Journal for the Philosophy of Science* 61 (4): 729–68. http://dx.doi.org/10.1093/bjps/axq011.

Scarantino, Andrea, and Paul E. Griffiths. 2011. "Don't Give Up on Basic Emotions." *Emotion Review* 3 (4): 444–54. http://dx.doi.org/10.1177/1754073911410745.

Scherer, Klaus R. 1999. "Appraisal Theory." In *Handbook of Emotion and Cognition*, edited by Tim Dalgleish and Mick Power, 637–63. Chichester, UK: John Wiley and Sons.

Sinnott-Armstrong, Walter, ed. 2008. *Moral Psychology*, vols. 1–3. Cambridge, MA: Bradford Books.

Solomon, Robert C. 1976. *The Passions*. New York: Doubleday.

Starkey, Charles. 2007. "Manipulating Emotion: The Best Evidence for Non-cognitivism in the Light of Proper Function." *Analysis* 67 (3): 230–7. http://dx.doi.org/10.1093/analys/67.3.230.

Teasdale, John D. 1999. "Multi-Level Theories of Cognition-Emotion Relations." In *Handbook of Cognition and Emotion*, edited by Tim Dalgleish and Mick Power, 665–81. Chichester, UK: John Wiley and Sons.

Tye, Michael. 2008. "The Experience of Emotion: An Intentionalist Theory." *Revue Internationale de Philosophie* 62: 25–50.

Zajonc, Robert B. 1980. "Feeling and Thinking: Preferences Need No Inference." *American Psychologist* 35 (2): 151–75. http://dx.doi.org/10.1037/0003-066X.35.2.151.

Zajonc, Robert B. 2000. "Feeling and Thinking: Closing the Debate over the Independence of Affect." In *Feeling the Thinking: The Role of Affect in Social Cognition*, edited by Joseph P. Forgas, 31–58. Paris: Maison des sciences de l'homme / Cambridge University Press.

5 Are Our Emotional Feelings Relational?

GEORG NORTHOFF

The well-known James-Lange theory determined feelings to be perceptions of physiological changes in the body's autonomic, hormonal, and motor systems. Once we become aware of physiological bodily changes induced by danger, we feel fear and subjectively experience emotional feelings. William James (1884, 190) consequently considered bodily changes as being central to emotional feelings. "We feel sorry because we cry, angry because we strike, afraid because we tremble, and not that we cry, strike, or tremble, because we are sorry, angry, or fearful, as the case may be" (ibid.). Modern empirical versions of this theory resurface in current neuroscientific models of emotion, as, for instance, in Damasio (1999) and others (Craig 2003, 2004, 2005; Bechara 2004; Niedenthal 2007). Conceptually, the embodied approach to emotion emphasizes the crucial role of the body in emotional feeling. If the body and its vegetative and sensorimotor function play a crucial role in constituting emotional feelings, the body can no longer be considered in a merely objective way, but rather as subjective and experienced – the mere *Körper* as objective body must be distinguished from the lived body as subjectively experienced body in emotional feeling (Colombetti and Thompson 2005, 2007; Colombetti 2008).[1]

The emphasis on the body raises the question of the role of the environment in constituting emotional feelings. (For greater context, see Paul Griffiths's discussion, in chapter 4 of this volume, of naturalistic theories premised on the notion that emotions are perceptions of the body's reactions to stimuli.) The body stands in direct contact with the environment through its sensorimotor functions, which are emphasized in recent body-based – that is, embodied – concepts of emotional feelings (see Niedenthal et al. 2005; Niedenthal 2007). The body is supposed to represent the environment in sensorimotor terms, and it is these bodily representations that are considered crucial in constituting emotional feelings. As a result, the environment may have an indirect and modulatory role through the body in the constitution of emotional feelings. One could also imagine that the environment has a direct and constitutive role in emotional feeling; the environment may then directly constitute emotional feeling independent of the body's sensorimotor (and vegetative) functions. In this case, emotional feelings should be constituted directly, by a person's relation to the environment rather than indirectly, through bodily representations. Since the person-environment relation is crucial here, I call such an approach "the relational concept of emotional feeling." (See Georg Northoff [2004] and especially Northoff [2014a, 2014b] for a general outline of this relational approach and Aaron Ben-Ze'ev [1993] for the characterization of perception as relational.)

The general aim of the present chapter is to briefly outline the characteristics of such a relational concept of emotional feeling and to investigate its empirical plausibility with respect to current neuroscientific data. More specifically, the first aim is to investigate current human imaging data on emotion processing and anatomical connectivity and to point out whether they lend supportive evidence to the relational concept of emotional feeling. I describe various studies on human imaging and anatomical connectivity in the first part and discuss their implications for an empirically plausible concept of emotional feeling. The second aim of the chapter is to briefly discuss some neurophilosophical implications of the relational concept for how to characterize emotional feeling in terms of phenomenal consciousness and intentionality; this will be done in the last part of the chapter.

Brain Imaging, Anatomical Connectivity, and the Relational Concept of Emotional Feeling

A discussion of all neuroscientific data on emotion processing would be beyond the scope of this chapter. I focus on two specific issues: human imaging data and anatomical connectivity. Concerning human imaging, I discuss studies that specifically focus on the subjective experience of bodily states – that is, interoceptive awareness. If interoceptive awareness involves only interoceptive stimuli in isolation, remaining independent of exteroceptive stimuli, empirical data may lend support to the body-based and embodied approach to emotional feelings. If, in contrast, interoceptive awareness involves exteroceptive stimuli by relating them to interoceptive ones, empirical data may rather be assumed to lend support to the relational approach. Accordingly, depending on the kind of recruited regions, which may be either intero- or exteroceptive, human imaging during interoceptive awareness may lend some empirical plausibility to either the embodied or the relational concept of emotional feeling. Anatomical connectivity may also yield some insight into the empirical plausibility of either concept. A body-based and embodied concept of emotional feeling presupposes more or less segregated anatomical connections and processing between intero- and exteroceptive stimuli, which, at best, may interfere at some node points for extero-interoceptive translation and exert modulatory or instrumental (but not constitutive) effects. On the other hand, a relational approach to emotional feeling requires that intero- and exteroceptive stimuli are always already processed in relation to each other, and for this, in turn, close anatomical connectivity between intero- and exteroceptive processing at all levels is necessary. As a result, the pattern of anatomical connectivity may provide some clue as to which concept of emotional feeling is empirically more plausible.

Brain Imaging of Interoceptive Awareness

Recent imaging studies using functional magnetic resonance imaging (fMRI) investigated neural activity during interoceptive stimulus processing, such as evocation of blood pressure changes during isometric and mental tasks, heartbeat changes and perception, anticipatory skin conductance during gambling, and heart rate modulation during a presentation of emotional faces (see Critchley 2005 for a review; Pollatos et al. 2007a, 2007b; Craig 2002, 2003, 2004). These studies observed neural activity changes in the right insula, the anterior cingulate cortex (ACC) extending from the supragenual (SACC) to the dorsal (DACC) regions, and the amygdala. This led to the assumption that specifically the right insula and the SACC/DACC integrally represent autonomic and visceral responses, which are transferred from the spinal cord through the midbrain, the hypothalamus, and the thalamocortical pathway to the right insular cortex (Craig 2002, 2003, 2004; Critchley 2005). Based on the results, these regions are assumed to be involved in representing the autonomic and visceral states of the body and thus interoceptive processing. Craig (2002, 2003, 2004) assumes, specifically, that the right insula is crucially involved in that it receives autonomic and visceral afferences from lower centres (see above) and represents the interoceptive body state in an integrated way. This allows the insula to give rise to a "mental image of one's physical state," which, according to A.D. Craig, provides the basis for subjective awareness of emotional feeling and one's self as "material me" (Craig 2002, 660).

If these regions mediate interoceptive processing, the question arises as to their role in the subjective experience of bodily, and thus interoceptive, changes as the basis for emotional feeling. Critchley et al. (2004) let subjects evaluate whether their own heartbeat was synchronous or asynchronous using an auditory feedback note, which allowed them to compare interoceptive- and exteroceptive-directed attention. Interoceptive attention to one's own heartbeat increased activity in the right insula (as well as the SACC/DACC and the somatomotor cortex), while exteroceptive attention to the tone suppressed activity in the very same region. Activity in the right insula also correlated with both performance in the heartbeat detection task and subjective anxiety symptoms, which also correlated with each other. These findings suggest a close relationship between interoceptive awareness and emotional feeling.

Other studies demonstrated the modulation of these interoceptive stimulus changes by exteroceptive stimuli. For instance, using fMRI, Critchley et al. (2004) investigated changes in regional neural activity during the presentation of happy, sad, angry, and disgusted faces. They observed that heart rate changes depended on the emotional category, with sad and angry faces inducing the strongest heart rate changes. Emotional face-responsive regions like the right (and left) insula, the SACC/DACC, the midbrain/brain stem and the right amygdala were also found to be correlating with the changes in heart rate magnitude. These results indicate that different emotions may be mediated by differential interoceptive response patterns, which may themselves be mediated by neural activity in the right insula, the SACC/DACC, the midbrain/brain stem, and the amygdala. According to the authors, these results provide support for the hypothesis that interoceptive stimulus processing may be involved in differentiating among different types of emotional feelings.

The group around Olga Pollatos conducted a series of studies on heartbeat perception and emotional feeling. Pollatos et al. (2007a, 2007b) investigated attention towards heartbeats and cardiovascular arousal. Regions implicated in both conditions included the right insula, the somatomotor cortex, the SACC/DACC, and the dorsomedial prefrontal cortex (DMPFC). They observed activity in the right insula and the

DACC to be correlating with the degree of interoceptive awareness, while negative feelings correlated with the blood-oxygenation-level-dependentBOLD response of the interoceptive awareness condition in the DACC and DMPFC. Using electroencephalography (EEG), they distinguished between good and poor heartbeat perceivers. Good heartbeat perceivers (Pollatos, Kirsch, and Schandry 2005; Pollatos et al. 2007a, 2007b) showed higher arousal ratings, as well as higher P300 amplitudes and slow-wave latency ranges, than poor heartbeat perceivers when they were presented with emotional pictures. Taken together, these studies show, behaviourally, a close relationship among interoceptive awareness, arousal, and emotional feeling, while neuroanatomically, they confirm the involvement of the right insula, the SACC/DACC, and the DMPFC in mediating the relationship between interoceptive awareness and emotional feeling.

Interoceptive Awareness and Its Relation to Exteroceptive Processing

The question is whether the above-described data support an embodied concept of emotional feeling, with exteroceptive stimuli being merely modulatory and instrumental or epiphenomenal; or, whether the data might rather be interpreted in favour of a relational concept of feelings, with interoceptive stimuli in relation to exteroceptive stimuli being constitutive and thus central. Presupposing the James-Lange theory, most of the above-cited authors have interpreted their data in favour of the interoceptive-based concept. However, I will argue that there are strong arguments that make the data rather compatible with what I call the intero-exteroceptive relational concept of emotional feelings. I argue that there seems to be a mismatch between the empirical data and their interpretation in current imaging studies on emotional feelings and interoceptive processing, which I want to support by making the three following points.

First, no paradigms employed investigated interoceptive stimuli in isolation from exteroceptive stimuli, but rather in relation to them. Critchley et al. (2004), for instance, investigated heartbeat perception in relation to auditory tones as exteroceptive stimuli, while Pollatos, Kirsch, and Schandry (2005) and Pollatos et al. (2007a, 2007b) directly compared both conditions with each other. Thus, changes in neural activity assumed to be specific for interoceptive awareness reflect a relation, or dynamic balance, between intero- and exteroceptive processing rather than mirroring isolated interoceptive stimulus processing and remaining (more or less) independent of exteroceptive stimulus processing. Dynamic modulation of right insula activity, as observed by Hugo D. Critchley, may thus reflect a dynamic balance between intero- and exteroceptive attention in the heartbeat-auditory tone-detection task rather than pure interoceptive heartbeat stimulus processing. Such an intero-exteroceptive relational concept would thus assume that the above-mentioned regions – the right insula, the SACC/DACC, and the DMPFC – are rather responsive to changes in intero-exteroceptive balance instead of isolated interoceptive changes remaining independent of exteroceptive changes.

Second, neither of the above-mentioned studies addressed the question of emotional valence, which indicates whether a feeling is positive or negative. (See also Colombetti [2005] for a discussion of the concept of emotional valence.) Pollatos, Kirsch, and Schandry (2005) and Pollatos et al. (2007a, 2007b) did not observe any significant difference between good and poor heartbeat perceivers in terms of their emotional valence ratings, while both groups did differ in emotional arousal. Interoceptive awareness may thus be linked to emotional arousal and subjective experience of emotional intensity, while it apparently does not seem to determine the valence of the emotional feeling. Regions that have been associated with emotional valence, as distinguished from emotional arousal, include the medial orbitofrontal cortex (MOFC), the SACC and pregenual anterior cingulate cortex, and the ventromedial prefrontal cortex (VMPFC) (Kringelbach 2005; Craig 2002; Critchley 2005; Phan et al. 2002; Grimm et al. 2006). Interestingly, these regions are densely and reciprocally connected with the right insula, the SACC/DACC, and the DMPFC, which are supposed to represent the body's interoceptive state (Ongür and Price 2000). The connectivity pattern thus argues strongly in favour of the intero-exteroceptive relational concept of emotional feeling, which seems to make isolated interoceptive processing and thus an interoceptive-based concept of emotional feeling rather unlikely. What, however, is needed to further support this point are investigations of both regional activity and connectivity patterns during intero- and exteroceptive stimulus processing (see Hurliman, Nagode, and Pardo 2005 for some first support).

My third point is that Pollatos, Kirsch, and Schandry (2005) and Pollatos et al. (2007a, 2007b) investigated the temporal course with EEG during the heartbeat-perception task. They observed that good heartbeat perceivers showed higher heart-evoked potential and stronger dipole strength in cortical sources, which included the SACC/DACC, the right insula, the DMPFC, and the secondary somatosensory cortex, when compared to poor heartbeat perceivers. Interestingly, they also observed the dipole sources in the SACC/DACC and DMPFC to occur earlier (around 280 milliseconds) than the ones in the insula and the somatosensory cortex (around 370 milliseconds). A similar temporal distribution is suggested by Naotsugu Tsuchiya and Ralph Adolphs (2007), who assume involvement of subcortical regions like brain stem nuclei and hypothalamus, which mediate interoceptive stimuli to occur after and later than activation in higher regions like the DMPFC. If the interoceptive-based model were true, one would rather expect the opposite temporal pattern with early insula and somatosensory involvement, indicating interoceptive processing, and late SACC/DACC and DMPFC involvement. Late SACC/DACC and DMPFC involvement may then reflect some abstract, internal, cognitive evaluation of interoceptive stimulus processing with consecutive top-down modulation of interoceptive brain regions, as interpreted by advocates of the interoceptive-based concept (Craig 2002; Tsuchiya and Adolphs 2007).

What is the role of the SACC/DACC and the DMPFC? These higher cortical regions have been associated with processing of higher-order exteroceptive stimuli, particularly those that are highly self-related to the organism (Northoff et al. 2006; Northoff and Bermpohl 2004). The fact that these regions are apparently implicated early on in interoceptive awareness gives some indirect support to the assumption that exteroceptive stimuli are involved early in interoceptive processing. Such early involvement indicates that the role of exteroceptive stimulus processing goes beyond mere modulation of interoceptive processing, which would be more compatible with late involvement. In other words, early involvement of these regions may indicate that interoceptive stimulus processing is coded in relation to exteroceptive stimuli, going beyond mere modulation of the former by the latter. The observed early spatio-temporal pattern may thus reflect neural coding of the relationship between intero- and exteroceptive stimulus processing, signifying their actual balance, since otherwise, there would be no need for regions predominantly associated with exteroceptive stimulus processing to be implicated so early, while this pattern seems to be less compatible with the assumption of primarily independent interoceptive processing that becomes secondarily modulated by exteroceptive stimuli.

Anatomical Connectivity and the Convergence of Intero- and Exteroceptive Stimulus Processing

The MOFC and the VMPFC have been demonstrated to be implicated in interoceptive processing. Using biofeedback arousal and relaxation tasks in fMRI, Yoko Nagai et al. (2004) demonstrated that resting-state neural activity in the VMPFC and MOFC covaried with the basal level of sympathetic skin conductance, whereas regions like the SACC/DACC, the insula, and the hypothalamus were related to the rate of change in skin conductance. The level of neural activity in the VMPFC and MOFC, which are part of the so-called anterior cortical midline structures (aCMS), may thus represent the basal sympathetic or autonomic tone independent of some actual stimuli. Since the aCMS have been shown to be also modulated by exteroceptive stimuli, neural activity in these regions may mirror a dynamic balance in attention between extero- and interoceptive stimuli (see also Nagai et al. 2004). This assumption is quite compatible with the connectivity pattern of these regions. The MOFC and VMPFC, as the entrance to the aCMS, receive connections from all regions associated with primary and/or secondary exteroceptive sensory modalities (olfactory, gustatory, somatosensory, auditory, and visual) (see Rolls, Tovée, and Panzeri 1999; Rolls 2000; Kringelbach and Rolls 2004; Barbas 2000; Damasio 2003a, 2003b).

The aCMS are also densely connected to regions (insula, brain stem regions like the hypothalamus, periaqueductal grey [PAG], colliculi, etc.) that process interoceptive sensory signals; these include the proprioceptive and vestibular senses, the visceral sense, and the sense of the interoceptive milieu, which can be taken together with that of pain and temperature (Barbas 2000, 2004; Damasio 2003a, 2003b; Rolls, Tovée, and Panzeri 1999; Rolls 2000; Kringelbach and Rolls 2004; Carmichael and Price 1996; Price 1999). The aCMS, especially the MOFC, VMPFC, and SACC/DACC, are also connected to regions associated with distinct functional domains, including the motor (premotor and motor cortex, basal ganglia), cognitive (lateral prefrontal cortex), and emotional (amygdala, brain stem) domains (Barbas 2000; Ongür and Price 2000; Carmichael and Price 1996; Rolls, Tovée, and Panzeri 1999; Rolls 2000; Kringelbach and Rolls 2004). Because such extensive intero- and exteroceptive connections involve different functional domains, the MOFC and VMPFC (and, in conjunction, the amygdala) can be characterized as a polymodal convergence zone (Rolls, Tovée, and Panzeri 1999; Rolls 2000; LeDoux 2002; Schore 2003).

This connectivity pattern predisposes the aCMS for neural processing, irrespective of the sensory modality of the respective stimulus – that is, supramodal processing. The assumption of supramodal processing in aCMS is supported by results from imaging studies. Emotions in either exteroceptive modality (visual, auditory, gustatory, olfactory) induced neural activity in various regions of the aCMS (see above as well as Phan et al. 2002; Northoff and Bermpohl 2004). Moreover, processing of interoceptive stimuli also induced activation in aCMS regions like the MOFC, VMPFC, and ACC (Critchley et al. 2004; Nagai et al. 2004; Craig 2002, 2003, 2004; Wicker et al. 2003). Finally, stimuli from different origins – that is, of different sensory modalities or of different functional domains (motor, emotional, cognitive, and sensory) induced analogous activation in aCMS (Northoff and Bermpohl 2004; Northoff et al. 2006). Taken together, connectivity pattern and imaging data suggest that neural processing in aCMS is supramodal and domain independent: what apparently matters for inducing neural activity in the aCMS is not so much the modality or domain – that is, the origin of the stimulus, be it either intero- or exteroceptive or cognitive, motor, sensory, or emotional – but how it is related to the respective intero- or exteroceptive stimulus (see further discussion below).

Neural activity in the aCMS may reflect bottom-up modulation by interoceptive processing in the subcortical regions, and this corresponds to their close connectivity with the aCMS (see above as well as Nagai et al. 2004). Analogous neural activity in the aCMS may also be induced by exteroceptive stimuli through bottom-up modulation, which may be traced back to the close connections of the aCMS to the sensory cortical regions. In addition to regions involved in intero- and exteroceptive processing modulating the aCMS in a bottom-up fashion, the aCMS may also top-down modulate the very same regions. For example, the aCMS may top-down modulate interoceptive processing in subcortical regions through the anterior insula (Critchley et al. 2004; Nagai et al. 2004; Craig 2002, 2003). Or as supposed by Davidson, Jackson, and Kalin (2000) and Davidson (2004), the medial prefrontal cortex may top-down modulate or inhibit neural activity in the amygdala, which receives strong intero- and exteroceptive inputs. Since aCMS regions like the MOFC and the VMPFC are regarded as polymodal convergence zones, intero- and exteroceptive processing may interfere through top-down and bottom-up modulation. This could result in mutual adjustment and reciprocal modulation between intero- and exteroceptive processing, which in subjective experience may be reflected in figure-background relationships. The bodily state may be the continuous background against which we subjectively experience our environment. However, the relation may also be converse, whereby the body and its interoceptive changes are the figure and the environment remains in the background; this is the case in neuropsychiatric disorders like somatic depression and somatoform disorder, where subjects experience strong bodily feelings (see below for further details about bodily feelings) rather than showing feelings directed towards environmental events.

In addition to the aCMS, subcortical midline regions like the PAG, the colliculi, the dorsomedial thalamus, and the ventral striatum may also be considered to process interoceptive stimuli in relation to exteroceptive ones. Jaak Panksepp (1998; also Damasio 1999), for instance, assumes that these regions are crucial in constituting emotional feelings. Since the very same regions are also characterized by strong motor connections both afferent and efferent, he and others like Ralph D. Ellis (2005) (unlike Antonio Damasio [1999], who assumes a sensory-based view of feelings) assume emotional feeling to be motor-based, which is very compatible with Panksepp's characterization of emotional feeling as reaching out to the environment, thus reflecting what I have called the relational concept of emotional feeling. Unfortunately, subcortical regions have often been neglected in imaging studies of emotions; this may be due, at least in part, to the fact that neural activity in these regions is rather difficult to reliably visualize using current imaging techniques like fMRI. However, animal experiments demonstrate the crucial role of these subcortical midline regions in constituting emotional feelings (Panksepp 1998, 2005); thus, to bridge the current gap between animals and humans, future studies in humans are needed to investigate subcortical neural activity during emotional feeling. Furthermore, the relationship between emotional feeling and motor function needs to be investigated in detail by, for instance, investigating the dependence of emotional feeling on variation of motor function and its neural underpinnings (and vice versa).

Interoceptive-Based Translational versus Intero-exteroceptive Relational Coding of Neural Activity in Emotional Feeling

What is the implicit presupposition that drives most of the above-cited authors to interpret their data in favour of the James-Lange theory? They seem to presuppose a clear-cut distinction between intero- and exteroceptive stimulus processing, in which both systems are separate and distinct, interacting only at specific node points. According to such a view, exteroceptive stimuli are translated into interoceptive stimulus processing, whose perception, in turn, is supposed to induce feeling. Thus, exteroceptive stimuli have, at best, an only indirect and mediated impact on emotional feeling in that they must first be translated into interoceptive stimulus processing before they can modulate feelings. I therefore call this model the interoceptive-based translational concept of feeling. Since exteroceptive stimuli are only indirect and mediated, the interoceptive-based translational concept attributes no constitutive role to exteroceptive stimuli and the environment, thus presupposing an "embodied" rather than embedded concept of emotional feeling.

However, anatomical connectivity suggests otherwise. Throughout the brain, at both the subcortical and cortical levels, but especially in the subcortical-cortical midline system, there is convergence between intero- and exteroceptive inputs. This is especially true for regions like the colliculi, the PAG, the tectum, and the aCMS, where both intero- and exteroceptive afferences converge on common neurons (see Panksepp 1998, 2005; Rolls, Tovée, and Panzeri 1999). This suggests not only that interoceptive stimuli are modulated by exteroceptive stimuli at specific node points, but also that the relation – for example, the degree of convergence and divergence – between intero- and exteroceptive stimuli is coded in neural activity in the subcortical-cortical midline system. Exteroceptive stimuli are thus not so much translated into interoceptive stimulus processing, but are rather directly and unmediated related to them, and it is this relation that seems to be coded in neural activity. I therefore call this model the intero-exteroceptive-based relational concept of feelings (see Figure 5.1). Since exteroceptive stimuli have a direct and unmediated role in the relational model, they must be considered constitutive for feeling, which in turn must be considered embedded rather than remaining "disembedded." However, this assumption must be considered preliminary since further experiments – both imaging and computational – are necessary to lend further support to the assumption that intero-exteroceptive relational coding (or difference-based coding as the difference between intero- and exteroceptive stimuli is encoded in neural activity [see Northoff 2014a, 2014b]), rather than interoceptive-based translational coding, is involved in emotional feeling (Figure 5.1).

Is there any empirical evidence in favour of the intero-exteroceptive relational model of neural coding? Critchley (2005, 162), one of the

Figure 5.1. Translational versus Relational Models of Neural Coding in Emotional Feelings

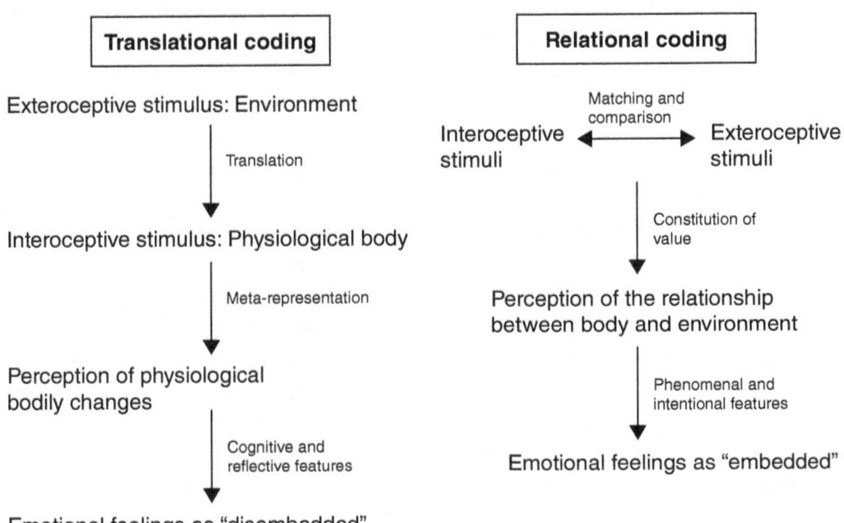

main investigators of interoceptive processing in imaging, states that the right insula maps bodily arousal states, and it does so contextually, which therefore represents an integration of external emotional information with peripheral states of arousal. What seems to be coded in the brain is not so much the interoceptive stimulus itself, but its relation to the respective exteroceptive stimulus. If neural activity codes the actual relationship and balance between intero- and exteroceptive stimuli, one would expect strong contextual dependence of emotional feelings. The constitution of the emotional feeling, the type of feeling, should then depend on the respective context, which implies that different contexts may lead to different types of emotional feelings, even in identical situations. In other words, the environmental context not only modulates emotional feelings but also actively participates in constituting emotional feelings. This accords with the Schachter-Singer experiments (1962), in which different contexts resulted in different types of emotional feelings; if the role of context were merely modulatory, subjects would not have shown completely different and opposing emotional feelings in the two situations, but rather variants of the same feeling. Thus, these experiments lend further support to the assumption of a constitutive role of the environmental context in emotional feelings (rather than remaining merely modulatory).

How are intero- and exteroceptive stimuli related and balanced with each other in relational coding? Rather than coding the intero- or exteroceptive stimulus itself, the degree of correspondence between intero- and exteroceptive stimuli is coded, signalling their convergence or divergence. If, for instance, a lion approaches, the heart rate may increase, which may signal strong correspondence and convergence between intero- and exteroceptive stimuli and consequently lead to the constitution of a corresponding emotional feeling: the feeling of fright and anxiety. If, in contrast, the approach of the lion is not accompanied by heart rate increases – for instance, if one is not clear whether the lion is real or not – there may be a mismatch between intero- and exteroceptive stimuli, and this may result in a different emotional feeling: the feeling of doubt and hesitation. This means that the degree of convergence and divergence between intero- and exteroceptive stimuli may determine the kind of emotional feeling; this is consistent with the relational concept rather than the embodied one, which claims an interoceptive- and thus body-based approach.

All in all, I assume that our brain's design is such that there is no way for interoceptive stimuli to be processed other than in relation to exteroceptive stimuli and vice versa. Consequently, I assume that it is (principally) impossible that interoceptive stimulus processing remains isolated from, unrelated to, and independent of exteroceptive stimulus processing. This implies what I call intero-exteroceptive relational coding, while it excludes interoceptive-based translational coding. What does this imply in experimental regard? The experimental efforts to isolate interoceptive stimulus processing and to search for its specific neural correlates may be futile since exteroceptive stimulus processing may already be implicated in interoceptive stimulus processing. One might better focus on experimentally investigating different intero-exteroceptive stimulus configurations and thus different constellations between body and environment, as nicely demonstrated in the Schacter/Singer experiments. I assume, for instance, that strong activity in the right insula may signal a configuration whereby interoceptive input predominates and the body is subjectively experienced as the figure, while exteroceptive inputs are of minor importance, so that experientially, the actual environment remains in the background. This specific intero-exteroceptive stimulus configuration may be described phenomenologically by the concept of bodily feeling (discussed further below), which may thus be considered an extreme case on one end of the continuum of different possible body-environment constellations that may reflect different kinds of emotional feelings.

Neurophilosophical Implications

I have so far considered only the neuronal mechanisms underlying emotional feelings. This entailed a purely empirical view. But emotional feelings also carry significance in a conceptual and philosophical regard. Feelings denote experience and consciousness. This raises the question about the relationship between emotional feelings and consciousness, which will be tackled in the following on neurophilosophical grounds.

The Relational Concept of Emotional Feeling and Phenomenal Consciousness

How should emotional feelings be conceptualized on the basis of the intero-exteroceptive relational model of neural coding? What we subjectively experience as emotional feeling is not so much mere perception of an interoceptive stimulus like the heartbeat perception, but rather the relation between intero- and exteroceptive stimulus processing. Emotional feelings can no longer be determined in an interoceptive-based way as perceptions of physiological bodily changes; instead, they can be better described in an intero-exteroceptive relational way, thus focusing more on the relation between body and environment than on either the body or the environment itself.[2] What is constitutive of emotional feelings is thus the relation between body and environment, so that feelings reflect a person's relationship to the world.

This is paradigmatically reflected in what Matthew J. Ratcliffe (2005, 2008) calls existential feelings. Based on the writings of Heidegger, he considers existential feelings to be feelings that characterize our relation to the world – that is, as ways of "finding ourselves in the world." This is also pointed out by Robert C. Solomon (2004, 77–8, 84) when he makes a claim for "an existential notion of emotions," which he considers to be "subjective engagements within the world."[3] For instance, different existential feelings characterize different relations to the world, such as feelings of homeliness, separation, belonging, power, control, etc. Most important, emotional feelings like anger, grief, etc. presuppose existential feelings so that both emotional and existential feelings can be characterized as relational. If so, the body itself may be considered only the medium through which feelings can be constituted. Feelings are the relation between person/body and environment rather than some perception of either bodily or environmental changes; in other words, feelings are the relation implying that this relationship is felt.

Due to the very basic and foundational character of the person/body-environment relation, the relational concept considers emotional (and existential) feelings to be basic and primary for emotions – that is, feelings are the "core" of emotions. This is very much in line with the neuroscientific approach taken by Jaak Panksepp (1998, 2005), who assumes what he calls "primary affective consciousness." He regards primary affective consciousness as basic and crucial for all forms of subjective experience and thus for consciousness in general. Analogously, the relational view considers our relation to the world primary, basic, and crucial to our subjective experience, or, as Ratcliffe would probably say, the relation is existential. Since the relational concept characterizes the person/body-environment as basic, primary, and constitutive of feelings, the relational concept of emotional feelings advanced here seems to complement Panksepp's empirical approach in conceptual regard. Feelings and thus affective consciousness can be only primary and basic, as Panksepp claims, because they are our relation to the world.

Another complementary point is Panksepp's insistence (and that of other authors, such as Maxine Sheets-Johnstone [1999] and Ellis [2005]) on the close link between motor function and emotional feeling – that is, the primary motor basis of affective consciousness. In contrast to Damasio, who opts for a rather sensory-based view of emotional feeling, Panksepp (and others, such as Ellis [2005]) argues for a primary "motor view" of affective consciousness and emotional feeling because all presumably involved subcortical regions, such as the PAG, the colliculi, etc., show strong connections to the motor system receiving motor afferences from, and sending out motor efferences to, other cortical and subcortical regions. Accordingly, Panksepp (and others, such as Ellis [2005]) claims that there is an intrinsic link between motor action and emotional feeling, resulting in what may be described as "I act, therefore I feel."

The assumption that motor underpinnings are crucial to emotional feeling is compatible with the relational concept. The relational concept presupposes a bilaterally dependent and constitutive link between person/body and environment. Mere linkage by sensory function would result in unilateral and rather instrumental linkage, whereby the person/body cannot directly impact the environment. It is only by motor function that the person/body becomes intrinsically anchored in and non-instrumentally – that is, constitutionally – linked to the environment. In other words, motor function must be considered the empirical means by which what I have conceptually described as relational becomes possible. Panskepp's insistence on the motor underpinnings of emotional feelings may thus be considered complementary to the relational concept of emotional feeling advanced here.

Once emotional feelings are considered to be the core of both emotions and consciousness, the commonly made distinction between "having an emotion" and "feeling an emotion" no longer applies. Following Maxwell R. Bennett and Peter M.S. Hacker (2003, 210–14), there is no principal distinction between having an emotion and feeling an emotion since, as Saul A. Kripke (1972) already pointed out, having pain is to be identified with feeling pain. Either we have pain and subjectively experience or feel pain, or we do not feel any pain and then have no pain. Having an emotion is consequently to be identified with feeling an emotion, and their distinction remains untenable and implausible. According to Bennett and Hacker (2003, 214), it would be better to differentiate between feeling an emotion – in other words, having an emotion – and "realizing what emotion one feels." Feeling an emotion might then indicate subjective experience and thus what is currently called phenomenal consciousness (see further explication below), whereas realizing what emotion one feels might be considered to implicate higher-order cognitive functions and thus be associated with what has been called reflective consciousness.

By considering feeling as constituting emotion and phenomenal consciousness, the relational concept of emotional feeling argues against explaining feelings in terms of higher-order cognitive and reflective functions, thereby mirroring what is called reflective consciousness. Roughly speaking, reflective consciousness describes a person's awareness of subjective experience and thus phenomenal consciousness – reflective consciousness may thus focus on higher-order cognitive functions. Phenomenal consciousness, in contrast, does not describe the cognitive and behavioural aspects associated with subjective experience. Instead, it focuses on the subjective experiential aspect itself, which is described as the "phenomenal aspect" (Chalmers 1995; Block 1996).

A number of alternative terms and phrases pick out approximately the same core property of phenomenal consciousness. These include "qualia," "phenomenology," "subjective experience," and "what it is like"; despite subtle differences, we consider them here to describe the same phenomenon for pragmatic purposes. I characterize emotional feeling as qualia and what it is like, thus presupposing phenomenal consciousness. This is in accordance with the approach of Peter Goldie, who emphasizes the phenomenal – for example, unreflective, qualitative, and what it is like – character of emotional feeling (Goldie 2000, 68–9). He (1–2, 41) argues that the phenomenal character of feelings is due to the involvement of a point of view, a perspective, through which they become "fundamentally personal." The relational concept claims that such a personal point of view is established by constituting the relationship between person/body and environment and thus by constituting feelings, be they existential or emotional. How such a personal point of view can be established by relating person/body to the environment remains to be discussed in detail, but it is, however, beyond the scope of this paper (see Northoff 2004; Northoff and Bermpohl 2004; Northoff et al. 2006).

The Relational Concept of Emotional Feeling and Intentionality

This constitutive interdependence between body and environment may account for what philosophers describe as the intentionality of emotions – that is, that they are about something and that they are directed at or about objects, events, or states of affairs in the environment (see Northoff 2014b, chap. 25, on intentionality; Griffiths, chap. 4 of this volume). According to Goldie (2000, 16–17), emotional feelings are not mere beliefs or desires, but are directed towards objects in the world; therefore, he (17–9) speaks of "world-directed intentionality," which characterizes what he calls "feeling towards." "Feelings towards" are an "unreflective emotional engagement with the world beyond the body" (Goldie 2002, 241), which thus mirror the relation between person/body and environment in a paradigmatic way – in other words, feeling towards mirrors the relational concept of emotional feeling that has been advanced here in a paradigmatic way.

Goldie distinguishes feeling towards from "bodily feelings." Bodily feelings do not concern objects, events, or states of affairs in the environment, but rather the phenomenal (or, as he says, unreflective) consciousness of bodily changes – that is, the "phenomenology or qualitative nature of our personal experience of these changes" inside our body (muscular, hormonal, autonomic) (Goldie 2000, 51–2). In contrast to feeling towards, bodily feelings show no direct intentionality towards objects in the world – that is, "world-directed intentionality" – since they are rather directed towards one's body (55–8). Although bodily feelings themselves refer only to the body, they nevertheless seem to include feelings that are directed towards objects in the world. Consequently, Goldie assumes that bodily feelings and feelings towards are "united in consciousness in being directed towards an object" in the world. "For example, sexual desire is felt with the whole being – body and soul – for the one we desire. And likewise, our whole being aches in grief for the one we have lost" (55). Due to their associative unity with feeling towards in consciousness, bodily feelings can quasi-participate in and "borrow" the world-directed intentionality of feelings towards, which Goldie describes using the concept of "borrowed intentionality."

My neurophilosophical hypothesis is that what Goldie calls borrowed intentionality of bodily feelings on a conceptual level may correspond empirically to what I described above as intero-exteroceptive relational coding. Bodily feeling may be considered an extreme case at one end of the continuum of possible intero-exteroceptive stimulus configurations, in which interoceptive stimuli predominate over exteroceptive stimuli. However, predominance does not imply elimination, so that even the predominating interoceptive stimuli are still coded in relation to exteroceptive ones, which conceptually may well correspond to Goldie's concept of borrowed intentionality. The participation of bodily feelings in the world-directed intentionality of feeling towards may empirically be possible only on the basis of the neural coding of interoceptive stimuli from one's body in relation to exteroceptive ones from the environment.

This relationship between borrowed intentionality and intero-exteroceptive relational coding may become even more apparent when one imagines the converse empirical case in a thought experiment. In the case of interoceptive-based translational coding, bodily feeling would remain isolated and disconnected from feelings towards, so that the two types of feelings would no longer share world directedness and intentionality. This, in turn, would make both the associative unity between bodily feelings and feeling towards in consciousness and the participation of the former in the world-directed intentionality of the latter impossible. This thought experiment demonstrates that intero-exteroceptive relational coding may be considered a necessary empirical condition of the borrowed intentionality of bodily feelings – that is, that "bodily feeling is thoroughly infused with the intentionality of the emotion; and, in turn, the feeling towards is infused with a bodily characterization" (Goldie 2000, 57). Due to intero-exteroceptive relational coding, even bodily feelings mirror some relation to the environment, so that they, similar to feelings towards, must be considered relational and intentional rather than merely embodied, as presupposed in the James-Lange theory and its modern advocates.[4]

Characterization of both feeling towards and bodily feelings by intentionality raises the question of their phenomenological distinction in subjective experience. I assume that world-directed intentionality of both types of feeling presupposes what I call the relational concept. The relational concept characterizes emotional feelings by the body-environment relationship, which may be constituted in different ways, with either the body or the environment predominating or both being balanced equally. Empirically, either intero- or exteroceptive stimulus processing may imprint more strongly on the relational coding of neural activity. In the case of strong physical bodily activity, for instance, interoceptive stimulus inputs may be much stronger than and predominate over exteroceptive ones. The intero-exteroceptive relational coding may thus allow for variable balances between intero- and exteroceptive inputs. The balance between intero- and exteroceptive inputs may then provide the empirical basis for the organization of subjective experience along the phenomenological distinction between figure and background (see also Ratcliffe 2005, 49).

What appears empirically as predominant interoceptive input when compared to exteroceptive input may subjectively be experienced as bodily feeling, with the body as figure and the environment remaining in the background of subjective experience. This is, for instance, the case after strong physical activity, when one's body aches, leading to strong bodily feelings. If, conversely, exteroceptive inputs predominate over interoceptive ones, the environment may shift into the centre – that is, as figure – of subjective experience, with the body remaining in the background. Even if you experience bodily pain, it remains experientially and thus phenomenologically in the background once a lion approaches and you are in severe danger. It is the virtue of the intero-exteroceptive relational coding, which I have assumed here, that it allows coding of different intero-exteroceptive stimulus configurations or balances, which, phenomenologically, may provide the basis for different possible body-environment constellations, ranging along a continuum between both extremes, where either the body (e.g., as in the example with physical activity) or the environment (e.g., as in the example with the lion) predominates as figure, with the respective other remaining in the background.

I characterized both bodily feelings and feeling towards by intentionality, intero-exteroceptive balance, and figure-background relationship. This implies that both types of feelings may be considered to be two extremes on a continuum, the relation between person/body and environment rather than two distinct conceptual types of feelings. This raises the question of whether Goldie's distinction between bodily feelings and feeling towards as two different types of feeling is really justified. Ratcliffe (2005, 47), for instance, agrees with Goldie that feelings "are inextricable from experience of the world and have a directedness towards things," whereas he does not share Goldie's distinction between feeling towards and bodily feelings by means of intentionality. He argues that the location of bodily feelings in the body does not determine their directedness and thus "what it is a feeling of" (48). Touching a snowball, for instance, feels cold in the hand, and it is this bodily feeling of coldness that predominates subjective experience. One should not, however, forget that the bodily feeling of coldness is directed towards the snowball; in other words, the bodily feeling of coldness reflects the relation between hand/body and snowball/environment, with the former predominating over the latter.

Thus, what is subjectively experienced in the body reflects something in the environment, which leads Ratcliffe (2005, 48) to assume that "feeling of the body and feeling towards objects in the world are two sides of the same coin." If so, the conceptual distinction between bodily feeling and feeling towards, as suggested by Goldie, can no longer be maintained. This can be supported even further by considering the conceptual implications of the relational concept of emotional feelings with regard to the concept of intentionality. The relational concept assumes that the person/body–environment relation provides the very basis of both bodily feelings and feelings towards. If so, the respectively associated types of intentionality, borrowed intentionality and world-directed intentionality, may be traced back to a common, underlying, and more basic concept of intentionality that can account for what I have called here the person/body–environment relation.

This common basic concept of intentionality may be characterized as being pre-reflective and pre-theoretical, something that Maurice Merleau-Ponty (1962), relying on Husserl, characterized as "operative intentionality" and distinguished from the concept of cognition, what he calls "act intentionality." "This is why Husserl distinguishes between intentionality of act, which is that of our judgments and of those occasions when we voluntarily take up a position – the only intentionality discussed in the *Critique of Pure Reason* – and operative intentionality (*fungierende Intentionalität*), or that which produces the natural and antepredicative unity of the world and of our life" (Merleau-Ponty 1962, xx). Although it is beyond the scope of this paper, future investigation is needed, of course, to characterize operative intentionality in further detail (see Zahavi 2005) and to link it conceptually to the borrowed intentionality and world-directed intentionality of bodily feelings and feeling towards (see also Ellis [2005], who speaks of "preconscious emotional intentionality"). Most important, my neurophilosophical hypothesis is that such common basic intentionality – that is, operative intentionality – corresponds on the conceptual level to what I have here empirically described as intero-exteroceptive relational coding. If this can be demonstrated, one may be able to develop a truly neurophilosophical and unifying theory of emotional feelings in which bodily feelings and feeling towards are no longer distinguished conceptually as being characterized by different types of intentionality (in the sense of Goldie), but only phenomenologically as being distinct figure-background configurations in subjective experience (in the sense of Ratcliffe).

Conclusion

The often favoured James-Lange theory, and many current neuroscientific approaches that consider feeling as mere perception of bodily changes and thus as embodied, may be extended by considering the crucial role of the environment in directly constituting emotional feelings. I have therefore suggested in this paper complementing the embodied concept of emotional feelings with a relational concept, which assumes that emotional feelings are constituted by the person/body–environment relationship. The relational concept assumes that the environment is instrumental, thus having not only an indirect impact on emotional feelings through the body but also a direct – for example, non-instrumental – impact and thus having a constitutive role in emotional feelings.

The present paper focuses on whether such a relational concept of emotional feelings is compatible with current empirical data on the neuroscience of emotion processing. If the relational concept of emotional feeling is empirically plausible, even interoceptive awareness should implicate brain regions that process exteroceptive stimuli, and both – that is, intero- and exteroceptive brain regions – should be closely linked to each other through anatomical connectivity. Human brain-imaging data show strong involvement of the VMPFC and other anterior cortical midline structures in emotional feelings. These regions can be characterized by a strong convergence in intero- and exteroceptive inputs, which suggests what I call an intero-exteroceptive relational mode of neural coding, or difference-based coding (Northoff 2014a), rather than interoceptive-based translational neural coding. This intero-exteroceptive relational mode of neural coding may well correspond, on the empirical level, to what, conceptually, I call the relational concept of emotional feeling. The merely embodied concepts of emotional feelings may correspond instead to an interoceptive-based translational neural coding, and thus a bodily-based concept of emotional feelings, as in the James-Lange theory and its current neuroscientific versions. In addition to empirically presupposing different forms of neural coding, the relational concept has conceptual implications, which concern the characterization of emotional feeling by phenomenal consciousness and a basic form of intentionality. I therefore conclude that, if further elaborated, my relational concept of emotional feeling may provide the opportunity to develop a coherent neurophilosophical concept of emotional feeling.

NOTES

1 It should also be pointed out that feelings cannot be considered to be conscious perceptions of the neural activity in those brain regions that induce emotion, as, for instance, Joseph E. LeDoux assumes. We cannot become conscious of neural activity in the first-order emotion regions (see also Bennett and Hacker 2003, 208) since we remain principally unable to perceive our brain's neural activity as such, something I recently called "autoepistemic limitation" (Northoff 2004; Northoff and Musholt 2006).

2 This is compatible with the relational approach to meaning and personal significance, as suggested by Ben-Ze'ev (1993, 2000), which undercuts the traditional assumption that higher-order cognitive functions are necessary to give meaning and personal significance to otherwise meaningless and personally insignificant sense data.

3 One may, of course, argue that we can have subjective experience without emotion; this occurs, for instance, in so-called cold cognitions. Cold

cognitions may, however, be considered just as an extreme case on a continuum between emotion and cognition, where feelings may still be involved in the background, although being maximally suppressed.

4 Taken together, Goldie (2002, 252) characterizes emotional feelings by both their phenomenal and their intentional nature, and he considers them to be intrinsically and "inextricably linked" with each other. The conditions for such links between phenomenality and intentionality in emotional feelings remain, however, unclear. Empirically, I assume intero-exteroceptive relational coding, which, conceptually, may implicate the constitution of a personal point of view (see above), to be crucially involved in intrinsically linking phenomenal and intentional features in emotional feelings. This, however, is a rather speculative hypothesis, and it needs both empirical and conceptual elaboration.

REFERENCES

Barbas, Helen. 2000. "Complementary Roles of Prefrontal Cortical Regions in Cognition, Memory, and Emotion in Primates." *Advances in Neurology* 84: 87–110.

Barbas, Helen. 2004. "Dead Tissue, Living Ideas: Facts and Theory from Neuroanatomy." *Cortex* 40 (1): 205–6. http://dx.doi.org/10.1016/S0010-9452(08)70951-1.

Bechara, Antoine. 2004. "The Role of Emotion in Decision-Making: Evidence from Neurological Patients with Orbitofrontal Damage." *Brain and Cognition* 55 (1): 30–40. http://dx.doi.org/10.1016/j.bandc.2003.04.001.

Bennett, Maxwell R., and Peter Michael Stephan Hacker. 2003. *Philosophical Foundations of Neuroscience*. Oxford: Blackwell.

Ben-Ze'ev, Aaron. 1993. *The Perceptual System: A Philosophical and Psychological Perspective*. New York: Peter Lang.

Ben-Ze'ev, Aaron. 2000. *The Subtlety of Emotions*. Cambridge, MA: MIT Press.

Block, Ned. 1996. "How Can We Find the Neural Correlate of Consciousness?" *Trends in Neurosciences* 19 (11): 456–9.

Carmichael, S. Thomas, and Joseph L. Price. 1996. "Connectional Networks within the Orbital and Medial Prefrontal Cortex of Macaque Monkeys." *Journal of Comparative Neurology* 371 (2): 179–207.

Chalmers, David J. 1995. "The Puzzle of Conscious Experience." *Scientific American* 273 (6): 80–6. http://dx.doi.org/10.1038/scientificamerican1295-80.

Colombetti, Giovanna. 2005. "Appraising Valence." *Journal of Consciousness Studies* 12 (8–10): 103–26.

Colombetti, Giovanna. 2008. "Emotion, Sense-Making and Enaction." In *Enaction: Towards a New Paradigm for Cognitive Science*, edited by John Robert Stewart, Olivier Gapenne, and Ezequiel A. Di Paolo, 145–64. Cambridge, MA: MIT Press.

Colombetti, Giovanna, and Evan Thompson. 2005. "Enacting Emotional Interpretations with Feeling." *Behavioral and Brain Sciences* 28 (2): 200–1. http://dx.doi.org/10.1017/S0140525X05280044.

Colombetti, Giovanna, and Evan Thompson. 2007. "The Feeling Body: Towards an Enactive Approach to Emotion." In *Developmental Perspectives on Embodiment and Consciousness*, edited by Willis F. Overton, Ulrich Müller, and Judith Newman, 45–68. Erlbaum.

Craig, A.D. 2002. "How Do You Feel? Interoception: The Sense of the Physiological Condition of the Body." *Nature Reviews Neuroscience* 3 (8): 655–66. http://dx.doi.org/10.1038/nrn894.

Craig, A.D. 2003. "Interoception: The Sense of the Physiological Condition of the Body." *Current Opinion in Neurobiology* 13 (4): 500–5. http://dx.doi.org/10.1016/S0959-4388(03)00090-4.

Craig, A.D. 2004. "Human Feelings: Why Are Some More Aware Than Others?" *Trends in Cognitive Sciences* 8 (6): 239–41. http://dx.doi.org/10.1016/j.tics.2004.04.004.

Craig, A.D. 2005. "Forebrain Emotional Asymmetry: A Neuroanatomical Basis?" *Trends in Cognitive Sciences* 9 (12): 566–71. http://dx.doi.org/10.1016/j.tics.2005.10.005.

Critchley, Hugo D. 2005. "Neural Mechanisms of Autonomic, Affective, and Cognitive Integration." *Journal of Comparative Neurology* 493 (1): 154–66. http://dx.doi.org/10.1002/cne.20749.

Critchley, Hugo D., Stefan Wiens, Pia Rotshtein, Arne Öhman, and Raymond J. Dolan. 2004. "Neural Systems Supporting Interoceptive Awareness." *Nature Neuroscience* 7 (2): 189–95. http://dx.doi.org/10.1038/nn1176.

Damasio, Antonio. 1999. *The Feeling of What Happens: Body and Emotion in the Making of Consciousness*. New York: Harcourt Brace.

Damasio, Antonio. 2003a. "Mental Self: The Person Within." *Nature* 15 423 (6937): 227.

Damasio, Antonio. 2003b. "Feelings of Emotion and the Self." *Annals of the New York Academy of Sciences* 1001 (1): 253–61. http://dx.doi.org/10.1196/annals.1279.014.

Davidson, Richard J. 2004. "What Does the Prefrontal Cortex 'Do' in Affect: Perspectives on Frontal EEG Asymmetry Research." *Biological Psychology* 67 (1–2): 219–34. http://dx.doi.org/10.1016/j.biopsycho.2004.03.008.

Davidson, Richard J., Daren C. Jackson, and Ned H. Kalin. 2000. "Emotion, Plasticity, Context, and Regulation: Perspectives from Affective Neuroscience." *Psychological Bulletin* 126 (6): 890–909. http://dx.doi.org/10.1037/0033-2909.126.6.890.

Ellis, Ralph D. 2005. *Curious Emotions: Roots of Consciousness and Personality in Motivated Action*. New York: John Benjamin. http://dx.doi.org/10.1075/aicr.61.

Goldie, Peter. 2000. *The Emotions: A Philosophical Exploration*. Oxford: Oxford University Press.

Goldie, Peter. 2002. "Emotions, Feelings and Intentionality: Phenomenology and the Cognitive." *Sciences* 1: 235–54.

Grimm, Simone, Conny F. Schmidt, Felix Bermpohl, Alexander Heinzel, Yuliya Dahlem, Michael Wyss, Daniel Hell, Peter Boesiger, Heinz Boeker, and Georg Northoff. 2006. "Segregated Neural Representation of Distinct Emotion Dimensions in the Prefrontal Cortex: An fMRI Study." *NeuroImage* 30 (1): 325–40. http://dx.doi.org/10.1016/j.neuroimage.2005.09.006.

Hurliman, Elisabeth, Jennifer C. Nagode, and Jose V. Pardo. 2005. "Double Dissociation of Exteroceptive and Interoceptive Feedback Systems in the Orbital and Ventromedial Prefrontal Cortex of Humans." *Journal of Neuroscience* 25 (18): 4641–8. http://dx.doi.org/10.1523/JNEUROSCI.2563-04.2005.

James, William. 1884. "What Is an Emotion?" *Mind* 9: 185–205.

Kringelbach, Morten L. 2005. "The Human Orbitofrontal Cortex: Linking Reward to Hedonic Experience." *Nature Reviews Neuroscience* 6 (9): 691–702. http://dx.doi.org/10.1038/nrn1747.

Kringelbach, Morten L., and Edmund T. Rolls. 2004. "The Functional Neuroanatomy of the Human Orbitofrontal Cortex: Evidence from Neuroimaging and Neuropsychology." *Progress in Neurobiology* 72 (5): 341–72.

Kripke, Saul A. 1972. "Naming and Necessity." In *Semantics of Natural Language*, 2nd ed., edited by Donald Davidson and Gilbert Harman, 253–355. Dordrecht, The Netherlands: Reidel. http://dx.doi.org/10.1007/978-94-010-2557-7_9.

LeDoux, Joseph E. 2002. *Synaptic Self: How Our Brains Become Who We Are*. New York: Viking.

Merleau-Ponty, Maurice. 1962. *Phenomenology of Perception*. London: Routledge.

Nagai, Yoko, Hugo D. Critchley, E.ric Featherstone, Michael R. Trimble, and Raymond J. Dolan. 2004. "Activity in Ventromedial Prefrontal Cortex Covaries with Sympathetic Skin Conductance Level: A Physiological

Account of a 'Default Mode' of Brain Function." *NeuroImage* 22 (1): 243–51. http://dx.doi.org/10.1016/j.neuroimage.2004.01.019.

Niedenthal, Paula M. 2007. Review of *Embodying Emotion. Science* 316 (5827): 1002–5. http://dx.doi.org/10.1126/science.1136930.

Niedenthal, Paula, Lawrence Barsalou, Piotr Winkielman, Silvia Krauth-Gruber, and Francois Ric. 2005. Review of *Embodiment in Attitudes, Social Perception, and Emotion. Personality and Social Psychology Review* 9 (3): 184–211. http://dx.doi.org/10.1207/s15327957pspr0903_1.

Northoff, Georg. 2004. "Why Do We Need a Philosophy of the Brain?" *Trends in Cognitive Sciences* 8 (11): 484–5. http://dx.doi.org/10.1016/j.tics.2004.09.003.

Northoff, Georg. 2014a. *Unlocking the Brain*. Vol. 1, *Coding*. New York: Oxford University Press.

Northoff, Georg. 2014b. *Unlocking the Brain*. Vol. 2, *Consciousness*. New York: Oxford University Press.

Northoff, Georg, and Felix Bermpohl. 2004. "Cortical Midline Structures and the Self." *Trends in Cognitive Sciences* 8 (3): 102–7. http://dx.doi.org/10.1016/j.tics.2004.01.004.

Northoff, Georg, Alexander Heinzel, Moritz de Greck, Felix Bermpohl, Henrik Dobrowolny, and Jaak Panksepp. 2006. "Self-Referential Processing in Our Brain: A Meta-analysis of Imaging Studies on the Self." *NeuroImage* 15: 31 (1): 440–57.

Northoff, Georg, and Kristina Musholt. 2006. "How Can Searle Avoid Property Dualism? Epistemic-Ontological Inference and Autoepistemic Limitation." *Philosophical Psychology* 19 (5): 589–605. http://dx.doi.org/10.1080/09515080600901889.

Ongür, Dost, and Joseph L. Price. 2000. "The Organization of Networks within the Orbital and Medial Prefrontal Cortex of Rats, Monkeys and Humans." *Cerebral Cortex* 10 (3): 206–19. http://dx.doi.org/10.1093/cercor/10.3.206.

Panksepp, Jaak. 1998. *Affective Neuroscience: The Foundations of Human and Animal Emotions*. Oxford: Oxford University Press.

Panksepp, Jaak. 2005. "Affective Consciousness: Core Emotional Feelings in Animals and Humans." *Consciousness and Cognition* 14 (1): 30–80. http://dx.doi.org/10.1016/j.concog.2004.10.004.

Phan, K. Luan, Tor Wager, Stephan F. Taylor, and Israel Liberzon. 2002. "Functional Neuroanatomy of Emotion: A Meta-analysis of Emotion Activation Studies in PET and fMRI." *NeuroImage* 16 (2): 331–48. http://dx.doi.org/10.1006/nimg.2002.1087.

Pollatos, Olga, Beate M. Herbert, Ellen Matthias, and Rainer Schandry. 2007a. "Heart Rate Response after Emotional Picture Presentation Is Modulated by Interoceptive Awareness." *International Journal of Psychophysiology* 63 (1): 117–24. http://dx.doi.org/10.1016/j.ijpsycho.2006.09.003.

Pollatos, Olga, Wladimir Kirsch, and Rainer Schandry. 2005. "On the Relationship between Interoceptive Awareness, Emotional Experience and Brain Processes." *Cognitive Brain Research* 25 (3): 948–62. http://dx.doi.org/10.1016/j.cogbrainres.2005.09.019.

Pollatos, Olga, Eva Traut-Mattausch, Heike Schroeder, and Rainer Schandry. 2007b. "Interoceptive Awareness Mediates the Relationship between Anxiety and the Intensity of Unpleasant Feelings." *Journal of Anxiety Disorders* 21 (7): 931–43. http://dx.doi.org/10.1016/j.janxdis.2006.12.004.

Price, Joseph L. 1999. "Prefrontal Cortical Networks Related to Visceral Function and Mood." *Annals of the New York Academy of Sciences* 877: 383–96. http://dx.doi.org/10.1111/j.1749-6632.1999.tb09278.x.

Ratcliffe, Matthew J. 2005. "The Feeling of Being." *Journal of Consciousness Studies* 12 (8–10): 43–60.

Ratcliffe, Matthew J. 2008. *Feelings of Being: Phenomenology, Psychiatry and the Sense of Reality*. Oxford: Oxford University Press. http://dx.doi.org/10.1093/med/9780199206469.001.0001.

Rolls, Edmund T. 2000. "The Orbitofrontal Cortex and Reward." *Cerebral Cortex* 10 (3): 284–94. http://dx.doi.org/10.1093/cercor/10.3.284.

Rolls, Edmund T., Martin J. Tovée, and Stefano Panzeri. 1999. "The Neurophysiology of Backward Visual Masking: Information Analysis." *Journal of Cognitive Neuroscience* 11 (3): 300–11.

Schachter, Stanley, and Jerome E. Singer. 1962. "Cognitive, Social, and Physiological Determinants of Emotional State." *Psychological Review* 69 (5): 379–99. http://dx.doi.org/10.1037/h0046234.

Schore, Allan N. 2003. *Affect Regulation and the Repair of the Self.* New York: W.W. Norton.

Sheets-Johnstone, Maxine. 1999. "Emotion and Movement." *Journal of Consciousness Studies* 6 (11–12): 259–77.

Solomon, Robert C., ed. 2004. *Thinking about Feeling: Contemporary Philosophers on Emotions*. Oxford: Oxford University Press.

Tsuchiya, Naotsugu, and Ralph Adolphs. 2007. "Emotion and Consciousness." *Trends in Cognitive Sciences* 11 (4): 158–67. http://dx.doi.org/10.1016/j.tics.2007.01.005.

Wicker, Bruno, Christian Keysers, Jane Plailly, Jean-Pierre Royet, Vittorio Gallese, and Giacomo Rizzolatti. 2003. "Both of Us Disgusted in My Insula:

The Common Neural Basis of Seeing and Feeling Disgust." *Neuron* 40 (3): 655–64. http://dx.doi.org/10.1016/S0896-6273(03)00679-2.

Zahavi, Dan. 2005. *Subjectivity and Selfhood. Investigating the First-Person Perspective*. Cambridge, MA: MIT Press.

6 The Interpersonal Is the Political: The Role of Social Belongingness in Emotional Experience and Political Orientation

KRISTINA TCHALOVA AND GEOFF MACDONALD

The human drive to establish positive and lasting relationships with other individuals transcends cultural and geographical boundaries. Around the world, people readily form groups (Coon 1946) and experience profound distress at the dissolution of close social ties, or the threat thereof (Hazan and Shaver 1994; Reiss 1986). Social psychologists view the motivation to secure and sustain feelings of interpersonal connection as a fundamental human need – a need that has become embedded in the psychobiological makeup of humans and other social animals because it has served an important adaptive purpose in the course of evolutionary history (Baumeister and Leary 1995; Bowlby 1973).

Like any other human need, the deeply held desire for close relationships can evoke powerful emotional experiences (MacDonald and Leary 2005). Further, secure connection with other people is perhaps the most potent tool for soothing emotional distress (Mikulincer and Shaver 2007). Thus, if one wishes to understand the role of emotion in political life, then unpacking the contribution of interpersonal connection would appear to be a crucial task. In this chapter, we first provide evidence for the power of social disconnection to elicit profound emotional experience by highlighting research showing that hurt feelings really hurt – that is, social exclusion activates physiological systems associated with the experience of physical pain. Next, we use attachment theory (Bowlby 1973; Mikulincer and Shaver 2007) to show the crucial role of social connection in regulating emotional states. Finally, we speculate on how feelings of attachment insecurity might contribute to political orientation. (This latter point may be read in conjunction with chapter 8, where James Jasper explores how shared emotion can be harnessed to social and political movements.)

Social Pain and the Evolution of the Need to Belong

Our evolutionary ancestors had to contend with a variety of survival and reproductive challenges (Baumeister and Leary 1995). While early humans were highly vulnerable on their own, group living provided a multi-purpose tool amid the perils and demands of their environment. Cooperative affiliation with others afforded increased protection from predators and antagonistic out-groups, improved access to mates, and allowed optimization of foraging, hunting, shelter-building, and resource-sharing strategies. Furthermore, as the prolonged separation of an infant from its caregivers is certain to lead to death, the need for connection is an especially acute fact of life in childhood (Bowlby 1982; Panksepp 1998).

Given the life-and-death stakes of reliable social connection, our ancestors would have benefited from mechanisms that supported the maintenance of social proximity and punished withdrawal from sources of social support. That is, feeling good in response to social inclusion and feeling badly in response to social exclusion would have provided enormous evolutionary advantage. Such affective patterns of responses to social stimuli are influenced by genes (Way and Taylor 2011) and are therefore subject to natural selection in a manner similar to physical traits. Those individuals who possessed genetic variants that sensitized them to cues of imminent social exclusion (e.g., increased interpersonal distance or averted gaze) and motivated them to act to restore and maintain belongingness were more likely to have survived and passed their genetic constitution on to modern humans (MacDonald and Leary 2005). In this way, gene forms that provided individuals with mechanisms to react appropriately to cues of social inclusion and exclusion would be perpetuated and eventually come to proliferate in the gene pool of the population, enshrining the need to belong as a central feature of human life (Baumeister and Leary 1995).

In recent years, much research has converged on the view that one such mechanism is pain (Panksepp 1998; Eisenberger and Lieberman 2004; MacDonald and Leary 2005; MacDonald and Jensen-Campbell 2011; Tchalova and Eisenberger 2015). A growing body of work supports the idea that social pain – the sense of hurt that stems from social rejection, loss, or the failure to obtain desired social rewards – is elaborated by the same neurophysiological mechanisms that underlie the aversive experience of physical pain. That is, hurt feelings are literal and real; social distress signals an alarm by activating feelings of pain, thereby drawing our attention to the threatening situation that must be remedied and thus limiting injury (Eisenberger and Lieberman 2004; MacDonald 2009).

There is considerable evidence for this overlap between physical and social pain. The anguish associated with injury to social bonds is often expressed in terms of physical pain; for example, people frequently describe the loss of an intimate other, a lover's slight, or exclusion by admired peers as causing "heartbreak," "wounding to the core," "crushing," or leaving "scars." Indeed, MacDonald and Leary (2005) found that many languages, as diverse as German and Inuktitut, rely on physical pain metaphors to convey the emotional distress of being rejected or devalued by others (i.e., what we commonly refer to in English as "hurt feelings"). However, this relation between social and physical pain increasingly appears to extend beyond metaphor, reflecting the physiological reality that social and physical pain share extensive overlap in neural and biochemical substrata (Panksepp 1998; MacDonald and Leary 2005; Tchalova and Eisenberger 2015; but see also Eisenberger 2015 for an in-depth discussion of caveats and controversial findings in the field). Neuroimaging studies show multiple points of commonality in brain regions activated during the experience of physical and socio-emotional pain (see Tchalova and Eisenberger 2015 for a recent review). For example, Eisenberger, Lieberman, and Williams (2003) took functional magnetic resonance imaging scans of participants' brains while they engaged in a computerized ball-toss game (Cyberball) with what participants believed were two other players (but were actually computer players preprogrammed by the researchers). Participants who stopped receiving ball tosses from their fellow players showed increased activation of the dorsal part of the anterior cingulate cortex and the anterior insula, brain structures involved in encoding physical pain unpleasantness (Rainville et al. 1997).

One corollary of the idea that social and physical pain systems share an extensive overlap in neurophysiological mechanisms is that any factors that reduce physical pain should exert similar effects on social pain. In one study (DeWall et al. 2010), participants were given acetaminophen or placebo every day for three weeks and asked to report on the amount of hurt feelings they experienced in the course of their daily social interactions. From day 15 on, individuals in the acetaminophen condition reported significantly attenuated levels of hurt feelings relative to the placebo group. In addition, a second group of participants who took acetaminophen every day for three weeks demonstrated less activation in pain-related brain regions when excluded by fellow ball players during Cyberball.

Given that reactions to social inclusion and exclusion have been evolutionarily linked to reactions as fundamental as pain, it seems reasonable to conclude that social conditions may also be deeply and profoundly tied to emotional experience. In the next section, we provide an overview of attachment theory, which proposes that humans' primary response to emotional distress, including social pain, is to turn to intimate others for support. Furthermore, internalization of the interactions we have with those intimate others powerfully impacts our experience and expression of emotion. We argue, therefore, that a sense of secure social connection is crucial for managing negative emotions (Mikulincer and Shaver 2007).

Attachment Theory: Normative Attachment Processes

John Bowlby (1973, 1980, 1982) argued that all human beings are endowed with an innate attachment-behavioural system, which drives people to seek proximity to caring and supportive persons (attachment figures) in times of danger or distress. As noted earlier, humans' very underdeveloped state at birth renders them highly reliant on their caregivers for support. Bowlby postulated that this evolutionary pressure favoured the emergence of a coordinated repertoire of care-seeking and caregiving behavioural responses displayed by infants and their mothers, respectively, which promoted the species' preservation by safeguarding the infants' welfare.

In this model, a child's confrontation with a physical or symbolic threat activates the primary attachment strategy of proximity seeking, bringing the child near its caregiver and so sheltering it from harm, alleviating distress, and evoking feelings of security. The attachment figure, therefore, is said to provide a safe haven that helps weather life's hardships. Once distress is sufficiently allayed, the child feels reassured enough to venture away from the attachment figure and engage in exploratory behaviour, using the attachment figure as a secure base to return to in the event that he or she encounters danger (Bowlby 1988).

Because the stakes of the attachment bond are quite literally life or death, this relationship is accompanied by some of life's most potent emotions (Bowlby 1982). While the attachment figure's presence is generally a source of intense relief and/or joy, his or her departure triggers a universal and highly predictable sequence of aversive emotional reactions. Bowlby observed that infants separated from their caregivers initially exhibit protest, which is characterized by acute distress, crying, vigorous searching for the attachment figure, and refusing others' comforting overtures. This stage is succeeded by a passive and desolate despair. If the separation continues, despair is followed by detachment, an apathetic avoidance of the caregiver when he or she eventually returns.

Although Bowlby's analysis centred on a discussion of attachment bonds in childhood, researchers have since extended the main tenets of his theory to the study of adult relationships and emotional experiences (Hazan and Shaver 1987; see Mikulincer and Shaver 2007 for a review). That is, the attachment system remains active in adulthood, but people other than parents, such as romantic partners, often play the role of attachment figures. It is important to note that, with the sophisticated conceptual abilities that emerge in adulthood, attachment strategies do not always necessitate the pursuit of physical proximity; they can also involve symbolic satisfaction – for example, by activating a mental representation of a caregiver (Shaver and Mikulincer 2002). This seeking of "symbolic proximity" (Mikulincer and Shaver 2007) may serve as a source of comfort and reinstate emotional equanimity in the attachment figure's absence.

Individual Differences in Attachment Security

In addition to delineating the normative patterns of attachment system functioning, Bowlby (1973) and his colleague, Mary Ainsworth (Ainsworth et al. 1978), described individual differences in the quality of attachment and the implications that these differences have for emotion regulation. A history of comforting interactions with attachment figures – whether caregivers in childhood or other attachment figures in adulthood (Mikulincer and Shaver 2007) – wherein one's bids for proximity and reassurance are attended to sensitively, fosters a sense of attachment security based on positive representations ("working models") of the self as lovable and of others as trustworthy and benevolent. However, the physical or emotional unavailability of attachment figures thwarts the emergence of attachment security and requires the individual to develop alternative strategies for managing distress (Mikulincer, Shaver, and Pereg 2003).

The shape that these strategies take depends on the precise nature of the caregiving deficits (Ainsworth et al. 1978; Mikulincer, Shaver, and Pereg 2003), and they can vary along the two orthogonal continua of attachment anxiety and attachment avoidance. Individuals high in attachment anxiety are theorized to experience erratic support and anxiety alleviation from their attachment figures. As a result, they develop a negative working model of themselves as being unworthy of love, leading to a relatively chronic sense of threat and distress, which in turn leads their attachment system to be chronically activated. This "attachment system hyperactivation" means that the system that promotes seeking proximity to attachment figures is essentially always "on." This manifests as an anxious, excessive, and persistent preoccupation with attachment figures and relationships, hypervigilant watch for signs of the attachment figure being unavailable, and an escalation of negative thoughts and emotions. Anxiously attached individuals display persistent worries about rejection and abandonment as well as the intense needs for reassurance and acceptance that are to be expected if their attachment system is continually active.

In contrast, individuals who are high in attachment avoidance are theorized to have caregivers who are consistently cold or who punish support seeking. As a result, avoidants, as they are called, form negative working models of others as being untrustworthy and suppress distressing emotions to minimize any activation of their attachment system ("attachment system deactivation"). This chronic deactivation of the attachment system essentially means that the system that promotes proximity seeking to attachment figures is effortfully kept "off" whenever threat or distress starts to switch it on. That is, avoidant individuals strive to maintain distance from attachment figures by downplaying their own emotional distress and need for support, instead emphasizing self-reliance, control, and independence. Avoidantly attached individuals display low emotionality and the disinterest in intimacy and emotional closeness that is to be expected if the attachment system is effortfully deactivated.

These hyperactivating and deactivating regulatory strategies characteristic of insecurely attached individuals are referred to as secondary attachment strategies because they are deployed after the primary attachment strategy, proximity seeking, has repeatedly failed to assuage distress (Shaver and Mikulincer 2002). Although people first learn to navigate attachment relationships in childhood, it should be noted that their working models of self and others remain changeable throughout life, allowing them to continuously revise and adjust in response to changes in the quality of their attachment interactions (see Mikulincer and Shaver 2007 for a review).

Attachment Insecurity and Political Orientation

Research on the need to belong suggests that insecurities at the interpersonal level might translate into predictable preferences at the political level. Baumeister and Leary (1995) forwarded the "substitution hypothesis," or the idea that belongingness needs can be met by multiple sources. That is, if one social entity does not satisfy their needs for belonging, individuals will seek out other sources that do (e.g., Spielmann et al. 2013). Further, research has suggested that when belongingness needs are frustrated at the interpersonal level, people will turn to non-interpersonal sources to receive at least a symbolic sense of connection (Aydin, Fischer, and Frey 2010; Knowles and Gardner 2008; McConnell et al. 2011). For example, Megan Knowles and Wendi Gardner (2008) showed that participants who had just written about an episode of social rejection demonstrated heightened identification with in-groups; this heightened identification buffered them from the negative emotional consequences of rejection. Thus, given that individuals high in attachment anxiety and avoidance experience chronic belongingness deficits, one compensatory strategy may be to identify more strongly with political in-groups. (This can be compared with Jasper's discussion in chapter 8 on the way in which a need for individual and group honour can motivate political action.)

Despite the theoretical link between attachment insecurity and group identification, there has been very little empirical research on the associations between the two dimensions of attachment insecurity and political orientation. What research has been conducted has focused on self-definition as liberal versus conservative in the American context, and it has produced very mixed results. Curtis Dunkel and Michelle Decker (2012) showed anxious attachment to be associated with liberalism, whereas Randy Thornhill and Corey Fincher (2007) found no relationship between anxious attachment and conservatism or liberalism. Christopher Weber and Christopher Federico (2007) showed no direct effect of attachment anxiety on political orientation, but did find evidence suggesting that anxious attachment was indirectly associated with higher levels of conservatism through links with associated variables. In the case of attachment avoidance, two separate studies found it to be associated with higher levels of liberalism (Dunkel and Decker 2012; Thornhill and Fincher 2007), although the effect of avoidance in the Dunkel and Decker data is not conventionally significant when accounting for variance from anxious attachment (Dunkel, personal communication). Weber and Federico (2007) found no relation between avoidance and conservatism or liberalism.

Thus, the research conducted so far on the relationship between attachment insecurity and political orientation is highly incomplete and mixed at best. One difficulty that has hindered this early research is the use of suboptimal attachment measurement instruments. Attachment orientation is commonly assessed in social psychology using self-report questionnaires. The measurement properties of these scales have improved over time, so studies that use older scales do not have the level of precision afforded by studies using more recent scales. For example, research by David Weise et al. (2008) suggests that attachment insecurity is associated with higher levels of conservatism, especially under conditions of threat. However, the measurement instrument used in this study does not allow insight into the relative contributions of anxious and avoidant attachment. Attachment researchers have achieved a fair degree of consensus that measurement instruments such as the Experiences in Relationships Questionnaire – Revised (Fraley, Waller, and Brennan 2000) are best suited to investigations of attachment insecurity using self-report measures.

In addition, conservatism/liberalism may be too broad a variable to use to gain much insight into the influence of attachment insecurity on political orientation. Instead, research may need to focus on how specific political issues intersect with the emotion-regulation strategies of anxious and avoidant individuals. Thus, we next consider the emotional lives of those with high levels of anxious and avoidant attachment, and speculate how these emotional profiles may influence political preferences. Such speculation should be treated very cautiously as we offer only theoretical conjectures, which need empirical validation. Our expertise is in interpersonal processes and not political orientation; thus, our speculation on the latter is likely to lack some degree of nuance and precision. Further, as attachment researchers, we are acutely aware of the danger of projecting our own political world views onto this work. It would be all too tempting to paint political philosophies we do not share as being motivated by insecurity, while simultaneously considering our own political views to be both objectively correct and impelled by feelings of security. Thus, the ideas below should be taken as a sort of conversation starter; they call for careful research rather than offer any kind of final word.

Emotional Sequelae of Anxious Attachment

Bowlby's extensive observations of attachment relationships led him to conclude that "the psychology and psychopathology of emotion is found to be in large part the psychology and psychopathology of affectional bonds" (Bowlby 1980, 40). While secure attachment representations enable honest acknowledgment and processing of emotional hurt (e.g., Cassidy et al. 2009), attachment insecurities impinge on the ability to effectively cope with emotion-eliciting events. According to attachment theory, individuals high on the dimension of attachment anxiety long for love and acceptance, but harbour deep-seated doubts about their worth and lovability, along with pervasive fears that their overtures for intimacy will be rejected (Mikulincer and Shaver 2007). This type of insecurity presumably stems from a history of frustrating interactions with highly inconsistent caregivers who were unreliably responsive to bids for proximity and reassurance and sometimes overly intrusive and unsupportive of independent exploration (Bowlby 1973; Ainsworth et al. 1978).

Without a secure sense of connection to an attachment figure, individuals high on the anxious attachment dimension are more prone to experience negative emotions, such as fear, depression, loneliness, sadness, and anxiety (e.g., Kobak and Sceery 1988; Simpson 1990; Magai, Distel, and Liker 1995; Cooper, Shaver, and Collins 1998; Wei, Heppner, and Mallinckrodt 2003; Diamond and Hicks 2005; Mikulincer and Orbach 1995). For example, in a study examining the psychological effects of missile attacks on a civilian population (Mikulincer, Florian, and Weller 1993), anxious individuals showed less emotional resilience in coping with adversity than securely attached persons (i.e., those lower in attachment anxiety). Further, the chronic negative emotional state of those higher in anxious attachment may increase access to a set of negative cognitions that further perpetuates distress. Negative affect induction leads individuals high in attachment anxiety to activate negative self-representations (Mikulincer 1998a) and attribute negative events to stable (unchangeable) and global (affecting all aspects of life) causes (Pereg and Mikulincer 2004). Altogether, compared to secure individuals, anxiously attached persons see life stressors as more threatening and enduring, and they appraise themselves as less capable of coping with these stressors (Mikulincer and Florian 1995, 1998).

One highly relevant line of enquiry has focused on attachment-style differences in regulating the terror of personal death (for reviews, see

Mikulincer and Florian 1998; Mikulincer and Shaver 2007), as might be made salient by factors like warnings of a terrorist attack or global environmental catastrophe. Research suggests that such reminders of mortality may leave anxiously attached individuals vulnerable to a sort of authoritarian mindset. For example, Mario Mikulincer and Victor Florian (2000) found that death reminders induced insecurely attached persons to make more severe judgments of, and endorse harsher punishments for, persons who had committed moral transgressions. Further, Mikulincer and Shaver (2001) showed that attachment anxiety was related to negative reactions to out-group members, possibly due to the propensity of anxious individuals to overestimate and be hypervigilant to potential sources of threat.

From a political-orientation perspective, individuals high in attachment anxiety see the world as a threatening and dangerous place, appraise themselves as unable to deal with that threat, and are chronically primed to search for the comfort of what Bowlby (1973) conceptualized as a stronger and wiser other. Arguably, then, political candidates who validate anxiously attached individuals' view of the world as dangerous (or heighten that sense through reminders of mortality), but present themselves as strong and unwavering in their ability to combat that threat may hold a special appeal. In essence, then, political leaders who offer the vigilance and protection akin to a strong parental figure may be playing to a very deep aspect of their more anxiously attached citizens.

In addition, anxiously attached individuals are especially vulnerable to mood-congruent memory biases during distress (Pereg and Mikulincer 2004). That is, when they are in a negative mood state (something that is relatively chronic for anxious individuals), they exhibit selective memory for negative events such as distressing newspaper headlines (Pereg and Mikulincer 2004). As a result, anxiously attached individuals may be particularly susceptible to the availability heuristic – the tendency to evaluate the probability of events based on the ease with which they come to mind. Anxious persons may overestimate the preponderance of negative events that receive disproportionate media coverage (such as violent gun crime) and be particularly swayed by political arguments that simultaneously describe these issues as catastrophes and promise to remedy them.

Given their history of receiving inconsistent care (a sort of variable reward schedule), anxious individuals learn that intensification of distress (i.e., an exaggerated protest response) may be a viable way to engage an erratic caregiver's attention and meet their unfulfilled needs for care and protection (Shaver and Mikulincer 2002). For example, anxious individuals may emphasize their sense of helplessness when their distress is aroused in a bid to win others' support and compassion (Mikulincer 1998a) – a strategy that comes at the expense of actual problem solving (Mikulincer and Shaver 2007). Arguably, a history of exaggerated helplessness in the personal sphere may also play out in the public sphere, as in the case of majority-group members who lay claim to being victims of discrimination.

One other potentially important aspect for the political world of the emotional experience of anxiously attached individuals is their propensity to experience feelings of shame (Magai, Distel, and Liker 1995; Lopez et al. 1997; Gross and Hansen 2000). While both guilt and shame are experienced in response to one's own misdeeds, guilt is characterized by a focus on the negative behaviour itself; attributing this behaviour to specific, unstable, and controllable aspects of the self; and feelings of self-efficacy in atoning for one's negative actions. In contrast, shame is characterized by a ruminative focus on one's personal shortcomings rather than the specific misbehaviour; attributing the negative behaviour to global, stable, and uncontrollable aspects of the self; and feelings of inferiority and helplessness (Mikulincer and Shaver 2005). In the words of C.A. Gross and N.E. Hansen, with shame "the whole self, rather than some correctable action or behaviour is experienced as flawed and intolerable" (Gross and Hansen 2000, 898). In essence, the shame of anxiously attached individuals appears to lead them to see their bad acts as indicating that they are bad, irredeemable people. If individuals who are high in anxious attachment generalize this view of negative actions to the actions of others, they may lend support to a harsh-punishment approach to issues such as crime. That is, if bad actors are seen as being evil and unlikely to change, then long prison sentences designed to remove those bad actors from the public sphere will be the response that seems to most naturally follow.

Arguably, one centrally important question that touches on both policy and attachment insecurity is how to manage the suffering of others. Questions around issues such as welfare and health care, for example, specifically call for a societal response to those in need. Bowlby (1982) postulated that lack of felt security and chronic preoccupation with unmet attachment needs hinder the engagement of humans' natural tendency to enact caregiving. Subsequent research has suggested that when confronted with the anguish of another person, individuals high in attachment anxiety become overwhelmed by crippling distress and self-focused ruminative worry (Mikulincer et al. 2001; Westmaas and

Silver 2001). How this personal discomfort with the distress of others influences the link between anxious attachment and support for social welfare policies is unclear, but it may depend on the extent to which anxiously attached individuals identify with those in distress.

When anxiously attached individuals feel part of the distressed group, or identify strongly with those who are in distress, they may advocate for policies that provide help. Given that anxiously attached individuals tend to view themselves as relatively helpless (Mikulincer 1998a; Shaver and Mikulincer 2002), they may see government support as being essential for resolving their difficulties. That is, the acute sense of vulnerability felt by those high in anxious attachment leads them to favour what could be called excessive care in interpersonal situations. For example, when anxiously attached individuals are placed in the role of caregiver, they often provide more care than those in distress actually want (Collins et al. 2006). Specifically, because anxiously attached persons feel relatively high levels of personal distress in caregiving situations, they are prone to overestimating the distress of others and providing a level of care consistent with that overestimation. Thus, if they are able to connect with others' suffering, or when they feel that they themselves are in need of government help, anxiously attached individuals may be particularly supportive of social welfare policies.

On the other hand, research suggests that anxiously attached individuals are often not able to fully engage with the suffering of others. For example, Mikulincer et al. (2001) observed in a series of studies that attachment anxiety was negatively related to empathy for others. Perhaps one strategy employed by anxiously attached persons to manage the personal distress they feel at the distress of others is to reduce empathy using strategies such as blaming the victim for his or her own suffering. In addition, anxiously attached individuals tend to exhibit what Mikulincer and Orbach (1995) have called unbridled "emotional spreading," wherein the evocation of one negative emotion leads to the activation of other negative, but unrelated, emotions. That is, a sadness-provoking episode may also elicit feelings of anger, fear, and disgust – emotions that are all likely to hinder helping. Such a response to distress seems likely to undermine support for social welfare policies and instead lead to support for policies that are consistent with an ideology of personal responsibility.

Overall, this analysis suggests that the difficulty that anxiously attached individuals have with down-regulating personal distress may be associated with a sense of victimization, harsh attitudes towards transgressors and those in need (at least when not identifying with their distress), and more attraction to leaders who project an image of strength. Of note, the issues we have identified fall largely into the category of social rather than economic concerns. As such, support for our conjectures may be found by examining political views on an issue-by-issue basis rather than on the basis of broader political identities.

Emotional Sequelae of Avoidant Attachment

Avoidant attachment is theorized to stem from a relational history in which expressions of distress and bids for reassurance were consistently met with impassiveness, rejection, or hostility from the caregiver, thereby fostering the belief that it may not be safe to express negative emotions (Ainsworth et al. 1978; Mikulincer, Shaver, and Pereg 2003). Like anxious persons, therefore, avoidant individuals lack a secure base on which to organize their emotional experiences; however, unlike anxious persons, they do not see that seeking support is a viable distress-management strategy (Shaver and Mikulincer 2002). As a result, avoidant individuals seek to restrict the experience, acknowledgment, and expression of distress and instead emphasize self-reliance to avoid attachment system activation and its attendant rejection and pain (Mikulincer and Shaver 2007). That is, if emotional distress activates the attachment system, then the solution for those who believe that attachment drives for security cannot be safely satisfied is to avoid the experience of strong emotion in the first place.

Therefore, the avoidant attachment style is characterized by deactivating affect-regulation strategies, including suppressing and denying negative feelings, thoughts, and memories, as well as making attempts to minimize exposure to strong emotion-eliciting events (Fraley, Davis, and Shaver 1998; Fuendeling 1998; Mikulincer and Shaver 2007). To achieve their goal of deactivating their attachment system, individuals high in attachment avoidance rely on both pre-emptive and post-emptive defensive processes in their confrontation with emotion-evoking stimuli (Mikulincer, Shaver, and Pereg 2003). Pre-emptive strategies circumvent experiences of emotional turmoil by deflecting attention away from distress-provoking material and excluding it from awareness and memory from the very beginning (Fraley, Davis, and Shaver 1998; Fraley, Garner, and Shaver 2000; Fraley and Brumbaugh 2007). However, if these strategies should fail, post-emptive defence mechanisms involve suppressing and dismissing extant emotionally charged memories, fears, and insecurities (Shaver and Mikulincer 2002).

Thus, a key feature of the experience of avoidantly attached individuals is a tendency to ignore and suppress emotional distress. This could have a number of implications in the political sphere. Similar to the argument made earlier for those high in anxious attachment, avoidants may be motivated to dismiss the suffering of others using mechanisms such as attributing blame. This strategy seems especially likely given that avoidant individuals tend to respond to distress arousal by establishing distance from other persons by overemphasizing self-other dissimilarity (Mikulincer, Orbach, and Iavnieli 1998).

Further, research suggests that when avoidant individuals attempt to suppress negative emotions, those emotions manifest themselves in subconscious or unintended ways. For example, avoidants exhibit what Mikulincer (1998b) has called "dissociated anger." Although avoidant participants in his study did not report feeling high levels of anger in response to anger-eliciting events, they exhibited more physiological signs of anger arousal, greater hostility, and a tendency to appraise other persons' negative behaviours as being motivated by hostility even when they were provided with clear indications of non-hostile intent. In addition, they reported a greater reliance on distancing strategies to cope with anger. Similarly, other research in the interpersonal domain shows that avoidants exhibit dissociation between emotional experience and behavioural strategies; for example, they may report feeling little distress in response to a transgressor's negative behaviour and yet act in an antagonistic manner (Cassidy et al. 2009). Indeed, avoidant attachment is consistently found to be associated with high levels of hostility (Kobak and Sceery 1988; Kobak et al. 1993; Mikulincer et al. 1993; Cooper, Shaver, and Collins 1998; Solomon et al. 1998) as well as contempt and disgust (Magai, Distel, and Liker 1995). The escapist responses employed by avoidants are likely to hinder constructive processing of the anger-provoking events and do not appear to be effective in alleviating tension (Mikulincer 1998b).

At a political level, this tendency to deny and externalize feelings of anger may be associated with lending less support to social welfare programs (but may also be associated with having less sympathy for any distress-relieving program, including calls for tax relief as a response to economic hardship). Overall, any argument that de-emphasizes the importance of emotional distress should appeal to those high in attachment avoidance. However, by consistently downplaying the effect that other individuals have on their own emotional experience, it is possible that avoidant persons may underestimate the role that their affective responses actually play in their political decision making, seeing it instead as guided solely by cold rationality.

Research indicates that the defensive strategies of individuals high in attachment avoidance are cognitively and physiologically effortful and prone to collapse (Mikulincer et al. 2000; Mikulincer, Dolev, and Shaver 2004; Gillath et al. 2005; Diamond, Hicks, and Otter-Henderson 2006). Indeed, research shows that avoidant individuals exhibit high levels of distress, depression, and feelings of helplessness when confronted with major life stressors (e.g., Berant, Mikulincer, and Florian 2001; Birnbaum et al. 1997; Solomon et al. 1998; Rodin et al. 2007). Thus, the emotional lives and political orientations of avoidantly attached individuals may be particularly sensitive to factors such as prevailing economic conditions. Their susceptibility to a sense of vulnerability under conditions of stress may increase their support for social welfare policies, particularly in difficult economic times. On the other hand, given their deep discomfort with the experience of personal insecurity, it is also plausible that avoidants may externalize their feelings of vulnerability, channelling those displaced negative emotions into hostility, blame, and punitive attitudes towards any scapegoats (e.g., immigrants) they perceive as an external threat to their stability.

One key feature of the emotional coping styles of avoidant individuals that seems especially relevant for political orientation is the value they place on independence and self-reliance. From an attachment perspective, those high in avoidant attachment display an overemphasis on independence that reflects a deeper fear that support will not be provided when it is asked for. In terms of political orientation, it might, at first glance, seem easiest to conclude that the premium placed on self-reliance would translate to traditionally conservative political positions, such as minimal government intervention in areas like taxation or gun control. However, traditionally liberal issues, such as access to abortion, can also be framed from a perspective of independence and non-interference. Overall, then, avoidantly attached individuals' emphasis on independence might best be framed as a libertarian value ultimately underpinned by unconscious fear that others simply cannot be relied on.

Conclusion

Our main goal in this chapter was to emphasize the central role of the interpersonal world in emotional life. We belong to a species that evolved to need each other. As such, our emotional reactions to the presence or absence of social support are as deep as they would be for any other life-or-death matter. In the most real sense, it hurts when we do not feel adequately connected to those around us. While it is true that people can cause us such great pain, attachment theory suggests that it is also true that other people are our greatest source of relief from pain. Individuals who feel that they can reliably turn to others for relief of their distress have an unparalleled emotional resource that allows them to experience the world as a less threatening place. However, those without such security reliably enact defensive strategies such as chronic neediness and relationship focus (i.e., attachment anxiety) or excessive self-reliance and unemotionality (i.e., attachment avoidance). Although our speculations as to how these forms of attachment insecurity influence political orientations may be off the mark in their specifics, it would be surprising to us if such a deep and fundamental aspect of human experience as attachment insecurity did not colour individuals' views of how the political world should be organized.

REFERENCES

Ainsworth, Mary D. Salter, Mary C. Blehar, Everett Waters, and Sally Wall. 1978. *Patterns of Attachment: Assessed in the Strange Situation and at Home.* Hillsdale, NJ: Lawrence Erlbaum Associates.

Aydin, Nilüfer, Peter Fischer, and Dieter Frey. 2010. "Turning to God in the Face of Ostracism: Effects of Social Exclusion on Religiousness." *Personality and Social Psychology Bulletin* 36 (6): 742–53. http://dx.doi.org/10.1177/0146167210367491.

Baumeister, Roy F., and Mark R. Leary. 1995. "The Need to Belong: Desire for Interpersonal Attachments as a Fundamental Human Motivation." *Psychological Bulletin* 117 (3): 497–529. http://dx.doi.org/10.1037/0033-2909.117.3.497.

Berant, Ety, Mario Mikulincer, and Victor Florian. 2001. "The Association of Mothers' Attachment Style and Their Psychological Reactions to the Diagnosis of Infant's Congenital Heart Disease." *Journal of Social and Clinical Psychology* 20 (2): 208–32. http://dx.doi.org/10.1521/jscp.20.2.208.22264.

Birnbaum, Gurit E., Idit Orr, Mario Mikulincer, and Victor Florian. 1997. "When Marriage Breaks Up: Does Åttachment Style Contribute to Coping and Mental Health?" *Journal of Social and Personal Relationships* 14 (5): 643–54. http://dx.doi.org/10.1177/0265407597145004.

Bowlby, John. 1973. *Separation: Anxiety and Anger*. Vol. 2 of *Attachment and Loss*. New York: Basic Books.

Bowlby, John. 1980. *Sadness and Depression*. Vol. 3 of *Attachment and Loss*. New York: Basic Books.

Bowlby, John. 1982. *Attachment*. 2nd ed. Vol. 1. of *Attachment and Loss*. New York: Basic Books.

Bowlby, John. 1988. *A Secure Base: Clinical Applications of Attachment Theory*. London: Routledge.

Cassidy, Jude, Phillip R. Shaver, Mario Mikulincer, and Shiri Lavy. 2009. "Experimentally Induced Security Influences Responses to Psychological Pain." *Journal of Social and Clinical Psychology* 28 (4): 463–78. http://dx.doi.org/10.1521/jscp.2009.28.4.463.

Collins, Nancy L., AnaMarie C. Guichard, Máire B. Ford, and Brooke C. Feeney. 2006. "Responding to Need in Intimate Relationships: Normative Processes and Individual Differences." In *Dynamics of Romantic Love: Attachment, Caregiving, and Sex*, edited by Mario Mikulincer and Gail S. Goodman, 149–89. New York: Guilford Press.

Coon, Carleton S. 1946. "The Universality of Natural Groupings in Human Societies." *Journal of Educational Sociology* 20 (3): 163–8. http://dx.doi.org/10.2307/2263780.

Cooper, M. Lynne, Phillip R. Shaver, and Nancy L. Collins. 1998. "Attachment Styles, Emotion Regulation, and Adjustment in Adolescence." *Journal of Personality and Social Psychology* 74 (5): 1380–97. http://dx.doi.org/10.1037/0022-3514.74.5.1380.

DeWall, C. Nathan, Geoff MacDonald, Gregory D. Webster, Carrie Masten, Roy F. Baumeister, Caitlin Powell, David Combs, David R. Schurtz, Tyler F. Stillman, Dianne M. Tice, and Naomi I. Eisenberger. 2010. "Acetaminophen Reduces Social Pain: Behavioral and Neural Evidence." *Psychological Science* 21 (7): 931–7. http://dx.doi.org/10.1177/0956797610374741.

Diamond, Lisa M., and Angela M. Hicks. 2005. "Attachment Style, Current Relationship Security, and Negative Emotions: The Mediating Role of Physiological Regulation." *Journal of Social and Personal Relationships* 22 (4): 499–518. http://dx.doi.org/10.1177/0265407505054520.

Diamond, Lisa M., Angela M. Hicks, and Kimberly Otter-Henderson. 2006. "Physiological Evidence for Repressive Coping among Avoidantly Attached Adults." *Journal of Social and Personal Relationships* 23 (2): 205–29. http://dx.doi.org/10.1177/0265407506062470.

Dunkel, Curtis S., and Michelle Decker. 2012. "Using Identity Style and Parental Identification to Predict Political Orientation." *Current Psychology* 31 (1): 65–78. http://dx.doi.org/10.1007/s12144-012-9131-8.

Eisenberger, Naomi I. 2015. "Social Pain and the Brain: Controversies, Questions, and Where to Go from Here." Annual Reviews of Psychology 66: 601-629. http://dx.doi.org/10.1146/annurev-psych-010213-115146.

Eisenberger, Naomi I., and Matthew D. Lieberman. 2004. "Why Rejection Hurts: A Common Neural Alarm System for Physical and Social Pain." *Trends in Cognitive Sciences* 8 (7): 294–300. http://dx.doi.org/10.1016/j.tics.2004.05.010.

Eisenberger, Naomi I., Matthew D. Lieberman, and Kipling D. Williams. 2003. "Does Rejection Hurt? An fMRI Study of Social Exclusion." *Science* 302 (5643): 290–2. http://dx.doi.org/10.1126/science.1089134.

Fraley, R. Chris, and Claudia C. Brumbaugh. 2007. "Adult Attachment and Preemptive Defenses: Converging Evidence on the Role of Defensive Exclusion at the Level of Encoding." *Journal of Personality* 75 (5): 1033–50. http://dx.doi.org/10.1111/j.1467-6494.2007.00465.x.

Fraley, R. Chris, Keith E. Davis, and Phillip R. Shaver. 1998. "Dismissing-Avoidance and the Defensive Organization of Emotion, Cognition, and Behavior." In *Attachment Theory and Close Relationships*, edited by Jeffry A. Simpson and W. Steven Rholes, 249–79. New York: Guilford Press.

Fraley, R. Chris, Joseph P. Garner, and Phillip R. Shaver. 2000. "Adult Attachment and the Defensive Regulation of Attention and Memory: Examining the Role of Preemptive and Postemptive Defensive Processes." *Journal of Personality and Social Psychology* 79 (5): 816–26. http://dx.doi.org/10.1037/0022-3514.79.5.816.

Fraley, R. Chris, Niels G. Waller, and Kelly A. Brennan. 2000. "An Item Response Theory Analysis of Self-Report Measures of Adult Attachment." *Journal of Personality and Social Psychology* 78 (2): 350–65. http://dx.doi.org/10.1037/0022-3514.78.2.350.

Fuendeling, James M. 1998. "Affect Regulation as a Stylistic Process within Adult Attachment." *Journal of Social and Personal Relationships* 15 (3): 291–322. http://dx.doi.org/10.1177/0265407598153001.

Gillath, Omri, Silvia A. Bunge, Phillip R. Shaver, Carter Wendelken, and Mario Mikulincer. 2005. "Attachment-Style Differences in the Ability to Suppress Negative Thoughts: Exploring the Neural Correlates." *NeuroImage* 28 (4): 835–47. http://dx.doi.org/10.1016/j.neuroimage.2005.06.048.

Gross, C.A., and N.E. Hansen. 2000. "Clarifying the Experience of Shame: The Role of Attachment Style, Gender, and Investment in Relatedness." *Personality and Individual Differences* 28 (5): 897–907. http://dx.doi.org/10.1016/S0191-8869(99)00148-8.

Hazan, Cindy, and Phillip R. Shaver. 1987. "Romantic Love Conceptualized as an Attachment Process." *Journal of Personality and Social Psychology* 52 (3): 511–24. http://dx.doi.org/10.1037/0022-3514.52.3.511.

Hazan, Cindy, and Phillip R. Shaver. 1994. "Attachment as an Organizational Framework for Research on Close Relationships." *Psychological Inquiry* 5 (1): 1–22. http://dx.doi.org/10.1207/s15327965pli0501_1.

Knowles, Megan L., and Wendi L. Gardner. 2008. "Benefits of Membership: The Activation and Amplification of Group Identities in Response to Social Rejection." *Personality and Social Psychology Bulletin* 34 (9): 1200–13. http://dx.doi.org/10.1177/0146167208320062.

Kobak, R. Rogers, Holland E. Cole, Rayanne Ferenz-Gillies, William S. Fleming, and Wendy Gamble. 1993. "Attachment and Emotion Regulation during Mother-Teen Problem Solving: A Control Theory Analysis." *Child Development* 64 (1): 231–45. http://dx.doi.org/10.2307/1131448.

Kobak, R. Rogers, and Amy Sceery. 1988. "Attachment in Late Adolescence: Working Models, Affect Regulation, and Representations of Self and Others." *Child Development* 59 (1): 135–46. http://dx.doi.org/10.2307/1130395.

Lopez, Frederick G., Mark R. Gover, Jennie Leskela, Eric M. Sauer, Lisa Schirmer, and James Wyssmann. 1997. "Attachment Styles, Shame, Guilt, and Collaborative Problem-Solving Orientations." *Personal Relationships* 4 (2): 187–99. http://dx.doi.org/10.1111/j.1475-6811.1997.tb00138.x.

MacDonald, Geoff. 2009. "Social Pain and Hurt Feelings." In *Cambridge Handbook of Personality Psychology*, edited by P.J. Corr and G. Matthews, 541–55. Cambridge: Cambridge University Press. http://dx.doi.org/10.1017/CBO9780511596544.034.

MacDonald, Geoff, and Lauri A. Jensen-Campbell, eds. 2011. *Social Pain: Neuropsychological and Health Implications of Loss and Exclusion*. Washington, DC: APA Books. http://dx.doi.org/10.1037/12351-000.

MacDonald, Geoff, and Mark R. Leary. 2005. "Why Does Social Exclusion Hurt? The Relationship between Social and Physical Pain." *Psychological Bulletin* 131 (2): 202–23. http://dx.doi.org/10.1037/0033-2909.131.2.202.

Magai, Carol, Nancy Distel, and Renee Liker. 1995. "Emotion Socialisation, Attachment, and Patterns of Adult Emotional Traits." *Cognition and Emotion* 9 (5): 461–81. http://dx.doi.org/10.1080/02699939508408976.

McConnell, Allen R., Christina M. Brown, Tonya M. Shoda, Laura E. Stayton, and Colleen E. Martin. 2011. "Friends with Benefits: On the Positive Consequences of Pet Ownership." *Journal of Personality and Social Psychology* 101 (6): 1239–52. http://dx.doi.org/10.1037/a0024506.

Mikulincer, Mario. 1998a. "Adult Attachment Style and Affect Regulation: Strategic Variations in Self-Appraisals." *Journal of Personality and Social Psychology* 75 (2): 420–35. http://dx.doi.org/10.1037/0022-3514.75.2.420.

Mikulincer, Mario. 1998b. "Adult Attachment Style and Individual Differences in Functional versus Dysfunctional Experiences of Anger." *Journal of*

Personality and Social Psychology 74 (2): 513–24. http://dx.doi.org/10.1037/0022-3514.74.2.513.

Mikulincer, Mario, Gurit Birnbaum, David Woddis, and Orit Nachmias. 2000. "Stress and Accessibility of Proximity-Related Thoughts: Exploring the Normative and Intraindividual Components of Attachment Theory." *Journal of Personality and Social Psychology* 78 (3): 509–23. http://dx.doi.org/10.1037/0022-3514.78.3.509.

Mikulincer, Mario, Tamar Dolev, and Philip R. Shaver. 2004. "Attachment-Related Strategies during Thought Suppression: Ironic Rebounds and Vulnerable Self-Representations." *Journal of Personality and Social Psychology* 87 (6): 940–56. http://dx.doi.org/10.1037/0022-3514.87.6.940.

Mikulincer, Mario, and Victor Florian. 1995. "Appraisal of and Coping with a Real-Life Stressful Situation: The Contribution of Attachment Styles." *Personality and Social Psychology Bulletin* 21 (4): 406–14. http://dx.doi.org/10.1177/0146167295214011.

Mikulincer, Mario, and Victor Florian. 1998. "The Relationship between Adult Attachment Styles and Emotional and Cognitive Reactions to Stressful Events." In *Attachment Theory and Close Relationships*, edited by Jeffry A. Simpson and W. Steven Rholes, 143–65. New York: Guilford Press.

Mikulincer, Mario, and Victor Florian. 2000. "Exploring Individual Differences in Reactions to Mortality Salience: Does Attachment Style Regulate Terror Management Mechanisms?" *Journal of Personality and Social Psychology* 79 (2): 260–73. http://dx.doi.org/10.1037/0022-3514.79.2.260.

Mikulincer, Mario, Victor Florian, and Aron Weller. 1993. "Attachment Styles, Coping Strategies, and Posttraumatic Psychological Distress: The Impact of the Gulf War in Israel." *Journal of Personality and Social Psychology* 64 (5): 817–26. http://dx.doi.org/10.1037/0022-3514.64.5.817.

Mikulincer, Mario, Omri Gillath, Vered Halevy, Neta Avihou, Shelly Avidan, and Nitzan Eshkoli. 2001. "Attachment Theory and Reactions to Others' Needs: Evidence that Activation of the Sense of Attachment Security Promotes Empathic Responses." *Journal of Personality and Social Psychology* 81 (6): 1205–24. http://dx.doi.org/10.1037/0022-3514.81.6.1205.

Mikulincer, Mario, and Israel Orbach. 1995. "Attachment Styles and Repressive Defensiveness: The Accessibility and Architecture of Affective Memories." *Journal of Personality and Social Psychology* 68 (5): 917–25. http://dx.doi.org/10.1037/0022-3514.68.5.917.

Mikulincer, Mario, Israel Orbach, and Daria Iavnieli. 1998. "Adult Attachment Style and Affect Regulation: Strategic Variations in Subjective Self-Other Similarity." *Journal of Personality and Social Psychology* 75 (2): 436–48. http://dx.doi.org/10.1037/0022-3514.75.2.436.

Mikulincer, Mario, and Philip R. Shaver. 2001. "Attachment Theory and Intergroup Bias: Evidence That Priming the Secure Base Schema Attenuates Negative Reactions to Out-Groups." *Journal of Personality and Social Psychology* 81 (1): 97–115. http://dx.doi.org/10.1037/0022-3514.81.1.97.

Mikulincer, Mario, and Philip R. Shaver. 2005. "Attachment Theory and Emotions in Close Relationships: Exploring the Attachment-Related Dynamics of Emotional Reactions to Relational Events." *Personal Relationships* 12 (2): 149–68. http://dx.doi.org/10.1111/j.1350-4126.2005.00108.x.

Mikulincer, Mario, and Philip R. Shaver. 2007. *Attachment in Adulthood: Structure, Dynamics, and Change*. New York: Guilford Press.

Mikulincer, Mario, Phillip R. Shaver, and Dana Pereg. 2003. "Attachment Theory and Affect Regulation: The Dynamics, Development, and Cognitive Consequences of Attachment-Related Strategies." *Motivation and Emotion* 27 (2): 77–102. http://dx.doi.org/10.1023/A:1024515519160.

Panksepp, Jaak. 1998. *Affective Neuroscience: The Foundations of Human and Animal Emotions*. New York: Oxford University Press.

Pereg, Dana, and Mario Mikulincer. 2004. "Attachment Style and the Regulation of Negative Affect: Exploring Individual Differences in Mood Congruency Effects on Memory and Judgment." *Personality and Social Psychology Bulletin* 30 (1): 67–80. http://dx.doi.org/10.1177/0146167203258852.

Rainville, Pierre, Gary H. Duncan, Donald D. Price, Benoît Carrier, and M. Catherine Bushnell. 1997. "Pain Affect Encoded in Human Anterior Cingulate but Not Somatosensory Cortex." *Science* 277 (5328): 968–71. http://dx.doi.org/10.1126/science.277.5328.968.

Reiss, Ira L. 1986. "A Sociological Journey into Sexuality." *Journal of Marriage and the Family* 48 (2): 233–42. http://dx.doi.org/10.2307/352390.

Rodin, Gary, Andrew Walsh, Camilla Zimmermann, Lucia Gagliese, Jennifer Jones, Frances A. Shepherd, Malcolm Moore, Michal Braun, Allan Donner, and Mario Mikulincer. 2007. "The Contribution of Attachment Security and Social Support to Depressive Symptoms in Patients with Metastatic Cancer." *Psycho-Oncology* 16 (12): 1080–91. http://dx.doi.org/10.1002/pon.1186.

Shaver, Phillip R., and Mario Mikulincer. 2002. "Attachment-Related Psychodynamics." *Attachment & Human Development* 4 (2): 133–61. http://dx.doi.org/10.1080/14616730210154171.

Simpson, Jeffry A. 1990. "Influence of Attachment Styles on Romantic Relationships." *Journal of Personality and Social Psychology* 59 (5): 971–80. http://dx.doi.org/10.1037/0022-3514.59.5.971.

Solomon, Zahava, Kami Ginzburg, Mario Mikulincer, Yuval Neria, and Abraham Ohry. 1998. "Coping with War Captivity: The Role of Attachment Style." *European Journal of Personality* 12 (4): 271–85. http://dx.doi.org/10.1002/(SICI)1099-0984(199807/08)12:4<271::AID-PER309>3.0.CO;2-U.

Spielmann, Stephanie S., Samantha Joel, Geoff MacDonald, and Aleksandr Kogan. 2013. "Ex Appeal: Current Relationship Quality and Emotional Attachment to Ex-Partners." *Social Psychological & Personality Science* 4 (2): 175–80. http://dx.doi.org/10.1177/1948550612448198.

Tchalova, Kristina, and Naomi I. Eisenberger. 2015. "How the Brain Feels the Hurt of Heartbreak: Examining the Neurobiological Overlap between Social and Physical Pain." In *Brain Mapping: An Encyclopedic Reference*, Vol. 3, edited by Arthur W. Toga, 15–20. Oxford: Elsevier.

Thornhill, Randy, and Corey L. Fincher. 2007. "What Is the Relevance of Attachment and Life History to Political Values?" *Evolution and Human Behavior* 28 (4): 215–22. http://dx.doi.org/10.1016/j.evolhumbehav.2007.01.005.

Way, Baldwin M., and Shelley E. Taylor. 2011. "Genetic Factors in Social Pain." In *Social Pain: Neuropsychological and Health Implications of Loss and Exclusion*, edited by Geoff MacDonald and Laurie A. Jensen-Campbell, 95–119. Washington, DC: APA Books. http://dx.doi.org/10.1037/12351-004.

Weber, Christopher, and Christopher M. Federico. 2007. "Interpersonal Attachment and Patterns of Ideological Belief." *Political Psychology* 28 (4): 389–416. http://dx.doi.org/10.1111/j.1467-9221.2007.00579.x.

Wei, Meifen, Puncky P. Heppner, and Brent Mallinckrodt. 2003. "Perceived Coping as a Mediator between Attachment and Psychological Distress: A Structural Equation Modeling Approach." *Journal of Counseling Psychology* 50 (4): 438–47. http://dx.doi.org/10.1037/0022-0167.50.4.438.

Weise, David R., Tom Pyszczynski, Cathy R. Cox, Jamie Arndt, Jeff Greenberg, Sheldon Solomon, and Spee Kosloff. 2008. "Interpersonal Politics: The Role of Terror Management and Attachment Processes in Shaping Political Preferences." *Psychological Science* 19 (5): 448–55. http://dx.doi.org/10.1111/j.1467-9280.2008.02108.x.

Westmaas, Johann L., and Roxane C. Silver. 2001. "The Role of Attachment in Responses to Victims of Life Crises." *Journal of Personality and Social Psychology* 80 (3): 425–38. http://dx.doi.org/10.1037/0022-3514.80.3.425.

7 Revising Emotions of Three Post-9/11 Moments

JOSEPH F. FLETCHER AND JENNIFER HOVE

The last fifteen years have seen a wealth of research involving emotional responses to terror and war. While the role of emotions in conflict and reconciliation has long occupied scholarly interest, the post-9/11 political context has generated new work, particularly on the relationships between information and emotion, as Western publics have attempted to make sense of new political realities. The explicitly emotional components of political responses to terrorism and the subsequent missions in Afghanistan and Iraq have been on clear display since 9/11: Western citizens and governments have expressed shock, fear, anger, and sadness as well as pride and solidarity.

We approach our work with the basic understanding that these emotions have been shaped by the political information on offer. Governments and politicians have, of course, selectively used information as part of their emotional appeals to buttress support both for security policy that limits domestic freedoms and for the exercise of military force abroad. But even the potent images associated with 9/11 and the war on terror, such as burning buildings and flag-draped coffins, carry basic information that gives rise to heightened emotional response.

It is against this backdrop that we reconfigure some of our previous work, looking to achieve a better understanding of the role of emotion in public support for military engagement (Fletcher, Bastedo, and Hove 2009; Fletcher and Hove 2012). What began with a focus on the influence of information in determining public support for the war in Afghanistan evolved to emphasize the role of emotion. While this work documents the interplay of information and emotion, it does so without decomposing the associations we find to expose the causal mechanisms involved. Since then, we have come to appreciate that emotion typically mediates the effect of information. In this chapter, we extend what we have done previously by focusing directly on some of the ways in which emotion has mediated the influence of information on public preferences. (This can be read in tandem with James Jasper's discussion in chapter 8 to develop a comparison of the process of preference formation and political action.)

The focus of our discussion here is thus on three moments in the post-9/11 era. They are not arranged chronologically, but rather in terms of the complexity of the emotions involved. The first case is the simplest. It concerns the political marketing of the Afghanistan mission in early 2007. The Canadian government, in an effort to stave off rapidly declining public support, mounted an information campaign aimed at instilling greater pride in the Canadian mission (Fletcher, Bastedo, and Hove 2009). The second moment we consider came just a short time later, as the Canadian public struggled to come to terms with some of the human cost of military engagement in Afghanistan. As Canadian casualties increased from 2006 on, crowds of ordinary citizens gathered along overpasses on what became known as the Highway of Heroes, to stand with mixed emotion in silent tribute as the bodies of fallen soldiers were brought home to their families (Fletcher and Hove 2012). The third moment we revisit draws on data that have languished, incompletely analysed, in our files. They were gathered in the emotional distress of the weeks immediately following the attacks of 9/11. As such, their analysis involves a more complex emotional story.

Theoretical Considerations

Consistent with common practice (Druckman and McDermott 2008), our paper on the political marketing of the Afghan mission (Fletcher, Bastedo, and Hove 2009) treats information and emotion as interacting to produce public preferences. This approach implies that emotion acts as a moderator variable, not as a mediator. In simple terms, a moderator variable influences the strength (and/or direction) of a relationship between two other variables, whereas a mediator explains the relationship between two other variables (Baron and Kenny 1986). Theoretically and conceptually, then, "A moderation effect in a causal model postulates 'when' or 'for whom' an independent variable most strongly (or weakly) causes the dependent variable" (Wu and Zumbo 2008, 370). As such, a moderator is generally conceptualized as an "inanimate attribute (i.e. gender or ethnicity), a relatively stable trait (i.e. personality type or disposition), or a relatively unchangeable background, environmental or contextual variable (i.e. parents' education level or neighborhood)" (379). Emotion does not quite fit into these categories.

Although the interaction of cognition and affect in determining political attitudes often appears in the literature (Way and Masters 1996a), on reflection it makes perhaps more sense to view emotion as a response to political information, not as an auxiliary variable that modifies the causal impact of the information. In other words, emotion can perhaps be better conceptualized as a mediator, not a moderator (Baron and Kenny 1986). As Amery Wu and Bruno Zumbo (2008, 368) further explain, "A mediator is a third variable that links a cause and an effect." Hence, "in mediation an analyst attempts to identify the intermediary process that leads from the independent variable to the dependent variable" (369). Moreover, a mediator is "often a cognitive, affective, physiological, or motivational *state* that functions as a person's psychological process after receiving a stimulus such as intervention treatments" (373). This conceptualization is closer to what we typically have in mind when we think about the role of emotion in determining public preferences. It also accords with the tried and true political strategy of using rhetoric and information as a means of shifting popular support for a given policy by eliciting specific emotional responses. The 2007 information campaign mounted by the Canadian government is a case in point.

The basic theoretical idea that motivates the following analyses, therefore, is to consider emotion as a mediating or intervening variable between information and support for war. Graphically, this might be most simply depicted as Information → Emotional response → Support for war. We use this simple model to discuss the dynamics of public opinion underpinning support for the use of military force on three post-9/11 occasions. In the first, we extend our earlier analysis using cross-sectional data to show that the effect of information provided by the government is mediated by the influence of emotion. In the second, we present data from a survey experiment to reveal a bit more of the causal mechanism. And in the third, we rely again on cross-sectional data to trace some of the ways that emotion can mediate the effect of information on public preferences.

Emotion and Support for War

Ideas concerning the effects of information on emotion find expression in popular understanding about politics – namely, that "leaders long have manipulated emotion for their benefit" (Way and Masters 1996b, 48). Take, for instance, voting. The potential for specific kinds of information to alter emotional response and hence political favour may explain why "candidates kiss babies; utilize balloons, bands, and banners at political rallies; and fundraise over lunch or dinner" (ibid.). Such behaviour extends, of course, well beyond the campaign trail. Writing about emotion and the war on terror, Emma Hutchinson and Roland Bleiker (2008) document the manner in which leaders manipulated citizens' fear to justify particular policy approaches. They argue, in particular, that "the US government and its allies employed a strong rhetoric of evil to gain broad support for their 'war on terror,' most notably for their invasions of Afghanistan and Iraq. Such an appropriation of emotions builds a sense of identity and political community that rests on maintaining a stark separation between a safe haven inside and a threatening outside" (ibid., 57). This perspective points to two related questions concerning the role of emotion in determining support for war. First, does emotion mediate between political information and public preferences? And second, are different emotions involved, such as fear, anger, and pride?

Emotion as Mediator

Treating emotion as a mediating variable is a familiar approach among scholars working on questions of political marketing and communication (Brader 2006) as well as those employing methods of experimentation (Brader, Valentino, and Suhay 2008). Framing effects are also increasingly seen as being mediated by emotion (Gross 2008; Fletcher and Schatten 2012). The fundamental logic remains the same: that information – presented as advertising, political rhetoric, or imagery – has the potential to elicit particular emotions, which in turn influence political evaluations. In keeping with the wide array of studies employing this basic approach, the content of information under investigation also varies – from perceived threat (Halperin, Canetti-Nisim, and Hirsch-Hoefler 2009; Merolla and Zechmeister 2009), to government communications (Hutchinson and Bleiker 2008), to imagery (Huddy and Gunnthorsdottir 2000).

Notwithstanding differences in the type of information being delivered (or by whom), its effects on emotional response bring to mind the long-standing military tactic of "winning hearts and minds," which can be applied here. The underlying assumption is that political judgments have an emotional core. Appealing to citizens' cognitive understanding of a political issue, but failing to address its emotional "heart" – especially on a contentious and fraught question – is not likely to be a winning political strategy (Fletcher, Bastedo, and Hove 2009). Political scientists are increasingly embracing this conclusion in their own work as "it seems clear that politics is about feeling as much as it is about thinking" (Civettini and Redlawsk 2009, 125).

The Influence of Discrete Emotions

That emotion can mediate the relationship between information and public preferences also gives rise to the question of what effect particular emotions are thought to have on support for, or opposition to, war. Prior work on attitudes towards the Iraq war draws on appraisal tendency theory (Lerner and Keltner 2001)[1] to differentiate between the effects of anxiety and anger (Huddy, Feldman, and Cassesse 2007). Specifically, Leonie Huddy and her colleagues find that anxious people are more likely to oppose a war than angry individuals. In the American context, the same effects of anxiety have been found in research concerning reactions to 9/11 and opposition to military intervention in Afghanistan (Huddy et al. 2005). Subsequent studies have confirmed the finding that anger predicts support for military action, while fear predicts avoidance behaviours (Cheung-Blunden and Blunden 2008), and these studies have extended the research agenda to include "prosocial tendencies" such as empathy, guilt, and moral outrage (Pagano and Huo 2007).

An interesting dimension to this discussion, however, is whether findings travel well to other "emotional communities" (Rosenwein 2006). In our experimental work on the influence of war-based imagery on support for the Afghan mission among Canadians, we find the effects of anger and anxiety to be slim at best (Fletcher and Hove 2012). Rather, in the Canadian case, it is a composite emotion of sadness and pride that determines attitudes towards military engagement; this will be discussed in greater detail below. This discontinuity underscores the importance of both examining the influence of discrete emotions and understanding the particularity of political and emotional communities.

Investigating the Three Moments

In approaching our three post-9/11 moments, we consider not only the influence of political information and emotion but also people's basic orientation towards politics, which we capture through measures of political realism. Together, these three variables of information, emotion, and orientation act as the cornerstones of our models. Accordingly, we investigate a number of hypotheses. First, we anticipate varying levels of information to be associated with differing policy preferences. The effect of emotion should rival that of information, although we expect it to be weaker than that of political orientation. Further, we expect emotion to mediate the influence of information on political attitudes. Last, in addition to its direct effect on support for war, we expect emotion to have an indirect effect via political orientation. In other words, we anticipate that emotion will influence attitudes towards specific military engagements, both directly and indirectly, through general "hawk vs. dove" orientations (to borrow common parlance).

As do Eran Halperin, Daphna Canetti-Nisim, and Sivan Hirsch-Hoefler (2009), we test these hypotheses using structural equation modelling (SEM), which provides us with a statistical approach to investigating plausible patterns of mediation (Shrout and Bolger 2002, 422). Moreover, SEM allows us to conduct both measurement and predictive analysis using maximum likelihood estimation. In the following analyses, rectangles represent observed or manipulated variables, while ovals represent latent variables constructed of multiple observed indicators (not shown). Effects are shown as standardized coefficients on the arrows and can be interpreted as regression weights.

Moment 1: Marketing the Afghan Mission

Looking first to our 2007 cross-sectional data, political information is conceptualized to reflect a major information campaign by the federal government of Canada to "educate" the public on the motivations for undertaking the mission in Afghanistan as well as the potential consequences of withdrawal. Specifically, in early 2007, government communications on the mission began to focus on the multilateral nature of international efforts in Afghanistan, the risk of Taliban resurgence, and the importance of rebuilding and supporting human rights (Fletcher, Bastedo, and Hove 2009). Political information is thus measured as an additive scale of indicators that tap these government "talking points" ($\alpha > .8$).[2] (See Appendix A for the wording of the questions.)

In using survey data collected by a national polling firm, we are limited in our analysis to using pride as an indicator of emotional response. Realism is measured by respondents' preference that the Canadian military act as a combat-ready force rather than serving exclusively in a peacekeeping capacity. We use a latent variable of three indicators of support for the Afghan mission: support for the initial deployment of troops, support for a long-term engagement, and willingness to bear casualties. The investigation is also placed in the context of a number of additional factors, including region, party identification, age, gender, and education. While these demographic variables are controlled for in the following model, for the sake of simplicity in presenting results, their effects are not shown.[3]

Turning to Figure 7.1, we find that political information, pride, and realism all positively influence support for Canada's engagement in Afghanistan, with the strongest effect being one's agreement with the information communicated by government.[4] This is to be expected: the more a respondent has internalized the federal government's preferred narrative on the motivations for using a military solution in Afghanistan, the more supportive he or she is of the mission. A positive emotive response – in this case, pride – also leads to greater support for Canada's role in Afghanistan, as does an orientation towards realism, or the belief in Canada's military as a combat-ready fighting force.

Beyond these relatively straightforward findings, Figure 7.1 also shows that both emotion and realism mediate the effects of information on support for the mission in Afghanistan. The relationship from government information to pride, however, is far stronger than that from information to realism, as shown by the respective standardized coefficients of .60 and .14.[5] These findings align well with the government's communications strategy. In the face of mounting opposition to the war in 2007, the Canadian government sought to disseminate greater information on the mission in an attempt to emphasize the existence of a new "post-Pearsonian" reality, in which the nature of global threats demanded something more than peacekeeping. Moreover, government officials attempted to give Canadians something to feel good about, particularly around the rights of women and children and giving hope to "the long-suffering Afghan people," as stated in a speech by former prime minister Stephen Harper (quoted in Fletcher, Bastedo, and Hove 2009).

The results in Figure 7.1 show greater support for this second strategy focusing on emotional connection, and they likely tell us something about the nature of political persuasion. Although the federal government sought to influence basic political orientations among the Canadian public, this proved difficult, as can be gathered from the consistently low levels of support for the Afghan mission from 2007 on.[6]

Figure 7.1. Mediating Role of Emotion on Support for the Afghan Mission (2007 Cross-Sectional Analysis)

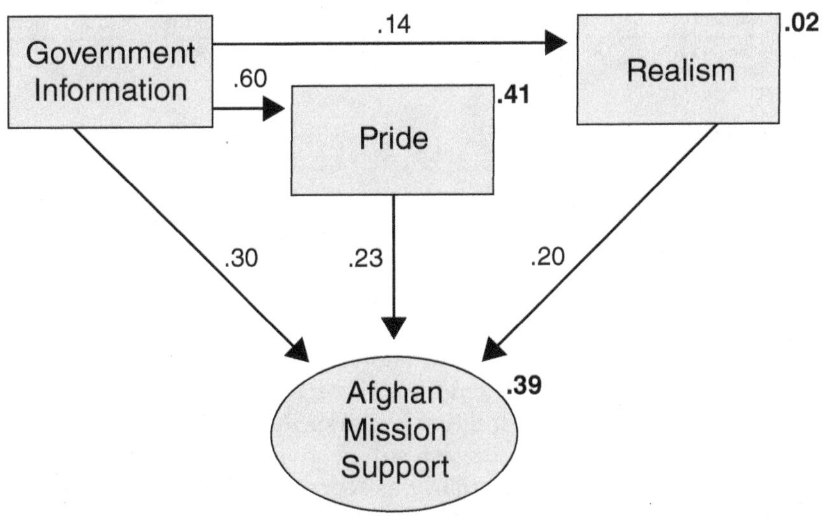

chi-square = 114.269; *df* = 79; *p* = .006; RMSEA = .021 (.012–.029)

Source: The Strategic Counsel – Globe and Mail/CTV national poll, July 2007.

The government's information campaign seems to have had a greater effect on Canadians' emotive responses towards the political considerations of the mission.

Moreover, contrary to expectations, we do not find emotion to have an indirect effect on support for the mission via respondents' orientation towards realism.[7] This suggests, instead, that the effect of government information on support for the mission in Afghanistan had two distinct mediation processes: one through emotion and the other through changes towards more "realist" orientations. And again, the point can be made that the former mediation had a greater influence on perceptions of war, as shown by examining the indirect effects in Table 7.1. When disaggregating information's indirect effect by its two "routes," we see that the path via emotion represents a more substantial proportion (nearly 30%) of the total effect than that via realism (almost 6%). Of course, the largest proportion of the impact of information on support

Table 7.1 Standardized Direct, Indirect, and Total Effects of Information on Support for the Afghan Mission (2007 Cross-Sectional Analysis)

Type of effect	Standardized coefficient	Proportion of total effects
Direct	.2969	.6457
Indirect	.1629	.3543
Via emotion	.1359	.2956
Via realism	.027	.0587
Total	.4598	1.0000

Source: Derived from Figure 7.1.

for the mission is direct (approximately 65%). Nevertheless, the effect of information via through emotion is roughly half as big, while the indirect effect via basic orientation is markedly smaller.

What we conclude from these results is twofold. First, the effects of political information – particularly as represented by a major government communications campaign – are complex and may alter citizens' attitudes in several ways. Second, the influence of both emotion and political orientation underscores the extent to which political attitudes are shaped by both emotive and cognitive processes. Appreciating these pathways can deepen our understanding of the bases of support for military engagement and bring more specifically into focus the role of emotion in mediating policy preference.

Moment 2: Dealing with the Human Cost of the Mission

Having demonstrated the basic plausibility of information affecting policy preferences via emotional responses, we now turn to an approach whereby information is not simply observed but also experimentally manipulated by randomly assigning respondents to condition.[8] This can establish the causal influence of information on emotion.[9] In this experimental analysis, the focus is on the emotions associated with dealing with the casualties of war. Thus, political information is presented as images of flag-draped coffins, a particularly potent example of war-based imagery that figures prominently in studies of public support for war (Gartner 2008).[10] We learned by conducting over 125 qualitative interviews along the Highway of Heroes that the dominant emotive response elicited in witnessing the repatriation of Canadian war dead is a composite emotional response of sadness and pride. In a survey-based experiment, we therefore include the appropriate emotional indicators and use a multiplicative term to estimate this sad-proud hybrid (Fletcher and Hove 2012). The same measures of realism and support for the Afghan mission are again employed, just as in the preceding investigation. Again, we control for a host of demographic factors – in this case, gender, political partisanship, and objective knowledge. As in the previous section, these variables are present in the analysis, but not shown here.

As we see in Figure 7.2, information again has a direct influence on support for the Afghan mission, although this time, the direct effects of emotion and political orientation are stronger.[11] And again, we see that emotion mediates the effect of information in determining attitudes towards military engagement. Further, consistent with what we originally anticipated, here there is a secondary mediation of the effect of information on support for the mission via emotion *and* realism. These effects are, of course, in addition to the direct effect of information on support for the mission and are net of controls for the available demographic variables.

In other words, exposure to an image of flag-draped coffins positively influences support for the mission in Afghanistan both on its own accord, and indirectly, through an emotional "hybrid" response of sadness and pride. This emotive response, in turn, produces a change in one's orientation towards realism, which also positively influences support. This finding of a positive effect stemming from having viewed the image of flag-draped coffins is precisely the opposite of what is found in the United States (Gartner 2008) and again speaks to the importance of considering distinctions among particular emotional communities. As these results suggest, there may be vital differences in our social and historical understanding of war between and even within political contexts.

In contrast to the findings presented in the previous section, it is also important to note that there is no direct pathway from information to realism.[12] Substantively, the effect of information provided by the experimental manipulation is mediated by emotion, but not realism. Some portion of the effect of emotion, however, is nevertheless mediated by a change in realism. By conventional standards, both indirect effects must be regarded as small, as shown in Table 7.2. Nevertheless, the contribution of information's indirect effect that can be attributed to emotion is markedly greater than the contribution of political orientation. The

Figure 7.2. Mediating Role of Emotion on Support for the Afghan Mission (2009 Experimental Analysis)

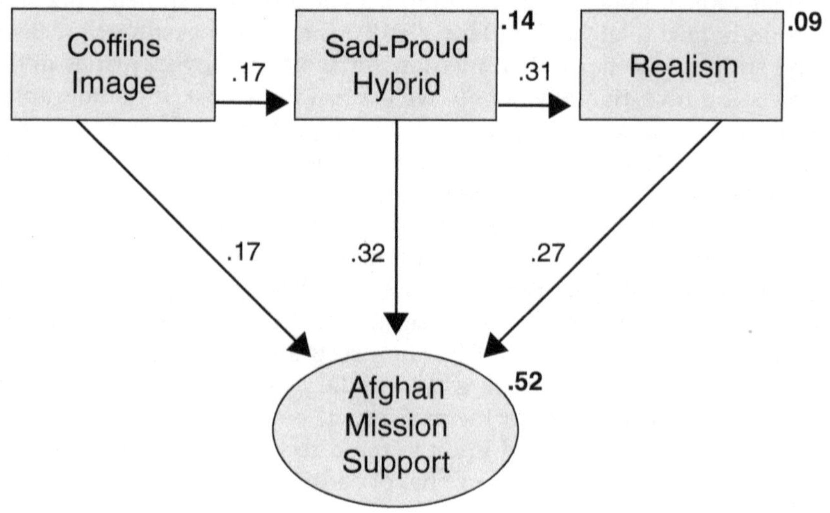

Source: Authors' experimental survey.

former pathway accounts for nearly a quarter of information's total effect on support for the mission. By comparison, the indirect effect via political orientation represents less than 6% of the total effect.

Again, these findings help to clarify the potential mediating role of emotion in shaping support for the use of military force. In this case, the emotions involved are more complex, but the mediation effect remains. And importantly, having been derived from an experimental approach, they allow the link between information and emotion to be established as causal. Moreover, the disparity between this model and the first – in the link between emotion and realism – suggests that the receipt of political information may influence both cognition and affect, as is commonly understood (first model), or it may influence cognition *through* emotional response and, consequently, a different interpretation (present model).

Table 7.2 Standardized Direct, Indirect, and Total Effects of Information and Emotion on Support for the Afghan Mission (2009 Experimental Analysis)

	Information		Emotion	
Type of effect	Standardized coefficient	Proportion of total effect	Standardized coefficient	Proportion of total effect
Direct	.1652	.6762	.3157	.7922
Indirect	.0691	.2828	.0828	.2078
Via emotion	.0547	.2239	–	–
Via emotion and realism	.0144	.0589	–	–
Total	.2443	1.0000	.3985	1.0000

Source: Derived from Figure 7.2.

Moment 3: Distress in the Wake of the Attack

We take as our third moment the months following 9/11. We reconsider public support for the war on terror at this iconic moment because it offers us a broader picture of the way in which emotion can mediate the influence of cognitive factors on policy preferences. Like our neighbours to the south, Canadians were severely shaken by the events of 11 September 2001. Survey data collected shortly thereafter show a similar degree of emotional distress in both countries, including disrupted sleep, work, and sex lives as well as seeking the support of a counsellor or health care professional.

The nub of our analysis remains a relationship between what respondents think to be the case (the information they have on hand) and their policy preferences. And once again, analysing the effects of information on emotion and political orientation along the lines we have used above shows us that emotion plays an important role in mediating the relationship between information and policy preferences. More specifically, we find that the complex relationship between information and views on public policy is clarified by the mediating role involving respondents' emotional responses.

In keeping with the political context in the months following 9/11, the operationalization of the variables is somewhat different in this case than in the previous ones. Political information is measured as respondents' appraisal of risk, or the perceived likelihood of threat, of another terrorist attack on North American soil. Emotion is operationalized by expressions of emotional distress. (See Appendix A for the wording of the questions.) Realism is measured by the respondents' willingness to give up freedom and sovereignty as part of the war on terror, a position related to support for aggressive foreign policy stances abroad (Merolla and Zechmeister 2009).[13] Support for war is now focused on the American-led war on terror more generally, rather than the mission in Afghanistan specifically.

Nevertheless, the basic analytic set-up remains essentially the same. What respondents know (information), feel (emotional distress), and prefer politically (realism) all directly influence support for military engagement. Information also has an indirect effect on foreign policy preferences via emotional response and political orientation. We again control for relevant demographic characteristics, including education, gender, urban residence, age, and language (French/English), although these effects are not shown. Turning to Figure 7.3, we see an expected pattern emerging.[14] As in the previous cases, information, emotion, and realism all directly influence support for war, and again we see indirect effect of information via emotion and realism.

What is noteworthy in this case is that the indirect effects involving emotional distress and realism are positive, while the direct effect of emotion is negative. Together they take the form of statistical suppression (MacKinnon, Krull, and Lockwood 2000). In particular, emotional distress directly undercuts support for an aggressive response to terror (as shown by the standardized coefficient of –.21); however, the very same distress leads to greater support for political realism (.21), which in turn augments support for the use of military force (.52).[15] The former negative effect is consistent with the findings of Huddy et al. (2005, 2007): that in times of international conflict, emotion can lead to reluctance to strike back. Moreover, as shown in Table 7.3, information's effects – both direct and indirect – are relatively limited. Emotion, by contrast, has more substantial effects, both direct and indirect, on support for responding to terror. But as discussed above, the coefficients for its direct and indirect effects are in opposite directions, leading to suppression. As a result, the overall effect is sharply diminished. In short, the effects of emotion are complex: in addition to its positive indirect effects, emotional distress also leads to reticence at striking back at terrorism. The very same emotional response, in other words, supports retaliatory action on the one hand and undermines it on the other. A full picture of the influence of emotional distress entails both positive and negative effects. This finding of mutually offsetting effects may well have broader

Figure 7.3. Responding to Terror (2001 Cross-Sectional Analysis)

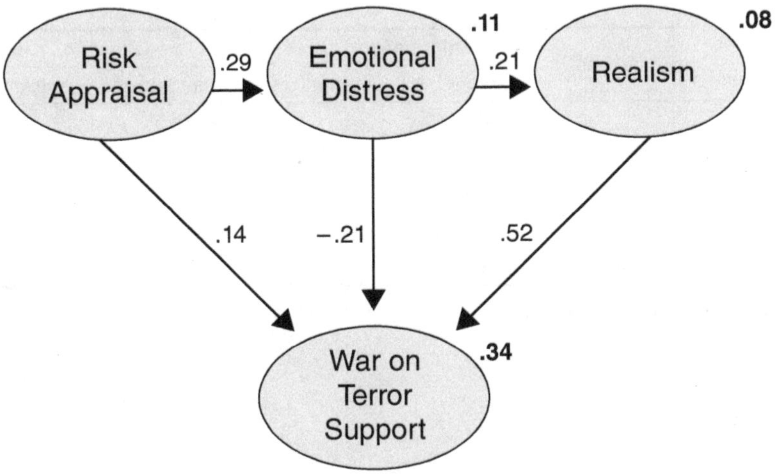

chi-square = 166.343; df = 87; p = .000; RMSEA = .028 (.021–.034)

Source: The Strategic Counsel – Maclean's/CBC national poll, December 2001.

implications for understanding how emotion shapes political attitudes, insofar as a "suppression system can explain why a theoretically interesting relation is not strong" (Shrout and Bolger 2002, 430).

Placing the investigation into the context of Canadian responses to terror in the months immediately following 9/11 allows us to accomplish three things. First, we are able to reinforce the findings of the two previous cases vis-à-vis a different (albeit related) context. Although the central variables are operationalized differently, in accord with the political realities of late 2001, our main findings pertaining to the relationship among information, emotion, and political orientation hold. Second, we are able to examine the mediating role of emotion in the context of a different set of emotions. While our first two cases involved pride (mixed with sadness in the second instance), this one explores emotional distress. And third, while we still find emotion functioning as an intervening factor between information and policy attitudes, the suppression effect found here brings to light a deeper level of complexity in the mediating role that emotion can play in determining political preference.

Table 7.3 Standardized Direct, Indirect, and Total Effects of Information and Emotion on Support for the War on Terror (2001 Cross-Sectional Analysis)[16]

	Information	Emotion
Type of effect	Standardized coefficient	Standardized coefficient
Direct	.1450	–.2085
Indirect	–.0284	.1105
Via emotion	–.0604	–
Via emotion and realism	.0320	–
Total	.1166	–.0980

Source: Derived from Figure 7.3.

Discussion

By approaching emotion as a mediating rather than a moderating variable, each of the three moments in the post-9/11 era that we have examined has added to our understanding of the ways in which emotion can influence foreign policy attitudes. Looking at the Canadian government's 2007 information campaign, we found evidence that emotion effectively supplements the role of information in forming public preferences. The information the government provided not only had a direct effect in increasing support for the Afghan mission but also did so indirectly by promoting a sense of pride in the mission. In this instance, the effects are relatively familiar in that they are consistent with the efforts that politicians and governments often make to influence public preferences.

In our second post-9/11 moment, emotion again played a mediating role, this time demonstrated through a combination of qualitative research and an experimental approach. Watching the procession of casualties returning home from the battlefields of Afghanistan stirred complex feelings among the public; Canadians were both sad and proud. This hybrid had unexpected consequences, leading to increased support for the mission in Afghanistan, an outcome contrary to what has been found in the American context. Moreover, the political relevance of this finding is made evident by the disjuncture between the complexity of Canadians' emotional responses to military casualties, on one hand, and efforts by the federal government to ban media coverage of repatriation ceremonies, on the other (Fletcher and Hove 2012).

The third moment that we examined occurred in the immediate wake of 9/11. Again we found evidence that emotion acted as a mediator in influencing public preferences. But we also found that emotion's effects can be multifaceted. Contrary to what one might expect, the overall effect of the emotional distress experienced 9/11 appears to be inconsequential. Looking only at the simple associations between emotion and policy preferences, there seems to be little connection. Understanding emotion as a mediator, however, allows us to decompose the overall effect. And beneath the surface, we find cross-cutting influences, leading in equal measure to both support for, and opposition to, military action.

These three investigations provide a view of the interplay between cognition and affect in shaping public policy preferences. The role of emotion is shown to be complex and having a real political effect on how citizens come to view military engagement. Importantly, not only does emotion influence support for war in its own right, it also mediates the impact of political information and may elicit a change in citizens' basic political orientations. Such patterns bring into clearer focus the bases of support for the use of military force, and they allow us to comprehend better the role of emotion in the formation of political attitudes.

Appendix A: Wording of Questions

2007

SUPPORT FOR THE MISSION

- Deploy: Overall, do you strongly support, support, oppose or strongly oppose the decision to send Canadian troops to Afghanistan?
- Long-term: The Chief of Canada's Defence Staff, General Hillier, has said that it may take up to 10 years or more to make real progress in Afghanistan. Would you strongly support, somewhat support, somewhat oppose or strongly oppose Canada being in Afghanistan for that length of time?
- Casualties: Some say that is the price that must be paid by countries like Canada to help bring stability and peace to Afghanistan. Others say it is too high a price to pay. Which is closer to your point of view?

REALISM

Given the state of today's world and the changing nature of conflict, which of the following is the most relevant role that Canada can play?

To work with the United Nations as peacekeepers, that is to maintain peace by monitoring and observing peace processes and implement peace agreements.

To work with the United Nations to enforce peace and defend countries or groups around the world that are being attacked by terrorists.

PRIDE

Please tell me whether you agree or disagree with the following statements using a 7-point scale, where 7 means you strongly agree, 1 means you strongly disagree, and the mid-point, 4, means you neither agree nor disagree.

I am proud of Canada's role in protecting the rights and freedoms of the Afghan people.

GOVERNMENT INFORMATION

- Consequences of withdrawal: Canada has made a commitment to be in Afghanistan until 2009. In considering whether Canada should stay beyond 2009, how important are each of the following. … Would you say this is a very important, somewhat important, or not very important consideration, or is it not important at all?
    - The Taliban will regroup and come back into power in Afghanistan.
    - The authority and legitimacy of the United Nations would be severely damaged.
    - Canada's reputation within the international community would suffer.
    - The rights of women and children will be negatively affected.
    - More terrorist attacks on Western nations such as Canada will occur.
    - Afghanistan's economy would become more reliant on the cultivation of poppies for the production of opium and heroin.
- Motivations for the mission: Please tell me whether you agree or disagree with the following statements using a 7-point scale, where 7 means you strongly agree, 1 means you strongly disagree, and the mid-point, 4, means you neither agree nor disagree.
    - The Afghan people want the assistance of Canada and other countries to remove the Taliban threat.
    - Canada's contribution to reconstruction and development in Afghanistan is making a real difference to improving the lives of Afghan people.

2009

SUPPORT FOR THE MISSION (AS ABOVE)

REALISM

Some people say that Canada's role in international conflicts should be limited to peacekeeping and humanitarian missions – that is, we should not be actively engaged in combat situations. Others say that this is unrealistic and that our armed forces have to be prepared to participate in active, armed combat duty. Which one of these two views best represents your own?

Emotion (only those items used in the present analysis are shown here)

On a scale running from 0 through 10, where 10 means you strongly feel this way and 0 means you do not at all feel this way, would you say that the mission in Afghanistan makes you feel …

- Proud At whom or about what? ____________________________
- Sad About what? ____________________________

2001

SUPPORT FOR THE WAR ON TERROR

Overall, do you approve or disapprove of US military action against terrorism? Is that strongly or somewhat?

In the fight against terrorism, the US has said that it might also consider using additional military force above and beyond that which has been used already. In general, would you support or oppose (the following)?

Using military force against suspected terrorist targets in other Middle Eastern countries, including Iraq.

(Is that strongly or somewhat?)

REALISM

Now I'd like to read you a number of statements that various people have made and have you tell me if you agree or disagree with each one. You can do this by telling me if you strongly agree, somewhat agree, neither agree nor disagree, somewhat disagree, or strongly disagree.

- I am prepared to give up some of my freedoms in order to combat terrorism more effectively.
- Canada should be prepared to give up some of its sovereignty in order to combat terrorism.

EMOTIONAL DISTRESS

As a result of the terrorist attacks and the US-led response, have you changed plans or experienced any of the following lately? (Yes/no)

- Had trouble sleeping
- Been less interested in sex
- Been less driven to succeed at work
- Sought advice from a health care professional or a counsellor

RISK APPRAISAL

And for the following potential types of attacks on the US, I'd like you to tell me how likely you consider each to be; is it very likely, somewhat likely, not too likely, or not at all likely?

- A serious chemical or biological attack, such as smallpox, that could kill millions of people.
- An attack on a nuclear power station.
- The hijacking of jetliners for use as weapons.

NOTES

1 See Kristina Tchalova and Geoff MacDonald (chap. 6 in this volume) for a discussion of the connections between attachment and appraisal.

2 To maintain consistency with our previous paper, which examines the same data, we measure political information as an additive scale (thus, represented as a rectangle in Figure 7.1) rather than constructing it as a latent variable, as could be done in SEM. Results are comparable when using the latter approach.

3 In constructing the models, significant intercorrelations among the demographic variables were included, as were all significant effects of the demographic variables on the key independent variables as well as the dependent variables. These coefficients, along with those for all paths from the demographic variables to the dependent variables, are included in the model, but not shown in Figure 7.1.

4 The fit of the model to the data is estimated by correspondence between the parameters estimated by the model and those produced by the data as a whole. The two measures of model fit reported here are chi-square and Root Mean Square Error of Approximation (RMSEA). The significance of chi-square ($p = .006$) suggests that there are significant differences between the relationships summarized in the model and those evident in

the covariance matrix produced by the data. However, the RMSEA value shows that the imprecision of the coefficients shown in the model is nearly zero, with a confidence interval extending to .029. Current interpretative standards for RMSEA suggest that values less than .06 indicate a good fit, while values up to .08 suggest an adequate fit (see Byrne 2010, 80).

5 All coefficients shown in Figure 7.1 are significant at $p < .001$. The entire model (including demographic variables not shown) explains 39% of the variance in support for the mission, as indicated by the coefficient to the right of the dependent variable.

6 National polling in December 2010 found that a majority of Canadians (56%) were opposed to the combat mission, but there was a closer split on the decision to keep some Canadian forces in Afghanistan in a training capacity until 2014: 48% of Canadians supported the decision, while 44% opposed it (Angus Reid Public Opinion 2010).

7 This was tested by first running a model that includes both information → realism and emotion → realism. We find that a model with only the path from emotion → realism is significantly worse than this initial model (Δ chi-square 4.532 with 1 *df*; $p = .0333$). In contrast, the model that includes only the path from information → realism is not significantly worse (Δ chi-square 1.579 with 1 *df*; $p = .2089$).

8 See Fletcher and Hove (2012) for study details.

9 To verify a link between emotion and policy preference as more than plausible would also require an experimental approach (Bullock and Ha 2011); however, we cannot practically manipulate emotion without losing the realism required in this kind of work, any more than we can manipulate basic political orientations.

10 In fact, our experimental survey presented respondents with three images on a random basis: the flag-draped coffins (loss of life), a solider saluting the Canadian flag (martial pride), and a soldier helping a young Afghan boy (humanitarian aid). The "soldier saluting" image was chosen as the control condition. The "helping" image is also included in the following model, although its effects are insignificant and not shown.

11 The fit of the model is good, as shown by the insignificance of the chi-square statistic ($p = .105$) and the RMSEA value of .04. All coefficients shown in Figure 7.2 are significant at $p < .001$ save those for the paths between information and emotion ($p = .039$) and information and mission support ($p = .048$). The model explains 52% of the variance in support for the Afghan mission.

12 The path from information → realism is not significant ($p = .71$), and thus the overall fit of the model is not significantly improved if this link is included (Δ chi-square = .139 with 1 *df*; $p = .7093$).

13 In the months immediately following 9/11, realism found greater expression in issues of freedom and sovereignty than in preferences about the Canadian military's role abroad.

14 Although the significance of the chi-square statistic (p = .000) suggests significant differences between the relationships summarized in the model and those evident in the covariance matrix produced by the data, the fit of the model is good, as shown by the RMSEA value of .028. All coefficients shown in Figure 7.3 are significant at $p < .01$. The model explains 34% of the variance in support for the war on terror.

15 This model is not significantly improved by adding a path from risk appraisal to realism (Δ chi-square = .631 with 1 *df*; p = .4270). Moreover, if included, the path parameter is not significant (p = .40945).

16 We do not calculate proportions of the total effect represented by direct and indirect effects since these can exceed 1.0 or, in the case of suppression, become negative. Patrick Shrout and Niall Bolger (2002) recommend that the effect ratio be computed only when there is no strong evidence of suppression.

REFERENCES

Angus Reid Public Opinion. 2010. "Canadians Divided on Assuming Non-Combat Role in Afghanistan: Canadian Public Opinion Poll, December 13." Accessed 21 August 2016. http://angusreid.org/canadians-divided-on-assuming-non-combat-role-in-afghanistan/.

Baron, Reuben M., and David A. Kenny. 1986. "The Moderator-Mediator Variable Distinction and Social Psychological Research: Conceptual, Strategic, and Statistical Considerations." *Journal of Personality and Social Psychology* 51 (6): 1173–82. http://dx.doi.org/10.1037/0022-3514.51.6.1173.

Brader, Ted. 2006. *Campaigning for Hearts and Minds: How Emotional Appeals in Political Ads Work*. Chicago: University of Chicago Press.

Brader, Ted, Nicholas A. Valentino, and Elizabeth Suhay. 2008. "What Triggers Public Opposition to Immigration? Anxiety, Group Cues, and Immigration Threat." *American Journal of Political Science* 52 (4): 959–78. http://dx.doi.org/10.1111/j.1540-5907.2008.00353.x.

Bullock, John G., and Shang E. Ha. 2011. "Mediation Analysis Is Harder Than It Looks." In *Cambridge Handbook of Experimental Political Science*, edited by James N. Druckman, Donald P. Green, James Kuklinski, and Arthur Lupia, 508–22. New York: Cambridge University Press. http://dx.doi.org/10.1017/CBO9780511921452.035.

Byrne, Barbara M. 2010. *Structural Equation Modelling with AMOS*. 2nd ed. New York: Routledge.

Cheung-Blunden, Violet, and Bill Blunden. 2008. "The Emotional Construal of War: Anger, Fear, and Other Negative Emotions." *Peace and Conflict* 14 (2): 123–50. http://dx.doi.org/10.1080/10781910802017289.

Civettini, Andrew J., and David P. Redlawsk. 2009. "Voters, Emotions, and Memory." *Political Psychology* 30 (1): 125–51. http://dx.doi.org/10.1111/j.1467-9221.2008.00683.x.

Druckman, James N., and Rose McDermott. 2008. "Emotion and the Framing of Risky Choice." *Political Behavior* 30 (3): 297–321. http://dx.doi.org/10.1007/s11109-008-9056-y.

Fletcher, Joseph F., Heather Bastedo, and Jennifer Hove. 2009. "Losing Heart: Declining Support and the Political Marketing of the Afghanistan Mission." *Canadian Journal of Political Science* 42 (4): 911–37. http://dx.doi.org/10.1017/S0008423909990667.

Fletcher, Joseph F., and Jennifer Hove. 2012. "Emotional Determinants of Support for the Canadian Mission in Afghanistan: A View from the Bridge." *Canadian Journal of Political Science* 45 (1): 33–62. http://dx.doi.org/10.1017/S0008423911000916.

Fletcher, Joseph F., and Will Schatten. 2012. "Framing the Toronto G20 Protests: The Role of Ambivalence and Emotion." Paper presented at the 84th Annual Meeting of the Canadian Political Science Association, Edmonton, 13–15 June.

Gartner, Scott Sigmund. 2008. "The Multiple Effects of Casualties on Public Support for War: An Experimental Approach." *American Political Science Review* 102 (1): 95–106. http://dx.doi.org/10.1017/S0003055408080027.

Gross, Kimberly. 2008. "Framing Persuasive Appeals: Episodic and Thematic Framing, Emotional Response, and Policy Opinion." *Political Psychology* 29 (2): 169–92. http://dx.doi.org/10.1111/j.1467-9221.2008.00622.x.

Halperin, Eran, Daphna Canetti-Nisim, and Sivan Hirsch-Hoefler. 2009. "The Central Role of Group-Based Hatred as an Emotional Antecedent of Political Intolerance: Evidence from Israel." *Political Psychology* 30 (1): 93–123. http://dx.doi.org/10.1111/j.1467-9221.2008.00682.x.

Huddy, Leonie, Stanley Feldman, and Erin Cassesse. 2007. "On the Distinct Political Effects of Anxiety and Anger." In *The Affect Effect: Dynamics of Emotion in Political Thinking and Behavior*, edited by W. Russell Neuman, George E. Marcus, Ann N. Crigler, and Michael MacKuen, 202–30. Chicago: University of Chicago Press.

Huddy, Leonie, Stanley Feldman, Charles Taber, and Gallya Lahav. 2005. "Threat, Anxiety, and Support for Antiterrorism Policies." *American Journal of Political Science* 49 (3): 593–608. http://dx.doi.org/10.1111/j.1540-5907.2005.00144.x.

Huddy, Leonie, and Anna H. Gunnthorsdottir. 2000. "The Persuasive Effects of Emotive Visual Imagery." *Political Psychology* 21 (4): 745–78. http://dx.doi.org/10.1111/0162-895X.00215.

Hutchinson, Emma, and Roland Bleiker. 2008. "Emotions in the War on Terror." In *Security and the War on Terror*, edited by Alex J. Bellamy, Roland Bleiker, Sara E. Davies, and Richard Devetak, 57–70. New York: Routledge.

Lerner, Jennifer S., and Dacher Keltner. 2001. "Fear, Anger, and Risk." *Journal of Personality and Social Psychology* 81 (1): 146–59. http://dx.doi.org/10.1037/0022-3514.81.1.146.

MacKinnon, David P., Jennifer L. Krull, and Chondra M. Lockwood. 2000. "Equivalence of the Mediation, Confounding and Suppression Effect." *Prevention Science* 1 (4): 173–81. http://dx.doi.org/10.1023/A:1026595011371.

Merolla, Jennifer L., and Elizabeth J. Zechmeister. 2009. *Democracy at Risk: How Terrorist Threats Affect the Public*. Chicago: University of Chicago Press. http://dx.doi.org/10.7208/chicago/9780226520568.001.0001.

Pagano, Sabrina J., and Yuen J. Huo. 2007. "The Role of Moral Emotions in Predicting Support for Political Actions in Post-War Iraq." *Political Psychology* 28 (2): 227–55. http://dx.doi.org/10.1111/j.1467-9221.2007.00563.x.

Rosenwein, Barbara H. 2006. *Emotional Communities in the Early Middle Ages*. Ithaca, NY: Cornell University Press.

Shrout, Patrick E., and Niall Bolger. 2002. "Mediation in Experimental and Not Experimental Studies: New Procedures and Recommendations." *Psychological Methods* 7 (4): 422–45. http://dx.doi.org/10.1037/1082-989X.7.4.422.

Way, Baldwin M., and Roger D. Masters. 1996a. "Political Attitudes: Interactions of Cognition and Affect." *Motivation and Emotion* 20 (3): 205–36. http://dx.doi.org/10.1007/BF02251887.

Way, Baldwin M., and Roger D. Masters. 1996b. "Emotion and Cognition in Political Information-Processing." *Journal of Communication* 46 (3): 48–65.

Wu, Amery D., and Bruno D. Zumbo. 2008. "Understanding and Using Mediators and Moderators." *Social Indicators Research* 87 (3): 367–92.

PART III

Emotions and Citizenship

8 Constructing Indignation: Anger Dynamics in Protest Movements

JAMES M. JASPER

In the last twenty years, emotions have returned to the sociological study of social movements as part of a paradigm shift from macro-level structures, such as state formations and economic inequality, to micro-level processes, such as cultural framing and identification with groups. Protest has proven a useful site for studying emotions because organizers self-consciously use emotion displays to coordinate action, to attract and retain participants, and to pressure other strategic players with whom they interact. They "experiment" with emotional images and words, much as social scientists do in their laboratories. Because we can observe emotional transformations in natural settings, we should find lessons for the study of emotions in other areas of social life.

Research on protest movements poses distinct questions (in this chapter, I use the terms *social movement*, *protest movement*, and *protest* interchangeably): Why do individuals join or drop out? Why do new movements and themes emerge? How are strategic decisions made? How do opponents, authorities, and other players react? What impacts do movements have? Explanations that include emotions have been given, especially for the first of these questions, regarding motivations for participation (van Stekelenburg and Klandermans 2013), but emotions are important for the other topics as well. Emotional factors have forced themselves on a generation of researchers whose training and presuppositions never allowed them to expect or look for emotions among the protestors they studied. Most sociologists who have incorporated emotions into their accounts of protest have adopted a cultural approach compatible with most versions of cognitive appraisal theory, reflecting the dominant cultural constructionism of sociology as a whole.

Anger and indignation, the morally grounded form of anger, are crucial to many aspects of protest. They not only motivate participation (van Stekelenburg and Klandermans 2013) but also direct blame for social problems, create sympathy and admiration for protestors, and guide strategic choices. Yet anger is tricky, often linked to aggression and generally disapproved of in modern societies. I examine several arenas in which strategic action occurs – both internal and external arenas – to summarize a few of the emotional mechanisms described in recent years. (Jasper 2011 provides a lengthier review.) Collective identity has come to play a central role in sociological theories of social movements, as it has in many other fields throughout the social sciences and humanities (McGarry and Jasper 2014), including social identity theory in social psychology (Tajfel and Turner 1979). Its central explanatory role has been to help explain why individuals engage in collective action on behalf of their group: they love and are proud of their group, and they wish to advance its respect and other advantages, even independently of their personal gains (van Zomeren et al. 2004). But collective identity is not always purely an advantage: it imposes dilemmas on organizers. Solidarity with one grouping may conflict with solidarity with others; loyalty to an organization may undermine it to one's family and vice versa (Goodwin 1997; Klatch 2004). Efforts to arouse solidarity with an entire movement may instead result in allegiance to a small subgroup, such as a cell or affinity group, in the "band of brothers dilemma" (Jasper 2004, 13), adapted from the intense loyalty that members of combat units feel towards each other. (Protest often feels like combat.)

Queer theorists and others have attacked each and every collective identity as a distortion of individual needs on the Foucaultian assumption that all such subject positions result from systems of power (Beltrán 2010; Butler 1990). But all collective solidarities include both advantages and disadvantages. Internally, they can generate pride and a sense of agency, and they can strengthen networks and trust; externally, they allow a group to project strength and make demands. On the negative side, internal risks include an imperfect fit with individual identities and the reification of existing identities; external risks include the restriction of solidarities with outsiders, prevention of individual assimilation to the broader society, and the creation of overly strong leaders who are seen as representing the group. The combination of advantages and disadvantages poses an "identity dilemma" for organizers about how and how strongly they should promote a movement's collective identity (McGarry and Jasper 2014).

Two kinds of emotions help keep groups together (Jasper 1998). Reciprocal emotions are what group members feel towards each other, including love, respect, trust, but also potentially envy, jealousy, and betrayal. Members of a group also experience shared emotions towards objects outside the group. Every demonstration of shared anger or hatred towards a policy or a group reinforces the reciprocal emotions: they feel the same way I do, therefore they must be good people. Even negative shared emotions, such as fear, can reinforce positive reciprocal emotions: we have survived this together (Eyerman 2005, 43; Whittier 2009). A successful collective identity fuses reciprocal and shared emotions by imagining an object of attachment (the group) consisting of its individual members taken as a whole. They love both the group and its members (Rupp and Taylor 1987), often fused into a feeling of home and community (Duyvendak 2011).

Because scholars of movements tend to study groups they admire or belong to, they have been reluctant to acknowledge the binding power of unsavoury emotions such as anger, hate, and revenge. These emotions play a motivating role in murder-suicides such as the Palestinian bombers in Israel (Brym 2007). The pleasure of revenge, particularly after a long series of humiliations, may be a sufficient motivation for individuals, especially when they are encouraged and aided by political organizations. Honour is one of the oldest of recognized motivations, prominent in the founding document of Western culture, the *Iliad*, and it motivates international relations and politics even today (Lebow 2008). It is often acknowledged in the form of the need for recognition (Honneth 1995).

Social psychologists have traced the impact of group-based emotions (Mackie and Smith 2002). Identities become political when an external enemy can be blamed for a group's problems and the struggle moves into political arenas (Simon and Klandermans 2001). Some scholars see group efficacy and anger as the link between identities and action. "People who perceive the in-group as strong are more likely to experience anger and desire to take action; people who perceive the in-group as weak are more likely to feel fearful and to move away from the out-group" (van Stekelenburg and Klandermans 2013, 893). Other scholars see group-based anger and group efficacy as two distinct pathways to collective action (van Zomeren et al. 2004).

People attend protest events because they expect a "positive" experience. Randall Collins's (2004) interaction ritual model is a theory of emotional energy, created in face-to-face situations, that in turn provides a sense of group solidarity and the joys of crowds that can motivate recurring participation. By describing the "emotional entrainment" of successful interactions – a shared focus of attention, bodies oriented towards each other, synchronized locomotion and singing – he can also posit the causes and consequences of failed interaction rituals. The good or bad moods created in interactions accompany us to our next interactions, affecting them in turn. The confidence and good moods that come from successful rituals are vital for political action, raising energy and activity levels and probably boosting a feeling of group efficacy (Smith and Kessler 2004).

Emotions can also work to prevent mobilization. As mentioned, alternative commitments, especially to one's family, often prevent participation. Adumbrating the band of brothers dilemma, Jeff Goodwin (1997) demonstrates how the Huk rebels in the Philippines struggled to contain the romantic dyads that formed in the jungle as well as the commitments to families that often drew participants away from the struggle. We also find emotions at work in avoidance and denial, as Kari Marie Norgaard (2011) shows in an ethnography of a small Norwegian town whose skiing industry was harmed by global warming. To acknowledge global warming, and by extension other social problems, would entail unpleasant emotions that most people try to avoid: feelings of helplessness, guilt over their own role in global warming, fear that their physical surroundings are no longer safe and dependable, and an unsettling threat to their own individual and collective identities. Her subjects deflected these emotions through irony, teasing humour, and cynicism, steering conversations to safer, more mundane topics. Finding no one to blame, they were unable to sustain anger.

Emotions are also part of demobilization. Many disagreements over strategic dilemmas grow more accusatory when a movement is declining as different factions attribute blame for failures. In his study of the collapse of the Amsterdam squatters' movement, Lynn Owens (2009) shows how sadness, anger, and despair led to mutual recriminations. When turned against comrades, anger can destroy a movement. The despairing mood also exacerbated several kinds of fear, he says, and the factions arose around these: existential fear, fear of violence, and fear of isolation.

Just as group honour motivates political action, so does a desire for individual honour, in the form of dignity. Even in situations where success seems unlikely, people often join movements simply to assert their dignity as human beings who are suffering and can make some noise. Dignity can motivate even high-risk activities such as revolutionary warfare. "Through rebelling," remarks Elisabeth Jean Wood (2003, 18), "insurgent campesinos [in El Salvador] asserted, and thereby constituted in their own eyes, their dignity in the face of condescension, repression, and indifference." The very act of rebelling improved their self-reputation (and reduced their reputation for passivity, at least in the eyes of others); it was a goal in itself as well as a means to additional demands. Some protestors have nothing left to lose except their humanity, having lost loved ones, been frustrated or attacked by their own governments, and been driven to passionate outrage (Fisher 1989, 28).

Protestors must create and sustain a sense of moral obligation and justice. They use a variety of emotional processes to promote their own moral visions, suggesting that morality affects human action partly or primarily through emotions (cf. the discussion of emotions and a sense of moral obligation and justice in chapter 10 of this volume). Scholars of movements have implicitly or explicitly begun to rely on a neo-Aristotelian view of morality as character training, which guides our actions intuitively, in contrast to a Kantian view of morality as a calculation of universally desirable choices (Monroe 2004). Our morality is more likely to be intuitive than to consist of explicit principles, although one of the tasks of movements is to develop and articulate principles from those intuitions (Jasper 1997).

Moral shocks help explain initial and continued participation, consisting of a visceral unease in reaction to information and events that signal that the world is not as it seemed, thereby demanding attention and re-evaluation (Jasper 1997). Political scientists have used anxiety in the same way: "generated when norms are violated; the more they are violated, and the more strategically central those norms are to people, then the greater the anxiety" (Marcus, Neuman, and MacKuen 2000, 138). Moral shocks were originally used to account for initial recruitment in the absence of strong network ties (Jasper and Poulsen 1995), and a number of studies have used the concept in this way to explain recruitment to the movement for peace in Central America (Nepstad and Smith 2001), abolitionism (Young 2001), anti-racism (Warren 2010), and the Madres of Buenos Aires (Risley 2011).

Other studies have found that moral shocks can rekindle or radicalize the commitment of those already active in a protest movement. Deborah Gould (2009) describes the moral shock – the Hardwick decision by the US Supreme Court in 1986 – that produced radical direct action out of the desperate mood that gays and lesbians had initially felt under the onslaught of the AIDS epidemic. They formed ACT UP, based on explicit anger, when they concluded that their own government was against them and complicit in the deaths. (On the similar generation of anger by ACT UP in France, see Christophe Broqua and Olivier Fillieule [2009].) With a new attribution of blame, AIDS was no longer an epidemic, but a genocide. "If you believed that AIDS was a holocaust, then 'business as usual' in the political realm, which by then was clearly ineffective, was not much of a response" (Gould 2009, 170). Fear and grief developed into anger, outrage, and indignation. Moral emotions came to the fore.

Groups are often most shocked when something is taken away that they take for granted (Heirich 1971). For instance, Verta Taylor et al. (2009) found that same-sex marriage became a much more central issue for the LGBTQ community in California when the right was suddenly rescinded by the courts in 2010, generating moral shock and anger. This view of emotions as embedded in flows of action, stabilized by resources, organizations, and routines, appears implicitly in Ziad Munson's (2009) account of recruitment to the US anti-abortion movement. He shows that new recruits do not usually have a well-developed ideology or moral system, but only develop these once they have begun to participate. Instead, they are drawn into protest activities through their social networks, which are themselves a combination of structural opportunities and emotional solidarity with selected others.

Massed demonstrators are always playing with or against traditional images of crowds as angry, dangerous, and irrational. Most groups wish to undermine this image through displays of calm and purpose and a commitment to non-violence, but some hope to appear threatening enough to be taken seriously. According to Frances Fox Piven and Richard Cloward (1977), poor people attain concessions only when they disrupt activities valued by elites through riots, sit-down strikes, and other aggressive activities. They have to frighten and not just inconvenience their targets. Although Piven and Cloward were writing in a period when scholars denied the emotions of protestors, the insurgent mood they describe can be explained only on the basis of anger and outrage.

Because the women's and LGBTQ movements challenged emotion rules in political arenas, they encouraged scholars to re-evaluate the emotions of protest. In the 1970s and 1980s, feminist scholars criticized liberal theories of autonomous individuals, modelled on market transactions, in favour of models of humans as emotionally connected to others, inspired instead by the paradigm of nurturing family ties (Ruddick 1989). At the same time, feminist activists battled against the norms by which women were not supposed to express anger, realizing that anger is essential to demanding rights and fighting in political arenas (Hochschild 1975). As we saw, queer activists formed ACT UP to overcome similar constraints. Anger is a pathway to indignation, pride, and other ingredients of self-assertion. A lesbian separatist group from the early 1970s, the Furies, used its name to both acknowledge the importance of political anger and to play on classical stereotypes demeaning angry women.

Feminists fought against other emotion norms that constrained and damaged women, including forms of shame that had traditionally been attached to women's bodies, as during menstruation. The bestselling *Our Bodies, Ourselves* (Boston Women's Health Book Collective 1973), for instance, was meant to demystify women's bodies in their own eyes. Taylor (1996) attacked the norm of the happy mother in examining the politics of post-partum depression, as mothers formed self-help groups to deal with having the "wrong" feelings. In her research on survivors of child sexual abuse, Nancy Whittier (2009, 68) observed their efforts to deal with shame by making abuse a public problem so that "undertaking emotional work in self-help groups and speaking publicly about one's experiences was not simply psychological change, but social change." Sue Campbell (1994) observed that women's anger is often framed by others as bitterness, inappropriate to public arenas.

In many cases, women remain reluctant to express anger. Research has documented a gendered division of labour in many social movements, which implies an emotional specialization as well. Women, especially, provide the glue for social-movement networks through their emotion work (Robnett 1997), while men are more likely to deploy their anger in militant tactics (Fillieule and Roux 2009) and angry public rhetoric (Roberts 2013, 119). In a classic work on an alternative health organization, Sherryl Kleinman (1996) found that men were more likely than women to be rewarded for expressing their emotions, thereby breaking gender-role expectations, although it seems likely that women are still punished for being too "masculine" when they display anger.

We rarely experience a single emotion at a time, so research has begun to examine combinations of emotions in protest. For purposes of clarity, the focus has been on pairs of emotions. James Jasper (2011, 2012) suggests that pairs of positive and negative emotions form "moral batteries" that indicate a direction for action, away from the unattractive state and towards the attractive one. These batteries might be nothing more than a condemnation of the status quo combined with a utopian hope for an alternative future, a pair that defines protest for Manuel Castells (2012).

The most studied moral battery is the combination of shame and pride: groups with stigmatized identities often form movements to replace one with the other. Although identified in other groups as well (Jasper 2010), this dynamic has been most thoroughly studied in the lesbian and gay rights movements, where "coming out" has been a dramatic and empowering transition from the passivity of shame to more active pride (Whittier 2012). Gould (2009) shows how unacknowledged shame first led to an assimilative politics of respectability, but was replaced, after the moral shock of the Hardwick Supreme Court decision, with an angry, defiant, often separatist assertion of pride. American "dreamers" (whose parents brought them to the United States illegally when they were young) also speak of coming out in their efforts to transform shame into pride (Nicholls 2013). Lory Britt and David Heise (2000) show that anger can aid the transition from shame to pride.

Pride often depends on externalizing instead of internalizing anger and blame for a group's plight. In a study of women incarcerated for infanticide, Taylor and Leitz (2010, 267) show that writing to pen pals helped the women to blame an illness, post-partum depression, for their actions. This "allowed women to minimize their shame and emotional distress and to shift blame for their actions to the medical and legal systems, enabling them to remake their identities as mothers." Whether individuals internalize or externalize their anger has broad implications for their mental health (Rosenfield, Phillips, and White 2006).

Some combinations of emotions resolve themselves into sequences, often carefully orchestrated by activists who understand how to recruit and retain participants. Katherine Lively and David Heise (2004) discuss emotional segues, including the important transformation of shame or fear into anger. Elizabeth Williamson (2011) examined "emotion chains" deployed by a feminist New Age religious group to ensure that members returned to future events. Initial confusion, followed by understanding and hope, increased the odds of someone returning; those who ended with hope were more likely to return, while those who ended up feeling fear were less likely to do so. The transformation of frustration into the joy of accomplishment, even in simple tasks, is an example that applies far beyond protest (Walby and Spencer 2012).

Some of the most important emotions of protest arise out of interactions with authorities (Gamson, Fireman, and Rytina 1982). Government repression of protest (through police ineptitude as well as regime policies) can infuriate more participants than it intimidates, and it can draw newcomers who are angrier about governmental actions than about the original grievance (Brockett 2005). These "procedural grievances" can be powerful as they involve a sense of betrayal by one's own government, the same agent that is supposed to protect citizens and process complaints (Gordon and Jasper 1996; Tyler and Smith 1998). In such cases, blame shifts from third parties to government (Hess and Martin 2006). Much protest involves a standard cycle of interaction: public protest, police repression, even more protest, and so on, reflecting waves of indignation over procedural grievances (Kurzman 2004, chap. 6).

Attention to emotions, and especially to combinations and interactions among emotions, challenges the means-end models that have dominated research on protest movements. There is a constant stream of emotions in any flow of action, and the balance between positive and negative emotions largely determines whether the action is continued. It is difficult to distinguish among the emotions involved in the efforts to attain certain goals and those that come from their accomplishment. The abilities to express righteous anger and to avoid debilitating shame are ends in themselves, but also the means to further political activity. Each victory yields a good mood of confidence, on which the next round of action can build.

Anger is the core of many of the processes we have observed. Shame must be transformed into pride to allow oppressed groups to feel indignant; the paralysis of shock must become activating anger; inchoate anger must be directed at someone to blame; and anger must take on a moral basis, becoming indignation. Activists deploy apparatuses to create anger during interactions and to display it to audiences (Broqua and Fillieule 2009). But we need to know far more about the many forms that anger can take, the many ways it can be displayed.

Scholars of protest can incorporate the study of emotions into most of the techniques they already use: depth interviews; ethnographic fieldwork; surveys, often conducted at protests; the interpretation of texts and other artefacts; and participant introspection. In addition, there are innumerable video recordings of crowds and protests, allowing careful scrutiny of facial expressions and other signs of mutual entrainment, often by slowing the videos down to capture and code relatively fleeting emotion displays (Collins 2004). Even though most sociologists of protest work in natural settings, other social scientists have successfully reproduced a number of emotional dynamics in experimental settings (e.g., Sanfey et al. 2003) and conducted sophisticated analyses of surveys completed by protestors (van Stekelenburg and Klandermans 2013). This young field needs dialogue with these other traditions so that our concepts can be made more rigorous and our insights from the field can better inform experiments and surveys.

REFERENCES

Beltrán, Cristina. 2010. *The Trouble with Unity*. New York: Oxford University Press.

Boston Women's Health Book Collective. 1973. *Our Bodies, Ourselves*. New York: Simon and Schuster.

Britt, Lory, and David R. Heise. 2000. "From Shame to Pride in Identity Politics." In *Self, Identity, and Social Movements*, edited by Sheldon Stryker, Timothy J. Owens, and Robert W. White, 252–70. Minneapolis: University of Minnesota Press.

Brockett, Charles D. 2005. *Political Movements and Violence in Latin America*. Cambridge: Cambridge University Press. http://dx.doi.org/10.1017/CBO9780511614378.

Broqua, Christophe, and Olivier Fillieule. 2009. "Act Up ou les raisons de la colère" [Act Up, or the reasons for anger]. In *Emotions ... Mobilisations!*, edited by Christophe Traïni, 141–67. Paris: Presses de Science Po.

Brym, Robert J. 2007. "The Six Lessons of Suicide Bombers." *Contexts* 6 (4): 40–5. http://dx.doi.org/10.1525/ctx.2007.6.4.40.

Butler, Judith. 1990. *Gender Trouble*. New York: Routledge.

Campbell, Sue. 1994. "Being Dismissed." *Hypatia* 9 (3): 46–65. http://dx.doi.org/10.1111/j.1527-2001.1994.tb00449.x.

Castells, Manuel. 2012. *Networks of Outrage and Hope*. Cambridge: Polity.

Collins, Randall. 2004. *Interaction Ritual Chains*. Princeton, NJ: Princeton University Press. http://dx.doi.org/10.1515/9781400851744.

Duyvendak, Jan Willem. 2011. *The Politics of Home*. New York: Palgrave Macmillan. http://dx.doi.org/10.1057/9780230305076.

Eyerman, Ronald. 2005. "How Social Movements Move." In *Emotions and Social Movements*, edited by Helena Flam and Debrah King, 41–56. New York: Routledge.

Fillieule, Olivier, and Patricia Roux, eds. 2009. *Le sexe du militantisme* [The sex of militancy]. Paris: Sciences Po.

Fisher, Jo. 1989. *Mothers of the Disappeared*. Boston, MA: South End Press.

Gamson, William A., Bruce Fireman, and Steve Rytina. 1982. *Encounters with Unjust Authority*. Homewood, IL: Dorsey Press.

Goodwin, Jeff. 1997. "The Libidinal Constitution of a High-Risk Social Movement." *American Sociological Review* 62 (1): 53–69. http://dx.doi.org/10.2307/2657452.

Gordon, Cynthia, and James M. Jasper. 1996. "Overcoming the 'NIMBY' Label." *Research in Social Movements, Conflicts and Change* 19: 153–75.

Gould, Deborah B. 2009. *Moving Politics*. Chicago: University of Chicago Press. http://dx.doi.org/10.7208/chicago/9780226305318.001.0001.

Heirich, Max. 1971. *The Spiral of Conflict*. New York: Columbia University Press.

Hess, David, and Brian Martin. 2006. "Repression, Backfire, and the Theory of Transformative Events." *Mobilization: An International Quarterly* 11 (1):249–67.

Hochschild, Arlie Russell. 1975. "The Sociology of Feeling and Emotion: Selected Possibilities." *Sociological Inquiry* 45 (2–3): 280–307. http://dx.doi.org/10.1111/j.1475-682X.1975.tb00339.x.

Honneth, Axel. 1995. *The Struggle for Recognition*. Cambridge, MA: MIT Press.

Jasper, James M. 1997. *The Art of Moral Protest*. Chicago: University of Chicago Press. http://dx.doi.org/10.7208/chicago/9780226394961.001.0001.

Jasper, James M. 1998. "The Emotions of Protest." *Sociological Forum* 13 (3): 397–424. http://dx.doi.org/10.1023/A:1022175308081.

Jasper, James M. 2004. "A Strategic Approach to Collective Action: Looking for Agency in Social-Movement Choices." *Mobilization: An International Quarterly* 9 (1): 1–16.

Jasper, James M. 2010. "Strategic Marginalizations, Emotional Marginalities." In *Surviving against Odds: The Marginalized in a Globalizing World*, edited by Debal K. SinghaRoy, 29–37. Delhi, India: Manohar.

Jasper, James M. 2011. "Emotions and Social Movements." *Annual Review of Sociology* 37 (1): 285–303. http://dx.doi.org/10.1146/annurev-soc-081309-150015.

Jasper, James M. 2012. "Choice Points, Moral Batteries, and Other Ways to Find Strategic Agency at the Micro Level." In *Strategies for Social Change*, edited by Gregory M. Maney, Rachel V. Kutz-Flamenbaum, Deana A.

Rohlinger, and Jeff Goodwin, 23–42. Minneapolis: University of Minnesota Press. http://dx.doi.org/10.5749/minnesota/9780816672899.003.0002.

Jasper, James M., and Jane D. Poulsen. 1995. "Recruiting Strangers and Friends: Moral Shocks and Social Networks in Animal Rights and Anti-Nuclear Protests." *Social Problems* 42 (4): 493–512. http://dx.doi.org/10.2307/3097043.

Klatch, Rebecca E. 2004. "The Underside of Social Movements." *Qualitative Sociology* 27 (4): 487–509. http://dx.doi.org/10.1023/B:QUAS.0000049244.69218.9c.

Kleinman, Sherryl. 1996. *Opposing Ambitions*. Chicago: University of Chicago Press.

Kurzman, Charles. 2004. *The Unthinkable Revolution in Iran*. Cambridge, MA: Harvard University Press.

Lebow, Richard Ned. 2008. *A Cultural Theory of International Relations*. Cambridge: Cambridge University Press. http://dx.doi.org/10.1017/CBO9780511575174.

Lively, Katherine J., and David R. Heise. 2004. "Sociological Realms of Emotional Experience." *American Journal of Sociology* 109 (5): 1109–36. http://dx.doi.org/10.1086/381915.

Mackie, Diane M., and Eliot R. Smith, eds. 2002. *From Prejudice to Intergroup Emotions*. New York: Psychology Press.

Marcus, George E., W. Russell Neuman, and Michael MacKuen. 2000. *Affective Intelligence and Political Judgment*. Chicago: University of Chicago Press.

McGarry, Aidan, and James M. Jasper, eds. 2014. *The Identity Dilemma*. Philadelphia: Temple University Press.

Monroe, Kristen Renwick. 2004. *The Hand of Compassion*. Princeton, NJ: Princeton University Press.

Munson, Ziad W. 2009. *The Making of Pro-life Activists*. Chicago: University of Chicago Press.

Nepstad, Sharon Erickson, and Christian Smith. 2001. "The Social Structure of Moral Outrage in Recruitment to the U.S. Central America Peace Movement." In *Passionate Politics*, edited by Jeff Goodwin, James M. Jasper, and Francesca Polletta, 158–74. Chicago: University of Chicago Press. http://dx.doi.org/10.7208/chicago/9780226304007.003.0010.

Nicholls, Walter. 2013. *The DREAMers: How the Undocumented Youth Movement Transformed the Immigrant Rights Debate in the United States*. Palo Alto, CA: Stanford University Press.

Norgaard, Kari Marie. 2011. *Living in Denial*. Cambridge, MA: MIT Press. http://dx.doi.org/10.7551/mitpress/9780262015448.001.0001.

Owens, Lynn. 2009. *Cracking under Pressure*. Amsterdam: Amsterdam University Press.

Piven, Frances Fox, and Richard A. Cloward. 1977. *Poor People's Movements*. New York: Vintage.

Risley, Amy. 2011. "Rejoinder." In *Contention in Context*, edited by Jeff Goodwin and James M. Jasper, 108–13. Stanford, CA: Stanford University Press.

Roberts, Catriona M.L. 2013. "The Role of Emotions in Social Movement Participation." Unpublished doctoral thesis. European University Institute, Fiesole, Italy.

Robnett, Belinda. 1997. *How Long? How Long?* New York: Oxford University Press.

Rosenfield, Sarah, Julie Phillips, and Helene White. 2006. "Gender, Race, and the Self in Mental Health and Crime." *Social Problems* 53 (2): 161–85. http://dx.doi.org/10.1525/sp.2006.53.2.161.

Ruddick, Sarah. 1989. *Maternal Thinking*. Boston, MA: Beacon Press.

Rupp, Leila J., and Verta. Taylor. 1987. *Survival in the Doldrums*. New York: Oxford University Press.

Sanfey, Alan G., James K. Rilling, Jessica A. Aronson, Leigh E. Nystrom, and Jonathan D. Cohen. 2003. "The Neural Basis of Economic Decision-Making in the Ultimatum Game." *Science* 300 (5626): 1755–8. http://dx.doi.org/10.1126/science.1082976.

Simon, Bernd, and Bert Klandermans. 2001. "Politicized Collective Identity: A Social Psychological Analysis." *American Psychologist* 56 (4): 319–31. http://dx.doi.org/10.1037/0003-066X.56.4.319.

Smith, Heather J., and Thomas Kessler. 2004. "Group-Based Emotions and Intergroup Behavior." In *The Social Life of Emotions: The Case of Relative Deprivation*, edited by Larissa Z. Tiedens and Colin Wayne Leach, 292–313. New York: Cambridge University Press. http://dx.doi.org/10.1017/CBO9780511819568.016.

Tajfel, Henri, and John Turner. 1979. "An Integrative Theory of Intergroup Conflict." In *The Social Psychology of Intergroup Relations*, edited by Stephen Worchel and William G. Austin, 33–47. Monterey, CA: Brooks-Cole.

Taylor, Verta. 1996. *Rock-a-by Baby*. New York: Routledge.

Taylor, Verta, Katrina Kimport, Nella Van Dyke, and Ellen Ann Andersen. 2009. "Culture and Mobilization: Tactical Repertoires, Same-Sex Weddings, and the Impact on Gay Activism." *American Sociological Review* 74 (6): 865–90. http://dx.doi.org/10.1177/000312240907400602.

Taylor, Verta, and Lisa Leitz. 2010. "From Infanticide to Activism." In *Social Movements and the Transformation of American Health Care*, edited by Jane C. Banaszak-Holl, Sandra R. Levitsky, and Mayer N. Zald, 266–82. New York: Oxford University Press. http://dx.doi.org/10.1093/acprof:oso/9780195388299.003.0016.

Tyler, Tom R., and Heather J. Smith. 1998. "Social Justice and Social Movements." In *Handbook of Social Psychology*, edited by D. Gilbert, S.T. Fiske, and G. Lindzey, 595–631. New York: McGraw-Hill.

van Stekelenburg, Jacquelien, and Bert Klandermans. 2013. "The Social Psychology of Protest." *Current Sociology* 61 (5–6): 886–905. Advance online publication. http://dx.doi.org/10.1177/0011392113479314.

van Zomeren, Martijn, Russell Spears, Agneta H. Fischer, and Colin Wayne Leach. 2004. "Put Your Money Where Your Mouth Is! Explaining Collective Action Tendencies through Group-Based Anger and Group Efficacy." *Journal of Personality and Social Psychology* 87 (5): 649–64. http://dx.doi.org/10.1037/0022-3514.87.5.649.

Walby, Kevin, and Dale Spencer. 2012. "How Emotions Matter." In *Emotions Matter*, edited by Dale Spencer, Kevin Walby, and Alan Hunt, 181–200. Toronto: University of Toronto Press.

Warren, Mark R. 2010. *Fire in the Heart*. New York: Oxford University Press.

Whittier, Nancy. 2009. *The Politics of Child Sexual Abuse*. New York: Oxford University Press. http://dx.doi.org/10.1093/acprof:oso/9780195325102.001.0001.

Whittier, Nancy. 2012. "The Politics of Coming Out." In *Strategies for Social Change*, edited by Gregory M. Maney, Rachel V. Kutz-Flamenbaum, Deana A. Rohlinger, and Jeff Goodwin, 145–69. Minneapolis: University of Minnesota Press. http://dx.doi.org/10.5749/minnesota/9780816672899.003.0007.

Williamson, Elizabeth. 2011. "The Magic of Multiple Emotions." *Sociological Forum* 26 (1): 45–70. http://dx.doi.org/10.1111/j.1573-7861.2010.01224.x.

Wood, Elisabeth Jean. 2003. *Insurgent Collective Action and Civil War in El Salvador*. Cambridge: Cambridge University Press. http://dx.doi.org/10.1017/CBO9780511808685.

Young, Michael P. 2001. "A Revolution of the Soul: Transformative Experiences and Immediate Abolition." In *Passionate Politics*, edited by Jeff Goodwin, James M. Jasper, and Francesca Polletta, 99–114. Chicago: University of Chicago Press. http://dx.doi.org/10.7208/chicago/9780226304007.003.0007.

9 Compassion and the Public Sphere: Hannah Arendt on a Contested Political Passion

SOPHIE BOURGAULT

Generally speaking, the role of the "heart" in politics seems to me altogether questionable.

– Hannah Arendt, *The Jew as Pariah* (247)

In his book *In Defense of Sentimentality* (2004, 43), Robert Solomon writes that "in contemporary politics, compassion is an endangered and often ridiculed sentiment." Ambivalence towards compassion characterizes not only present-day politics, according to Solomon, but also moral and political philosophy more generally – where the status of compassion is "anything but obvious" (ibid.). This reading stands in sharp contrast with those of Clifford Orwin (1997), Richard Boyd (2004), and Myriam Revault d'Allones (2008). Orwin claims, for instance, that compassion possesses a rather "lofty and *uncontroversial* status" (2008, n.p.; emphasis added) and that it has, in fact, become the object of a "cult" in both our private and our public lives (1997, 20).[1] If such a cult exists, its disciples have grown in number in recent years. If Orwin could write in 1997 that compassionate, "moist eyes" are mostly the affair of soft-hearted liberals (read: American Democrats) and that American Republicans' hearts "rarely seem to brim with compassion" (1997, 16), we can likewise point to a long tradition of the American right deploying the term. From Marvin Olasky to George W. Bush, *en passant par* the arch-conservative Roger Scruton,[2] neoconservatives have equally sought to plant their flag on the territory of compassion. In American politics (and increasingly in Canadian politics),[3] the virtue of compassion is fought over by both the left and the right, with each side accusing the other of counterfeit compassion (Woodward 2004; Scruton 2009).

In the midst of this scuffle between right-wing and left-wing fans and critics of compassion, the work of Hannah Arendt has often been invoked and, in particular, her book *On Revolution* (1963).[4] Hannah Arendt (1906–75) was one of the most important political theorists of the twentieth century. Her oeuvre, featuring an insightful analysis of totalitarianism and an extremely influential theory of political liberty, offers an important account of the passions and their political effects. Given her vast number of devotees and the widespread popular interest in her work, it is worthwhile exploring the troubling and novel things she has to say about the place of compassion in political life. It is in this comparative study of the American and French revolutions that Arendt offers her most explicit and most brutal indictment of compassion: she refers to it as the "most powerful and perhaps the most devastating of all passions" (OR, 66).[5] Arendt considers compassion to be radically antithetical to freedom (OR, 249)[6] and, thus, argues that it should remain out of politics.

It is partially on the basis of her harsh critique of compassion (and of its perverted twin brother, pity) that interpreters like George Kateb (1983) have suggested that Arendt seeks to purge politics of all affects and inner motives. Such a suggestion can be found not only among critics of Arendt but also among her most loyal admirers. For instance, Deborah Nelson (who is generally sympathetic to Arendt) believes that it is appropriate to summarize *On Revolution* as "an extended defense of coldness and *heartlessness*" in politics (2004, 226; emphasis added). But is it entirely appropriate to describe Arendtian politics as "heartless?" Are emotions "under siege" in Hannah Arendt – and, if so, what is the significance of this siege?

This chapter proposes to tackle these questions through an extended analysis of Arendt's treatment of compassion – which Kateb (1983, 27) has referred to as "the most intricate and yet one of the most disturbing segments in Arendt's works." The primary task of this chapter will thus be to spell out the Arendtian critique of compassion. What I hope to underscore is, first, that Arendt's treatment of human emotions is marred by some serious imprecision and, second, that it is incorrect to see in Arendt an unwavering enemy of emotions in public life. While she desperately tries to confine compassion to the heart and the household, her political ideal ultimately rests on an *affective* foundation. (We could also compare this project with the similarly reconstructive approach taken to the work of John Rawls, and how it reveals the affective basis of his political thought, in chapter 10 of this volume.)

The second aim of this chapter is to indicate that, paradoxically, the Arendtian case *against* compassion partially mirrors the neoconservative apology *for* compassion in politics – especially with regard to the neoconservative insistence that compassion ought to be tied to the private realm and to charity. This is not to suggest that Arendt ought to be labelled a neoconservative; I tend to agree with Margaret Canovan's (1996) suggestion that Arendt ultimately eludes political labels (as Arendt herself liked to note).[7] Nevertheless, there is something fruitful about drawing a parallel between Arendt's thought and the neoconservative deployment of the vocabulary of compassion because it underscores a troubling part of her work – one that cannot simply be dismissed as a minor "blind spot," as some have suggested. Stated differently, this chapter hopes to give us grounds for a sober reassessment of what Walter Laqueur (1998) has called the "Arendt Cult." More importantly, the chapter seeks to indicate the political implications of denigrating compassion as anti-political. For we live in an era in which the political role of compassion is very much a live issue: social psychologists tout the political virtues of empathy and compassion, and educational theorists promise miraculous transformations of society through the cultivation of these emotions (Armstrong 2011; Trout 2009; De Waal 2009). At the same time, voices claiming the mantle of "realism" denounce "bleeding hearts" and leftist politics of compassion as being ineffectual at best and despotic at worst (Brooks 2007). Much depends, then, on whether we accept the Arendtian critique of compassion as a political emotion.

Before we turn to Arendt's attack against compassion, a few words need to be said about terminology. Lauren Berlant, who has written extensively about compassion, once noted that "there is nothing clear about compassion" (2004, 1). And indeed, there is not. While some scholars insist that compassion is a sentiment, but not a virtue (Boyd 2004; Orwin 2008; Woodward 2004), others insist that it is a most significant political virtue – one that is tied to fairly elaborate cognition processes (Blum 1980; Nussbaum 2001; Porter 2006; Reilly 2008; Solomon 2004; Snow 1991; Whitebrook 2002). And if many have insisted on how important it is to distinguish between pity and compassion (Whitebrook 2002; Blum 1980), others have called into question such a distinction (Orwin 2008; Nussbaum 1996).[8] Arendt's own position (which we will flesh out in greater detail throughout this chapter) is that compassion is a passion ("a capacity for suffering *with* others" [OR, 76; emphasis added]);[9] it is *not* a virtue. Also, Arendt insists that there is an important distinction to be made between pity and compassion (a distinction that she nevertheless does not always uphold, as we will see). In the following pages, we will try to sort out the intricate relationships between Arendt's conception of compassion and her views concerning speech, reason, action, and poverty.

Compassion's Insignificance: The Dullness and Speechlessness of the Passions

> Compassion ... remains, politically speaking, irrelevant and without consequence.
>
> – Arendt, *On Revolution* (81)

While Arendt touches briefly on compassion in *On Violence* (1970) and in her essays on Brecht and Lessing, it is in *On Revolution* that she offers her most sustained analysis of the subject. We learn here that compassion is largely what explains the "success"[10] of the American Revolution and the "failure" of most modern revolutions. Because massive poverty was largely absent from eighteenth-century America, the "most powerful passion" that accompanies poverty – compassion – was also absent (OR, 66).[11] Whereas the American founders were able to remain "men of action" dedicated to freedom and had the good sense to embrace the "age-old rule model of the rule of reason over the passions" (OR, 91), the French revolutionaries' desire for freedom collapsed "under the impact of [their] compassion with human misery" (OR, 249). Ever since that time, Arendt laments, "the passion of compassion has haunted and driven the best men of all revolutions" (OR, 65).

If compassion is a most overwhelming and destructive passion for revolutions, how can Arendt simultaneously argue that compassion is, "politically speaking ... irrelevant and *without consequence*" (OR, 81; emphasis added)? How can a passion be held responsible for the Terror and for the "failures" of *all* (or at least most) revolutions since 1789 and at the same time be deemed inconsequential for politics? Clearly, when Arendt writes that compassion is without consequence, she is making a normative rather than a descriptive claim: she is convinced that compassion *can have* grave repercussions for the world of politics, but that it rather should not.

There are at least two (related) bases for Arendt's belief that compassion ought to be excluded from politics. First, she claims that compassion is irrelevant for action because it – like most passions – is "mute" (dumb, *alogos*) or "awkward with words" (OR, 81). In *The Human Condition* (1998), Arendt writes that intense feelings are simply not communicable (HC, 50–1). At best, affects and passions can produce sounds and gestures, but not speeches or elaborate arguments (OR, 81–2; HC, 51) – a distinction that is reminiscent of Aristotle's own famous dichotomy between *phonê* and *logos*.[12] However, Arendt suggests elsewhere that some political passions (e.g., the love of liberty) might be loquacious and conducive to dialogue. It would thus be legitimate to ask the following question: Why is compassion necessarily mute, whereas courage and ambition (both defined by Arendt in some places as passions) can give birth to speeches (e.g., OR, 280)?

A partial (albeit not fully convincing) answer might be derived from an enigmatic observation she makes in her essay on Lessing (*Men in Dark Times* 1970a). Here, she briefly suggests that passions tied to joy may be slightly more capable of "talk" (and thus potentially of politics?) than those based on pain and suffering – which she seems to regard as decisively mute (MDT, 15).[13] Her claim appears to rest on the conviction that the experiences of joy and pleasure (on which courage might be based?) tend to be favourable to sharing and to openness to others, whereas sadness and pain (on which compassion is more obviously based) tend to make individuals retreat from the world in utter speechlessness.

Now, as all readers of *The Human Condition* will recall, it is precisely speech that is essential for action (one could even suggest that speech *is* action).[14] In the absence of words, no persuasion or argumentation is possible and, therefore, no public realm either, according to Arendt. She insists not only that, without speech, there is no politics (a somewhat reasonable claim) but also more controversially that, without speech, feelings are hardly human or meaningful.

> However much we are affected by the things of the world, however deeply they may stir and stimulate us, they become human for us only when we can discuss them with our fellows. … We humanize what is going on in the world and in ourselves by speaking of it, and *in the course of speaking of it we learn to be human.* (MDT, 25; emphasis added)

While it may be reasonable to argue that our feelings tend to acquire greater depth and significance as we communicate them or as we formulate political claims on their basis, it is not as convincing to assert that there is *nothing* specifically human or valuable about the mere experiencing of emotions. (The work of Martha Nussbaum, Jerome Neu, Solomon, Ronald de Sousa, and Antonio Damasio might be instructive here.)

To better illustrate her point about the "speechlessness" of compassion, Arendt draws on the examples of Billy Budd (Melville) and Christ's compassion for the "Grand Inquisitor" (Dostoevsky).

> Both Jesus' silence (and kiss) and Billy Budd's stammer indicate the same, namely their incapacity (or unwillingness) for all kinds of predicative or argumentative speech, in which someone talks *to* somebody *about* something that is of interest to both because it *inter-est*, it is between them. Such talkative and argumentative interest in the world is entirely alien to compassion, which is directed solely, and with passionate intensity, toward suffering man himself; compassion speaks only to the extent that it has to reply directly to the sheer expressionist sound and gestures through which suffering becomes audible and visible in the world. (OR, 81-82; emphasis in the original)

Setting aside the speechlessness and political "insignificance" of compassion for a moment, let us note Arendt's important claim here (one that sets her apart from most critics of compassion). We are told that compassion is fundamentally *other* directed – or, as some would put it, that it is an "altruistic" passion.[15] While noble, such "selflessness" is not entirely a good thing, according to Arendt: she insists that she who offers compassion becomes so enthralled *in* the other's suffering that the space between them completely vanishes.[16] While some might want to argue that this intense experience of fusion and shared humanity is precisely what makes compassion so valuable for morality and living together (e.g., Blum 1980), Arendt would respond that blurring the distinctions between self and others is, in fact, equivalent to eradicating the political world altogether. Political life should "relate" us, but it should also "separate" us (HC, 52).[17] One of the great perils of compassion is that it fails to do the latter: compassion is too intimate – if not, perhaps, too bodily. It strikes "one in the flesh," observes Arendt, and it is as contagious as a virus (e.g., OR, 80, 84). While it may be quite appropriate for intimate relationships, compassion has no place in politics: it is incapable of arguments and persuasion, and what is more, it tends to culminate in kisses, hugs, and tears.[18] One suspects that Arendt would have had little sympathy for Neu's thesis that "a tear is an intellectual – and an *interesting* – thing" (Neu 2000).

We see here that Arendt's eulogy for the dignity of politics is accompanied by some significant distaste for, if not loathing of, bodily intimacy (as some Arendt scholars have previously noted).[19] And it also comes, more generally, with considerable disregard for the inner motives and emotions that energize the political actor – with the very significant exception of a handful of good "political passions."[20] If Arendt believes that citizens can show their uniqueness and greatness through deeds and speeches – their "psychological qualities" – motives or passions are, on the whole, rather uninteresting.[21] Inside, she insists, we are all the same.

We are presented here with the second basis for Arendt's claim that compassion is politically insignificant: in *The Life of the Mind* (1978b), for instance, she writes that passions and emotions do not allow one to shine or become a hero – only individuals struggling with a serious mental illness can distinguish themselves with their inner life (LM, 35). Not surprisingly, then, she considers the scientific study of emotions and the heart to be a rather insignificant discipline. She goes on to say, "Psychology ... discovers no more than the ever-changing moods, the ups and downs of our psychic life, and its results and discoveries are neither particularly appealing nor very meaningful in themselves" (LM, 35). Contrary to political deeds (which, according to her, are always distinct), passions and inner forces are rather "typical" and "*never unique*" (HC, 206; emphasis added). Unlike the "monotonous sameness and pervasive ugliness" of the inner realm described by modern psychology, the world of action, the world of "overt human conduct," is the only one that can (potentially, at least) be filled with variety and virtuosity (LM, 35).[22]

In this sense, one could argue that Arendt is much more Machiavellian than Aristotelian – since she puts the claims of glory, deeds, and theatre[23] well above those of soul craft. In fact, one could claim that she turns against the latter in the name of the former.[24] In the context of her discussions of compassion and love, Arendt repeatedly cites – with admiration – the famous words from Machiavelli's *The Prince* (1532) that "one must learn how not to be good" (quoted in HC, 77). In her view, the Florentine correctly understood that what is needed to face the world of politics is not the "effeminate" virtues that are goodness or compassion, but a much "harsher" kind of virtue – more specifically, one that is highly *demonstrative*.[25]

We have seen thus far that compassion is "politically irrelevant," according to Arendt – because it cannot generate speech and is too intimate, and because it cannot be "seen":[26] compassion generates no outer manifestation. It cannot *appear*. We might want to add here that if compassion could, by some miracle, produce an outward manifestation, this would immediately destroy the passion itself, according to Arendt. Like all actions performed out of "goodness," compassionate acts vanish as soon as they are seen by others or made conscious to the self.

> When goodness appears only, it is no longer goodness. ... Goodness can exist only when it is not perceived, not even by its author; whoever sees himself performing a good work is no longer good. ... Therefore: "Let not thy left hand know what thy right hand doeth." (HC, 74)

Once made public or an object of people's admiration, a compassionate act may be useful as a kind of handout or as an act of solidarity, but it is no longer a true act of compassion, according to Arendt (HC, 74).[27] A "compassionate state," a "compassionate statesman," and a "compassionate policy" are therefore all oxymorons: only compassionate gestures performed in the privacy of the home are significant. What we see here is that behind Arendt's critique of political compassion lies an implicit apology for *private* compassion (one rarely noted by interpreters). In the obscurity of our intimate relationships, compassion – the "noblest form of passion" – is redeemed (OR, 66).

In her longing to sever compassion from publicity, Arendt appears to be motivated by the Christian conviction (shared by many American neoconservatives) that true charity ought to be secretive and, hence, free from pride.[28] Indeed, the list of Arendtian heroes does not merely include Pericles and Socrates, but also, let us not forget, Jesus Christ (the archetype of compassion, who, in spite of his compassion for all men, was able to elude the great sin of pride) (e.g., OR, 80; HC, 238–43, 246–7). If Jesus of Nazareth is, strictly speaking, not a fully political figure in the strict Arendtian sense, it is nevertheless him whom Arendt credits for the discovery of one of the most important human faculties required for action: forgiveness (e.g., HC, 238, 247).[29]

Compassion: Particular and Passive?

Now, in all fairness to Arendt, to suggest that compassion is politically irrelevant or "uninteresting" need not mean that this passion is *entirely* meaningless or that it may not be part of what a "normal" human being looks like. In her essay on Lessing, for instance, Arendt writes that

> compassion is unquestionably a *natural, creature affect which involuntarily touches every normal person at the sight of suffering*, however alien the sufferer may be, and would therefore *seem* an ideal basis for a feeling that reaching out to all mankind would establish a society in which men might really become brothers. (MDT, 14; emphasis added)

But she goes on to insist that the latter kind of large-scale "brotherhood" is accessible only to pariah peoples and that it certainly cannot be artificially "acquired" by financially privileged individuals who try to improve the lot of the poor (regardless of these individuals' best intentions [MDT, 14]). Unlike pity, compassion cannot be felt for a large group, a class, or an entire people, according to Arendt: it can be felt only for a specific individual with whose suffering one is confronted. "[Compassion's] strength hinges on the strength of passion itself, which, in contrast to reason, can comprehend only the particular, but has no notion of the general and no capacity for generalization" (OR, 80).[30] But could one not argue, contra Arendt, that, without this "particular," the general could hardly ever be "accessed" or become significant?[31] For Arendt, the point is moot: it is never *possible* to feel compassion for a group, and even if it could be (in compassion's "perverted" version, pity), it would not be desirable. Indeed, good politics is impartial and seeks "to establish justice *for all*," rich and poor (MDT, 14; emphasis added) – it is not concerned with the plight of a particular class.

Let me come back briefly to Arendt's claim that compassion is a natural[32] affect possessed by all human beings, for it is here that one can locate a third ground for Arendt's perplexing claim that compassion is politically irrelevant. Because compassion is a passion over which we seem to have little control ("it *involuntarily* touches every normal person" [MDT, 14]),[33] Arendt claims that it cannot be "active" (OR, 82) and, thus, that it cannot translate into concrete political change. (But we will see later that Arendt considers *some* passions to be capable of action.)

> *As a rule, it is not compassion which sets out to change worldly conditions in order to ease human suffering*, but if it does, it will shun the drawn-out wearisome processes of persuasion, negotiation, and compromise, which are the processes of law and politics, and lend its voice to the suffering itself,

> which must claim for swift and direct action, that is, for action with the means of violence. (OR, 82; emphasis added)[34]

We are thus presented with a two-fold charge. First, compassion is *insufficiently* potent to be political (it is mute and "passive," hence incapable of action); and yet compassion is also considered to be *too* potent to be a legitimate ground for politics: it eschews speech and "reasonable" procedures – and may even, when it turns into pity, translate into boundless rage and violence. Emotions thus have a unique capacity to overwhelm us against our wills, according to Arendt (a common accusation levelled against "the heart" in the history of ideas, needless to say).[35]

Many critics of compassion share Arendt's concern about the possible excess and lack of reliability of such an emotion. Orwin (1997, 20), for instance, writes, "Almost always too much or too little, too intense or too sporadic, liable alike to mindless excess and to calculated hypocrisy, compassion is anything but a reliable basis for public policy." To these widespread concerns, one could offer the following brief responses. First, laws, speech, and rational procedures (which Arendt often presents as the safe *alternatives* to compassion and pity) have also failed to prove perfectly reliable.[36] Also, all emotions could potentially be appealed to "hypocritically" – it is not clear why compassion should be singled out on that point. More important, one could also indicate that Arendt's concern regarding the risk of passionate excess or inflexibility could equally be levelled at some of the principles and virtues she espouses (e.g., honour, ambition, courage).[37] It is certainly far from obvious why the principle of honour or the virtue of courage could not make for a wrathful and bloody politics.[38]

Before we turn to another central reason for Arendt's attack on compassion, I would like to pause here and comment briefly on her use of the terms *passion* and *emotion*, for it is remarkably imprecise. In *On Revolution*, Arendt argues that there is a clear distinction to be made between compassion (which she refers to as a passion) and pity (which she refers to as a sentiment or an emotion) (OR, 83–4). While Arendt considers compassion and pity to be related phenomena of the human heart, she nevertheless treats them as different things. If the passion of compassion is mute, the emotion of pity is talkative. If compassion can be felt for only one individual, pity can be felt for a multitude – it can "enter the market-place" (OR, 76). But beyond these pages, Arendt fails to apply this distinction systematically: she interchangeably refers to compassion as an emotion, as an affect, as a passion, and as a sentiment.[39] By doing so, she undermines many of the arguments that rested on her distinction between passion and emotion (e.g., the one that concerned the speechlessness of compassion).

It seems that Arendt did not carefully work out the basis for her distinction between passion and emotion. While some scholars have sought to elucidate the distinction between these two things by appealing to a historical explanation (e.g., emotion is but a secular equivalent to passion, one that made its appearance in the late eighteenth century; see Dixon 2003), Arendt proposes no such explanation. There are some passages in her work that suggest that passions (such as compassion) are to be regarded almost solely as physiological phenomena (MDT, 14), whereas emotions are more complex cognitive feelings. (But, if anything, this distinction should raise emotions *above* compassion in her estimation.) Unfortunately, Arendt is not meticulous here either; she suggests in *The Life of the Mind* that individuals are equally at the mercy of their emotions (i.e., that these are involuntary) and, elsewhere, that compassion is not a *necessary* physiological reaction[40] (e.g., LM, 32–3; OR, 65). In short, one must take the significance of the distinction Arendt makes between compassion as a passion and pity as an emotion, and the implications she draws from this distinction, with a large grain of salt.

If the difference between passion and emotion, and between compassion and pity, in Arendt's work is unclear, what is a little clearer is that both compassion and pity are treated as the opposites of solidarity. What is more, Arendt maintains that solidarity's superiority to compassion and pity is largely due to solidarity's inherent rationality, thereby implying that compassion and pity are irrational.[41] For instance, in contrast with pity, solidarity is said to be a *dispassionate* way to establish "a community of interest with the oppressed and exploited" (OR, 84) – one that would be built not on "love," but rather on the basis of "ideas" or "principles" (e.g., honour, dignity, greatness). Solidarity "partakes of reason, and hence generality" – and, as such, it can do what compassion cannot: it can "comprehend a multitude conceptually" (OR, 84) without negating the uniqueness of each individual.

It may therefore be tempting to conclude that Arendt opts for reason and ideas over the "irrationality of emotions." Much of Arendt's work would lend itself to such a conclusion: she tells us that feelings obscure the "hard facts" of reality and put "thinking in jeopardy" (OR, 75);[42] she shows her admiration for the "cold and abstract" (OR, 84) character of solidarity; she calls for a type of political friendship that is "sober and cool rather then sentimental" (MDT, 25); and finally, she likes to describe her ideal politics as a friendship "without intimacy and without closeness" (HC, 243). Nelson's thesis regarding Arendt's "heartlessness" seems to be sensible: a rule of reason over the passions appears to be called for (2004).

But this conclusion would be a little hasty: Arendt's conception of the relationship between emotion and reason is not that straightforward. It would obviously be incorrect to claim that Arendt is a rationalist or that she believes that emotions can be entirely separated from reason – even though Ken Reshaur (1992) is right to stress that Arendt tries, not without difficulty, to "keep *distinct* the *contributions* of emotion and cognition" (723; emphasis added). And it would be too simple to say that, in *Between Past and Future* (2006), she calls for a radical *disciplining* of our emotions (BPF, 147; emphasis added). After all, she did not conceal her disapproval of Plato's "tyranny of reason," and in *On Violence*, she bluntly notes that "absence of emotions neither causes nor promotes rationality" (1970b, 64).[43] Finally, and most important, when we look to the principles she exposes as the legitimate basis for politics (and here she draws heavily on Montesquieu), we are forced to note that these are entirely affective. Many of them are indeed defined in terms of love and joy: Arendt's ideal politics is to be filled with *love* of the world, the *love* of honour, a *passion* for equality, the *love* of distinction, the *desire* for glory, etc. If above we saw Arendt suggest that emotions are to be separated from politics altogether, here we see that some political emotions are redeemed.

But the emotions that Arendt embraces are far from being everyday feelings. Arendtian passions (like her political agent) have to be exceptional; they have to be Periclean.

> Political passions – courage,[44] the pursuit of public happiness, the taste of public freedom, an ambition that strives for excellence regardless not only of social status and administrative office but even of achievement and congratulation – are perhaps not as rare as we are inclined to think, living in a society which has perverted all virtues into social values; but *they certainly are out of the ordinary under all circumstances.* (OR, 280; emphasis added)

Now, what is remarkable is the degree to which Arendt sometimes seems to have been blind to the affective nature of her political principles – she almost constantly describes the latter in terms of an *anti-affective* quality. In *On Revolution*, for instance, she desperately seeks to underscore the distinction between emotions and the principle of solidarity: she describes the latter as *dispassionate*, cold, and abstract (OR, 84). Moreover, she seems remarkably eager to separate all her (Montesquieu-inspired) principles (e.g., virtue, honour, fear) from psychological life. In one of her pieces included in *Essays in Understanding, 1930–1954* (2005, 332), she insists that Montesquieu's principles of virtue and honour are not to be seen primarily as "psychological motives," but rather as objective "criteria according to which all public life is led and judged." Under Arendt's pen, Montesquieu becomes astonishingly "dispassionate."

It may be the case that Arendt was, in the end, uninterested in working out the details of the relationship between the world of human affect and that of cognition – perhaps because she considered the exercise to be pointless. Even if one could figure out what the difference between passions and emotions is, and what kind of "cognitive" potential the passions may have, the heart *should* remain a place of "darkness." Arendt thus does not "solve" some of the problems she raises, but instead gives us the following triviality (which is poetically if not physiologically correct): "Whatever the passions and the emotions may be, and whatever their true connection with thought and reason, they certainly are located in the human heart" (OR, 91). What she has attempted to emphasize with this, as we will see below, is that certain things ought to be sheltered from the bright light of public scrutiny.

Of Hearts, Homes, and Poverty

Nothing ... could be more obsolete than to attempt to liberate mankind from poverty by political means; nothing could be more futile and more dangerous.

– Arendt, *On Revolution* (110)

This brings us to another important part of Arendt's indictment of compassion (and of emotions more generally). Despite the fact that she wants to hold onto a handful of political emotions (as we noted above), she repeatedly claims that feelings do not belong in the public realm. The heart is a dark place, and so it should remain.

> Not only is the human heart a place of darkness which, with certainty, no human eye can penetrate; the qualities of the heart need darkness and protection against the light of the public to grow and to remain what they are meant to be, innermost motives which are not for public display. (OR, 91)

There are at least three reasons why feelings should remain hidden, according to Arendt. The first is that regardless of how hard we try, it is impossible to really know them. Not only are our feelings hidden from others, but they are also bound to remain hidden from ourselves (e.g., BPF, 143; OR, 91–4). Second, presuming that we could, somehow, catch a good glimpse of the sea of emotions that dwells in our soul, we would not be able to bear such a sight. In a Nietzschean moment, Arendt writes that "nobody but God can see (and perhaps, can bear to see) the nakedness of a human heart" (OR, 92). And finally, there are additional problems with trying to have feelings displayed in public: at best, this leads to a distasteful sentimentality, but at worst, it distorts our emotions altogether or leads to a wrathful obsession with hypocrisy (ibid.).

The comfort afforded by our private "hiding places" (our homes, our souls) is precisely what makes Arendt attribute such great importance to the virtue of courage. She believes that political actors require temerity if they are to face the bright light of publicity: "courage and boldness are already present *in leaving one's private hiding place* and showing who one is, in disclosing and exposing one's self" (HC, 186; emphasis added).[45] If one allows the life of the heart to invade the public stage and thus to blur the line between public and private (as modernity has done, according to Arendt), one loses a large part of what is meaningful about entering the world of action. We noted above that while Arendt was generally dismissive of emotions in political life, she nevertheless held onto the love of distinction and the desire for immortality. True Arendtian courage – a passion, in her view – is fiercely political: it can be found only on the public scene and must be accompanied by danger. (This suggests a more distinct version of courage than that offered by Plato, discussed by Ryan Balot in chapter 1 of this volume, which was informed by practices of deliberation and democratic education.) As Arendt would put it, "The world has to be at stake" – and not simply "mere life" (BPF, 155).

> The daily fight in which the human body is engaged to keep the world clean and prevent its decay bears little resemblance to heroic deeds; the endurance it needs to repair every day anew the waste of yesterday is not courage, and what makes the effort painful is not danger but its relentless repetition. (HC, 101)

In the household, in our private relationships, and in the quotidian passions that are implicated in labour, the world is not at stake. The indignation of an underpaid factory worker, the love of a child, or the courage it takes a poor single mother to scrape by are not politically significant – they leave no significant traces behind. Like the human body, they are destined to oblivion and thus do not factor into the system of "organized remembrance" that is politics (e.g., HC, 198).

I noted in the previous section of this essay that compassion made Arendt uneasy because she regarded this passion as excessively intimate and bodily. And to this we might now add that, for Arendt, what belongs to the body should remain in the obscurity of the household (HC, 31–5, 57). There is thus an implicit link between Arendt's concerns about "sentimentality" in politics and her famous attack on "the social," and it is a connection that is underlined by her critique of compassion. Indeed, another ground for her wariness of compassion is that when one is overwhelmed by the misery of another individual, the issue of poverty (and its relief) attains such great importance that the cause of freedom tends to be discarded (OR, 110). This is precisely what she says happened with the French Revolution.

> Since the revolution had opened the gates of the political realm to the poor, this realm had indeed become "social." It was overwhelmed by the cares and worries which actually belonged in the sphere of the household and which, even if they were permitted to enter the public realm, could not be solved by political means, since they were matters of administration. (OR, 86)

Like the heart, then, poverty and physical necessity more generally should remain in the dark – they should not be the basis for, or the essential concerns of, action.[46] Alas, modernity failed to heed this important lesson and destroyed the separation between the private and the public realms: overwhelmed by sentimentality, it let the biological concerns of the social pollute the political sphere.[47] In the Arendtian account of modernity, the (political) emancipation of the emotions, women, and labourers all seem to be related.

> It is striking that from the beginning of history to our own time it has always been the bodily part of human existence that needed to be hidden in privacy, all things connected with the necessity of the life process itself, which prior to the modern age comprehended all activities serving the subsistence of the individual and the survival of the species. *Hidden away were the laborers who "with their bodies minister to the [bodily] needs of life," and*

> *the women who with their bodies guarantee the physical survival of the species. ...* The fact that the modern age emancipated the working classes and the women at nearly the same historical moment must certainly be counted among the characteristics of an age which no longer believes that bodily functions and material concerns should be hidden. (HC, 72–3; emphasis added)

To Arendt's dismay, pregnant women, large-scale bureaucracies, Rousseauian "moist eyes" (Orwin 1997), and the interests and concerns of the labouring class have all invaded the public space. This, in her view, worked to undermine the dignity of the *vita activa* – a realm where boldness, warfare, and great speeches[48] – rather than sentimentality, welfare, and governmental "housekeeping" – should matter (HC, 33, 28).[49]

If Arendtian politics are defined by talk, the object of our conversations should not be economic issues or "arithmetic" matters like grain quotas and health care funding. Issues such as hunger, health coverage, and the struggling farming industry are to be pushed outside politics – not only because grain quotas or the price of dented cans of tuna rarely make for heroic Periclean speeches but also because Arendt believes that they are issues that *can be solved* mathematically and with administrative precision. Indeed, with remarkable naiveté, Arendt asserts that, contrary to the "great political questions" (which are to remain open-ended, but about which Arendt is incredibly vague),[50] poverty and other economic matters can be "resolved" by experts with the help of a calculator and technology. For Arendt, "political economy" is an oxymoron (HC, 29). In language slightly reminiscent of social conservatives grumbling about the "nanny state," Arendt laments the fact that our family and biological concerns have been taken over "by a gigantic nation-wide administration of housekeeping" (HC, 28).[51]

Now, Arendt certainly did not mean to suggest that hunger and poverty were acceptable, or that women (pregnant or not) should stay at home in darkness. But she could hardly have been blind to some of the concrete repercussions that her theoretical musings on compassion and the social, if acted on, would have had on women. In the absence of generous welfare programs that are directed at infants, children, the elderly, or the disabled (any of which could be said to fall under the Arendtian category of housekeeping), it is women who tend to shoulder the weight of these necessities. And if this was true of antiquity (as Arendt herself acknowledged [HC, 119]), it was equally applicable to the 1950s American women Arendt was surrounded by. (This is not to suggest that compassion is a virtue of women, as a few care theorists have suggested, but only that what is at stake in the debate over compassion may be of particular significance for women – and, naturally, the poor). Contra "compassionate conservatives," women may wish to insist that true political compassion does *not* mean private charity, but, above all, a strong welfare state.

If some of Arendt's devotees have noted that we have here a blind spot in her work, I would argue that this is in fact much more. It is hardly convincing to claim, as Elizabeth Young-Bruehl has done, that the social and the issues connected to the household were simply not Arendt's "thing" and that we should focus on the fascinating things Arendt wrote regarding action or totalitarianism.[52] Arendt's distinction between public and private, just like her distinction between good public passions and bad private ones, are central to her political theory. They are not minor and detachable parts of her enterprise – which is to rehabilitate the dignity of action at (almost) any cost.

Hannah Arendt and "Compassionate Conservatism"

Orwin (1997, 16) once noted that at the heart of the academic and popular debate about compassion lies the question of the welfare state. As I have intimated above, I think that Orwin is absolutely right. If the philosophical debate surrounding compassion focuses largely on its rationality, or on its inegalitarian and condescending overtones, what is at stake, in practice, is the welfare state. Compassion obviously raises the problem of human suffering, but it also raises the very crucial question of what constitutes an appropriate *answer* to this suffering: Should we attempt to relieve misery mostly through private charity or largely through the provision of state-regulated and state-funded social services?

Forced to choose between these two paths, it may be that Arendt would have preferred the first. And it is here that one can identify a certain parallel between Arendt's thought and the discourse of "compassionate conservatives" (a primarily American discourse, but certainly one that has found some sympathizers in England and Canada). Compassionate conservatives (who like to market themselves as critics of left-wing political compassion) are convinced that compassion belongs principally to the private realm and that it is not really up to the state to take care of issues of health, drug addiction, or poverty. In their view, all this is better done by private enterprises, families, or faith-based charities. While Arendt's discussion and personal experience of statelessness suggest that she might have had some awareness of the limitations of private charity, she nevertheless refused to entertain the idea that one could derive valuable, strong welfare state measures from a civic experience of compassion.

We witnessed, in Arendt, great concern about the risk posed by "totalitarian sentimentality" for plurality as well as much discomfort about the idea of making economic issues a matter of political discussion and political control. These concerns are certainly mirrored in the writings of some neoconservatives. To briefly quote Scruton,

> As the state takes charge of our needs, and relieves people of the burdens that should rightly be theirs – the burdens that come from charity and neighborliness – serious feeling retreats. In place of it comes an aggressive sentimentality that seeks to dominate the public square. *I call this sentimentality "totalitarian" since – like totalitarian government – it seeks out opposition and carefully extinguishes it,* in all the places where opposition might form. Its goal is to "solve" our social problems. ... The result is to replace old social problems, which should have been relieved by private charity, with the new and intransigent problems fostered by the state. (Scruton 2009, n.p.; emphasis added)

Even though Arendt never systematically spelled out what she would want the American government to do regarding welfare policies or various economic matters (not surprisingly, given what has been said in the previous section), she nevertheless explicitly deplored the fact that American income tax was unbearably high (2007, 107). Moreover, she often noted that private property should not only be carefully protected but also actively encouraged. (She stated this, however, without giving her full loyalty to market capitalism [ibid.].) And finally, as we noted earlier, Arendt repeatedly lamented the fact that large state agencies were increasingly taking over the realm of "necessity." It would be most unfair to suggest that Arendt was indifferent to questions of social justice or that she explicitly embraced a kind of neoliberal economics. Nevertheless, what I would like to suggest here is that her relegation of compassion to the private sphere, combined with her refusal to regard *economic* issues as matters of concern for action, indicate that her work is not fully compatible with the kind of radical politics with which her left-wing champions would like to associate her.

Naturally, this essay can only touch on the question of economics in Arendt. My first concern was to help make sense of what Kateb (1983) considered to be disturbing and obscure in Arendt: her indictment of compassion. I have argued that although Arendt certainly puts compassion on trial, she does not totally discard it. She briefly acknowledges its attentiveness to the particular, its disinterestedness, and its intensity in intimate relationships. But for these very reasons, Arendt was unwilling to consider it fit for politics. In the end, what we see in this chapter is that Arendt did not put all emotions "under siege," but rather tried to sort through them to identify those political passions that are amenable to plurality and dialogue and those that are not. What she failed to do, however, was to provide us with a convincing philosophical account of the criteria on which her sorting of emotions would rest.

NOTES

1 For a fuller exposition of Orwin's case against compassion and a thoughtful analysis of Rousseauian pity, see Orwin and Tarcov (1997).

2 While he is an Englishman, Scruton likes to lend his pen to the cause of American neoconservatism.

3 Recall former prime minister Stephen Harper's transparent attempt, during past electoral campaigns, to decrease his so-called compassion deficit by adjusting his wardrobe and discourse and by appealing to arguments espoused by "compassionate conservatives." Compassion thus seems to have a large fan club – not only among politicians but also among academics and the general public. American news media got momentarily excited some years ago by a poll suggesting that "compassion counts more than ever." (See, e.g., http://www.parade.com/news/what-america-cares-about/featured/100307-compassion-counts-more-than-ever.html, accessed 30 March 2010.)

4 Some have tried to appeal to Arendt's work to redeem "true" compassion – by comparing it with its "perversion," pity; see, e.g., Beran (2003). For an appeal to Arendt as a way of *criticizing* the "fake" compassion of the right, see Nelson (2004).

5 Unless otherwise stated, the following abbreviations and editions will be used when referring to the following works by Arendt: *On Revolution* 1963 (OR), *The Human Condition* 1998 (HC), *Men in Dark Times* 1970a (MDT), *Between Past and Future* 2006 (BPF), and *The Life of the Mind* 1978b (LM).

6 The "taste of public liberty," Arendt writes, "died away under the impact of compassion with human misery" (OR, 249).

7 Arendt once noted, "You know the left think that I am conservative, and the conservatives sometimes think I am left or I am a maverick or God knows what. And I must say I couldn't care less" (quoted in Canovan 1996, 11). This statement was made by Arendt in the context of a conference dedicated to her work, held in Toronto at York University in 1972. For the transcript, see "On Hannah Arendt," in *Hannah Arendt: The Recovery of the Public World*, ed. Melvyn A. Hill ed. (New York: St Martin's Press, 1979).

8 Most scholars who have argued for a distinction between compassion and pity have emphasized the fact that the latter is condescending, whereas the former is not (e.g., Blum 1980, 512).

9 In MDT, she refers to compassion as "an affect," but also as an emotion (15).

10 The success is indeed not total, according to Arendt. For a good discussion of the "relative" character of the "success," see Enégren (1984).

11 Pity is also the product of poverty – and it is, as we will see below, the perverted outgrowth of compassion.

12 In her essay on Lessing, she also notes, "The decisive factor is that pleasure and pain, like everything instinctual, tend to muteness, and while they may well produce sound, they do not produce speech and certainly not dialogue" (MDT, 16). For an insightful critique of the Aristotelian/ Arendtian perspective on the relation among *phonê, logos,* and politics, see Jacques Rancière (2001).

13 "Gladness, not sadness, is talkative, and truly human dialogue differs from mere talk or even discussion in that it is entirely permeated by pleasure in the other person and what he says. It is tuned to the key of gladness, we might say" (MDT, 15); cf. the quotation in note 27 below. And as we will see below, the political passions that Arendt "redeems" (e.g., love of freedom, love of the world) are essentially joyful passions.

14 Deeds matter as well. But since Arendt is remarkably vague as to what she means by deeds (military acts? dances? a heroic moment of crowd control?), the "heroic deeds" she repeatedly celebrates in *The Human Condition* seem to come down to the performance of a good speech.

15 See also MDT (15). Most critics of compassion insist that it is self-regarding or selfish. But most of them also tend to equate pity and compassion (whereas Arendt separates them).

16 It is this type of objection that has led Nussbaum to insist on the fact that compassion need not be about a complete communion. Rather, true compassion requires awareness of one's separateness. "If one really had the experience of feeling the pain in one's own body, then one would precisely

have failed to comprehend the pain of another *as other*" (Nussbaum 1996, 35; emphasis added).

17 "To live together in the world means essentially that a world of things is between those who have it in common, as a table is located between those who sit around it; the world, like every in-between, relates and separates men at the same time" (HC, 52).

18 According to Arendt, it can also eventually end in violence (a much worse prospect, evidently). More specifically, it is pity (the perversion of compassion) that ends in violence.

19 E.g., Pitkin (1998, 271); also Kateb (1983, 29).

20 E.g., courage, the love of liberty, the love of distinction (OR, 280; HC, 41). More on these "political passions" will be said below.

21 And this regardless of their "purity" or intensity. In "What Is Freedom?," Arendt writes, "Action, to be free, must be free from motive on one side, from its intended goal as a predictable effect on the other" (BPF, 150).

22 It is, therefore, the only realm that can be cause for remembrance.

23 The *polis* is defined as "a kind of theatre where freedom could appear" (BPF, 152); for glory, see HC (76).

24 Arendt repeatedly criticized the French revolutionaries for having failed to respect the "legal masks" worn by political actors (*personae*) and for having sought to unmask with much violence, rage, and futility all hypocrisy and emotional delusions.

25 "Goodness ... is not only impossible within the confines of the public realm, it is even destructive of it. Nobody perhaps has been more sharply aware of this ruinous quality of doing good than Machiavelli, who, in a famous passage, dared to teach men 'how not to be good'" (HC, 77); see also MDT (236).

26 "The inner feeling, since it is without manifestation, is by definition politically irrelevant"; see "What Is Freedom?" (BPF, 145).

27 For a discussion of charity on its more "emotional" level – as Christian love (rather than *material* offerings), see HC (53–5).

28 *Hubris* seems to be appropriate in politics, but only up to a point. (Arendt notes, in *The Human Condition*, that pride can indeed become "the" great vice of politics and that it needs to be tempered by moderation; see, e.g., HC [191].)

29 See also HC (318), where she writes, "The only activity Jesus of Nazareth recommends in his preachings is action."

30 In this regard, pity is quite different, according to Arendt: with pity, one is "not stricken in the flesh" (OR, 84). The consequences of this are significant to Arendt: since the pitier is not "absorbed" by the sufferer, he can experience pity for a multitude.

31 A similar argument is put forth by Elisabeth Porter, who argues that compassion can mediate between the particular and the universal (Porter 2006, 102).

32 Elsewhere, her claim is a bit more nuanced – see, e.g., OR (65).

33 Arendt stops short of saying, however, that passions are purely physiological phenomena. Compassion, at least, does seem to involve some cognition (although she does not sufficiently elaborate on this for me to make a substantive claim).

34 Human passions are exclusive, whereas principles and "ideas" are inclusive and capable of generality.

35 For discussions of these accusations, see, e.g., Solomon (1993) and Kingston and Ferry (2008).

36 One might also argue that we are not confronted with an either-or situation here: there is no reason why law and the cultivation of character (including the cultivation of compassion) could not be combined.

37 More on this below. For a distinction between principles (which inspire "from without") and motives (which operate "within"), see also "What Is Freedom?" (BPF, 150–1).

38 She suggests that there will be "limits" on politics (those afforded by man's capacities for forgiving and making promises) – but what is not evident is why these limits could not equally apply to a "politics of compassion" rather than just one based on courage or honour.

39 In her essay on Brecht, e.g., she explicitly refers to "the emotion of compassion" (MDT, 236), and elsewhere, she refers to fear and compassion as "emotions"; see also MDT (15).

40 Also, if fear is sometimes considered to be an affect or passion, Arendt refers to it as an "emotion" (LM, e.g., 36).

41 Although it seems that Arendt extols the value of solidarity, she also seems to have had reservations about it. According to Nelson, Arendt in fact much preferred solitude to solidarity (Nelson 2006). But see Reshaur (1992).

42 See Nelson (2006, 92–5; 2004, 229).

43 See also OR (91), where she notes briefly the naiveté of the Enlightenment project of bringing the "irrationality of desires and emotions under the control of rationality."

44 Incidentally, courage is a virtue rather than a passion, but Arendt uses the terms interchangeably at times.

45 Not only is the meaningfulness of political courage threatened by compassion/pity being on display, so is the "courage" required for thinking. Indeed, thinking requires "facing up to reality" without consolation or communion with others (Nelson 2004, 222).

46 They should be the concerns of technology and "experts" – not of those involved in politics.
47 Naturally, many commentators have discussed this problematic distinction in Arendt (e.g., Pitkin 1981, 1998; Benhabib 2000). Cf. the interpretation proposed by Patchen Markell in his "Arendt's Work: On the Architecture of *The Human Condition*" (2011). Markell argues that Arendt's conception of private property and work muddles not only the famous triad labour/work/action but also the public/private dichotomy. In the end, however, even Markell is forced to admit that while work and action are quite closely intertwined, the same claim cannot be made about labour and work or, for that matter, labour and action.
48 Since her primary examples of the deeds of action are speeches taken from Thucydides (where the main topic is warfare), it does not seem to be totally unreasonable to suggest that part of the "content" of Arendtian politics would be war related (as Arendt's friend Mary McCarthy also suggested). See also "What Is Freedom?" (BPF, 154–5).
49 "With the rise of society, that is, the rise of the 'household' (*oikia*) or of economic activities to the public realm, housekeeping and all matters pertaining formerly to the private sphere of the family have become a 'collective' concern" (HC, 33). I thus disagree with Anne Amiel's claim, *"Il n'y a aucun mépris de la sphère de l'intimité chez Arendt"* ("There is no contempt for the sphere of intimacy in Arendt") (Amiel 1996, 69).
50 Even McCarthy once expressed her frustration with Arendt's fuzziness regarding the content of political speech. In a public discussion they had in Toronto in 1972, McCarthy observed that "discourses cannot simply be discourses. They have to be discourses *about something*." If all "social" and economic questions are pushed outside politics, what is left to talk about? To this, Arendt could simply answer, "You are perfectly right, and I acknowledge that I have asked myself this question as well" (Arendt 2007, 101–2; translation mine).
51 It concerns her not only because this has compromised the formerly sacred privacy of our family lives but also because it tends to produce conformity and uniformity and kills the dignity of our political lives.
52 Young-Bruehl (1996, 310) writes that Arendt "did not ask how 'the social' shaped life in households, setting the subordination of women there more on a specifically sexual and reproductive basis, less on a labouring basis. 'The personal is the *social*' was not her topic." For one of the many commentators who acknowledges the link between Arendt's work on totalitarianism and the dichotomies she proposes in *The Human Condition,* see Markell (2011).

REFERENCES

Amiel, Anne. 1996. *Politique et Évènement*. Paris: PUF.

Arendt, Hannah. 1963. *On Revolution*. New York: Macmillan.

Arendt, Hannah. 1970a. *Men in Dark Times*. London: Lowe & Brydone.

Arendt, Hannah. 1970b. *On Violence*. New York: Harcourt Brace.

Arendt, Hannah. 1978a. *The Jew as Pariah*. Edited by Ron Feldman. New York: Grove.

Arendt, Hannah. 1978b. The *Life of the Mind*. New York: Harcourt Brace.

Arendt, Hannah. 1998. *The Human Condition*. 2nd ed. Chicago: University of Chicago Press. http://dx.doi.org/10.7208/chicago/9780226924571.001.0001.

Arendt, Hannah. 2005. *Essays in Understanding, 1930–1954*. New York: Random House.

Arendt, Hannah. 2006. *Between Past and Future*. New York: Penguin.

Arendt, Hannah. 2007. "Édifier un monde": *Interventions, 1971–1975*. Paris: Éditions du Seuil.

Armstrong, Karen. 2011. *Twelve Steps to a Compassionate Life*. London: Random House.

Benhabib, Seyla. 2000. *The Reluctant Modernism of Hannah Arendt*. Lanham, MD: Rowman and Littlefield.

Beran, Michael Knox. 2003. "Conservative Compassion vs. Liberal Pity." *City Journal* (New York). http://www.city-journal.org/html/conservative-compassion-vs-liberal-pity-12438.html.

Berlant, Lauren, ed. 2004. *Compassion: The Politics and Culture of an Emotion*. New York: Routledge.

Blum, Lawrence. 1980. "Compassion." In *Explaining Emotions*, edited by Amélie Oksenberg Rorty, 507–17. Berkeley: University of California Press.

Boyd, Richard. 2004. "Pity's Pathologies Portrayed: Rousseau and the Limits of Democratic Compassion." *Political Theory* 32 (4): 519–46. http://dx.doi.org/10.1177/0090591703258118.

Brooks, Arthur C. 2007. *Who Really Cares: The Surprising Truth about Compassionate Conservatism*. New York: Basic Books.

Canovan, Margaret. 1996. "Arendt as a Conservative Thinker." In *Hannah Arendt: Twenty Years Later*, edited by Larry May and Jerome Kohn, 11–32. Cambridge, MA: MIT Press.

De Waal, Frans. 2009. *The Age of Empathy: Nature's Lessons for a Kinder Society*. New York: Harmony.

Dixon, Thomas. 2003. *From Passions to Emotions: The Creation of a Secular Psychological Category*. Cambridge: Cambridge University Press. http://dx.doi.org/10.1017/CBO9780511490514.

Enégren, André. 1984. *La pensée politique de Hannah Arendt*. Paris: PUF.

Kateb, George. 1983. *Hannah Arendt: Politics, Conscience, Evil*. Totowa, NJ: Rowman & Allanheld.

Kingston, Rebecca, and Leonard Ferry. 2008. *Bringing the Passions Back In: The Emotions in Political Philosophy*. Vancouver: UBC Press.

Laqueur, Walter. 1998. "The Arendt Cult: Hannah Arendt as Political Commentator." *Journal of Contemporary History* 33 (4): 483–96. http://dx.doi.org/10.1177/002200949803300401.

Markell, Patchen. 2011. "Arendt's Work: On the Architecture of *The Human Condition*." *College Literature* 38 (1): 15–44.

Nelson, Deborah. 2004. "Suffering and Thinking." In *Compassion: The Politics and Culture of an Emotion*, edited by Lauren Berlant, 219–44. New York: Routledge.

Nelson, Deborah. 2006. "The Virtues of Heartlessness: Mary McCarthy, Hannah Arendt, and the Anesthetics of Empathy." *American Literary History* 18 (1): 86–101. http://dx.doi.org/10.1093/alh/ajj004.

Neu, Jerome. 2000. *A Tear Is an Intellectual Thing*. New York: Oxford University Press.

Nussbaum, Martha. 1996. "Compassion as the Basic Social Emotion." *Social Philosophy & Policy* 13 (1): 27–58. http://dx.doi.org/10.1017/S0265052500001515.

Nussbaum, Martha. 2001. *Upheavals of Emotions*. Cambridge: Cambridge University Press. http://dx.doi.org/10.1017/CBO9780511840715.

Orwin, Clifford. 1997. "Moist Eyes – From Rousseau to Clinton." *The Public Interest* 128: 3–20. Accessed 13 March 2010. http://www.nationalaffairs.com/public_interest/detail/moist-eyesfrom-rousseau-to-clinton.

Orwin, Clifford. 2008. "How an Emotion Became a Virtue: It Took Some Help from Rousseau." *In Character* (blog). http://incharacter.org/archives/compassion/how-an-emotion-became-a-virtue-it-took-some-help-from-rousseau-and-montesquieu/.

Orwin, Clifford, and Nathan Tarcov. 1997. *The Legacy of Rousseau*. Chicago: University of Chicago Press.

Pitkin, Hannah. 1981. "Justice: On Relating Private and Public." *Political Theory* 9 (3): 327–52.

Pitkin, Hannah. 1998. *The Attack of the Blob: Hannah Arendt's Concept of the Social*. Chicago: University of Chicago Press.

Porter, Elisabeth. 2006. "Can Politics Practice Compassion?" *Hypatia* 21 (4): 97–123. http://dx.doi.org/10.1111/j.1527-2001.2006.tb01130.x.

Rancière, Jacques. 2001. "Ten Theses on Politics." *Theory & Event* 5 (3). Online journal.

Reilly, Richard. 2008. *Ethics of Compassion: Bridging Ethical Theory and Religious Moral Discourse*. Lanham, NJ: Lexington Books.

Reshaur, Ken. 1992. "Concepts of Solidarity in the Political Theory of Hannah Arendt." *Canadian Journal of Political Science* 25 (4): 723–36. http://dx.doi.org/10.1017/S0008423900004479.

Revault d'Allones, Myriam. 2008. *L'homme compassionnel*. Paris: Éditions du Seuil.

Scruton, Roger. 2009. "Totalitarian Sentimentality." *American Spectator* (Dec. 2009–Jan. 2010). Accessed 14 April 2010. http://spectator.org/archives/2009/12/09/totalitarian-sentimentality.

Snow, Nancy. 1991. "Compassion." *American Philosophical Quarterly* 28 (3): 195–205.

Solomon, Robert. 1993. *The Passions: Emotions and the Meaning of Life*. Indianapolis, IN: Hackett.

Solomon, Robert. 2004. *In Defense of Sentimentality*. Oxford: Oxford University Press. http://dx.doi.org/10.1093/019514550X.001.0001.

Trout, J.D. 2009. *The Empathy Gap: Building Bridges to the Good Life and the Good Society*. New York: Viking.

Whitebrook, Maureen. 2002. "Compassion as a Political Virtue." *Political Studies* 50 (3): 529–44. http://dx.doi.org/10.1111/1467-9248.00383.

Woodward, Kathleen. 2004. "Calculating Compassion." In *Compassion: The Politics and Culture of an Emotion*, edited by Lauren Berlant, 59–86. New York: Routledge.

Young-Bruehl, Elizabeth. 1996. "Hannah Arendt among Feminists." In *Hannah Arendt: Twenty Years Later*, edited by Larry May and Jerome Kohn, 307–24. Cambridge, MA: MIT Press.

10 Envy, Shame, and Self-Respect: Situating the Emotions in the Work of John Rawls

KIRAN BANERJEE AND JEFFREY BERCUSON

As part of a broader turn in the discipline, political theorists have increasingly come to recognize the central role of affect in social and political life; indeed, many scholars, coming from a number of distinct theoretical traditions, have drawn our attention to the importance of the emotions to the tradition of the history of political thought as well as to normative political theory.[1] This attentiveness to affect is often cast as a break with earlier, primarily Enlightenment-inspired, liberal approaches towards politics. On such a view, liberalism and liberal theorists have a deeply ingrained tendency to either neglect or marginalize the emotions, dismissing affect as inconsequential or potentially dangerous (Solomon 1995; Hall 2002, 2005; Walzer 2002, 2006). The view of liberalism as a project committed to distancing politics from the passions is often characterized as anchoring political life in deliberative public reason and a neutralist state. Consequently, according to such a portrayal of contemporary liberal theory, emotions are said to have no place in the public sphere, while proceduralist institutions abstract away from the affective attachments, now cast as private preferences, of individuals qua citizens. Emotions, so the argument goes, ought not to have any place in the consideration of liberal principles of justice or in the design of political institutions. In this chapter, we challenge this prevalent view. We argue that no less a liberal theorist than John Rawls is deeply attentive to the place of emotions in his account of liberalism. In doing so, we hope to contribute to upending the conventional view that liberalism is affect blind and thus encourage a more nuanced reading of the liberal tradition more generally.

Rawls's Unreasonable Rationalism?

Casting Rawls as a theorist sensitive to affect and emotional experience may strike many readers as counterintuitive. Indeed, Rawls's work has been frequently criticized for epitomizing some of the deepest problems of contemporary liberal theory as a result of the emphasis on rationalism and reasonableness in his account of liberal justice. Whether this is a residual of his earlier attempt to bring rationality and justice together, or a consequence of the explicitly neo-Kantian foundations of his political thought, Rawls has frequently been taken to be guilty of the propensity of contemporary theory to ignore or marginalize the emotions (Sandel 1982; Okin 1989; Barry 1995; Solomon 1995; Blackburn 1998; Fisher 2003; Hall 2002, 2005).[2] Far from attending to the embedded and affective dimensions of human nature, so this argument goes, Rawls is an exemplar of the misguided liberal propensity to articulate a politics of illusory neutrality grounded in a deracinated and "unencumbered" understanding of the individual.

Indeed, it is precisely this perspective on Rawls that has informed a number of prominent critiques of his account of justice. To situate our own reading, it is helpful to sketch this prevalent perspective on the Rawlsian project, from its beginnings in the initial critical response to *A Theory of Justice* (1971) to more recent challenges from communitarian, feminist, and Marxist perspectives. This important, and by no means marginal, understanding of Rawls's project, which focused primarily on the conceptual architecture of the first two parts of *A Theory of Justice*, characterized much of the early reception of Rawls's work, on the sides of both critics and defenders. In this reading, the main task of *A Theory of Justice* was to offer a conception of justice that "generalizes and carries to a higher level of abstraction" the central insights of the liberal contractual tradition to justify fundamental principles to govern the institutions and basic structure of society (Rawls 1971, 11).[3]

To generate such principles, Rawls asks us to imagine an original position of rational and mutually disinterested individuals tasked with choosing principles of justice, under the condition of a veil of ignorance requiring them to bracket morally arbitrary facts, such as their individual characteristics and talents, as well as knowledge of their own actual position and status in society. Under such circumstances, Rawls suggests that the parties would select two principles of justice: legitimate political institutions must secure the basic liberties of persons in the most extensive manner possible, and they must arrange social and economic inequalities so that they are conducive to both fair equality of opportunity and the maximum improvement of the socio-economic condition of society's least advantaged (TJ, 52). The latter principle, known as the difference principle, specifically tied the commitment of *A Theory of Justice* to relative economic egalitarianism to the rationalist assumptions of decision theory, suggesting that under the conditions of uncertainty meant to model an appropriate moral situation, individuals would choose a distributive paradigm that would severely curtail inequalities, only allowing them if they benefited the standing of the representative least well-off individual. Indeed, Rawls appeared to claim that the general project of *A Theory of Justice* was itself "a part, perhaps the more important part of the theory of rational choice" (TJ, 16), suggesting that a central aspect of his project was to marry rational self-interest maximization and justice.

Picking up on Rawls's emphasis on rationality in his attempt to articulate a procedure for deciding on the principles of liberal justice, a number of works in the early critical literature focused on whether Rawls's principles of justice were, in fact, congruent with the assumptions of rational choice. Scholars, such as the utilitarian John Harsanyi (1975), as well as more sympathetic writers such as James Fishkin (1975) and Allen Buchanan (1982), criticized various aspects of Rawls's rationality assumptions, asking whether they would, in fact, lead to the adoption of Rawls's conception of justice. Would the difference principle actually be the outcome of a rational decision procedure under the original position's conditions of uncertainty? Did Rawls's argument rely on an implausible model of rational choice, or did his account smuggle in dubious assumptions about the significance of the diminishing marginal value of Rawlsian primary basic goods? Key features of this broader perspective and critical reception of Rawls's project concern his purported insistence on the need to abstract away from the particular features and social positions of individuals as well as his attempt to graft aspects of rational choice theory to his account of the original position.

It was precisely this focus on rationality and abstraction that motivated some of the strongest critiques of those who dissented from the Rawlsian project. Early on, the libertarian theorist Robert Nozick (1974) raised doubts about the implications of the original position, suggesting that the difference principle generated by this device of representation violated the project's purportedly Kantian commitment to the integrity of the person. This was because it appeared to take a person's individual attributes and talents as a collective good, thereby seeming to treat individuals as mere means. In a similar vein, communitarian theorists, such as Michael Sandel (1982, 1984), objected to what they took to be an unrealistic and highly problematic concept of the human subject at the centre of Rawls's approach. According to Sandel, as a result of the project's problematic Kantian legacy, Rawls's attempt to develop a deontological liberalism presupposed an unencumbered "noumenal" moral agent and, with that, a conception of the individual that deeply misrepresented our status as socially embedded and embodied beings (Sandel 1982, 1984).

Feminist critics, such as Susan Okin (1987, 1989), Iris Marion Young (1990), and Amy Baehr (1996), saw cause for concern in what they saw as Rawls's tendency to privilege reason and abstraction in his account of justice. If the original position as a device of representation was supposed to model features relevant to the subject of justice in liberal societies, the emotions, gender, and the family were curiously absent from the Rawlsian picture. For Okin, in particular, the difficulties apparent in Rawls's project were largely a result of his Kantian assumptions regarding rationality and autonomy, leading him to neglect the role of the "human qualities of empathy and benevolence" in establishing principles of justice (Okin 1989, 234). Drawing inspiration from the feminist critique of Rawls, G.A. Cohen criticized Rawls's project from a Marxist perspective, arguing that there is a tension between the sense of justice that would characterize a just society and the appeal to self-interest implicit in Rawls's account of the rationality of his principles of justice; rather, a just society requires an ethos of justice that supports equality-enabling choices, and such an ethos must go beyond narrow self-interest (Cohen 1992, 1997, 2008). Underlying Cohen's critique were deeper worries regarding the motivational resources of Rawls's project and whether a truly just society would need to rely on rational incentives – such as the permissible inequalities of the difference principle – to motivate just action.

But is Rawls quite the arch-rationalist that these prevalent readings seem to suggest? Does Rawls provide us with an account of justice grounded in an abstract, unencumbered self, in which the embodied and affective dimensions of human experience have no place? Contrary to the prevalent view implicit in these critiques, we argue that Rawls *is*, in fact, attentive to the role of emotions in the political lives of citizens and that affect has a central place in his understanding of the liberal regime.

Rawlsian Sentimentalism

In line with the reading that we propose, in recent years there has been a notable increase in scholarly attention to the presence of the emotions in Rawls's political philosophy. As we have already noted, this is emblematic of a more general turn towards affect in political theory. Michael Frazer and Sharon Krause, in particular, are on the vanguard of this reappraisal of Rawls. In this section, we will focus our attention on an important contribution by each thinker: Frazer's "John Rawls: Between Two Enlightenments" (2007) and Krause's "Desiring Justice: Motivation and Justification in Rawls and Habermas" (2005). While both authors are right to emphasize the centrality of affect in the landscape of justice as fairness, it is our contention that Frazer and Krause tell only a *part* (albeit an important, under-appreciated part) of the story. In this chapter, we hope to give a more thorough and complete picture of Rawls's thinking on the role of affect in political philosophy and political life.

What, then, are the merits and limitations of this more recent account? At first glance, it seems to be the case, according to Krause and Frazer, that Rawls treats the emotions as a kind of post hoc *justificatory mechanism*: citizens look back on the principles (and institutions) that govern them, hopeful that these social structures are worthy of their assent as free and equal persons. Reflection, in other words, is not exclusively a matter of *rational* reflection, of the hierarchical privileging of my true, noumenal self over my contingent emotions and attachments. On this sentimentalist account, our chosen principles of justice have normative authority because of their compatibility with *both* the exercise of reason *and* the complex emotional psychology characteristic of human beings; again, our concern for justice is a "display [of *both* our] independence from the accidental circumstances of our world" *and* our "natural sympathy with other persons and an innate susceptibility to the pleasures of fellow feeling" (TJ, 403). Frazer and Krause are thus (rightly) engaged in the attempt to "re-embody" Rawls: the principles of justice are justified (in part) by virtue of their compatibility with the kinds of emotions citizens actually happen to have. There is no sense, in other words, that the possibility of justice depends on the transcendence of our empirical, contingent, affective selves.

Of course, there are important, insuperable limits to the justificatory work that the emotions can do. This, according to Frazer, is a conspicuously Humean moment in Rawls's political philosophy. "The fact that we can have higher order moral sentiments – that we can approve or disapprove of our own approval and disapproval – allows for a process of reflection in which the mind as a whole repeatedly turns on itself as a whole, and winnows out those sentiments which cannot pass the test of reflection" (Frazer 2007, 761).[4] This reason-emotion dialectic is captured by the Rawlsian notion of reflective equilibrium: the elaboration and adaptation of justice principles is, according to this sentimentalist rereading of Rawls, the product of the mutual adjustment and enlargement of reason and affect as we collectively argue and reflect on what a just political community ought to be like (see, e.g., TJ, 44, 507). The outcome of this process must be acceptable to our thoroughly interrogated, and therefore rightly authoritative, reasons and emotions. Not *any* reason can function as the justificatory basis of a given principle, law, or policy: reasons must respect the freedom and equality of all citizens. And the same goes for the emotions: only those politically constructive emotions, such as our natural sympathy for, and empathy with, our fellow citizens, are the legitimate basis of political obligation. This is an important point worth emphasizing: on this sentimentalist rereading, it is our natural sense of empathy that motivates our attachment to legitimate, other-regarding principles of justice. We are attached to principles of justice, in other words, because they reflect our natural empathetic inclinations towards our fellows. Such sentiments then receive institutionalized expression in the basic structure of society – that is, in the principle-guided institutional structure that protects the freedom and equality of all citizens. *This* is why the sense of justice itself is rightly thought of as an affective attachment.

Citizens' commitment to the principles of justice (i.e., the sense of justice itself) is thus conceived (in part) as the "reflective outgrowth of basic human emotions" (Frazer 2007, 768). This is the main thrust of Krause's argument too. "To have a conception of the good … is to have an affective attachment to it or a desire to realize it; hence when we are rational we are also desiring" (Krause 2005, 366). Elsewhere, Krause describes the sense of justice itself as an "affective attachment" to the idea of being a just person and to the good of justice (364, 367). According to this reading of Rawls, citizens in a just liberal regime are thus appropriately understood as *desirous* of justice. What both Frazer and Krause recognize is that Rawls's account of justice is implicated in the politics of affect and that the emotions *always* play a central role in providing the motivational resources necessary in any stable, legitimate political community. This reading therefore goes beyond earlier engagements with Rawls's project, which emphasized the exclusive place of reason and rationality in the choice of justice principles, thereby neglecting the central role of the emotions in *A Theory of Justice*. We are reminded, again, of Hume. "Human nature [is] compos'd of two principal parts, which are requisite in all its actions, the affections and understanding ... these two component parts of the mind ... [are] uncompounded and inseparable" (Hume 2000, 317).[5]

This is a very important point: what both Frazer and Krause hope to show is that this emphasis on affect is present in Rawls's thought *from the very beginning* precisely because of the ultimate inextricability of reason and affect. After all, the desire to live with others on just terms, says Rawls, "exercises a *natural* attraction upon our *affection*," and so the principles of justice themselves are conscientiously designed to be "continuous with our *natural sentiments*" (TJ, 477–8; italics added). This ought to correct our initial (post hoc, justificatory) impression of the role of affect in Rawls's political philosophy: far from offering a retrospective defence of the (mere) compatibility of Rawls's project with the affect turn in political theory, Frazer and Krause rightly emphasize how an attentiveness to the role of emotion is present at the *start* of justice as fairness. In the later section "Institutions, Affect, and the Embedded Self," we will take this important insight even further.

It is patently the case, then, that the principles of justice are designed with explicit reference to feeling, sentiment, and affect – with emotions that citizens actually happen to have, such as sympathy, empathy, care, trust, fellow feeling, and even love. Indeed, in a revealing moment in *A Theory of Justice*, Rawls goes so far as to call justice as fairness a "theory of the moral sentiments" (TJ, 51). This lends Rawls's theory an additional basis of legitimacy and, by extension, stability (for the right reasons). The question of the relation between justice and affect thus boils down to a question of motivation: we care about the principles of justice, and are motivated to act according to their dictates, precisely because they take into account and reflect our care for fellow citizens and our affective attachment to the ideal of a just political community (cf. Paul Griffiths in chapter 4 of this volume). And this continues to be true even after the revisions in *Political Liberalism* (2005) to the original doctrine: the fact that the political conception of justice is now embedded *in* citizens' deeply held (but ultimately reasonable) comprehensive doctrines constitutes another affective basis of motivation and stability; that is, we care about the principles of justice precisely because obedience to them is a constitutive expression of our commitment to much more existentially robust comprehensive doctrines (Krause 2005, 370–1; Frazer 2007, 772–4).

However, as we have already indicated, this is only a *part* of the story about the role and place of the emotions in Rawls's political philosophy. On our view, the emotions do not merely function as a source of motivation to comply with justice principles. Rather, what we hope to show below is that a liberal regime is *always already* concerned with the affective dimension of citizenship and that justice as fairness, in particular, is better understood when we incorporate this concern for the relationship between politics and affect in an even more robust manner.

Institutions, Affect, and the Embedded Self

While the recent turn towards the affective dimensions of Rawls's project has focused on how Rawls does recognize the need for desire, sentiment, and emotion as motivational resources in his account of liberal justice, our reading of Rawls wishes to push further in suggesting that, at the core of Rawls's project, is an even thicker conception of an embedded and affective subject. To demonstrate this, we draw on the extra-Kantian resources of Rawls's project. As we argue, supplementing his Kantian-inspired account of liberal autonomy is a richer relational conception of the human subject. This moves the question of the place of affect in Rawls's theory beyond the motivational issues posed by a reason-driven justificatory liberalism. Rather, as we indicate, Rawls's conception of the just liberal regime presupposes an intersubjectively constituted individual.

What we find in Rawls, then, is a theorist sensitive to the embedded nature of the individual and the extent to which subjectivity is the by-product of political and social relations; that is, for Rawls, *subjectivity* is always already *inter*subjectivity. In the end, we hope to decisively rebut those communitarian critics who disregard justice as fairness because (in their view) it is based on a philosophically, psychologically, and metaphysically incoherent conception of the person (see, e.g., Sandel 1982; Solomon 1995; Blackburn 1998; Fisher 2003; Hall 2002, 2005). What is the basis of this critical view? Contracting parties in the original position, recall, are denied any information about their ends, values, or conceptions of the good; they are, in other words, radically detached from any sense of particularity and from their constitutive attachments. And so, according to his critics, Rawls takes for granted or, rather, he fully neglects, the extent to which individuals are fundamentally shaped by their social and political milieu; he subscribes to a kind of unencumbered, asocial individualism. How can contracting parties thus conceived adequately reason about *social* justice?

This image of the asocial and unencumbered chooser of justice principles – which, as we have already seen, is so pervasive in the secondary literature on *A Theory of Justice* and Rawls more generally – is, quite simply, wrong. In this spirit, we hope to show two things in the remainder of this section and in the paper more generally: (1) the extent to which Rawls regards the self as deeply embedded in – *as importantly determined by* – its social and political-institutional milieu and (2) the extent to which Rawls regards these selves as deeply affective, as desirous of a certain kind of recognition from the institutions that coerce them and from the fellows with whom they are engaged in social cooperation. In the end, justice as fairness is best characterized by its attempt to secure the self-respect of citizens; and, for Rawls, proper self-respect is not just a quality of individuals; it is a quality of the configuration of societies.

In turning to the Rawlsian conception of the embedded self, this thicker conception of the human subject can be brought into sharper relief if we attend to Rawls's own critical engagements and criticisms of the Kantian approach with which he is so frequently identified; instead, we will attend more carefully to the deep influence of Rousseau and Hegel on the Rawlsian project. Here, a crucial resource for reconstructing Rawls's view can be found in his attempt to distinguish the nature of his project from that found in Kant. Whereas Kant is primarily concerned with moral *individuals,* Rawls is concerned with moral *institutions*. "Justice as fairness assigns a certain primacy to the social. By contrast, Kant's account of the categorical imperative applies to the personal maxims of sincere individuals in everyday life" (Rawls 1999b, 339; see also Rawls 2000, 204). In distinguishing his project from Kant's, Rawls thus signals his departure from this Kantian perspective; unlike Kant, Rawls is deeply interested in the institutional contours of social life. Again, "Kant proceeds from the particular, even personal case of everyday life; he assumed that this process carried out correctly would eventually yield a coherent and sufficiently complete system of principles, including principles of social justice. *Justice as fairness moves in quite the reverse fashion*" (ibid.; italics added).

It is of crucial importance, in Rawls's account, that public justice – justice at the level of institutions – comes first. And Rawls ultimately justifies the primacy of the political with reference to the educative function fulfilled by principle-guided institutions; that is, we begin by focusing on institutions because of the educative and socializing purposes they fulfil. Simply put, Rawls does not see Kant *in the world* – as the *Lectures on the History of Moral Philosophy* (2000) constantly emphasize, Rawls reads Kant as fundamentally interested in the transcendence of the social and political world. And so Rawls turns to Hegel, for whom the first principle of political philosophy is "deep social rootedness of people within an established framework of their political and social institutions" (Rawls 2000, 366). *This* is the appeal of Hegel's moral and political philosophy for Rawls. "*A Theory of Justice* follows Hegel when it takes the basic structure of society as the *first* subject of justice" (ibid.). Rawls, unlike Kant, in his view,[6] is deeply concerned with the constitutive role of institutions in forming the background conditions for just liberal citizens.

Indeed, Hegel's view of freedom is "distinctively *institutional*" (Rawls 2000, 330). This connects, says Rawls, "with [Hegel's] view of persons as *rooted in and fashioned by the system of political and social institutions under which they live*" (ibid.; italics added). Of course, this Hegelian view is a response to – it is *a direct critique of* – Kant's transcendentalism: freedom is realized not in the pangs of the abstract and isolated conscience, but *in* the world, through political and social institutions at a particular historical moment (Hegel 1991, §28, §30, §39–45, §77, §147, §265A; Rawls 2000, 189, 263–7, 299–301). In other words, Hegel rejects the Kantian view that one is capable of genuine moral freedom by virtue, exclusively, of one's humanity and the concomitant possession of conscience; moral freedom is indivisible from the political institutional conditions in which it develops and evolves. Principle-guided institutions lead us to an idea of ourselves and of our fellows as capable of certain kinds of action and worthy of certain kinds of treatment. We have freedom, in other words, *because* political institutions recognize (and concomitantly institutionalize) "our dignity as persons who are free" (Rawls 2000, 331).

For Rawls, as for Hegel, the "basic structure" is the first subject of justice because of "the profound effects of these institutions on the kinds of persons we are" (Freeman 2003, 4; see also Rawls 1999b, 304). What Rawls recognizes is the powerful and pervasive effects of institutions, which always already deeply shape the moral psychology of citizens and so necessarily have a transformative effect on the character and ethos of those subject to their coercive effects. Rawls's most explicit statement of the socializing function of principle-guided institutions is to be found in Book I of *Political Liberalism* (2005). "Think of the principles of justice [and the political institutions established in light of them] as *designed to form the social world* in which our character and our conception of ourselves as persons are *first acquired*. These principles must give priority to those basic freedoms and opportunities in background institutions of civil society that enable us to *become* free and equal citizens in the first place, *and to understand our role as persons with that status*. … We have no prior identity before being in society" (Rawls 2005, §I.7.1; see also Rawls 1999a, 173; Rawls 2000, 333; Rawls 2001, §55.2). Political institutions (for Rawls as for Hegel) have "decisive long-term social effects and importantly shape the character and aims of the members of society, the kinds of persons they are and want to be" (Rawls 1999b, 326). Rawls and Hegel share the foundational belief that institutions (and their guiding principles) determine the kind of people we become. Citizenship is the outcome of an educative process. If, as Charles Taylor succinctly puts it, "the doctrine of *Sittlichkeit* is that morality reaches its completion in a community," then Rawls is better understood in light of his engagement with Hegel (Taylor 1979, 84).

In a certain sense, then, the communitarian critics *are* right: the original position *is* based on an unrealistically unencumbered conception of the person. But, unlike the communitarians, *we* must avoid falling into a familiar trap in Rawls scholarship: treating the original position as *historical fact* – as a kind of founding moment – and not as a (mere) hypothetical thought experiment designed to represent, or "model," our intuitions about justice as they happen to have evolved over time (see, e.g., Sen 2009, esp. 56, 60, 69, 79; see also Rawls 2001, §7.2, §8.2, §9.1, §11.3, §23.4). The centrality of the original position in *A Theory of Justice* is not, in the end, a claim about the possibility or desirability of stripping away the social identity and attachments of citizens; neither does its inclusion strip Rawls's theory of its emphasis on the social-institutional constitution of identity. While the abstract capacity for agency is, for Rawls, a central feature of our moral life, it is not the only such feature: for Rawls, the relationship of citizens is intrinsically social and other-oriented. It follows that *the* political problem is the proper institutional support for salutary intersubjective relations – what Rawls calls the social basis of self-respect. After all, for Rawls, self-respect is not only a matter of having a secure sense of self, a secure sense that one's life has meaning, and that one is well suited to pursue and revise one's system of ends. Self-respect also has an intersubjective or relational dimension: genuine self-respect requires that "our person and deeds [are] appreciated and confirmed by others who are likewise esteemed ... unless our endeavors are appreciated by our associates it is impossible for us to maintain the conviction that they are worthwhile" (TJ, 386).

As we have tried to indicate in this account, far from embracing an implausibly disembodied and affectless subject of political life, Rawls not only acknowledges these aspects of individuals but also insists that political and social institutions harness these affective resources. Of course, the central claim of our discussion – that, for Rawls, individuals are *constituted* or *determined by* principle-guided institutions – presents a conspicuously one-sided image of political life: it is easy to get the impression that egalitarian institutions are somehow in place and that these institutions are then able to fulfil their educative or socializing function. But Rawls does not believe that political life begins *in media res*: we must move beyond the *constitution* paradigm, according to which individuals are spontaneously constituted (as liberal egalitarians) by their prevailing institutional milieu, towards *co-constitution.* What, exactly, do we mean by co-constitution? We hope to show in this section that Rawls does not merely think of institutions as educating citizens to a particular ideal of recognition and reciprocity (although he certainly does think this). Rawls also thinks of persons as fundamentally subject to the psychological need for recognition and self-respect, which itself possesses a powerful affective dimension in Rawls's account: we desire to be recognized *as equals* by the institutions that coerce us and by the fellows with whom we are engaged in political cooperation, and it is these ideals of mutual recognition and universal self-respect that inform and guide our shared political labours. In other words, proper self-respect is configured through our relations with others and through the sort of community in which we live.

Justice as fairness is therefore deeply implicated in the politics of recognition; the ideal of self-respect at its core is characterized by an intersubjective and affective quality. Indeed, the extent to which justice as fairness is motivated by psychological concerns – namely, the need for recognition and self-respect – has not been fully appreciated by Rawls's interpreters and critics. In many respects, Rawls reminds us of Rousseau here. Indeed, like Rousseau, Rawls starts from the human proclivity for interpersonal comparisons, accepts the negative consequences of unfavourable comparisons, and (still following Rousseau) includes these psychological tendencies – to compare and to feel shame – as a fundamental consideration for constitutional and institutional design. It is in this spirit that Rawls claims that self-respect is "perhaps the most important primary good" (TJ, 386). And, as we shall see in a moment, like Rousseau Rawls's solution to the lack of recognition – and, concomitantly, to the lack of self-respect – is to institutionalize the rights of citizenship in the basic structure of society.

This is a very important point: Rawls is not only deeply interested in the mental states of citizens but also recognizes the political salience of socially destructive psychological sentiments, such as envy and shame. Such feelings are often associated with inequalities of political and social status. In other words, envy-producing arrangements undermine the empathetic identifications necessary for stable, productive social cooperation; in Rawls's mind, envy is the obverse (and deeply counterproductive) psychic phenomenon of empathy. It follows that a constitutive aim of justice as fairness is to negotiate the emergence of such sentiments (TJ, 469–71, 478).

How are these destructive emotions mediated or prevented? On Rawls's view, the solution to the lack of recognition – and to the concomitant lack of self-respect among those disadvantaged members of society – is to institutionalize political and relative economic equality in the basic structure of society (TJ, 477). In other words, equality at the highest level – at the level of citizenship – is the social basis of self-respect (TJ, §15). Social and political conditions, in other words, are the fundamental determinant of a person's self-respect: to be a citizen is to be secure about one's place in society. Again, we are reminded of Rousseau: even in *A Theory of Justice*, Rawls gives us an institutional–basic structure solution to the problem of socially destructive envy; he is permanently sensitive to all the ways in which self-respect is potentially undermined by inegalitarian political and economic institutions and of the ways in which empathetic identification is undermined by envy-generating arrangements.

It follows that a central purpose of justice as fairness is to mitigate the natural human propensity to envy, which undermines the stability of the political community. Envy, on Rawls's view, is "a reaction to the loss of self-respect in circumstances where it would be unreasonable to expect someone to feel differently" (TJ, 468). In this vein, the interpretation of justice as fairness presented here emphasizes the principles of justice – and the political and distributive institutions established in light of them – as the essential source not only of autonomy but also of intersubjectively grounded self-respect, understood here as in part an affective disposition. Indeed, an essential dimension of Rawls's project is to use principle-guided institutions to combat the socially destructive forms of envy that arise from the lack of self-respect felt by society's least advantaged members. After all, according to Rawls, the problem of envy cannot be permanently ignored in any theory of justice: such sentiments do exist in society; this is opposed to the information-deficient original position, where envy has no basis. And for Rawls, political institutions are often the basic instigating cause of these sentiments. In this sense, Rawls views liberalism as in part constituting an affective economy for its citizens – living under a just liberal regime leads to the cultivation of emotions and affective attachments appropriate to the psychology of mutual recognition.

Indeed, if the basic structure of society gives rise to feelings of pervasive envy – on account of the inequalities permitted by our principles of redistribution, say – this gives us reason to question those guiding principles. For feelings of envy, to reiterate, may lead to mutually destructive policies and actions. "The individual who envies another is prepared to do things that make them both worse off, if only the discrepancy between them is sufficiently reduced" (TJ, 466). And so it is with the spite of the advantaged members of society, who are also subject to the redistributive difference principle. "The spiteful man is willing to give up something to maintain the distance between himself and others" (TJ. 468). Envy, in other words, obscures the mutual (economic) advantageousness of social cooperation (when governed by fair principles of justice). But Rawls does not spend much time contemplating the economic or distributive consequences of widespread envy. Instead, his main concern is the *psychological* consequences of unfavourable interpersonal comparisons (TJ, §81). Again, an essential function of political institutions is to support the self-esteem of citizens, as grounded in egalitarian relations of mutual respect. And when individual self-esteem is secure, the pleasures of community are apparent. "One who is confident in himself is not grudging in the appreciation of others" (TJ, 387).

There is, in Rawls's thought, a kind of dialectic in operation (albeit one that will never come to a complete resolution) between the natural psychological needs of persons and the design of the basic structure of the political community. Hence, the necessity of going beyond (mere) constitution towards *co*-constitution: institutions educate, but the design of those institutions is fundamentally informed by – it is a response to – the psychological needs of those subject to institutional coercion. We are, simply put, naturally desirous of egalitarian recognition and self-respect; we need only recall the Rousseauian inspiration for Rawls's characterization of self-respect and self-esteem as basic primary goods. The more important point, however, is that both Rawls and Rousseau believe that self-respect and self-esteem are sentiments that are most effectively satisfied by well-designed political and economic institutions. A just liberal society thus necessarily has an affective economy, one that aims to secure the conditions of mutual respect, which are in turn the necessary grounding for self-respect and self-esteem. This leads to a new, holistic image of the historical evolution of this or that political community: our institutional milieu evolves from being a source of destabilizing envy – on account of political and radical economic inequalities – to being the essential guarantor of deeply sought-after recognition and self-respect.[7] Only the latter milieu is the legitimate and likely object of citizens' affective attachment.[8] This insight has important implications for the place of what we might call a liberal character, or ethos of justice, in Rawls's project.

As we have suggested above, far from enjoining us to embrace an unrealistically simplistic conception of the human subject, at the centre of Rawls's project is a vision of individuals as both embodied as well as intersubjectively and institutionally constituted. Moreover, Rawls not only acknowledges these aspects of individuals but also repeatedly insists that political and social institutions harness these affective resources. Consequently, his project *is* highly attentive to the necessary role of affect in enabling appropriate relations of reciprocity and mutual respect among liberal citizens. What is more, these fundamental psychological needs of citizens themselves possess an affective dimension; proper self-esteem and self-respect are sentiments cultivated and supported by just liberal institutions.

And what is the mechanism for cultivating these dispositions – for creating the conditions necessary to avoid the socially destructive forces of envy and for cultivating appropriate relations of self-love and self-esteem? As we have noted, Rawls's answer is institutional: he appeals to the basic structure of society precisely because of the profound socializing capacity he sees it playing in social life, precisely because of the profound effects it has on the values, choices, and motivations of affected citizens. The rules of a just basic structure, in other words, cannot help but transform the psychology of individuals subject to those rules.[9] The basic structure of a just liberal society not only promotes egalitarian relations that minimize the socially destructive force of envy; it also promotes the necessary intersubjective conditions of equality necessary for the affective dispositions of proper self-respect and self-esteem. After all, the latter rest on satisfying individual citizens' desire for a particular kind of recognition – recognition as equals. Liberalism, on Rawls's view, therefore, depends explicitly on the creation of institutions that satisfy fundamental human desires – most fundamentally, our desire for recognition and respect. But it is equally necessary that such institutions play a role in developing the affective dispositions and attachments conducive to just and stable social cooperation. This highlights the sense in which Rawls's project describes an ongoing historical process, a process by which liberal institutions and liberal citizens are mutually transformed, with the latter developing what we might call a liberal character, or ethos of justice.

A Liberal Soul Craft?

Our reconstruction of Rawls's political project, *pace* prevalent although ultimately misleading readings, is now complete. As we have shown, affect does have a central, fundamental, and yet unappreciated place in Rawls's attempt to constitute and defend a liberal theory of justice. The emotions *are* present in Rawls's thought from the very beginning, in his account of both the natural constellation of psychological needs and the role that the emotions must play in the articulation of justice principles and in the institutional arrangements characteristic of a just liberal order. In the end, Rawls does have a rather capacious understanding of the self, and he does see that such an understanding is an essential element in the articulation of any compelling theory of justice.

We must concede, however, that there are deep tensions in Rawls's project and that his incorporation of affect into his understanding of the liberal subject is far from uncomplicated. Although we can only do so in a cursory manner, by way of conclusion we wish to draw attention to some of these potential issues. For one, Rawls's incorporation of the emotions into his account of liberal justice must certainly trouble our understanding of Rawls as a key representative of traditional liberal, and especially Kantian-inspired, visions of autonomy. As we have shown, Rawls anchors his account of liberal society in an intersubjectively and affectively constituted conception of the self, as signalled in his self-avowed departure from the (purportedly) Kantian conception of the person. The individual can no longer rightly be conceptualized as the purely rational, unencumbered chooser of ends; citizens' ends (and the value systems used to evaluate and choose those ends) must now be thought of as fundamentally constituted by their institutional milieu. All this suggests that we must dispense with the image of the original position as capturing Rawls's conception of the autonomous self. Instead, Rawls follows Rousseau and Hegel: he views *autonomy as an accomplishment*, the contingent by-product of institutional circumstances that are themselves part of a larger historical process.

What is more, this suggests that the general liberal repugnance towards soul craft is simply not present in Rawls: he clearly recognizes that institutions cannot avoid having a decisive effect on our moral and emotional development as individuals and citizens. Indeed, this is precisely why the basic structure must be governed by principles of justice: the basic structure of a just society not only *facilitates* self-development, but liberal institutions also inform and quintessentially *determine* the nature of self-development. Liberalism is therefore fundamentally implicated in the cultivation of a liberal *character* or *ethos*. Of course, this puts Rawls in tension with the liberal aspiration to neutrality, and it may demand that we move away from the typical liberal aversion to viewing political life as always already implicated in the project of character formation. And given the centrality of the idea of neutrality in the later iteration of justice as fairness – political liberalism – our view raises important questions about the coherence of Rawls's later political philosophy.

However, it is only once we first acknowledge the place of affect in Rawls's thought that we can begin to grapple with these matters. Far from banishing the emotions from the domain of politics, Rawls's account of liberalism seeks to harness these embodied aspects of liberal citizens to bring about and sustain the stability of just liberal institutions. And while we may ultimately find ourselves dissenting from the vision of an affective economy that emerges in Rawls's project, with its implications of a distinctively liberal soul craft, surely the starting point for such an evaluation must be a serious reckoning with the place of the emotions in his thought. Moreover, while recognizing this dimension of Rawls's project does raise deeper questions, it is worth considering that often the hallmark of a great thinker consists, in part, in these very tensions and ambiguities. Indeed, when read in this light, Rawls can be seen as an iconic representative of the complicated and ongoing engagement of liberal theory with the question of the place of the emotions in political life.

NOTES

1 An outpouring of material has sought to highlight the important place of affect in political life and political theorizing. Some recent examples, in addition to those in this volume, include Michael L. Frazer, *The Enlightenment of Sympathy: Justice and the Moral Sentiments in the Eighteenth Century and Today* (2010); Rebecca Kingston and Leonard Ferry, eds., *Bringing the Passions Back In: The Emotions in Political Philosophy* (2008); Sharon R. Krause, *Civil Passions: Moral Sentiment and Democratic Deliberation* (2008); Michael Walzer, *Politics and Passion: Toward a More Egalitarian Liberalism* (2006); Cheryl Hall, *The Trouble With Passion: Political Theory Beyond the Reign of Reason* (2005).
2 Solomon (1995, 300) goes so far as to interpret Rawls's apparent invocations of the moral sentiments as merely "cosmetic plaster that [Rawls] adds between the structural struts to give his deductive theory some sense of humanity."
3 Hereafter, this work is cited as "TJ."
4 "A mind will never be able to bear it[s] own survey," Hume writes, "that has been wanting in its part to mankind and society" (Hume 2000, sec. 3.3.6.6, 395).
5 Another important merit of both Frazer's and Krause's articles is that they highlight Rawls's unrecognized debt to the Scottish Enlightenment despite its association with the kind of utilitarian politics that justice as fairness was designed to rebut. In the end, as we emphasize below, Rawls himself thinks of justice as fairness as a "theory of the moral sentiments," which clearly evokes its eighteenth-century Scottish heritage (TJ, 51).
6 Of course, Rawls's reading of Kant may itself miss the affinities between his sensibilities and Kant's, as the growing critical literature on the embodied dimensions of Kantian moral judgment and Kant's so-called "impure ethics" would seem to suggest. See, for instance, O'Neill (1990), Herman (1996), Louden (2002). But this potential interpretive myopia on Rawls's part need not detract from our account of his position.
7 The conspicuously (and yet underappreciated) historical orientation of Rawls's thought is well captured by the introduction to *Political Liberalism* (2005), which proposes a kind of historical genealogy of liberal toleration. There Rawls gives a more concrete expression to the notion of the educative function of institutions: properly designed institutions show the theologically inclined that a shared religious world view is *not* a necessary prerequisite of civic co-existence (and perhaps even civic vitality). Institutions make potentially unreasonable doctrine holders reasonable by showing,

over time, that equal rights and toleration are the only stable bases of civic association in a religiously plural community. But certainly this is not a necessary, causal relationship: the institutionalized practice of toleration is not logically possible in the absence of a world view that acknowledges the political manageability of religious diversity. Says Rawls, "Intolerance was accepted as a condition of social order and stability. The weakening of that belief helps to clear the way for liberal institutions" (Rawls 2005, xxv). Unreasonable religions must go through a process of "liberalization" before political liberalism is possible (Beiner 2010); hence the existence, and operation, of a kind of institutional-behavioural dialectic in Rawls's work: institutions educate, but citizens must be open to such processes of socialization. According to our argument, there is a similar logic at work when it comes to the question of self-respect.

8 And Rawls goes even further: *peoples* also have a constitutive interest in recognition and self-respect. In other words, Rawls is concerned not only with the cultivation of the affective resources necessary to proper self-respect and esteem among liberal citizens but also with the affective orientation of peoples. That this is the case is revealed even more clearly in Rawls's last major theoretical contribution, *The Law of Peoples*, where Rawls explicitly draws on the Rousseauian language of "*amour-propre*," understood as the proper self-respect of peoples (Rawls 1999c, 34).

9 For this reason, Cohen's critique of Rawls misses the mark (1992, 1997, 2008). The project of *A Theory of Justice*, and Rawls more generally, *is* attentive to the place of an ethos of justice in a well-ordered society, although the contours of that ethos may not quite conform to Cohen's expectations. For an excellent discussion of what a Rawlsian ethos ought to resemble, and why it would most likely not be compatible with the radical egalitarianism of Cohen, see Titelbaum (2008).

REFERENCES

Baehr, Amy R. 1996. "Toward a New Feminist Liberalism: Okin, Rawls, and Habermas." *Hypatia* 11 (1): 49–66. http://dx.doi.org/10.1111/j.1527-2001.1996.tb00506.x.

Barry, Brian. 1995. "John Rawls and the Search for Stability." Reviews of *A Theory of Justice* and *Political Liberalism*. *Ethics* 105 (4): 874–915. http://dx.doi.org/10.1086/293756.

Beiner, Ronald. 2010. *Civil Religion: A Dialogue in the History of Political Philosophy*. Cambridge: Cambridge University Press. http://dx.doi.org/10.1017/CBO9780511763144.

Blackburn, Simon. 1998. *Ruling Passions*. Oxford: Clarendon Press.

Buchanan, Allen. 1982. "A Critical Introduction to Rawls's Theory of Justice." In *John Rawls's Theory of Social Justice: An Introduction*, edited by H. Gene Blocker and Elizabeth H. Smith, 5–41. Athens: Ohio University Press.

Cohen, G.A. 1992. "Incentives, Inequality, and Community." In *Tanner Lectures on Human Values*, edited by G.B. Peterson, 262–329. Salt Lake City: University of Utah Press.

Cohen, G.A. 1997. "Where the Action Is: On the Site of Distributive Justice." *Philosophy & Public Affairs* 26 (1): 3–30. http://dx.doi.org/10.1111/j.1088-4963.1997.tb00048.x.

Cohen, G.A. 2008. *Rescuing Justice and Equality*. Cambridge, MA: Harvard University Press. http://dx.doi.org/10.4159/9780674029651.

Fisher, Philip. 2003. *The Vehement Passions*. Princeton, NJ: Princeton University Press.

Fishkin, James. 1975. "Justice and Rationality: Some Objections to the Central Argument in Rawls's Theory." Review of *A Theory of Justice*. *American Political Science Review* 69 (2): 615–29. http://dx.doi.org/10.2307/1959092.

Frazer, Michael L. 2007. "John Rawls: Between Two Enlightenments." *Political Theory* 35 (6): 756–80. http://dx.doi.org/10.1177/0090591707307325.

Frazer, Michael L. 2010. *The Enlightenment of Sympathy: Justice and the Moral Sentiments in the Eighteenth Century and Today*. Oxford: Oxford University Press. http://dx.doi.org/10.1093/acprof:oso/9780195390667.001.0001.

Freeman, Samuel. 2003. Introduction to *The Cambridge Companion to Rawls*, edited by Samuel Freeman, 1–61. Cambridge: Cambridge University Press.

Hall, Cheryl. 2002. "'Passions and Constraint': The Marginalization of Passion in Liberal Political Theory." *Philosophy and Social Criticism* 28 (6): 727–48. http://dx.doi.org/10.1177/019145370202800607.

Hall, Cheryl. 2005. *The Trouble with Passion: Political Theory beyond the Reign of Reason*. New York: Routledge.

Harsanyi, John. 1975. "Can the Maximin Principle Serve as a Basis for Morality? A Critique of John Rawls's Theory." Review of *A Theory of Justice*. *American Political Science Review* 69 (2): 594–606. http://dx.doi.org/10.2307/1959090.

Hegel, G.W.F. 1991. *Elements of the Philosophy of Right*. Edited by Allen W. Wood. Translated by H.B. Nisbet. Cambridge: Cambridge University Press.

Herman, Barbara. 1996. *The Practice of Moral Judgment*. Cambridge, MA: Harvard University Press.

Hume, David. 2000. *A Treatise of Human Nature*. Edited by David Fate Norton and Mary J. Norton. Oxford: Oxford University Press.

Kingston, Rebecca, and Leonard Ferry, eds. 2008. *Bringing the Passions Back In: The Emotions in Political Philosophy*. Vancouver: UBC Press.
Krause, Sharon R. 2005. "Desiring Justice: Motivation and Justification in Rawls and Habermas." *Contemporary Political Theory* 4 (4): 363–85. http://dx.doi.org/10.1057/palgrave.cpt.9300154.
Krause, Sharon R. 2008. *Civil Passions: Moral Sentiment and Democratic Deliberation*. Princeton, NJ: Princeton University Press. http://dx.doi.org/10.1515/9781400837281.
Louden, Robert B. 2002. *Kant's Impure Ethics: From Rational Beings to Human Beings*. Oxford: Oxford University Press.
Nozick, Robert. 1974. *Anarchy, State, and Utopia*. New York: Basic Books.
Nussbaum, Martha C. 2002. "Rawls and Feminism." In *The Cambridge Companion to Rawls*, edited by Samuel Freeman, 488–520. Cambridge: Cambridge University Press.
Okin, Susan. 1987. "Justice and Gender." *Philosophy & Public Affairs* 16 (1): 42–72.
Okin, Susan. 1989. "Reason and Feeling in Thinking about Justice." *Ethics* 99 (2): 229–49. http://dx.doi.org/10.1086/293064.
O'Neill, Onora. 1990. *Constructions of Reason: Explorations of Kant's Practical Philosophy*. Cambridge: Cambridge University Press. http://dx.doi.org/10.1017/CBO9781139173773.
Rawls, John. 1971. *A Theory of Justice*. Cambridge, MA: Harvard University Press.
Rawls, John. 1999a. "The Idea of Public Reason Revisited." In *The Law of Peoples*, 131–80. Cambridge, MA: Harvard University Press.
Rawls, John. 1999b. "Kantian Constructivism in Moral Theory." In *Collected Papers*, edited by Samuel Freeman, 303–58. Cambridge, MA: Harvard University Press.
Rawls, John. 1999c. *The Law of Peoples*. Cambridge, MA: Harvard University Press.
Rawls, John. 2000. *Lectures on the History of Moral Philosophy*. Edited by Barbara Herman. Cambridge, MA: Harvard University Press.
Rawls, John. 2001. *Justice as Fairness: A Restatement*. Edited by Erin Kelly. Cambridge, MA: Harvard University Press.
Rawls, John. 2005. *Political Liberalism*. New York: Columbia University Press.
Sandel, Michael. 1982. *Liberalism and the Limits of Justice*. Cambridge: Cambridge University Press.
Sandel, Michael. 1984. "The Procedural Republic and the Unencumbered Self." *Political Theory* 12 (1): 81–96. http://dx.doi.org/10.1177/0090591784012001005.

Sen, Amartya. 2009. *The Idea of Justice*. Cambridge, MA: Harvard University Press.

Solomon, Robert C. 1995. *A Passion for Justice: Emotions and the Origins of the Social Contract*. Oxford: Rowman & Littlefield.

Taylor, Charles. 1979. *Hegel and Modern Society*. Cambridge: Cambridge University Press.

Titelbaum, G. Michael. 2008. "What Would a Rawlsian Ethos of Justice Look Like?" *Philosophy & Public Affairs* 36 (3): 289–322. http://dx.doi.org/10.1111/j.1088-4963.2008.00140.x.

Walzer, Michael. 2002. "Passion and Politics." *Philosophy and Social Criticism* 28 (6): 617–33. http://dx.doi.org/10.1177/019145370202800602.

Walzer, Michael. 2006. *Politics and Passion: Toward a More Egalitarian Liberalism*. New Haven, CT: Yale University Press.

Young, Iris Marion. 1990. *Justice and the Politics of Difference*. Princeton, NJ: Princeton University Press.

PART IV

Seeking Common Ground

Epilogue: Integrating Multiple Perspectives into the Study of Emotions

REBECCA KINGSTON

Emotions concern those things that are important to us, including our relations to others, our relations to ourselves, and our most central commitments and desires. So how might we address the conundrum of the disjuncture between the centrality of the phenomenal experience for all of us and the broad lack of agreement in the theoretical and experimental domains? Some of the differences are grounded in fundamentally divergent methodological commitments. The divide between interpretive and naturalistic approaches to the study of the human sciences is revisited, and perhaps magnified, in the literature on emotions.

Despite recent calls for fuller interdisciplinary collaboration in the study of emotions, attempts of more integrated study (apart from the pioneering work associated with the journal *Emotion Review*) are either limited to the study of one emotion or offer a series of pieces written from within separate disciplinary enclaves (Lewis, Haviland-Jones, and Barrett 2008) and with limited cross-references.[1] As a first step in exploring the possibility of greater in-depth interdisciplinary collaboration, it might be helpful to make a distinction between two levels of interdisciplinary thinking. At one level, we can discern ways in which a study of emotion in one field integrates the conclusions or findings about emotions from another, such as the way in which affect theory can draw on neuroscience or how a number of contemporary philosophers can draw on the conclusions of Antonio Damasio or the experiments of Stanley Schachter and Jerome Singer. We might call this approach "light" collaboration. However, we can think of how deeper integration might be possible, while still avoiding the pretension of providing an overarching meta-theory. In the following analysis, I attempt to build bridges (informed by my own place in the discipline of political theory), taking approaches and methods seriously and examining ways in which discourses, assumptions, and broad contours as well as conclusions provide points of continuity and contrast with others. Using a consciously situated attempt at deep comparison and contrast (itself, perhaps, informed by general hermeneutical methods of interpretation), I come to one articulation of what I understand to be points of basic convergence in emotion studies and of how a more integrated field of emotion studies might be structured. Of course, this remains tentative and one articulation among many.

Close analysis of some of the patterns in subject and analysis can reveal possible patterns for organization and integration. As a step in this direction, I first explore some patterns in defining emotion. Second, I will look at ways in which individual emotion is deemed to be shaped by developmental, environmental, and institutional factors and then, third, explore some of the broad patterns that emerge from a consideration of the effects of emotion. This exploration offers a basic framework for thinking about the emotions in an integrated way, incorporating insights from across the human sciences. Of course, it does not pretend to be a definitive model, but rather an exploratory one, and it is suggested to help organize and reflect on insights from a number of fields.

In my closing remarks, I reflect on my own field of political theory, and, drawing from chapters from the field in this collection, I suggest broad ways in which greater cross-disciplinary considerations can provide us with insights for deeper reflection. The particular challenge of emotion studies, from my vantage point of political theory, stems from the reluctance of many scholars in the field to let a broad appreciation of emotional phenomena enter into a reconsideration of the nature and status of our core liberal democratic ideals – for example, equality and freedom. Can the possibility of new approaches to cross-disciplinary studies of the emotions lead to a reconsideration of the emotion-reason divide that still lingers at the core of the field?

Coming to Speaking Terms on the Phenomena of Emotion

Are there any matters over which we might say there is certain or relative agreement in the literature concerning the emotions? It is obvious that there is a great deal of definitional dispute about how to characterize emotion and its relationship to feeling. Nonetheless, we might suggest that, in broad terms, there is an acknowledgment that there are aspects of ourselves, our motivations, and the forces shaping our behaviour and our dispositions and orientation to our environment that are not always amenable to our control or, indeed, not always accessible immediately or without distortion to our self-consciousness. Whether this accounts for the vast majority of what is called emotion, or a certain subset of it, I think it is reasonable to suggest that, contrary to the staunchest of cognitivists, we cannot be deemed responsible for our emotions in their entirety. The study of the science of emotions has expanded enough beyond the early assertions of the Stoics that it can no longer be claimed that animals and individuals with few cognitive abilities (be it babies or those stricken with a disability – severe dementia, for instance) lack the capacity to share in emotional experience of one form or another. Children with full cognitive potential may often need to be taught to correctly identify the emotions that move them; in other words, in our moral development, our felt experience can often serve to inform our cognitive self-awareness of emotional phenomena. While it is true that individual, ill-defined motivational energy can lend itself to manipulation by imposing meaning from outside (as in the Schachter and Singer experiments), it is also the case that our emotions are often those things that help us *shape* our point of view or, as Aristotle claimed, those things through which we come to change our judgments (Aristotle 2006, 1378a 19–22).

This is not to say that the concept of judgment is not relevant to the nature of emotion, for clearly, judgment can either be implicit in the structural meaning of emotion or, as self-conscious judgment, play a role in matters of a cognitively complex nature (as is often apparent in politics or in what I have called in another work "public passion," for example), and it is one of those factors on which emotion can draw (Kingston 2012). However, for many individuals and in certain circumstances, those judgments are not ready to hand or fully amenable to full articulation, and sometimes the judgments that we are aware of in feeling an emotion are not always the judgments associated with an intensity of feeling in the first place (e.g., underlying jealousy that manifests itself as anger, or shame that can manifest itself as disdain), suggesting a more subtle and sometimes murky form of claim staking in the act of emoting.

A number of "feeling" theorists have recently sought to incorporate into their theories some mechanisms that allow for the identification of claims in the conceptual structure of emotion, but that are not reduced to cognitive judgments. These mechanisms are called, respectively, affective appraisal (Robinson 2007), perceptual theories (Prinz 2007; de

Sousa 2011), and attitudinal theories (Deonna, Rodogno, and Teroni 2012). While differing somewhat in degree, all these positions have in common the idea that the motivating force of many, if not all, forms of emotion emanating from the body also provides the evaluative content of the emotion; and so consequently, an emotion cannot be considered to be constituted by more cognitive forms of judgment (with cognition here used in a very narrow sense referring to conscious awareness). From these perspectives, judgment as understood in a cognitivist light is more apt to have been elicited by, rather than underlying, these emotive forces. So a first point that might be demonstrated to have some broad credibility is that emotion can often draw from or link to parts of the human person that remain to a certain degree inaccessible to the forces of immediate human reflexivity, although not always fully inaccessible and certainly amenable to modification through reflection. Related to this, perhaps some more detailed conceptual mapping of how the term *cognition* is used in the various disciplinary accounts would be useful to help come to terms in more specific ways with where the similarities lie within the broader field.

It is also the case that the various affect systems – that is, a variety of brain circuits that, when stimulated, can be said for some researchers to constitute emotions – can be identified through scientific experimentation. Some individuals may even be brought to feel or feel differently once their attention is brought to bear on the affective mechanism (hence the ability of certain individuals to "ride it out" when initially confronted with, but then being able to identify, extreme feelings of fear or panic). So while it is true that there is an aspect of the emotional universe of the individual (if defined largely) that can be, even if momentarily, beyond our immediate consciousness, the boundary here is not a fixed one, and it may shift with our own focus of attention. It is in part for this reason that Julien Deonna, Raffaele Rodogno, and Fabrice Teroni suggest that Paul Griffiths's distinction between basic emotions as one type and higher cognitive emotions as another is more complex in reality, given that aspects of both may be pervasive in much of emotional experience (Deonna, Rodogno, and Teroni 2012; Griffiths 1997). Attention paid to what were initially unacknowledged and unfelt signs of emotion, such as a furrowed brow showing the signs of anger or the resumption of a nervous habit showing distress, leads in some instances to recasting that emotion on a higher cognitive plane or invoking the moral emotions relevant to individual character (in the act of emotional regulation); in addition, an emotion triggered by conscious thoughts and thereby grounded in a cognitivist framework, such as imagining the loss of a loved one or a judgment concerning what should be an appropriate policy response to increased environmental devastation, may in turn activate the same neural circuits and behavioural symptoms of what have been called basic emotions in the experience of those same forms of fear and anger. In other words, the same emotion can be experienced in similar circumstances as both a type of basic emotion and the more complex emotion as defined by Griffiths.

This may not be enough to convince us of Deonna, Rodogno, and Teroni's position that we should continue to hold to the idea of emotion as a unitary category that constitutes "a natural kind" (Griffiths 2004; Scarantino 2012). In their favour, however, it may be the case that the interaction and complex relations among motivations related to basic biological needs of survival, those generated by deeper moral reflection and higher cognitive categories and those arising from social norms and cultural trends, do not provide evidence for three categorically distinct kinds of emotion, and some situations (the fear of losing one's job, for example) may be linked to both simultaneously. Furthermore, the notion of habit in the development of moral character is geared precisely to the idea that these categories are malleable, to make the appropriate moral emotions a matter of second nature. Nonetheless, in contrast to the position of Deonna, Rodogno, and Teroni, the "level," or type, of motivation to which an emotion may be traced – for example, distinguishing between a fear of snakes and the fear of the electoral success of a particular political candidate – does make a difference in how we deal with those emotions. While not necessarily less intense, the latter forms deriving from more clearly developed cognitive and cultural considerations may, in general, be more amenable to interpretive management.

What this suggests is that emotions can be composed of a number of factors, and different factors emerge as more salient or defining depending on a whole array of considerations, so different experiences of emotion draw from a different array of these factors and in different proportions. So while we might reject the idea of emotions as a natural kind in the basic sense of the term, as being amenable to discovery by the same "scientific" method, we can still argue for a certain *non-essentialist unity* in the phenomenon of emotion in that emotion can draw from and combine a circumscribed set of elements. We might use the analogy of culinary practice, a practice that can be considered to be both a science and an art, to illustrate the point. A set of basic ingredients can be combined in multiple ways to produce a whole array of results, and the interaction of the ingredients under pressure, or changes in temperature, can lead to a transformation in the end result. In a similar way, emotion can draw from a limited set of determined factors, some of which are deemed to be more fundamental in certain cases and less in others, and the manner and circumstances in which these elements combine can lead to different results of both quality and intensity. This analogy can apply both in the general category of emotion and to emotions that we tend to denote with the same term, such as love or anger.

This pluralist and non-essentialist understanding of emotion differs from the idea of emotion as a "family resemblance" in that it constitutes not only an intuitive unity for us but also a substantive one in many ways in that it draws on a limited number of constitutive elements combined in different ways (Russell 1991). This idea should not imply a rejection of the invocation of the term *emotion* in scientific terms, argued by Carroll Izard to be potentially lacking use as a category in scientific analysis (Russell and Widen 2010; Izard 2010). Instead, we might consider the complexity of the phenomenon of emotion as a positive challenge to science, which may have to come to terms more adequately with the various ways in which emotion can be generated, transformed, and transforming. There is no reason why a notion of plurality within certain limits, as described above – that is, emotion as non-essentialist, but constituted by a combination of a distinct and limited set of elements – could not be integrated into the very heart of the scientific study and use of the term *emotion*.

This discussion concerning the meaning behind the invocation of emotion helps shed light on the division between interpretive and naturalistic approaches, which provides an organizing principle of this collection and which mirrors a broader division of approaches found across the literature on the emotions in a number of disciplines. The essence of this division relates to how we perceive what we can claim to know about the emotions. Can the claims about emotions be shown through scientific and empirical evidence and/or principled logic to have timeless and universal validity, or do we need to perceive both the language and the cultural claims embedded in our particular understanding of emotion to be reflective of a specific time and place? On the interpretive side, it is relevant to recall that even the term *emotion* is a relatively recent invention, a word that replaced the more common invocation of *appetites, passions, affections*, and *sentiments* in the English language before the nineteenth century (Dixon 2012).

The contributions of Ryan Balot, Jan Purnis, and John Gunnell in this collection point to a defence of an interpretive position, the first two as a culturally and historically situated exposition of the terms through which emotion has been understood and the last as a principled defence of the perennial embeddedness of our understanding of emotion. As we have seen, Balot demonstrates that, even in the ancient world, the contrast between the Spartans and the Athenians involved a very distinct understanding of the emotions of shame and courage and the practices associated with them. The manifestation of courage in the Greek context depended on a particular understanding of the link between reason and emotion. In the case of the Spartans, at least according to Pericles, courage was unreflective and based largely on an immense fear of shame, rooted in the disapproval of others, whereas for the Athenians, again according to Pericles, courage was linked to a sense of a need to live up to discursively developed models of what it meant to be a good and responsible citizen. Still, it could be understood to some degree as a classical iteration of the general point of Schachter and Singer about the importance of cultural context giving meaning and form to more general emotional drives. Also, despite the different manifestations of courage, the upshot of this interpretive approach is not to distance the understanding of virtue from current practice, but instead to provide a normative model that is more amenable to modern appropriation and, in particular, to being adapted to a practice of good democratic citizenship. This demonstrates that a historical and interpretive approach need not undermine the search for transhistorical lessons and that experimental science could work hand in hand with historical evaluation in reflecting on worthy norms and the ways to promote them.

A similar lesson issues from the Purnis discussion of Renaissance discourses of emotion. Despite some of the ways in which the conceptualization of emotion in the Renaissance period in England appears to be foreign to modern sensibilities, Purnis acknowledges the way in which the pre-Cartesian outlook conforms to certain modern aspirations of espousing the important interconnectedness of mind and body. Nonetheless, the similarities mask an ambiguity, for they may not express reference to a singular underlying reality, but the possible cultural contingency of the very discourse of modern science itself. From this perspective, both naturalistic and interpretive approaches share in being historically situated and culturally conditioned.

This latter point is emphasised by Gunnell, who provides a spirited defence of an interpretive approach to the study of emotion in the social sciences through an analysis of the work of Ludwig Wittgenstein. For Gunnell, the central feature about theorists trying to come to terms with the social and political manifestations of emotions is less their historical embeddedness, as shown in the previous chapters, and more their linguistic embeddedness. The fact that human beings of whatever historical period seek to come to terms with the meaning of their emotions on a social plane needs to be understood as a cultural phenomenon that takes place fully within the existing linguistic frame of reference. This means that it would be misleading and misguided to seek to find explanations of emotion in social and political context through reference to the body or brain or some other substrate outside language and culture because the act of social science is one of interpretation and finding meaning within the strata of language. However, taking Wittgenstein seriously would not outlaw all naturalistic approaches to the study of emotion, but those scientific and experimental studies would be deemed only to provide an account of patterns in the brain, with no pretence of shedding deeper light on the social phenomenon of emotion, whose meaning lies outside the brain and body and within a social nexus. The position poses a radical challenge to the very possibility of a cross-disciplinary study of emotion, not because different approaches to something called *emotion* are not possible, but because it is misleading to think that the different approaches are actually all referring to the same phenomenon. For Gunnell, not only do emotions not constitute a natural kind, but the competing disciplinary invocations of emotion are also referring to things of a completely different nature.

How do naturalistically minded researchers in the field of emotion studies respond to such a challenge? We can look at scholarship from three different fields – neuroscience, developmental psychology, and behavioural social science – and try to discern from their discussion of emotion what they offer as a response to the radical interpretive challenge. I think it is fair to say that contemporary naturalistic approaches acknowledge the importance of interpersonal dynamics in extending and deepening the experience of emotion. Despite the important influence of the work of Paul Ekman, some theorists are questioning the notion that there is anything that might be called primary emotions that have a universal status and that are less dependent for their meaning on language and social networks than others (Smith and Schneider 2009). Instead, all emotions are deemed to share in some bodily component, along with implication in intersubjective networks that impact on their meaning.

While it is distinct from the level of language and social meaning, we have seen in the work of Georg Northoff, in the field of neuroscience, a close examination of processing mechanisms in the brain demonstrating that the environment impacts directly on feeling. What this relational understanding of emotion implies is that there is a mechanism that can help account for intentionality or that the basis for meaning of an emotion is not subsequent to the feeling, but partly constitutive of it. It suggests a more sophisticated, contextualized experience of feeling than previously discussed in a great deal of the scientific literature. Nonetheless, it indicates a formal structure for the possibility of meaning rather than the substance of the meaning itself. Such a conception appears to offer greater potential for compatibility with interpretive approaches than the standard approaches of neuroscience, for it acknowledges in a formal sense that the nature and meaning of the emotion is not exhausted by its bodily manifestation narrowly construed.

On a different level, reflections on emotion coming out of the field of attachment theory in psychology demonstrate the importance of another relational feature of emotion – namely, the central importance of a feeling of inclusion for individuals in a social setting. However, the work of Kristina Tchalova and Geoff MacDonald also invokes complex ways in which emotion can both be formed in and work to shape social settings. What the interpretive position does not fully reveal, but which comes to light in this literature, is that there are various levels at which emotion both records and reflects social meanings. Indeed, the implication of emotion in a social context appears to work as a recurrent loop. Far removed from the question of the fundamental ground for the intentionality of emotion, it appears here that feeling, as derived from a pattern of social interaction, gives rise in turn to a further array of emotion and choices, ultimately having an impact on a broader affective environment.

It is a position also reflected, albeit from a distinct theoretical framework, in the work of the behavioural political science of Joseph Fletcher and Jennifer Hove, where emotion is explored as a variable in helping to shape support for public policy. Despite the naturalistic premises of the psychological and behavioural literature, as dismissed in principle by the radical interpretive position, to some degree the former can offer a much more complex picture of the interplay of emotion and social practices and norms. It could be suggested, then, that what is mostly *at stake* in the division between broad interpretive and naturalistic approaches is less the awareness of possible social meanings and implications in emotional experience, or even the acknowledgment that these can shift over changing historical and cultural environments, than the question of whether the defined emotion can be only one thing or manifest itself in one particular way in a given context. Grounding the emotive experience in biology, or in the neural circuits of an affect system, carries the implication that the emotion manifests itself in a singular, identifiable way and thus can be measured in an unproblematic, seemingly objective way, whether this be by expression, activated neural circuits, behaviour, or subjective accounts of feeling (as in behavioural survey data, for example). So while the accounts in this volume on the naturalistic side of the equation do not fully respond to the interpretivist challenge as raised by Gunnell, there is nonetheless some evidence that the divide is not as great as sometimes it is thought to be. It is apparent that the science of emotion is evolving to acknowledge the importance of the embeddedness of the 'emotional' subject in a number of environments.

Certainly a challenge for an integrated field of emotion studies is a consideration of how naturalistic and interpretive approaches can come to some complementary relation. As I have been arguing, one way to facilitate greater exchange among these competing approaches might be to introduce a notion of pluralism into naturalistic approaches, with the idea that one emotion might be seen, felt, or manifested in different ways or generated from and impacted by multiple sources – indeed, even to consider that emotions might be overdetermined – and to acknowledge the broader consequences of defining emotion in a certain way. Those engaged in interpretive approaches might also do well to understand more deeply the science they may sometimes draw on to justify and legitimate their analysis and seek to come to terms with the bodily component of emotional experience.

Two Axes on Which to Compare the Study of Emotions across Disciplines: Factors Shaping Emotions and the Effects of Emotions

Another manner in which analysis might consider challenging the naturalistic and interpretive divide is to consider those factors that help to shape emotional experience as well as the upshot and effects of emotions in terms of both their effect on attitudes and behaviour as well as their possible place in a normative theory of social and political life. In drawing from, developing, and reorganizing some of the findings concerning how various disciplines are studying the emotions, I offer here a rudimentary framework for thinking about how studies in other disciplines can be more effectively introduced into the field of political science and political theory. In addition, it may provide us with a rough vision of how a more integrated field of emotion studies might look, at least as applied to the social sciences. The point of this conceptual map is not to provide a comprehensive account of all literature on the emotions in the social sciences, but rather to build a tentative and makeshift structure that might serve as conceptual scaffolding so that works on the emotions across the social sciences, in particular, could be more easily compared. The framework is composed of three levels: emotion at the individual level, emotion at a social and communal level, and the effects of emotion.

At the level of the individual, psychology is the most privileged discipline for studying the array of attributes and processes that help characterize and give rise to emotional feeling, exploring such matters as individual sensitivities, thresholds, processing, and response mechanisms as well as resources for attention and energy. But even here, one needs to make distinctions among the level of feeling, the level of function, and the neural level as well as acknowledge how certain theories combine the view of individual processes in their interaction with certain environmental factors (Frijda 2008, 69). Notions of situated affect or extended emotions in cognitive science and philosophy have given rise to the idea of embedded cognition, for which the context or the environment is not just seen as a trigger for emotion but can also act as a support or scaffold for the emotional experience itself (Stephan, Walter, and Wilutzky 2014).[2] It might be fruitfully compared to some approaches in anthropology, where emotion is studied as a part of the very process of social interaction and through the performance in which the emotion is expressed, perhaps akin to the idea of ritual approaches to emotion studies in sociology (exploring such things as the emotions involved in greetings or more institutionalized forms of community ritual) (Wilce 2014; Stets and Turner 2008). Phenomenologists also provide insightful analysis of the unfolding of the experience of emotion in a particular context (see, e.g., Schmitz, Mullan, and Slaby 2011).

In terms of the individual, another approach of sociological theory seeks to interpret emotion as issuing from individual self-conceptions and how they are matched or contested by the unfolding of events, or what is called the "symbolic interactionist approach" (Stets and Turner 2008, 38). This contrasts with theories of self-interest, which characterize rational actor theories in political science and what are called exchange approaches in sociological theory. In philosophy as well, there are enquiries into the structure and ontology of an emotional feeling and whether, depending on the particular feeling, there is a formal structure of reasons and beliefs that underlie that experience or some more particular relation to the object of feeling itself. So in terms of providing an articulation of the production, nature, and internal regulation of the emotional experience, its feeling, structure, logic, unravelling, and competing meanings and explanations, there appears to be a fair amount of ground for some meaningful and insightful cross-disciplinary exchange.

At a second level, reaching beyond the individual to the independent play of social norms themselves, the work of Norbert Elias has been of central importance in bringing attention to changing emotional expression across history (Elias 2000; see also Matt 2011). The array of factors beyond social norms helping shape the contours of emotional expression include social groupings (as in the work of Barbara Rosenwein and her notion of emotional communities), social and political institutions (seen especially in the work of William Reddy), cultural influences (the work of Peter Stearns comes to mind), as well as the economy and the workplace (Rosenwein 2006; Reddy 2001; Stearns 2008). In addressing broad norms across culture, sociologists have developed the notion of "feeling rules," through which culture guides what can be expressed and how, especially in studies on expressions of grief and sympathy (Stets and Turner 2008, 34). The theatrical resonance of exploring the rules of emotion expression is also matched in the field of anthropology. A perspective demonstrating the unequal social distribution of emotional capacity, especially along the lines of class and power in the patterns of acceptable emotional expression, is found in structural approaches to the study of emotions in sociology as well as in the work of Daniel Gross, following in a similar line, but through very different means, as the pioneering work by Arlie Hochschild on emotional labour (Gross 2006; Hochschild 1983; Stets and Turner 2008).

As a third area of possible cross-disciplinary comparison, in terms of the effects of emotions, one can look at the levels of individual behaviour, social and political change, and cultural impacts. These questions are taken up mostly in normative terms in this volume – that is, "What emotions *should* we have if we wish to have good politics?" – but the reader should be aware of the ways in which different fields have explored these questions in a more descriptive and explanatory way, like James Jasper's contribution to this volume. Economics is perhaps the privileged discipline for exploring the ways in which emotion can help determine or shape individual judgments, despite its many competing schemas of how decision making works (Loewenstein and Rick 2008). In terms of individual impacts, there has been discussion in the field of political science of the effects of anxiety on voting behaviour, especially the question of whether anxiety makes voters more attentive to the issues (Marcus 2002; Marcus and MacKuen 2011; Marcus, Neuman, and MacKuen 2000; Ladd and Lenz 2008, 2011; Nadeau, Niemi, and Amato 1995; Groenendyk 2011). At another level, studies of the impact of emotional appeals in advertising have demonstrated their great effectiveness in influencing political choices (Brader 2006). In broad terms, as noted by Eric Groenendyk, "Results suggest that emotions are vital to understanding when and why voters seek out political information, how this information is converted into political evaluations, and when citizens are sufficiently motivated to participate in politics" (Groenendyk 2011, 459).

There is a suggestion that, at the level of social and political change, the first step in the study of emotional changes that have a broader cultural impact stems from a growing interest in social history and, most important, the history of the family (Stearns 2008, 20). As one example, the history of emotion in the family realm of the Victorian era helps demonstrate how the sanctity of the family was consolidated and how class and gender divisions were accentuated (Stearns 2008, 24). Later, there were numerous studies of the impact of emotion on key historical events – for example, of the way in which a shared understanding of the "passion, sentiment and sensibility" helped ground the independence movement in America and the French Revolution or the growth of fear among peasants in the Guyenne, giving rise to the rebellions of the *croquants* (Matt 2011, 120; see also Burnstein 1999; Eustace 2008; Knott 2008; Muchembled 1985). Studies also demonstrate the importance of affective changes in culture to usher in the growth of consumer capitalism in the twentieth century, such as the promotion of envy (Matt 2003). Studies of the evolution of particular emotions, such as disgust, demonstrate how new manifestations of the emotion gave rise to new practices in sanitation and cosmetics (Corbin 1986). There are also a great number of contemporary studies that look to the pervasive climate of fear in the post-9/11 context and its impact on cultural, social, and political life.

There is a great deal of literature and possible commentary to be made about the possible directions of research on the impact of emotions in social and political life. The overlap is possibly too obvious to dwell on here, so to close this chapter, I will explore one other way of conceiving the impact of emotion, and that is in normative political theory. The reason I do so is that this approach to the study of emotions seeks to speak also to non-specialists by raising questions relevant to each individual's place in a broader social and political network.

Theorists have considered the force of emotions in collective life since the classical age. More recently, many theorists have sought to harness that tradition to gather insights into how emotion might best manifest itself in the lives of contemporary democratic citizens trying to think through what they consider to be both good and destructive manifestations of emotion in the context of a healthy democracy. A normative theory of politics seeks to build a picture of the conceptual framework that citizens might keep in mind as the best way to direct action and policy in public life. Are there particular emotions better suited, or ill suited, for good democratic practice in the modern era?

It might be suggested that the idea of normativity in emotions lends itself directly to an interpretive approach and that it does not combine well at all with the naturalistic approaches entertained here. Does the idea of political science, and political theory in particular, require a rejection of naturalism with regard to the emotions, as suggested by Gunnell in this volume? The argument for the division is built in part on the suggestion that the normativity built into political theory about which emotions can make for good citizenship and good social order cannot be justified by naturalistic principles alone, but requires a more cognitivist understanding of emotion, allied with an interpretive approach. Nevertheless, it is also suggested that if social norms are well entrenched in behavioural terms, then the perception of normativity in social and political behaviour can be felt without the intermediary of a strong cognitivist grounding for emotional feeling (see Hufendiek 2014). Thus, feelings of social guilt, anger, and justice will be felt in immediate terms (regardless of strong evidence of historical and cultural mediation), stemming directly from interaction with the environment and through a sense of an interruption of more traditional patterns of relation. Nonetheless, it would appear that, for our moral emotions and intuitions to be tested, they would ultimately need to be subject to some degree of reflective exercise, if only to ensure that the content of our choices conforms to the deeper contours of our commitments, although these commitments may also be subject to change based on a repeated pattern of emotional response.

I here compare and contrast the contributions to this volume as two examples of a much broader dialogue to give a brief demonstration of the potential of these approaches to engage with a broader ethos. Both the chapter on the thought of Hannah Arendt and the chapter on the thought of John Rawls raise the issue of what constitutes either a positive or a negative emotion for an effective practice of citizenship.

Arendt challenges the perhaps intuitive stance that compassion can serve as a positive force in public life, and while not discounting it fully, she suggests that it applies in a minimal fashion to the public realm, but serves better in the realm of social life. The reason for Arendt's stance, as discussed by Sophie Bourgault, appears to be linked to its status of what we might call, drawing from other areas of emotion studies, an emotion with negative valence – namely, that it involves feeling a deep sadness for the condition of the other, which, through its intensity, appears to shut off debate, deliberation, and openness. Of course, compassion may leave us open to the concerns of the object of our compassion, but Arendt's point is that this targeted emotion shuts us off from discussion with others who are not deemed to share in that compassion. Because of the particular dynamic of compassion for Arendt, it can be judged to be "anti-political" (in the admittedly narrow Arendtian sense) as compassion more readily invokes concealment over publicity and is really only authentic when it leads to hidden action. If taken as a motivating force for public action, it becomes a boundless weapon for the long-suffering and can usher in the biggest pathologies of mass politics, such as, Arendt argues, the Terror of the French Revolution. In broad terms, Arendt's rejection of compassion as a good public or political emotion mirrors Plato's rejection of the Spartan version of courage (and, indeed, Rawls's rejection of envy) insofar as they are deemed to inhibit public dialogue.

We do not need to fully endorse Arendt's position to take lessons from her analysis. Her broader point is that some collective emotional dynamics may detract from the vision of good citizenship we require.

Others may suggest that hate, disgust, shame, and contempt might also be good candidates for exclusion from public life (see, e.g., Nussbaum 2006). As we see in the piece by Kiran Banerjee and Jeffrey Bercuson, Rawls considered envy a pernicious emotion as it erodes a sense of equality that is an important precondition for justice. In more general terms, the fact that one of the more rationalist of contemporary liberal theorists can be seen to harbour a theoretical framework that carries, both implicitly and explicitly, a set of precise emotional conditions for contemporary citizens demonstrates how unavoidable questions of emotional quality are in matters of social and political organization.

On one level, as seen in the work analysing Plato, Arendt, and Rawls, among others, we can reflect on the degree to which various emotions can contribute to or detract from the ideals we establish as being regulative for our political and social communities. This leads to two observations: emotions can take competing political forms (as in Athenian versus Spartan courage), and in recognition of the complicated terrain of citizenship relations, as distinguished from family as well as cosmopolitan relations, emotions may be subject to a much more nuanced assessment given how they may impact each level in distinct ways and, indeed, give rise to competing claims of justice.

A broader challenge for political theory, and perhaps to the whole of the humanities and social sciences, is the degree to which our openness to things emotional should impact not only on our practices for implementing our most important public ideals, especially those of freedom and equality, but also the very content of those ideals. Equality perceived in terms of the distribution of goods, or procedural fairness, may take on quite different qualities if we begin to think about it as something like equal rights to well-being and happiness or having all feeling beings weigh equally in determining policy. In addition, a serious consideration of the centrality of emotion in our social and political lives, a feature made evident by the broad interest in the emotions across almost all fields of enquiry where human life is studied, may lead us perhaps to rethink what our core normative ideals should be. For example, can we envisage a society that is based on the principle of the avoidance of all forms of psychological damage and committed to the emotional flourishing of every being? How deeply might our standard liberal norms of justice be transformed if we were to re-conceptualize the structure of a society committed to such an ideal? Is this a desirable set of commitments?

It is only through a broad cross-disciplinary understanding, although possible in a vast number of ways, that we can begin to tackle the larger question of the links between emotion and human flourishing. Once this is done, there may be greater justification for rethinking the long traditions of self-governance and governance of others that have rested on a repression and marginalization of emotion and emotional practices. Ushering in the emotions in these multifaceted ways offers an exciting opportunity for new perspectives and insights.

NOTES

1 See, e.g., Part 1, "Interdisciplinary Foundations." A call for more cross-disciplinary collaboration comes from chap. 2 of that collection (Stearns 2008, 29).

2 The notion of extended emotions draws on and develops the notion of the "extended mind" first developed by Clark and Chalmers (1998); see also Colombetti and Roberts (2015).

REFERENCES

Aristotle. 2006. *On Rhetoric: A Theory of Civic Discourse.* 2nd ed. Translated by George A. Kennedy. Oxford: Oxford University Press, 1378a 19–22.

Brader, Ted. 2006. *Campaigning for Hearts and Minds: How Emotional Appeals in Political Ads Work.* Chicago: University of Chicago Press.

Burnstein, Andrew. 1999. *Sentimental Democracy: The Evolution of America's Romantic Self-Image. New.* York: Hill and Wang.

Clark, Andy, and David J. Chalmers. 1998. "The Extended Mind." *Analysis* 58 (1): 7–19.

Colombetti, Giovanna, and Tom Roberts. 2015. "Extending the Extended Mind." *Philosophical Studies* 172 (5): 1243–63.

Corbin, Alain. 1986. *The Foul and the Fragrant: Odor and the French Imagination.* Cambridge, MA: Harvard University Press.

Deonna, Julien, Raffaele Rodogno, and Fabrice Teroni. 2012. *The Emotions: A Philosophical Introduction.* New York: Routledge.

De Sousa, Ronald. 2011. *Emotional Truth.* Oxford: Oxford University Press.

Dixon, Thomas. 2012. "'Emotion': The History of a Keyword in Crisis." *Emotion Review* 4 (4): 338–44.

Elias, Norbert. 2000. *The Civilizing Process.* Oxford: Blackwell.

Eustace, Nicole. 2008. *Passion Is the Gale: Emotion, Power and the Coming of the American Revolution*. Chapel Hill: University of North Carolina Press.

Frijda, Nico H. 2008. "The Psychologists' Point of View." In *Handbook of Emotions*, 3rd ed., ed. Michael Lewis, Jeannette M. Haviland-Jones, and Lisa Feldman Barrett, 68–87. New York: Guilford Press.

Griffiths, Paul. 1997. *What Emotions Really Are: The Problem of Psychological Categories*. Chicago: University of Chicago Press.

Griffiths, Paul. 2004. "Is Emotion a Natural Kind?" In *Thinking about Feeling: Contemporary Philosophers on Emotions*, ed. Robert Solomon, 233–249. Oxford: Oxford University Press.

Groenendyk, Eric. 2011. "Current Research in Political Science: How Emotions Help Democracy Overcome Its Collective Action Problem." *Emotion Review* 3 (4): 455–63.

Gross, Daniel. 2006. *The Secret History of Emotion*. Chicago: University of Chicago Press.

Hochschild, Arlie. 1983. *The Managed Heart*. Berkeley: University of California Press.

Hufendiek, Rebekka. 2014. "Social Emotions between Normativity and Naturalism." Unpublished paper presented at the European Philosophical Society for the Study of the Emotions, Lisbon, July.

Izard, Carroll. 2010. "The Many Meanings/Aspects of Emotion: Emotion Definitions, Functions, Activation, and Regulation." *Emotion Review* 2 (4): 363–70.

Kingston, Rebecca. 2012. *Public Passion: Rethinking the Grounds for Political Justice*. Montreal, Kingston: McGill-Queen's University Press.

Knott, Sarah. 2008. *Sensibility and the American Revolution*. Chapel Hill: University of North Carolina Press.

Ladd, Jonathan McDonald, and Gabriel S. Lenz. 2008. "Reassessing the Role of Anxiety in Vote Choice." *Political Psychology* 29: 275–96.

Ladd, Jonathan McDonald, and Gabriel S. Lenz. 2011. "Does Anxiety Improve Voters' Decision Making?" *Political Psychology* 32: 347–61.

Lewis, Michael, Jeannette M. Haviland-Jones, and Lisa Feldman Barrett, eds. 2008. *Handbook of Emotions*. 3rd ed. New York: Guilford Press.

Loewenstein, George, and Scott Rick. 2008. "The Role of Emotion in Economic Behavior." In *Handbook of Emotions*, 3rd ed., ed. Michael Lewis, Jeannette M. Haviland-Jones, and Lisa Feldman Barrett, 138–156. London: Guilford Press.

Marcus, George. 2002. *The Sentimental Citizen*. University Park: Pennsylvania State Press.

Marcus, George, and Michael MacKuen. 2011. "Parsimony and Complexity: Developing and Testing Theories of Affective Intelligence." *Political Psychology* 32:323–36.

Marcus, George, W. Russell Neuman, and Michael MacKuen. 2000. *Affective Intelligence and Political Judgment*. Chicago: Chicago University Press.

Matt, Susan J. 2003. *Keeping Up with the Joneses: Envy in American Consumer Society 1890–1930*. Philadelphia: University of Pennsylvania Press.

Matt, Susan J. 2011. "Current Emotion Research in History: Or, Doing History from the Inside Out." *Emotion Review* 3 (1): 117–24.

Muchembled, Robert. 1985. *Popular Culture and Elite Culture in France, 1400–1750*. Trans. Lydia Cochrane. Baton Rouge: Louisiana State University Press.

Nadeau, Richard, Richard G. Niemi, and Timothy Amato. 1995. "Emotions, Issue Importance, and Political Learning." *American Journal of Political Science* 39 (3): 558–74.

Nussbaum, Martha. 2006. *Hiding from Humanity*. Cambridge, MA: Harvard University Press.

Prinz, Jesse. 2007. *The Emotional Construction of Morals*. Oxford: Oxford University Press.

Reddy, William M. 2001. *The Navigation of Feeling: A Framework for the History of Emotions*. Cambridge: Cambridge University Press.

Robinson, Jenefer. 2007. *Deeper than Reason: Emotion and Its Role in Literature, Music and Art*. Oxford: Oxford University Press.

Rosenwein, Barbara H. 2006. *Emotional Communities in the Early Middle Ages*. Ithaca, NY: Cornell University Press.

Russell, James A. 1991. "Natural Language Concepts of Emotion." In *Perspectives in Personality: Self and Emotion*, ed. Daniel J. Ozer, Joseph M. Healy, Jr., and Abigail J. Stewart, 119–137. London: Jessica Kingsley.

Russell, James A., and Sherri C. Widen. 2010. "Descriptive and Prescriptive Definitions of Emotion." *Emotion Review* 2 (4): 377–8.

Scarantino, Andrea. 2012. "How to Define Emotions Scientifically." *Emotion Review* 4 (4): 358–68.

Schmitz, Hermann, Rudolf Owen Mullan, and Jan Slaby. 2011. "Emotions outside the Box: The New Phenomenology of Emotions and Corporeality." *Phenomenology and the Cognitive Sciences* 10 (2): 241–59. http://link.springer.com/article/10.1007%2Fs11097-011-9195-1. Accessed 24 July 2014.

Smith, Herman, and Andreas Schneider. 2009. "Critiquing Models of Emotions." *Sociological Methods & Research* 37 (4): 560–89.

Stearns, Peter N. 2008. "The History of Emotion: Issues of Change and Impact." In *Handbook of Emotions*, 3rd ed., ed. Michael Lewis, Jeannette

M. Haviland-Jones, and Lisa Feldman Barrett, 17–31. New York: Guilford Press.

Stephan, Achim, Sven Walter, and Wendy Wilutzky. 2014. "Emotions beyond Brain and Body." *Philosophical Psychology* 27 (1): 65–81.

Stets, Jan E., and Jonathan H. Turner. 2008. "The Sociology of Emotions." In *Handbook of Emotions*, 3rd ed., ed. Michael Lewis, Jeannette M. Haviland-Jones, and Lisa Feldman Barrett, 32–46. New York: Guilford Press.

Wilce, James. 2014. "Current Emotion Research in Linguistic Anthropology." *Emotion Review* 6 (1): 77–85.

Contributors

Ryan K. Balot is Professor of Political Science and Classics at the University of Toronto. The author of *Greed and Injustice in Classical Athens* (Princeton University Press, 2001), *Greek Political Thought* (Blackwell, 2006), and *Courage in the Democratic Polis: Ideology and Critique in Classical Athens* (Oxford University Press, 2014) and editor of *A Companion to Greek and Roman Political Thought* (Blackwell, 2009), Balot specializes in early modern and classical political thought. He received his PhD in Classics at Princeton University and his BA degrees in Classics from the University of North Carolina, Chapel Hill, and Corpus Christi College, Oxford, which he attended as a Rhodes Scholar. Before moving to the Department of Political Science at Toronto, he taught for nearly a decade in the Classics departments at Union College and Washington University in St. Louis as both a Greek historian and a classical philologist. Balot's research has been funded by the National Endowment for the Humanities, the Social Sciences and Humanities Research Council of Canada, and the Teagle Foundation of New York. His essays and reviews have appeared in such venues as *Political Theory, Ancient Philosophy, Social Research,* and the *Journal of Hellenic Studies.* His current projects include work on Machiavelli's republicanism, Aristotle and the mixed regime, and Plato's Laws.

Kiran Banerjee received his PhD in 2016 with the Department of Political Science at the University of Toronto, where he was a Vanier Canada Graduate Scholar. He received his BA and MA degrees at the University of Chicago. He is currently a Postdoctoral Research Fellow at Columbia University's School of International and Public Affairs. His current research is focused on theorizing the normative dimensions of claims to membership as a subject of global justice, with a particular focus on statelessness and forced migration. Banerjee's research has been supported and recognized with numerous awards and fellowships, including the Vanier Canada Graduate Scholarship, and his work has been published in such venues as the *History of European Ideas*, the *Journal of International Law and International Relations*, the *European Journal of Political Theory*, and *Refuge*. Banerjee's broader research interests include international relations, migration studies, and human rights as well as political philosophy and legal theory.

Jeffrey Bercuson is a professor of Political Science at Seneca College of Applied Arts and Technology in Toronto. His first book, *John Rawls and the History of Political Thought*, was recently published by Routledge. He is currently at work on a book project that examines the role of religion in contemporary liberalism.

Sophie Bourgault is Associate Professor of Political Science at the University of Ottawa. Current research interests centre around the ethics of care, feminist political theory, and French Enlightenment thought. Her publications include articles published in *Eighteenth-Century Thought, Symposium, Women's Studies, Recherches Féministes,* and *Frontiers: A Journal of Women Studies.* She is also the co-editor of *A Companion to Enlightenment Historiography* (2013) and *Le* care: *Éthique féministe actuelle* (2015).

Yi-Chun Chien is a PhD candidate in the Department of Political Science at the University of Toronto. She received her BA in Political Science from National Taiwan University and an MA in politics and policy from the University of Toronto. Her areas of research include immigration, gender politics, and social policies in the East Asian countries. Through a comparative analysis of migrant care-worker policies in Taiwan and South Korea, Yi-Chun's doctoral dissertation investigates the relationships among the welfare state, care work, and international migration. Her broader research interests include gender and labour policy, comparative political theory, and emotions.

Joseph F. Fletcher, after forty years as a member of the Department of Political Science at the University of Toronto, is now visiting professor in the Politics Department at the University of California Santa Cruz and Department of Political Science faculty affiliate at the University of Victoria. His recent research publications focus on the application of statistical modelling techniques to political, psychological, biological, and educational processes.

Paul E. Griffiths is a philosopher of science with a focus on genetics and development. He is Professor in the Department of Philosophy, University of Sydney, and a Domain Leader at the Charles Perkins Centre, a major research institute of the university devoted to interdisciplinary approaches to lifestyle-related disease. He also serves as a Fellow of the American Association for the Advancement of Science and the Australian Academy of the Humanities. From 2011 to 2013, he was president of the International Society for History, Philosophy and Social Studies of Biology. His publications include *What Emotions Really Are: The Problem of Psychological Categories* (University of Chicago Press, 1997), *Sex and Death: An Introduction to the Philosophy of Biology* (University of Chicago Press, 1999) (with Kim Sterelny), and *Genetics and Philosophy: An Introduction* (Cambridge University Press, 2013) (with Karola Stotz).

John G. Gunnell is a Distinguished Professor Emeritus at the State University of New York at Albany and currently a research associate at the University of California, Davis. His work involves various aspects of political theory and the history and philosophy of social science. Recent work includes *Social Inquiry after Wittgenstein and Kuhn: Leaving Everything as It Is* (Columbia University Press, 2014); *Social Science and Political Theory: Cutting against the Grain* (Palgrave Macmillan, 2011); "The Reconstitution of Political Theory: David Easton and the Long Road to System," *Journal of the History of the Behavioral Sciences*, 2013; "Rise and Fall of the Democratic Dogma and the Emergence of Empirical Democratic Theory," in Mark Bevir, ed., *Modern Pluralism: Anglo-American Debates since 1880* (Cambridge University Press, 2012); and "Unpacking Emotional Baggage in Political Theory," in Frank Vander Valk, ed., *Essays in Neuroscience and Political Theory* (Routledge, 2012).

Jennifer Hove received her PhD in Political Science at the University of Toronto. Before that, she was vice-president of product development for a Vancouver-based strategic marketing firm and worked as an analyst for several high-profile organizations in North America, South Asia, and Africa. Jen is the recipient of numerous awards, including the 2012 Beattie Fellowship at the Munk School of Global Affairs,

University of Toronto; the Dr. F.M. Hill Ontario Graduate Scholarship in Public Policy; and a Social Sciences and Humanities Research Council of Canada Doctoral Fellowship.

James M. Jasper teaches sociology at the Graduate Center of the City University of New York. He writes about social movements, especially their cultural and emotional components. His most recent book is *Protest* (Polity, 2014).

Rebecca Kingston is Professor of Political Science at the University of Toronto. She is a specialist of the political thought of Montesquieu and the emotions in political theory. Her most recent book is *Public Passion* (McGill-Queen's University Press, 2011), and she is also editor (with Len Ferry) of *Bringing the Passions Back In* (University of British Columbia Press, 2008). She is now working on a book on the political thought of Plutarch and its iterations in the history of ideas in England and France (1500–1800).

Geoff MacDonald is Associate Professor of Psychology at University of Toronto. His research focuses on issues such as the role of attachment insecurity in romantic relationships, experiences of inclusion/exclusion, and human sexuality.

James McKee is the Director of Research for the Public Affairs Bureau, Executive Council in the government of Alberta. He is also a doctoral candidate (all but defended) in the Department of Political Science at the University of Toronto. His research interests focus on the intersection of emotions and public policy.

Georg Northoff, MD, PhD, FRCP, is the Canada Research Chair for Mind, Brain Imaging and Neuroethics at the University of Ottawa Institute of Mental Health Research in Ottawa. He is the author of *Unlocking the Brain* (Oxford, 2014), Vol. 1 *Coding* and Vol. 2 *Consciousness*, as well as *Minding the Brain* (Palgrave, 2014) (http://www.georgnorthoff.com/).

Keith Oatley is a cognitive psychologist and a novelist; he is professor emeritus at the University of Toronto. His research is on the psychology of emotions and the psychology of fiction. He is the author of seven books of psychology, most recently *The Passionate Muse: Exploring Emotion in Stories* (Oxford University Press, 2012), an original novella with psychological commentaries. The first of his novels, *The Case of Emily V.* (Secker & Warburg, 1993), won the Commonwealth Writers' Prize for Best First Novel in 1994. His most recent novel is *Therefore Choose* (Goose Lane Publications, 2010). He is a Fellow of the Royal Society of Canada, a Fellow of the British Psychological Society, and a Fellow of the Association for Psychological Science.

Jan Purnis is Assistant Professor of English Literature at Campion College at the University of Regina. She specializes in discourses of the body, particularly the digestive tract, in Renaissance literature, and has published on the stomach and early modern emotion, the belly-brain relationship, and early modern out-of-body experiences. She is currently working on a project on intersections of discourses of digestion, religion, colonialism, and cannibalism.

Kristina Tchalova is a PhD student in Social Psychology at McGill University. Her research examines the neurobiological substrates that contribute to the formation and maintenance of social bonds as well as the influence that these mechanisms exert on emotional and physical health. Kristina holds a BSc in Psychology from the University of Toronto and an MA in Psychology from the University of California, Los Angeles.

Constantine Christos Vassiliou is a PhD candidate in the Department of Political Science at the University of Toronto. He received his BA in Political Science at Mount Allison University and an MA in political theory at the University of Toronto. His core research investigates the tension between commerce and virtue in eighteenth-century political thought. More specifically, he compares Montesquieu with his seventeenth- and eighteenth-century contemporaries on questions concerning republicanism, commerce, religion, and the perceived relationship between republican Rome and Enlightenment England and France. He also does research on the political thought of Plutarch, and his recent work analyses the Chaeronean's reception in early modern and Enlightenment Europe.